GENDER EQUALITY
AND
AMERICAN JEWS

SUNY Series in American Jewish Society in the 1990s
Barry A. Kosmin and Sidney Goldstein, Editors

GENDER EQUALITY AND AMERICAN JEWS

MOSHE HARTMAN
and
HARRIET HARTMAN

State University
of New York
Press

Published by
State University of New York Press, Albany

© 1996 State University of New York

Production by Susan Geraghty
Marketing by Theresa Abad Swierzowski

Printed in the United States of America

For information, address State University of New York
Press, State University Plaza, Albany, N.Y., 12246

Library of Congress Cataloging-in-Publication Data

Hartman, Moshe, 1936-
    Gender equality and American Jews / Moshe Hartman and Harriet
Hartman.
        p.   cm. — (SUNY series in American Jewish society in the
1990s)
    Includes bibliographical references and index.
    ISBN 0-7914-3051-0 (hc : alk. paper). — ISBN 0-7914-3052-9 (pb :
alk. paper)
    1. Jews—United States—Social conditions. 2. Sex role—United
States. 3. Sexual division of labor—United States. I. Hartman,
Harriet. II. Title. III. Series.
E184.J5H345 1995
305.892′4073—dc20   95-45948
                                                                                           CIP

10 9 8 7 6 5 4 3 2 1

CONTENTS

List of Tables   *vii*

List of Figures   *xv*

Acknowledgments   *xix*

Chapter 1   Introduction   1

PART 1   Gendered Patterns of Secular Achievement
Among American Jews   21

Chapter 2   Education: Gatekeeper to
Gender Equality in the Economy   23

Chapter 3   The Labor Force Participation
of American Jewish Men and Women   61

Chapter 4   Occupational Achievement
of American Jewish Men and Women   115

Chapter 5   Gender Equality Within Jewish Couples   165

PART 2   Are We One? The Jewishness
of the Gendered Patterns of Secular Achievement   195

Chapter 6   Are We One? How Jewish Involvement
Is Related to Gendered Patterns of Secular Achievement   197

Chapter 7   Are We One? Gendered Patterns of
Secular Achievement Among Israeli and American Jews   249

Chapter 8   Conclusions   289

APPENDIXES   299

Appendix I   The Methodology of the 1990 Jewish National
Population Survey, by Joseph Walesberg   301

Appendix II   Jewishness Factors   323

Appendix III   Methods of Analysis   327

Appendix IV   Profile of Israeli Society   329

Notes   337

Bibliography   351

Name Index   365

Subject Index   369

LIST OF TABLES

2.1   Years of Education, by Sex, U.S. Jewish and Total White
      Population, 18 and over and 25 and over, 1990   31

2.2   Highest Academic Degree, by Sex, U.S. Jewish and Total
      White Population, 18 Years and over, 1990   33

2.3   Graduate Degrees Earned, by Sex, U.S. Jews 25 and over,
      1990   35

2.4   Mean Years of Education for an Academic Degree, by
      Sex, U.S. Jews 25 and over, 1990   36

2.5   Mean Years of Education, by Sex and Age, U.S. Jewish
      and Total White Population, 1990   39

2.6   Highest Academic Degree, by Sex and Age, U.S. Jews,
      1990   42

2.7   Percent of Women of Total U.S. Jews in Each Age and
      Degree Group, 1990   43

2.8   Percent with Four Years of College, by Marital Status
      and Sex, U.S. Jewish and Total White Population, 25 and
      over, 1990   46

2.9   Multiple Regression Analysis of Years of Education on
      Sex, Age, and Marital Status, U.S. Jews, 25 and over,
      1990   47

2.10 Multiple Regression Analysis of Years of Education on
      Age and Age at Marriage, U.S. Jews, 25 and over, 1990 49

2.11 Years of Education by Age at Marriage and Sex, U.S.
      Married Jews, 1990   50

2.12 Multiple Regression of Years of Education on Age at
      Marriage, Age at Birth of First Child, and Age, U.S.
      Married Jewish Women, 25 and over, 1990   52

2.13 Age at Birth of First Child, by Highest Academic Degree,
      U.S. Married Jewish Women, 25 and 0ver, 1990   53

2.14   Education by Number of Children, U.S. Jewish Married
        Women, 25 and over, 1990   55

2.15   Number of Children, by Education, U.S. Jewish Married
        Women, 25 and over, 1990   57

2.16   Age at Marriage, Age at Birth of First Child, Number of
        Children, and Age of Youngest Child, by Age, U.S.
        Jewish Married Women, 25 and over, 1990   58

2.17   Multiple Regression Analysis of Highest Academic
        Degree on Family Variables, U.S. Jewish Married
        Women, 25 and over, 1990   59

3.1   Percent in Paid Labor Force, by Sex and Age, U.S. Jewish
        and Total White Population, 1990   65

3.2   Percent in Paid Labor Force, by Marital Status and Age,
        U.S. Jewish Men, 1990   75

3.3   Percent in Paid Labor Force, by Age, Sex, and Marital
        Status, U.S. Jewish and Total White Population, 1990   78

3.4   Percent in Paid Labor Force, by Marital Status and Age,
        U.S. Jewish Women, 1990   79

3.5   Percent in Paid Labor Force and Mean Hours of Work,
        by Highest Academic Degree, Sex, and Age, U.S. Jews,
        1990   86

3.6   Percent in Paid Labor Force, by Years of Education and
        Sex, U.S. Jewish and Total U.S. Population, Ages 25–64,
        1990   88

3.7   Multiple Regression Analysis of Paid Labor Force
        Participation, U.S. Jewish Men and Women, 1990   90

3.8   Multiple Regression Analysis of Hours of Work per
        Week, U.S. Jewish Men and Women in the Paid Labor
        Force, 1990   93

3.9   Percent in Paid Labor Force, by Number of Children and
        Age of Mother, U.S. Jewish Married Women, 1990   97

3.10   Mean Hours Worked per Week in Paid Labor Force, by
        Number of Children and Age of Mother, U.S. Jewish
        Married Women Employed in the Labor Force, 1990   99

3.11   Percent in Paid Labor Force, by Age of Youngest Child,
        U.S. Jewish and Total White Married Women, Spouse
        Present, 1990   100

3.12   Percent in Paid Labor Force, by Age of Youngest Child
       and Age of Mother, U.S. Jewish Married Women, 1990   101

3.13   Percent of Workers Employed Full-Time, by Age of
       Youngest Child, Married U.S. Jewish and Total White
       Women, 1990   102

3.14   Percent in Paid Labor Force, by Number of Children and
       Years of Education, U.S. Jewish Married Women, 1990   103

3.15   Percent in Paid Labor Force, by Age of Youngest Child
       and Years of Education, U.S. Jewish Married Women,
       1990   104

3.16   Multiple Regression Analysis of Paid Labor Force
       Participation on Age, Education, Number and Ages of
       Children, U.S. Jewish Married Women, 1990   105

3.17   Multiple Regression Analysis of Hours of Work per
       Week, U.S. Jewish Married Women in the Paid Labor
       Force, 1990   107

3.18   Percent in Paid Labor Force, by Age at Birth of First
       Child, U.S. Jewish Married Women, 1990   108

3.19   Multiple Regression Analysis of Paid Labor Force
       Participation on Age, Education, Number of Children,
       Age at Birth of First Child, and Age at Marriage, U.S.
       Jewish Married Women, 1990   109

4.1   Occupation, by Sex, U.S. Jewish and
       Total White Population, 1990   118

4.2   Dissimilarity Coefficients of Occupational Distributions,
       by Sex, U.S. Jewish and Total White Population, 1990   119

4.3   The Ten Leading Occupations of U.S. Jewish Men and
       Women, 25 and over, 1990   121

4.4   Mean Years of Education, by Occupation and Sex, U.S.
       Jews, 25 and over, 1990   123

4.5   Occupation, by Years of Education and Sex, U.S. Jews,
       25 and over, 1990   124

4.6   Dissimilarity Coefficients for Occupational Distributions,
       by Years of Education and Sex, U.S. Jews, 25 and over,
       1990   126

4.7   Occupation, by Years of Education and Sex, U.S. Jewish
       and Total White Population, 1990   128

4.8   Percent of Part-Time Workers, by Occupation and Sex,
       U.S. Jews, 1990   130

4.9   Occupations of Full- and Part-Time Workers, by Sex,
       U.S. Jews, 1990   131

4.10   Family Characteristics of Occupations, by Sex,
       U.S. Jews, 1990   133

4.11   Dissimilarity Coefficients of Occupational Distributions,
       by Age and Sex, U.S. Jews, 1990   139

4.12   Occupation, by Age and Sex,
       U.S. Jews, 1990   140

4.13   Occupation, by Age, Years of Education, and
       Sex, U.S. Jews, 1990   144

4.14   Mean Occupational Prestige for Occupations,
       by Sex, U.S. Jews, 1990   146

4.15   Mean Occupational Prestige, by Education, U.S. Jews,
       1990   147

4.16   Estimated Direction of Life Cycle and Cohort Effects on
       Occupational Prestige at Different Ages   149

4.17   Stepwise Multiple Regression Analysis of Occupational
       Prestige, U.S. Jews, 25 and over, 1990   151

4.18   Mean Occupational Prestige, by Education, Part- and
       Full-Time Employment, Marital Status, Age, and Sex,
       U.S. Jews, 1990   154

4.19   Multiple Regression Analysis of Occupational Prestige
       for Men and Women Separately, U.S. Jews, 1990   158

4.20   Multiple Regression Analysis of Occupational Prestige,
       U.S. Jewish Married Women, 1990   161

5.1   Age Differences of Husbands and Wives, U.S. Jews (1990)
       and Total Population (1985, 1980)   173

5.2   Age Differences of Husbands and Wives, by Husband's
       Age, U.S. Jews, 1990   173

5.3   Mean Age at Marriage, by Age and Sex, U.S. Jews, 1990   174

5.4   Husband's Academic Degree, by Wife's Academic
       Degree, U.S. Jewish Couples, 1990   177

5.5   Highest Academic Degree of U.S. Jewish Husbands and
      Wives, and of All U.S. Jewish Men and Women, 1990   177

5.6   Types of Couples in Terms of Husband's and Wife's Paid
      Labor Force Participation, by Husband's and Wife's Age,
      U.S. Jewish and Total Couples, 1990   180

5.7   Mean Number of Children, by Cohort, for Male
      Breadwinner and Dual Earner Couples, U.S. Jews, 1990   181

5.8   Occupation of Husbands in Dual Earner
      and Male Breadwinner Couples, U.S. Jews, 1990   183

5.9   Logistic Regression of Wife's Labor Force Participation,
      U.S. Jews, 1990   185

5.10 Occupations of Husbands, by Occupations of Wives,
      U.S. Jews, 1990   190

5.11 Stepwise Multiple Regression Analyses of Husband's and
      Wife's Occupational Prestige, U.S. Jews, 1990   192

6.1   Mean Score on Jewishness Factors, by Denomination and
      Sex, U.S. Jews, 1990   205

6.2   Multiple Regression Analysis of Jewishness on Sex, Age,
      and Marital Status for Each Jewishness Factor, U.S. Jews,
      1990   209

6.3   Mean Score on Jewishness Factor, by Sex, Age, and
      Marital Status, U.S. Jews, 1990   211

6.4   Pairwise Pearson Correlation Coefficients Between
      Jewishness Factors and Highest Academic Degree, U.S.
      Jews, 1990   216

6.5   Mean Years of Education for the Most and Least Jewishly
      Involved for Each Jewishness Factor, by Age and Sex, U.S.
      Jews, 1990   218

6.6   Multiple Regression Analysis of Highest Academic
      Degree for Each Jewishness Factor, U.S. Jews, 1990   219

6.7   Multiple Regression Analysis of Highest Academic
      Degree for Each Jewishness Factor,
      for Selected Age Groups, U.S. Jews, 1990   221

6.8   Multiple Regression Analysis of Highest
      Academic Degree, for Denomination and Jewishness
      Factors, U.S. Jews, 1990   223

6.9   Multiple Regression Analysis of Highest Academic
      Degree on Jewishness Factor and Age, for Men and
      Women Separately, U.S. Jews, 1990   225

6.10 Spousal Inequality in Education, by Jewish Involvement
      for Each Jewishness Factor, U.S. Jews, 1990   226

6.11 Denomination, by Educational Characteristics of U.S.
      Jewish Couples, 1990   227

6.12 Percent in Paid Labor Force, for the Most and Least
      Jewishly Involved, for Each Jewishness Factor, Age, and
      Sex, U.S. Jews, 1990   230

6.13 Multiple Regression Analysis of Paid Labor Force
      Participation on Age, Education, and Jewishness, for Each
      Jewishness Factor and Sex, U.S. Jews, 1990   232

6.14 Multiple Regression Analysis of Paid Labor Force
      Participation on Age, Education, Marital Status, and
      Jewishness, for Each Jewishness Factor and Sex, U.S.
      Jews, 1990   236

6.15 Path Analysis of Paid Labor Force Participation, for Each
      Jewishness Factor, U.S. Jewish Married Women, 1990   240

6.16 Inequality in Spousal Occupational
      Achievement, by Jewish Involvement, U.S. Jews, 1990   244

6.17 Spousal Occupational Inequality, by Denomination, U.S.
      Jews, 1990   245

6.18 Gender Dissimilarity in Occupational Distributions
      Among the More and Less Jewishly Involved, for Each
      Jewishness Factor, U.S. Jews, 1990   247

7.1   Years of Education, by Sex, Second Generation
      European-American Israeli Jews (1983) and U.S. Jews
      (1990), 25 and over   259

7.2   Percent with 16 or More Years of Education, by Sex and
      Age, Second Generation European-American Israeli Jews
      (1983) and U.S. Jews (1990)   260

7.3   Mean Years of Education, by Age at Birth of First Child
      and Number of Children, for European-American Israeli
      Jewish (1988) and U.S. Jews (1990), Married Women,
      Ages 22–39   263

7.4 Percent in Paid Labor Force, by Sex and Age, Second Generation European-American Israeli Jews and U.S. Jews, 1990   264

7.5 Percent in Paid Labor Force, by Years of Education and Sex, Second Generation European-American Israeli Jews and U.S. Jews, 1990   266

7.6 Percent in Paid Labor Force, by Marital Status and Sex, Israeli Jews and U.S. Jews, 25 and over, 1990   268

7.7 Percent Participation in Paid Labor Force, by Number of Children, Second Generation European-American Israeli Ever-Married and U.S. Jewish Married Women, 1990   270

7.8 Percent of Part-Time Employment, by Marital Status, Israeli (1988) and U.S. Jewish Employed Women (1990)   271

7.9 Dissimilarity Coefficients Between Occupational Distributions of Second Generation European-American Israeli and U.S. Jewish Populations   272

7.10 Occupations, by Sex, Second Generation European-American Israeli and U.S. Jews, 1990   272

7.11 Occupations, by Sex and Years of Education, Israeli Jews, 1990   274

7.12 Dissimilarity Coefficients Between Occupational Distributions, by Sex and Years of Education, of Israeli and U.S. Jews, 1990   275

7.13 Age, Education, and Labor Force Differences of European-American Israeli (1988) and U.S. Jewish (1990) Husbands and Wives   278

7.14 Occupations of Husbands in Dual Earner and Male Breadwinner Couples, European-American Israeli (1983) and U.S. Jews (1990)   281

7.15 Multiple Regression Analysis of Wife's Labor Force Activity, European-American Israeli Women, 1988   285

7.16 Selected Couple Characteristics, by Religiosity, European-American Israelis, 1988   286

AI.1 Results of the Recontact Validation Phase   311

AI.2 Results of the Main Study Phase   312

AI.3   Jewish Households Qualified by Screener,
        by Reporting Status in Validation Interview   314

AI.4   Percentage of Sample with Distinctive Surnames
        (Base = Qualifiers with a Located Surname)   315

AI.5   Final Estimates of Jewish Households Reflecting
        Adjustments to "Not Qualified" Call Results   316

AII.1   Correlation Coefficients Between Jewishness Factors
        and Original Indicators, U.S. Jews, 1990   324

AII.2   Correlation Coefficients Between Jewishness Factor and
        Original Indicators, Israeli Married Women, 1988   326

LIST OF FIGURES

2.1   Years of Education, by Sex, for U.S. Jewish and Total
White Population, 18 Years and over, 1990   32

2.2   Mean Years of Education, by Age and Sex, U.S. Jewish
and Total White Population, 1990   39

2.3   Mean Years of Education, by Age at Birth of First Child,
U.S. Jewish Married Women, 1990   52

2.4   Highest Academic Degree, by Number of Children, U.S.
Jewish Married Women, 1990   56

2.5   Mean Number of Children, by Years of Education, for
U.S. Jewish (1990) and Total U.S. Women (1987)   58

3.1   Percent in Paid Labor Force, by Sex and Age, U.S. Jews,
Ages 18–34, 1990   67

3.2   Labor Force Participation, by Sex and Age, U.S. Jews and
Total White Population, Ages 18–34, 1990   68

3.3   Mean Hours of Work, by Sex and Age, U.S. Jews, 1990   69

3.4   Percent in Paid Labor Force, by Age at Marriage and Sex,
U.S. Jews, 1990   72

3.5   Percent in Paid Labor Force, by Age and Marital Status,
U.S. Jewish Men, 1990   76

3.6   Mean Hours of Work, by Age, Sex, and Marital Status,
for U.S. Jews, 1990   77

3.7   Percent in Paid Labor Force, by Age and Marital Status,
U.S. Jewish Women, 1990   80

3.8   Percent in Paid Labor Force, by Years of Education and
Sex, U.S. Jews, 1990   84

3.9   Percent in Paid Labor Force, by Age and Sex, U.S.
Jewish and Total White Population, 1990   111

3.10 Mean Hours of Work, by Age and Sex, U.S. Jews, Ages
50 and over, 1990   112

3.11   Percent in Paid Labor Force, by Years of Education and
       Sex, U.S. Jews, 50 and over, 1990   113

4.1   Mean Occupational Prestige, by Age, U.S. Jews,
       1990   150

6.1   Monotonic Multidimensional Scaling of Jewishness
       Factors, U.S. Jews, 1990   206

6.2   Mean Number of Children, for More and Less Jewishly
       Involved, for Five Jewishness Factors, U.S. Jewish
       Women, 1990   239

6.3   Path Model of Labor Force Participation, U.S. Jewish
       Women, 1990   239

7.1   Percent in Paid Labor Force, by Age, Marital Status, and
       Sex, Israeli Jews, 1990   269

8.1   Model of Jewish Economic Achievement   289

Dedicated to our 4 children—
Niv, Raz, Liat, and Maya.

ACKNOWLEDGMENTS

Many colleagues have provided feedback on various chapters in the book, and we are grateful for all of their comments. However, two colleagues stand out for their careful perusal of the entire book at various stages of its development. We are indebted to Professors Sidney Goldstein and Paul Hare for their diligent comments and constructive criticism. Of course, we must assume responsibility for the final product (for better or for worse).

CHAPTER 1

Introduction

THE ISSUES

Inequality between men and women has undergone extensive changes in the past few decades. The allocation by gender of both social roles and rewards has changed. Questions remain about whether equality in either sense is possible to achieve, the costs and benefits of such equality, to what extent it has been achieved, and under what conditions such equality is more likely to occur.

Gender Role Differentiation

One component of gender equality is how similar are the genders in a society, or what Chafetz (1990) calls *gender differentiation*—how males and females differ in terms of the roles they perform, their preferences, aspirations, language usage, and so on. Typically, men have more extensive roles in public domains in the various arenas of social action: political, religious, economic; whereas women's roles have been concentrated in the private domain. Further, even when women participate in public roles, they very often participate in different roles than men: women are teachers, men are more commonly managers; women are secretaries, men are more commonly sales agents; women are domestic maids, men are laborers. Similarly, within the domestic or private sphere, men take out the garbage, women cook.

In the last few decades, however, extensive changes have occurred in the distribution of economic roles or in the participation in the paid labor force by American women and women in industrialized countries the world over. These increases have been facilitated by a reduction in family roles. Delayed marriage and childbearing and a lowering of fertility have reduced the conflict between women's family roles and their participation in the paid labor force. Changes in the marriage patterns are also brought about by women's changes in labor force patterns: marriage and childbearing are postponed because of women's ambitions to train for and get ahead in a career before they get involved in family roles and mothering. Changes in the extent of women's roles in both the family and the economy have made the "dual earner" family prevalent among today's couples.

1

Nevertheless, role differentiation persists. Gender scholars have increasingly become aware that "doing" gender[1]—the actual practice of gender roles—is strongly affected by cultural contexts (West and Zimmerman, 1991), and there is increasing sensitivity to the differences in the context of gender relations among blacks, Hispanics, Catholics—and Jews—within the United States (Almquist, 1987; Fenstermaker, West, and Zimmerman, 1991). Further, the normative compatibility of familial roles and responsibilities with nonfamilial economic roles varies by culture and class (Lewis, 1992; Weller, 1969). In this book we consider how gender differentiation in economic roles is influenced by the American Jewish context, and what it is about the American Jewish context that is related to gender differentiation.

Differential Allocation of Rewards by Gender

Differential role allocation does not in itself imply that either gender is more or less highly valued on any particular dimension. Societies differ in the extent to which they value different roles and traits, and these roles and traits may be distributed differentially between the genders. This differential distribution may result in similar or different evaluation of men and women. Further, men and women may not be allocated the same *rewards* for performing the same roles. Such rewards (of scarce and valued resources) include material goods (such as money), access to services provided by others, leisure, power (the ability to influence other's actions or to control one's own), opportunities for psychic enrichment and gratification, and prestige (what others think about or how they evaluate what one does) (see also Chafetz, 1990).[2]

Men and women may have equal access to rewards for performance of different roles. Women in some societies are highly valued because of their role as mothers, but men receive less prestige for being fathers. Men, on the other hand, often receive social prestige for performing "breadwinning" roles rather than familial roles. This is, then, an example of similar rewards for different behaviors or roles performed. In our current American society, a higher value is generally placed on economic roles than on domestic roles—the occupation of housewife is not even considered "work" by most economic standards. To the extent that women are confined or concentrated in domestic roles, they are allocated into roles less valued by our society, even without any overt discrimination. By the same standards, men gain status and power within the family when they are sole "breadwinners"; and as they join in the economic contributions to the family, women's domestic power rises.

Rewards are not always allocated equally for similar behaviors of men and women, however. By law men and women should receive equal monetary pay for performing the same role; the whole issue of "comparable worth" addresses inequities in allocating social rewards (usually money) for performance of similar roles. But it has often been pointed out that authoritative women performing a managerial role, for instance, are evaluated differently by their subordinates than authoritative men. This is an example of unequal rewards for similar behaviors.

In the last several decades extensive research has established certain factors involved in role differentiation and stratification.[3] Gender differentiation has been related especially to norms about the differential ability or nature of men and women; norms about appropriate gender roles, which bring about differential socialization to fulfill these normative expectations; as well as differential access to training and formal preparation for the assumption of various roles. Although men and women do not generally perform the same occupational roles, they may have equal opportunity to perform these roles and for some other reason (possibly because of differential rewards associated with men and women performing these roles) not actualize this potential. Selective mating processes reinforce traditional gender differences as well. On the other hand, some roles in society are not open to men, or vice versa, not open to women: men for instance cannot (yet) give birth, and thus do not have equal access to the role of reproduction that women have. To the extent that women and men are considered to have inherently different natures, it may not be possible to allocate equal roles or rewards to them.

Variation in Gender Roles and Rewards

Research has shown that the allocation of rewards by gender varies within a society at least by social class and possibly by race, ethnicity, or religion (Almquist, 1987; Blumberg, 1984).

This variation by religion is of particular interest, because in the 1990s many have relegated religion to a specialized compartment that has little relevance to secular aspects of social behavior in the modern world. Several decades ago it was expected that one of the consequences of modernization was a secularization, which implied the end of religious influence on secular behavior (e.g., Berger, 1967; Wilson,1976). Remaining differences in the secular behavior of members of different religions were expected to be explained by variables outside the religious arena, such as socioeconomic status, family size, immigrant status. However, recent studies suggest that ethnic, cultural, and religious backgrounds still aid in the construction of social reality in the sense of setting priorities for behaviors, delimiting behavioral parameters, and reinforcing different types of achievement (e.g., Lorber and Farrell, 1991; McGuire, 1992). Further, secular achievement does not appear to come in exchange for religious commitment. Distinguishing characteristics of American Jews as well as other ethnic and religious groups lead us to reexamine the relationship between religious involvement and secular behavior. In this book we examine the relationship between involvement in the Jewish religion and other aspects of Jewish life, on the one hand, and patterns of gender equality in secular achievements, on the other.

Gender Differences and American Jews

Jews are distinguished in the United States by their socioeconomic achievement and in particular their upward mobility since the early part of this century (Goldscheider and Zuckerman, 1984; Lipset, 1995). Studies of gender equality have linked higher education to greater support of gender equality (Mason and Lu, 1988) and higher achievements of women (Bianchi and Spain, 1986; McLaughlin et. al., 1988), so that the gender gap among men and women of high levels of education is narrower than in other parts of the population. One question is whether the distinctive patterns of American Jews are attributable only to their higher educational achievements or should they be related to other elements in their cultural heritage.

American Jews are also distinctive in having low fertility in comparison to other American ethnic groups (Goldstein, 1992); they were among the most successful at family planning, adopting modern contraceptive measures when they first became available. A reduction in family roles minimizes the conflict with economic roles outside the home and is associated both with higher educational achievements and career commitment. However, the negative relationship between education and fertility is not as clear from previous research on American Jews (Goldscheider, 1986), and it is not clear how much of the distinctive achievements of American women can be attributed to reduced family roles.

One of the reasons that the relationship is complex is that Jews are known to be very familistic in a number of ways, which would indicate stronger gender role differentiation. Supporting this is the finding that the labor force participation of American Jewish women appears to be particularly sensitive to having children at home, for instance (Chiswick, 1986).

Therefore, there are contradictory implications about gender equality from a number of characteristics of American Jews. In this book we question the extent to which the high educational and occupational achievements of American Jews are shared by Jewish men and women alike. More generally, we consider whether the high achievement of the Jews eradicates the traditional gender differentiation or whether more common patterns of gender differences are just elevated to a higher level.

Because of the relatively high achievement of American Jews, we must consider whether the patterns of gender inequality observed among them are related to their level of achievement and thus may be shared by other populations who reach the same level of achievement and social status. At the same time, we consider whether the patterns we observe are related to more cultural aspects of the Jewish tradition and religion.

The Allocation of Roles and Rewards by Gender Among American Jews

This book addresses itself to gender differences in the roles and rewards of Jews in the United States. We focus on roles in education and the labor force and how they are related to family roles. Although family roles generally have more impact on women's nonfamilial roles than on men's, to some extent we consider the interrelationship of family roles with educational and labor force roles for both women and men and gender differences in the interrelationships.

The educational role of student is one that occupies a person for the most part until the ages of 18–24. More specialized graduate school may extend through the late twenties. With smaller families, the major child-rearing roles are often finished by the time mothers are in their forties, which has brought about another pattern of returning to school (or to work) after the children are more or less self-sufficient for most of the day. But most schooling, even among a college-educated population like American Jews, has been completed by the mid-twenties. Education may take place in different types of institutions, which lead to varying academic degrees and credentials. Our initial interest is in the length of engagement in educational roles (do Jewish men and women have the same amount of education?) and in the outcome of such education (what educational degrees are earned by Jewish men and women?).

These educational roles, completed early in the life cycle, act as gate-keepers for subsequent labor force activity and occupational achievement and are therefore of key importance even though they take place before the main ages of our analysis, the adult years starting from age 25.

The second set of roles we focus on are labor force roles or the extent to which Jewish men and women are active in the labor force. Labor force activity varies over the life cycle, and it varies differently for men and for women. Labor force activity is generally entered on a full-time basis only after education has been completed, although they may be engaged in simultaneously, mainly on a part-time basis. One of our interests is whether Jewish men and women enter the labor force at similar ages and in the same proportions. Once they are in, we consider how the labor force activity varies both in terms of whether or not they participate and how many hours a week they work for pay.

For men, labor force participation typically remains fairly constant through the working life cycle, with some periods characterized by more intense involvement. Retirement is usually around the age of 65, but men have begun to retire earlier, making for greater variation in the age of disengagement from the labor force. How do Jewish men's patterns of labor force participation compare with the general population's? How do they compare with Jewish women's patterns of participation?

Labor force participation has been one of the major areas of change among women in the United States in the last few decades. Women's labor force activity, unlike men's, is less stable and more variable in terms of how many hours per week are invested. It has been related to such factors as the woman's personal qualifications, her family situation, and cultural norms about when women should work outside the home. The educational qualifications of Jewish women and their small family size, on the average, seem to encourage high levels of labor force activity; but the familistic orientation of Jewish tradition, would seem to mitigate against this tendency. How do Jewish women combine family and economic roles? How is this related to their level of education? When they have the same educational qualifications as Jewish men, is their pattern of labor force activity similar?

In the labor force, the roles women and men traditionally have assumed are quite distinct. With their high educational background, and with some earlier discrimination against the entrance of Jews into certain types of firms and industries combined with cultural preferences, Jewish men have been characterized by a certain occupational concentration. Do Jewish women follow the same pattern?

As women have increasingly entered the labor force, their occupational roles have also expanded, although overall there still tends to be strong gender differentiation in occupational roles. With their high educational qualifications, have Jewish women been among the pioneers into nontraditional occupations? Do the occupations of Jewish men and women more closely resemble each other than men's and women's occupations do in the wider population?

There has been some indication that certain occupations are more conducive to combination with women's family roles than others. Given the familistic orientations of the Jewish background, we consider whether Jewish women have preferences for certain occupations, and whether their occupational roles vary by the extent and type of family obligations. Following this line, we ask whether family obligations therefore increase the gender differences in occupational roles among American Jews.

We thus consider the extent of gender differences in educational, labor force, and occupational roles; how differences in education are related to labor force and occupational differences; and how labor force differences are expressed in occupational differences as well.

The role that family obligations play in each of these areas is considered and serves to explain some of the gender differences that are found. We consider both marital roles (being married and the age at which marital roles were entered) and parenting roles (how many children there are, how young they are, and the age at which the parenting role was entered), the latter especially for women.

Gender inequality in rewards is a more difficult subject. Social rewards are considerably more difficult to measure and their sources sometimes well insulated from survey research. Many rewards come from within the family, for instance, and are not easily quantified for a survey. Some rewards, like power, are sensitive issues, and raise the question of whether the perceived power is the actual influence a person has over others. Further, the survey on which most of this book is based is limited in the personal rewards it measures. No personal income, for instance, is recorded (household income is, which lumps together the personal incomes of all household contributors).

With these limitations in the areas we are studying, we focus on the occupational prestige attached to the individual's occupation. Typically women have been excluded from both the most prestigious and the least prestigious occupations, whereas the variation in men's occupational prestige has had a wider range. Given the distinct patterns of Jewish men's and women's occupational roles, we consider gender differences in how much occupational prestige is rewarded. We then go on to consider the extent to which gender differences in prestige are related to the gender gap in educational achievement and labor force activity. In other words, is the same occupational prestige awarded to men and women given similar educational and labor force investments, or is there a gender gap in prestige that cannot be explained by their patterns of investment?

Once we have described the patterns of gender difference among Jews in these economic and educational roles and rewards, we attempt to understand their sources and explanations. Gender differences in the roles and rewards accruing from educational, labor force, and occupational activity are related to some factors distinct to American Jews (such as their strong familism), and some factors common to all Americans if not to all industrialized countries.

AMERICAN JEWS AS AN IMMIGRANT MINORITY GROUP

American Jewish patterns of socioeconomic achievement have been traced to their earlier minority and immigrant status in the United States. The majority of American Jews have now been in the the United States for two to three generations. Many of their ancestors immigrated from Eastern Europe. When they arrived, as a foreign minority with few material assets but with a tradition of scholarship and an urban mentality, the Jews turned to education as the major key to raise them out of their inferior social status. Without the possibility of returning to their countries of origin, from which most had fled persecution and pogroms, they became avid learners of English, the language of their new home. They took schooling very seriously, and if the first generation could not take advantage of the educational opportunities, they saw to it that their children did (see, for example, Karp, 1976).

Around the turn of the century, at the peak of Jewish immigration to the United States, educational opportunities were expanding. Free schooling was extended through high school, and gradually extended for a minimal fee to public colleges and universities. Their children increasingly entered occupations that made use of their educational investments, eventually raising the social status of Jews to its upper-middle-class average today.

But as in any immigration, the economic context of absorption had an influence on the Jewish situation as well. Assimilating the American success ideal of material wealth, the ideal for a Jewish man was transformed into becoming a secular success rather than the religious scholar of the old country. Such success was measured to some extent—among Americans in general, and among Jews as well—by being able to afford for the wife not to work. This ideal was related to the very immigration wave that many American Jews were part of: the supply of immigrant labor reduced the need for women and children in the labor force (McLaughlin et al.,1988), and social norms adjusted themselves accordingly. In fact, however, most immigrant women needed to contribute to the household economy, either in factory work or by having lodgers or selling in the family business (Baum, Hyman, and Michel, 1976; Hyman, 1991). The burdens of immigration also increased familial roles on the wife and mother (Hertzberg, 1989, Chapter 12), upon whose shoulders day-to-day adjustments were bound to fall. So the immigrant generation is renowned for its hardworking mothers as well as fathers.

But women's work was seen as a temporary necessity, and many aspired to days when their hard labor would not be needed or when their children could have an easier life. Further, the male ideal of being the "good provider" was undermined by having his wife need to work. To some extent this transformed the ideal woman from the traditional "woman of valor" contributing to the household economy, to an ideal wife-mother tending primarily to her domestic roles. Thus, gender role differentiation became an ideal if not a reality, and to the extent that the

Jewish "princesses" (the daughters) could be protected from such a hard life, the second generation and later the third were raised with aspirations for strong gender differentiation—the husbands as breadwinners and good providers, the wives as ladies of leisure and culture.

THE JEWISH TRADITION AND MALE DOMINANCE

Gender role differentiation can also be traced to the Jewish tradition. Although men and women were considered equal in terms of their inherent nature, gender role differentiation was both explicitly and implicitly encouraged. "Men and women are considered spiritually equal before God, but the rules governing their respective life-cycles and daily concerns are clearly intended to place them in separate domains; men and women are expected to follow different routes in the pursuit of the ideal life that God has prescribed for them . . ." (Webber, 1983, p. 143).

Men are differentiated from women in halachic provisions[4] for biologically linked rituals, such as circumcision, or using the mikveh (ritual bath) in relation to menstruation or childbirth—what is seen as "separate but equal" provisions (Bar-Yosef and Shelach, 1970). These provisions have few implications for secular achievement. More broadly, however, an implicit recognition of differentiated gender roles is expressed in some of the *halachic* differences. Women are not explicitly prescribed a specific role or confined only to their "biological" role. Marriage and procreation are mandatory obligations of men but not of women; the "law could have made mandatory for women not only marriage and procreation but also the entire range of household duties which would have defined an exclusive role for them . . . but Jewish law does not define with any precision a 'proper' or 'necessary' role for Jewish women" (Berman, 1976, p. 121). It does, however, encourage or support exercise of the wife-mother-homemaker choice, by assuring that no legal obligation could possibly interfere with the woman's performance of that role. Women appear to be granted privileges in that they are exempted from "time-bound" commandments—ritual activities and duties that must take place at a particular time. In many cases, however, women are not forbidden from performing the time-bound commandments, and in fact their optional performance of them is strongly commended (because optional performance of commandments is supposedly valued higher than obligatory performance) (Meiselman, 1978). However, they are not obligated to perform them.

Because the reasons for this gender differentiation are not given explicitly, the question has been raised as to whether this inequality in access to and performance of roles is simply "gender differentiation" or should be interpreted as "gender stratification"; that is, related to inequality in access to rewards and their allocation. If it derives from a difference in the inherent nature of men and women, it would suggest that women do not have access to the same rewards as men because of an inherent inferiority. However, the perception of women's roles and access to rewards is not allocated categorically to women but rather pertains to certain life-stages or statuses (Wegner, 1988). The nature of the genders does not seem to be conceived of as inherently different.

Women are considered "other"[5] when they are in certain statuses, but not qua woman. Thus, women in certain statuses (e.g., married women) have limitations that men in the same statuses do not have (e.g., on initiating divorce or bequeathing property while married without their spouse's consent). This differentiation results from their being women in particular statuses in terms of the life-cycle and their relation to others (particularly husbands and fathers).

However, women at other stages of life are not differentiated from men in the same way. Further, women are equal to men in such diverse areas as having the right to acquire, inherit, and bequeath property and in having the duty to observe all religious proscriptions (the so-called "positive" commandments). Hence, the inherent nature of men and women does not seem to be considered different.

The exclusion from obligatory time-bound commandments, however, made women ineligible for major leadership positions in the religion, such as leading prayers for congregations including men or bearing witness in a religious court. Not having access to the same religious roles as men resulted in an inequality in access to roles and the societal rewards (such as social prestige and power) accruing from them. The significance of this role differentiation became particularly acute in the Eastern and Central European Diaspora, where learning and teaching Torah became central to the community as the primary means of collective survival and transmission of culture. Internal political power was often linked to religious status, also excluding women because of their limited access to communal religious roles. Despite isolated role models in Jewish history (such as the biblical Deborah) and the contemporary Golda Meir, women did not generally assume communal leadership roles. To the extent that no other communal roles developed that gave similar social prestige and power for roles women did have access to, gender stratification in the religion resulted.

This gender stratification in the public religious arena persists among Orthodox and some of the Conservative denomination today. However, non-Orthodox denominations in the United States today have modified this gender differentiation in religious roles considerably (Monson, 1990; Umansky, 1985). The Reform pioneered the elimination of restrictions on whether women could officiate at religious ceremonies as rabbis in the

1950s,[6] and the Reconstructionists followed suit in the 1970's. The Conservatives officially allowed women to enter the rabbinate in the 1980s, but there is still controversy within the movement about the extent to which women may have access to traditionally male religious roles. In Reform and many Conservative congregations, for instance, women are counted as part of the official *minyan* of 10 persons needed to hold a communal service; among the Orthodox, only males are counted. In Reform and Conservative congregations there is no segregated seating in synagogue services. The Orthodox are the only denomination to have strictly upheld the traditional customs of gender differences in religious roles, and they are a minority in the United States.

If there are expectations that the gender stratification in religious roles might spill over into secular arenas of activity, it is limited by the extent to which this gender stratification is upheld among today's American Jewry. Further, even in traditional Judaism, the gender stratification in religious roles was balanced with a different perspective on familial and economic roles, as we shall see next.

THE JEWISH TRADITION AND FAMILISTIC VALUES

Another characteristic of Jewish tradition that might influence gender differentiation is the strong emphasis on the family. The importance of the family in Judaism is well known: many religious rituals and customs take place within the family, and the family's importance was strengthened by the Diaspora experience, where the main and most reliable channel of transmitting tradition from one generation to another became the family. Children are highly valued in the culture, as is the importance of the "Jewish mother" role. The proverbial saying that "the woman's honor faces inward" suggested internal power and respect for the woman in familial roles that was perhaps the basis for the modern-day powerful Jewish mother image. In any case, it served to compensate women for their exclusion from prestigious communal religious and leadership roles.

Men's family roles were also valued. They were supposed to satisfy their wife and discipline their children, and faced sanctions if they did not. They presided over ritual celebrations in the family and were responsible for teaching their children Torah. Although during the Torah period men were given complete power in their families, in later tradition a mutual understanding and respect in family roles was worked out (Berman, 1976). There was implicit role differentiation, but it did not seem to lead to the same type of gender stratification as could be seen in religious roles. Especially in Eastern and Central Europe, to which most American Jews trace their ancestry, the Jewish husband and father [was] no remote tyrant. Deprived of political independence and, in most places, the right to bear arms, Jewish men denigrated physical prowess as a cultural ideal. Instead, they cultivated intellectual and spiritual pursuits. They expressed their masculinity in the synagogue and in the house of study, not on the battlefield and not through the physical oppression of their women.

This absence of the "macho mystique" freed Jewish men and women from the sharpest differentiation of gender characteristics: the strong, emotionally controlled, yet potentially violent male vs. the weak, emotional and tender female. Jewish culture "permitted" men to be gentle and emotionally expressive and women to be strong, capable and shrewd. Sex-role differentiation was strict in many areas of Jewish life, but not in the sphere of human personality characteristics. (Hyman, 1983, pp. 24–25)

Thus the type of family roles expected of both women and men influenced also the conception of gender difference among the Jews.

Women's roles were by no means confined to the family. The proverbial "woman of valor"[7] is praised for her economic pursuits and successes; Jewish women have been noted throughout history as solid and successful businesswomen.

> [T]he Jewish working mother has a long and noble history we should make our own. The image of the *yiddishe mamma* spending all her time and energy *tsittering* over her children, cooking, scrubbing her home, and mothering her husband as well as her children, is only part of her historical role. . . . Ashkenazic women in Central and Eastern Europe, at least . . . were traditionally responsible for much of what we now describe as masculine roles. It was not uncommon, for example, for the Jewish wife to be the primary breadwinner of the family, particularly if her husband was talented enough to be able to devote himself to study. The halkhic tradition even accommodated itself to the expanding economic role of women. While halkhic prescriptions had traditionally prohibited a Jewish woman from being alone with any man other than her husband, that tradition was relaxed in those areas where women peddlers had to take business trips alone and enter Gentile homes to peddle their wares. In Western Germany in the eighteenth century, for example, religious authorities issued a dispensation to allow women to peddle, thus legalizing what was already accepted in practice. (Hyman, 1983, pp. 22–23)

Women were not prohibited from such economic pursuits, but on the contrary expected and encouraged to pursue them, to provide appropriately for the family. Economic roles were basically considered from a pragmatic point of view, as a means to provide for the family, and they were obligations of both the men and the women. The motivation for economic activity was not—for men or for women—self-actualization or a divine calling, but rather a means to an end, provision for family life. At the same time, the ideal activity for men was religious study. Women, on the other hand, were given special consideration to care for children, indicating that priority was given to their domestic responsibilities and secondarily to their contribution to the family economy.

The importance of the family thus elevated the prestige of women's roles in the family, on the one hand, and on the other, enabled women—as well as men—to participate in public economic roles to help provide for the family. At the same time, gender differentiation was encouraged by giving priority to women's domestic roles and to men's religious roles.

THE JEWISH TRADITION AND THE VALUE OF EDUCATION FOR MEN AND WOMEN

Because of the ideal of men's involvement in religious roles, and women's involvement in domestic roles, a tradition of differentiation in educational training also developed in traditional Judaism. A religion based on law and individual responsibility for knowing and performing commandments (as opposed to mediated access to knowledge, performance, and responsibility), the Jewish tradition attached strong importance to knowledge not only for an elite but for the general Jew (Eisenstadt, 1992) and hence to formal learning of these laws and their interpretations. At first this importance was attached mainly to religious learning and to those who needed the knowledge for obligatory performance (men). There was an ambivalence regarding women's education because of the value given to knowledge, on the one hand (an incentive to educate women), but on the other hand, fear that this education would mislead women into thinking they had to or should perform religious obligations that applied only to men (an obstacle to their education). Women's formal education was therefore quite neglected in traditional Judaism.

With the Enlightenment, however, as secular education became more widespread, among many Jews (but not all) the positive value of acquiring knowledge was generalized to include all education (including secular education). Both men and women were exposed to this new trend in education, and often women were exposed to it for practical reasons even when men concentrated on religious studies. While the men were to be engaged in religious study, the women were providing the economic needs of the families; and their ability to do so was enhanced by the skills taught in secular schools, such as reading, writing, mathematics (Katz, 1973; Webber, 1983).

Therefore, we see that from the Jewish tradition there is a difference in the orientation to secular achievement for men and women. Spiritually equal to men but not required to perform the same rituals and without access to the same rewards from these roles, women's pursuits were channeled to the domestic roles. These domestic family roles were highly valued; that is, different roles brought more social prestige or status for women than for men. But, in addition to family roles, women were expected and allowed to engage in multiple economic pursuits. This leads us to suggest a strong pattern of gender equality in secular achievement stemming from the Jewish heritage, mitigated by family roles for women that might interfere with such achievement, particularly at certain stages of life, and by devotion to religious study for men.

With the Enlightenment, some Jews broke away from the traditional way of life and began to participate more fully in the secular life of the wider society. As men and women both became more involved with their secular surroundings, they were, however, prey to the access allowed by the wider authorities. Such restrictions on full participation in the wider society coupled with outright persecution provided the main impetus for immigration to the United States.

THE AMERICAN SOCIAL ENVIRONMENT AND GENDER INEQUALITY

The wider American environment also provides us with some explanation for the patterns of gender differentiation that have developed among American Jews. In the last few decades, changes in the economy, in the educational opportunities, in marriage and family patterns, and in social norms all have bearing on the social environment related to gender differentiation in the United States.

In the past century changes in the industrial structure of the United States have increased the proportion of service and white-collar jobs and reduced the need for heavy manual labor. This has increased the types of jobs appropriate for an educated population like American Jews. It has also increased the kinds of jobs considered appropriate for the female labor force, and with it the demand for female labor has increased.

Dramatic changes in patterns of women's labor force participation have taken place especially since World War II, when women replaced the men who were drafted in a variety of jobs. Having shown that they were qualified as workers and responding to the economic pressures of the postwar economy, many women returned to the labor force after a brief respite following the war; and since then the female labor force has continued to grow and expand. At first, mainly older women, whose child-care responsibilities were minimal, entered the labor force; gradually mothers of younger children became the majority of the female workers.

This development was both a reflection of changing social norms about women's roles in the economy and the family and of economic pressures within the family, and a source of related social changes.

Women's labor force participation was in part enabled by changes in marriage and the family that were in the making since the beginning of the century. Increasingly dissociated from the economic and educational functions they once played, family roles play an increasingly small role in American lives, as the age of marriage is postponed, childbearing is postponed, the number of children is reduced, and the number of terminated marriages increases (Sweet and Bumpass, 1987).

American Jews have been at the forefront of these trends, with a decreasing family size of a proportion to worry the American Jewish community as to its future (DellaPergola, 1980; Goldscheider, 1986; Goldstein, 1992) and with increasingly delayed marriage and childbearing reinforced by the proportions going on to college and graduate school. This made it relatively easier for American Jewish women to take advantage of the changes in labor force and higher education norms that would characterize the United States from the 1960s.

This century has seen the expansion of both free compulsory secondary schooling and higher educational opportunities. Notable spurts in these educational developments have come from the need for Americanization of the very waves of immigration of which many American Jews were a part at the turn of the century; the compensation for education interrupted by World War II provided veterans by the GI bill; and the increasing awareness of racial and gender inequalities in education, which brought forth the Title IX Amendment of the Educational Act of 1972, ensuring equal educational opportunities for all and attempting to redress previous inadequacies.

American Jews were motivated to take full advantage of each of these advances. The immigrant situation coupled with an urban middle-class background pushed the Jews to utilize the higher education, which expanded around the turn of the century (Steinberg, 1974); the strong orientation to higher education enabled Jewish veterans to use the GI bill to finance professional training; and their value for higher education, their middle- to upper-middle-class status, and their relatively small family size made American women ready to take advantage of newly opened educational and occupational opportunities in the last two decades. Discrimination against Jews, which characterized the earlier part of the century, greatly declined in recent decades, facilitating the benefit American Jews could derive from these expanded opportunities.

It is therefore perhaps not coincidental that Jewish women have been at the forefront of the American struggle for gender equality.[8] Even though for many of these women their Jewishness seemed incidental to their feminism (Pogrebrin, 1991; Umansky, 1985), it seems that a number of issues converged to make American women prime movers in the movement for gender equality.[9] Nevertheless, apparent conflicts between the Jewish tradition and feminist orientations raise the question as to how Jewish is the drive for gender equality and how much of the involvement of Jewish women should be attributed to other causes, such as their white, middle-class, educated status in American society (Umansky, 1985).

The struggle for gender equality is reinforced by a trend toward individualism that has accompanied the other social changes of the past century or so. The value of individualism stresses the importance and right of each person to pursue his or her own self-actualization without the need for uncompromising conformity or bending to social frameworks such as the family. This has accompanied such normative changes as an increasing selectivity of family life that is individually satisfying and a belief that women as well as men should be able to seek a personally satisfying career without being restricted because of their biological sex.

The wider American social environment thus encompasses a number of forces pushing toward gender equality in secular achievement, especially in the last few decades.

THE INTIMATE FAMILY ENVIRONMENT
AND GENDER INEQUALITY

Gender differences respond not only to the wider social forces such as the wider American social environment or the Jewish tradition, but also to the more immediate family environment. Family characteristics such as socioeconomic status affect the need for wives to participate in the paid labor force, for instance. The number of children in the home affects the feasibility of the mother working outside the home. The division of labor within the couple or household unit are another of the characteristics that might intervene between the wider social forces and the individual's predispositions and qualifications.

In particular, the characteristics of the person one marries may have considerable influence on individual behavior. It has been suggested that wives who are more educated than their husbands may restrict their occupational aspirations to avoid status competition with their spouse. Wives may restrict geographic patterns of mobility to enhance their career more than their husbands. Wives who are married to husbands in their same profession show different patterns of promotion and "backstage support" than wives whose husbands are in different professions. Husbands whose wives are younger can afford to retire earlier if their wives will continue to receive an income. The educational level, labor force activity, and occupational characteristics of the spouse influence the educational advancement, labor force activity and occupational characteristics of the partner. With traditional mate-selection patterns of age and educational heterogamy, gender differences may persevere in the immediate family environment even as men and women become more equal in the wider society.

CHANGES IN GENDER ROLES AND REWARDS

All of these social forces have brought about changes in gender roles and the allocation of rewards to men and women in the last several decades. To some extent we look at these changes by comparing different cohorts of American Jews. We are limited by the survey on which most of the book is based in that it uses a cross-sectional sample at one point in time rather than a longitudinal study that follows the same people over several points in time. As a result, age cohorts double as our indicator of life cycle stages and birth cohort differences, which sometimes confuses the conclusions we can reach. Nevertheless, certain cohort differences are apparent, and we present them with appropriate reservations.

CAUSAL DIRECTIONS

Social scientists are frequently plagued with the question of what comes first. We find, for instance, a relationship between family roles and roles in the economy. The debate about whether women have fewer children because they have invested more in a career and do not want to give it up or whether women who are less interested in having children look for outside involvement is an example of a chicken-and-egg situation that has not been resolved. Decisions are apparently made at several life cycle stages that affect further courses of action. But family and economic roles are not related only for women. When we find that Jewish married men have higher occupational prestige, for instance, it is difficult to determine whether Jewish men who are more successful in their careers are more likely to marry or whether they are successful because they have a family to support them in their endeavors. Or whether the connection between marriage and career success is due to a third factor, such as ability to carry responsibility. A longitudinal survey over several points in time would be more helpful in determining the appropriate direction of interpretation, as would more in-depth interviews about attitudes, goals, and aspirations. Without these added insights, we rely on our understanding of current sociological analysis to make sense of the findings.

THE PRESENT ANALYSIS

In this book we attempt to determine the extent to which American Jews show a distinguishable pattern of gender equality. Are American Jewish women equal to Jewish men in secular achievement? And, if so, how much of it is atrributable to their Jewish heritage or in spite of it or because of their particular situation as American Jews? Does Jewish involvement foster more or less gender equality? Are the patterns we find universal for all types of Jews? We approach these questions in a number of ways.

First we try to determine the distinctiveness of gender role differentiation and reward achievement in comparison with the wider American society.

Second, we try to relate different degrees and types of Jewish involvement among American Jews to their patterns of secular achievement. We conceive of "Jewish involvement" as a multifaceted concept, which encompasses what we normally consider as religiosity (ritual observance), formal and informal communal involvement and affiliation, and formal Jewish training. We consider which of these aspects of Jewishness are related to men's and women's secular achievement; whether they are related in the same way for men and for women; and how the importance of these various dimensions of Jewishness differ over cohorts.

A competing explanation of why American Jews are distinct is their minority status and immigrant roots (cf. Goldscheider, 1986). We consider this explanation in two ways. If the minority status explains the distinctiveness of American Jewish patterns of behavior, then the greater involvement in that minority group, the more "Jewish" would be the behavior. On the other hand, it is assumed from this perspective that those less involved in Jewish life will be less likely to exhibit "Jewish" patterns of behavior. The relationship between "Jewishness" and the gendered patterns of achievement are considered from this perspective.

Another aspect of the minority thesis is tested by comparing American Jews to Jews with a similar background (second generation European immigrants) who live in Israel, where they do not have a minority status. The pressures that led American Jews to stress secular attainment as a goal seem to be integrally connected to their minority status and the values of this particular wider society (the United States). What happens when the wider environment is pervasively Jewish? As the majority in their own country, Israeli Jews may exhibit patterns of behavior less influenced by a wider non-Jewish environment than would a Jewish minority in a predominantly non-Jewish country.

THE DATA

Our analysis of American Jews is based primarily on the National Jewish Population Survey (NJPS) conducted by the Council of Jewish Federations and the North American Jewish Data Bank in 1990. The survey represented 6.8 million "Jewish" individuals living in 3.2 million households with at least one Jewish member (including persons born Jewish or of Jewish parents, but not currently calling themselves Jewish). (For a fuller description of the survey, see Appendix I.)

The original sample of respondents included 2,441 interviewees who gave information about themselves and other members of their households. For our purposes, we define *Jewish respondents* as those who had the opportunity to be influenced by Jewish tradition, which influence we were studying. Therefore to be included as Jewish in our sample, respondents either (1) said they were born Jewish and are currently Jewish, (2) said they were born Jewish and raised Jewish even if they do not currently identify themselves as Jewish, or (3) said they were raised Jewish and currently identify themselves as Jewish. Our rationale was that these three types of people had exposure to Jewish norms for the greater part of their lives, and therefore we could test whether their secular behavior was related to their Jewishness. Persons who were not "Jewish" on more than one of these three questions were excluded from our analysis.

This selection process resulted in a sample size of 1,800 respondents ages 18 or over who fulfilled our criteria of being Jewish. To these 1,800 we added the other adult household members who met the same criteria of Jewishness, expanding the sample from 1,800 to 3,020.

For simple calculations, "household" weights were used that make the sample representative of the wider Jewish population with the same attributes (see Appendix I for more explanation). Unless otherwise noted, the numbers reported in tables are weighted. For analyses based on correlations or using significance tests, including factor analyses and multiple regressions, the unweighted data were used.[10]

For the study of couple units, we included married respondents and their spouses if either the husband or the wife met the same criteria of Jewishness. Only married respondents whose spouse was currently living with them were included; 1,414 couples met these criteria.

To put the findings in perspective, we offer two kinds of comparison. (1) A comparison was made with the wider American population of which Jews are a small part (only 2.5 percent of the white population).[11] The data about the general American population are taken from published governmental statistics. When possible we have narrowed these data to the white population, because almost all Jews are white, and this constitutes the most probable reference group for American Jews. (2) A comparison was made with Israeli Jews. The Israeli data are taken from published data from the Israel Central Bureau of Statistics and from a special survey of urban married Jewish women that was conducted in 1987–88. More details about these data sources are found in Chapter 7.

A PREVIEW OF WHAT FOLLOWS

The first part of the book describes the extent of gender inequality in education, labor force participation, and occupational attainment among American Jews. We focus first on education and training, which act as key "gatekeepers" to roles in the economy (Chapter 2). Our focus on gender differences in educational attainment is seen as a key for access to similar occupational roles and the rewards that derive from them. We then assess the gender similarity in labor force behavior and occupational attainment (Chapters 3 and 4).

We then consider the differential allocation of rewards resulting from the secular attainment of Jewish men and women. In particular, we concentrate on the allocation of occupational prestige, and the extent to which it is linked to educational training and similar labor force roles (Chapter 4).[12] Hence, we concentrate on the allocation of rewards from the wider society rather than from within the Jewish community itself.[13] We do so first for the whole population of American Jewish men and women (Chapters 2–4) and then by comparing spouses within Jewish households (Chapter 5).

In the second part of the book we consider the extent to which the characteristics and behaviors we identify in the first part of the book are shared by all types of Jews. We do so first (in Chapter 6) by differentiating American Jews by different types and extents of involvement in being Jewish and comparing the patterns of achievement of men and women of different Jewish involvement. In Chapter 7, we compare patterns of gender inequality between American Jews and Israeli Jews of similar background, to determine the effect of being a minority group in the United States. The final chapter summarizes the findings and the conclusions that can be drawn from our analysis.

PART 1

Gendered Patterns of Secular Achievement Among American Jews

CHAPTER 2

Education: Gatekeeper to
Gender Equality in the Economy

INTRODUCTION

As the main ticket to roles in the economy, education is both a precursor of economic attainment and a result of societal norms and channeling, which are conditioned by the desired outcomes for men and women in society. How educated one becomes depends on many factors: socioeconomic status, which influences the ability to pay for higher education; family size (number of siblings), which influences both resources and attention available for children (Blake, 1989); mother's and father's educational level, which influences both socioeconomic status and parental aspirations for educational achievement (Sewell, Hauser, and Wolf, 1980); peer aspirations for educational achievement (Sewell et al., 1980); cognitive ability or intelligence (Jencks et al., 1972); one's own achievement orientations or educational aspirations, influenced in great part by the wider values and cultural environment; and school factors such as curriculum tracking (Oakes, 1985) and teacher encouragement (Rosenthal and Jacobson, 1968). The inequality of educational experiences in the United States for men and women has received considerable attention, and although legal remedies for gender inequality in education have been established and to a great extent enforced, a 1992 report could still be definitively entitled, "How Schools Shortchange Girls" (AAUW, 1992). Although formal requirements and opportunities are legally the same for boys and girls, teaching strategies, peer, parent, and teacher expectations, gender bias in testing, hidden curriculum bias, and staffing patterns all reinforce traditional gender differences in educational experiences, motivation, attainment, and outcomes.

Critical to the process of educational attainment are social expectations influenced not only by the school environment, but the family and informal social circles of friends and relatives (Sewell et al, 1980). Social norms about succeeding in school have a snowball effect, channeling efforts and talents either toward higher education (as among Jews) or against school achievement (see, for instance, the case of the Hallway

Hangers described in MacLeod, 1987). Not only does educational attainment differ by socioeconomic class, race, and ethnicity—for cultural as well as material reasons—but so do gender differences, given different gender role expectations in different cultures and subcultures (AAUW, 1992, Ch. 3).

We focus here on the subculture of American Jews to determine what are the gender differences in educational attainment among them. Jews are known as high achievers in education and economic roles. Is the orientation to high achievement extended to Jewish men and women alike?

The sources of the high educational orientations of American Jews are rooted both in the values derived from the Jewish heritage and manifest in parental, peer, and student aspirations for higher education, and in the socioeconomic situation of the Jewish immigrant to the United States, which provided both impetus and opportunity for higher education.

The Value of Education in the Jewish Tradition

Judaism has always placed a high value on learning. In the shtetl of Eastern Europe, from which most American Jews trace their background, status was a function of learning, and the whole family was involved in seeing that the children, especially the boys, received proper and adequate education (Zborowski and Herzog, 1962).

> In order to lead a moral and ethical life and to adhere to the laws that are believed to be divinely authored one had to study and interpret complex texts which further reinforced the central value of intellectual accomplishment and created the need for specialized institution (schools) to realize these primary religious-cultural goals.
>
> One who did not study, who did not gain Jewish knowledge, was labeled an *am ha'aretz*, an igonoramus, (literally, a person "close to earth"), outside the divine light of knowledge. It was a stinging rebuke to be considered devoid of learning, and even the very poor considered the education of their male children a vital necessity. (Brumberg, 1986, p. 21)

Education was traditionally linked primarily to religious study. "Jews conceived of learning as a religious act and as a prerequisite to leading a full and just life. Learning was almost wholly concerned with discovering how to lead one's life in accordance with the precepts and laws of God, as set forth in his Torah (the Pentateuch) as interpreted by the great rabbis of old and recorded in the collection of commentaries known as the Talmud" (Brumberg, 1986, p. 25).

It should be emphasized, however, that included in religious study was a considerable amount of applied knowledge to everyday life, because (as we have mentioned earlier) Jewish law prescribed a total way of life.

Major parts of the law related to such "secular" topics as economic relations between people, marriage, and divorce and were not confined to typically "religious" subjects concerning the human relationship to God and
the transcendental. The later extension of the value of learning to secular
learning was not as radical a change as it might be considered had the religious learning been confined to strictly religious matters.

Religious studies traditionally were valued primarily for males, as
females were not expected to fill the religious roles that required extensive
schooling and literacy. "The education of females was limited or neglected
because of the gender-related role differences encoded in traditional Jewish religious practices" (Brumberg, 1986, p. 25). Because women were not
required to perform religious roles to the extent that men were, schooling
in the appropriate performance and reasoning behind these laws was not
as necessary as it was for men. The Jewish tendency to rationalism, for
having a reason and a purpose behind actions, would limit "unnecessary" learning.

The primary roles of women in Jewish tradition are familial (related
to the family). Education, on the other hand, is an investment in nonfamilial roles, which usually prepares the student for an occupational career.
In the case of traditional Judaism, the purpose of educating women was
seen differently from educating men. The religious obligations and options
being much fewer for women, their religious education was minimal and
often informal. At some points in Jewish history, the education of girls in
religious matters was even considered threatening, as it would not be
properly applied and might raise the aspirations of girls for roles they
were not allowed to perform.

Throughout Jewish history, schooling was not confined to religious
learning, but the availability of secular learning and the value placed on it
fluctuated by historical circumstances and opportunities and the value
climate both within and outside of the Jewish society.[1] The Enlightenment movement that spread through Europe reached most of the European Jews who were later to immigrate to the United States, especially
those living in urban settings in Europe. When opportunities opened up in
the middle of the nineteenth century, many Jews were ready to generalize
their value on learning to secular spheres as well. In some communities,
daughters were encouraged to become schooled in secular matters even
while the sons were restricted to the more traditional religious education
(Fishman, 1993). In part this was due to the more time-consuming religious training of the boys; in part it was because girls could put their
secular training to practical use as they engaged in economic activity to
support the family.

But the Jews were dependent on wider authorities, who regulated
the availability of institutions of secular education. For instance, even

though the czarist government in Russia at first encouraged the secular education of Jews, by the end of the century it had placed restrictions on Jews' entry into secondary schools and universities (Brumberg, 1986, p. 25).

Thus many of the Jewish immigrants who arrived to America at the turn of the century had aspirations for a secular education, especially for their children, which had been frustrated abroad. Evidence of this comes from the aspirations of Jewish mothers, who in the Eastern European shtetl had prayed that their son be a rabbi, in the United States transformed their aspirations for sons to be doctors or lawyers.

American Jews as Immigrants and Educational Aspirations

The largest waves of Jewish immigration reached the United States around the turn of the century (1881–1924) just at the time when mass public education was spreading throughout the nation and extending to the secondary and post-secondary level, particularly in the Northeastern states where most of the Jewish immigrants settled.[2] Not only were the Jewish immigrants "in the right place at the right time" for public education (Steinberg, 1974, p. 31), their social and economic background (which gave them some money to invest in children's education and occupations that made aspirations for education sensible), family characteristics, and urban background were all conducive to taking advantage of the new educational opportunities (Goldscheider and Zuckerman, 1984). That most of the Jewish immigrants intended to stay in the United States permanently (unlike many of the other ethnic groups who immigrated to the United States during this same period) also motivated them more to learn the language by attending school (Steinberg, 1974; Goldscheider and Zuckerman, 1984). In other words, Jewish immigration coincided with the spread of mass education, and the settlement patterns and socioeconomic status of the Jews were such that it allowed them to take advantage of these new opportunities.

Another aspect of the immigration process affected the orientation of American Jews to educational attainment. The desire to become successful in the new culture, which regarded them as ascriptively different, channeled aspirations for mobility to achievement dimensions such as education and occupation. Jewish immigrants to the United States perceived of American education as the key to social mobility in that society. Jews were not the only immigrants to view education in the same way,[3] but the degree of aspiration and propensity for education were reinforced by the cultural characteristics in the Jewish heritage. If the first generation could not take full advantage of it, they sacrificed so that their children could, transferring the focus of their aspirations for social status onto their children (documented, for example, in Karp, 1976). The overambitious Jewish mother stereotype derived from this transferring of status aspirations onto the child, through which the mother could enjoy vicarious status if she could not experience it directly herself.

Socioeconomic Constraints on Educational Attainment
of the Immigrants and Implications for Gender Differences

However, the circumstances of immigration favored males over females in access to the educational opportunities in the United States, because of the strain in family resources it imposed. Generally, it may be said that immigration even in the best of circumstances imposes a financial burden on immigrants, as they relocate, repurchase household goods, spend more time and energy on solving daily problems that once were taken for granted, generally depleting immigrants' resources. This may result in a lack of resources to go beyond education that is free or reaches into economically productive years. Even children may have to leave school early to help support the family. Or one child must be chosen at the expense of others to be the one to pursue higher education. And, indeed, many American Jewish immigrants had to do just that.

Even though the distribution of family socioeconomic status cannot be said to differ for girls and boys, the willingness with which parents use their economic resources to pay for the education of girls and boys often differs (even today, see Stockard, 1980; Walters, 1986), because traditionally girls have not always utilized the capital investment of education (or at least their investments paid off less than investments in boys' education). With lower participation rates in the paid labor force and a greater probability of more interruptions in their labor force activity due to conflict with normative family roles, girls' education might have seemed more of a luxury than a necessity. When resources are scarce, girls' education may therefore be sacrificed before that of boys. In the circumstances of immigration, which imposed a long-term financial burden, girls' education may have been sacrificed before that of boys, even if there were aspirations for the education of both.[4] Because girls' educational achievements have been found to be strongly influenced by their mothers' educational achievements (more than boys'),[5] the historical experience of immigration may have set out a long-term and exaggerated pattern of unequal educational attainment for the American Jews.

Nevertheless, Jewish immigrants were exposed to an environment fostering gender equality of educational opportunity. The expansion of free public schooling for both sexes was an important factor in overcoming any gender differentiation in aspirations for secular schooling—at least through the free and compulsory level—stemming from traditional Judaism.

Both women and men took advantage of these new opportunities. "Even though sons were definitely favored when opportunities for secular education were limited, Jewish women were more likely to receive extended secular education than any other group of women [in the United States]. In New York in 1910, at a time when Jews made up about 19 percent of the population, 40 percent of the women enrolled in night school were Jewish; by 1916, 25 percent of the graduates of Hunter College were Jewish women of Eastern European origins; and by 1934 more than 50 percent of New York female college students were Jewish" (Fishman, 1993, p. 70).

The socioeconomic status of American Jewish families has improved with generations in the country, and scarcity of resources is less likely to be the cause for unequal access to higher education today. Nevertheless, the importance still attached to the familial roles of Jewish women and to the occupational roles of Jewish men may make investment in the education of Jewish women seem less profitable (from an economic point of view) and more necessary for the Jewish male.

Gender Differences in Education in the
Wider American Environment

We must remember that the environment affecting the education of American Jews is a combination of the wider American environment, the Jewish environment of their homes and social circles, and the environment that influenced their parents to aspire and provide education for their children. A more complete analysis would therefore look for the relationship between the achievement of today's Jewish population and the Jewish and other characteristics of their parents' environments. Unfortunately, little information is available from the NJPS or other data sets about the Jewishness of their parents' environment. In a later chapter (Chapter 6), we will examine whether the extent to which our samples' homes and social circles are Jewish is related to their educational attainment. Here, we will mention some of the changes that have happened since the turn of the century as regards gender and education in the wider American society.

Although compulsory elementary and secondary education for both girls and boys had become common in most states around the turn of the century and solidified by the 1930s, gender bias in higher education persisted longer, partly because of the association of higher education with preparation for professional careers that were not open to women (Hunter College, 1983) and partly because of the assistance offered men through the GI bill after World War II (McLaughlin et al., 1988). Only since 1960 have American women begun to catch up with the level of college education of American men, and the higher the level of education is, the greater the remaining gap.

The question of gender bias in the wider American educational environment became topical in the late 1960s, following the concern with educational inequality raised by the civil rights movement and its attentiveness to racial inequality in the schools, and the women's movement, which inspired research and attention to gender inequalities in education. Title IX of the 1972 Education Amendments Act took legal steps to prohibit sex discrimination in any education program or activity receiving federal financial assistance, going a long way to redress formally imbalances that had developed.

The increase in opportunities for women's higher education came about in great part as a response to the change in norms about women's roles, especially the increasing acceptance that women (especially married mothers) would participate in the labor force throughout their life cycle and that appropriate training for a woman's career was a worthwhile investment—a change that began with World War II and had wideranging effects especially from the 1950s (McLaughlin et al., 1988).

We know from reports like the 1992 report of the American Association of University Women (AAUW) that there is still a high degree of gender bias in the schools and in the environments surrounding the schools that depresses womens' educational aspirations, self-confidence, and ease in excelling in higher education to the same level and in the same areas as men (see also Sadker and Sadker, 1989). In higher education, men tend to be more professionally oriented, whereas more women attend general liberal arts colleges and seem to strive for a well-rounded but less career-defined educational background. This may be related to differential occupational aspirations, partly conditioned by educational experiences and partly by friends, family, and the media, as well as to different norms about how compatible men's and women's family roles are with the nonfamilial roles education enjoins. At lower levels of education, more males pursue vocational education whereas females of similar abilities get general education degrees (Vetter, 1989). Gender differences in education are also related to curriculum bias, since the motivation to achieve has been related to identification with the subject matter, and gender bias in educational content undoubtedly contributes to the lack of gender equity in educational attainment. Traditional subject matters such as history and the humanities have largely neglected women's contributions, not only in terms of individuals noted but also by their very definitions: history emphasizing political milestones and military events, which have traditionally been male domains; the humanities emphasizing rational objective logic (O'Barr, 1989; Gabriel and Smithson, 1990). The growth in women's studies courses and interdisciplinary departments in the last decade or so offers some redress to the previous neglect.[6] Other sources of gender bias derive from different perceived occupational opportunities on the parts of students, their counselors, and teachers. The changes toward gender equality in education are continuing gradually in the United States, but such change takes time, and there still is a long way to go.

Just as Jewish immigrants were at the "right place at the right time" and with the "right" characteristics to take advantage of the expansion of mass higher education at the turn of the century (Steinberg, 1974), American Jewish women might be seen as optimal beneficiaries of the expansion of educational opportunities for women since the 1970s. They were mainly from middle- and upper-middle-class families, who could afford to send their daughters (and wives) on to higher education. They came from relatively well-educated fathers (and sometimes mothers) who valued education and the horizons it broadened. Their cultural heritage had so transformed itself that it emphasized liberal and universalist values, which minimized ideologically the importance of ascriptive traits, like sex (Liebman and Cohen, 1990). Jewish families were shrinking in size and were characterized by delayed marriage and childbearing, which the American Jewish community had witnessed with apprehension as to its future, but nevertheless reduced the obstacles for women's higher education and its natural outcomes, such as employment and career commitment. The relatively small family size characterizing American Jews also contributed to the ability to provide higher education for all children (quality rather than quantity was invested in children) earlier than for populations with more children per family.

Even though some of the traditional barriers to equal secular education among Jewish men and women have diminished in influence in recent cohorts, differential role expectations within the Jewish tradition and in the wider American surroundings continue to generate gender differences in educational attainment. In this chapter, we consider the extent to which American Jews have realized gender equality in education, which infrastructure was reinforced in the 1970s, and whether their change in this direction has come about faster and more completely than the wider population whose characteristics did not foster the same receptiveness as American Jewish characteristics seem to.

Educational achievement in our survey is indicated by two main variables: (1) the number of years of formal education reported by the respondent (and especially the number of years of post-high school education); and (2) the highest academic degree earned (high school diploma, vocational degree/A.A., B.A., M.A., Ph.D., or professional degree[7]). This also allows us to consider the academic product of the years invested in education.

EDUCATIONAL ATTAINMENT AMONG
AMERICAN JEWISH MEN AND WOMEN TODAY

The Education of American Jews

In 1990, American Jews continue to be well educated in comparison to the rest of the American population (Table 2.1 and Figure 2.1). With a median education of 15.5, over 95 percent have attained a high school education, nearly 80 percent have gone on to college, and over half have completed 16 or more years of schooling. With an average level of education of 16.0 years, over 80 percent of the American Jewish men have completed some post-secondary schooling, and over 60 percent have 16 or more years of schooling. With an average of 14.9 years of schooling, three-quarters of the American Jewish women have some post-secondary schooling, and nearly half, 16 or more years of education.

TABLE 2.1
Years of Education, by Sex, U.S. Jewish and Total White Population,
18 and over and 25 and over, 1990

Years of Education	U.S. Jewish			U.S. White		
	Males	*Females*	*Total*	*Males*	*Females*	*Total*
Population 18 Years and Over						
11 or less	4.3	3.9	4.1	21.4	21.7	21.0
12	12.8	22.1	17.4	35.7	42.3	39.3
13–15	22.3	24.5	23.4	17.6	17.4	19.4
16 or more	60.6	49.5	55.1	25.4	18.4	20.2
Total (%)	100.0	100.0	100.0	100.0	100.0	100.0
Median	16.0	14.9	15.5	12.8	12.7	12.7
(*N* in thousands)	(1,871)	(1,815)	(3,687)	(74,830)	(88,393)	(163,223)
Population 25 Years and Over						
11 or less	4.3	4.2	4.3	21.8	22.2	22.0
12	13.1	23.1	18.1	35.8	41.0	38.5
13–15	19.1	21.6	20.3	17.9	18.3	18.1
16 or more	63.4	51.1	57.4	24.5	18.5	21.3
Total (%)	100.0	100.0	100.0	100.0	100.0	100.0
(*N* in thousands)	(1,710)	(1,672)	(3,382)	(74,056)	(82,398)	(156,449)

Source: 1990 NJPS; Kominski and Adams (1992), Table 1; for U.S. whites 25 and over, unpublished tabulations from the *Current Population Survey*, 1990 annual averages, U.S. Department of Labor.

FIGURE 2.1
Years of Education by Sex, for U.S. Jewish and Total White Population,
18 Years and Over, 1990

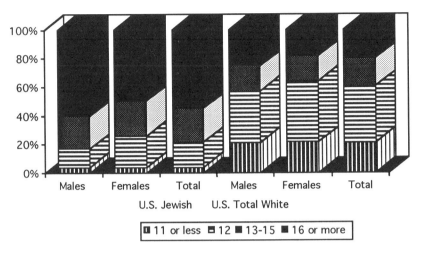

Sources: NJPS, 1990; Kominski and Adams (1992), Table 1.

In comparison, the median education of the white[8] population in the United States is 12.8, nearly 60 percent never went beyond grade 12, and only 22 percent completed 16 or more years of schooling. Over half of the men did not go beyond high school, and only a quarter completed 16 or more years of schooling. Clearly, American Jewish men are more educated than their counterparts in the general white population in the United States. More than twice as many Jewish men completed 16 or more years of education, and nearly five times as many whites did not complete even 12 years of education than among American Jewish men.

The differences between the general white population of women and the American Jewish women are similar to those found between the two groups of men. Nearly two-thirds of the women in the general white American population had no post-secondary schooling and only 18 percent completed 16 or more years of education. Nearly three times as many Jewish women completed 16 or more years of education, and more than five times as many of the women in the general white population completed less than 12 years of education.

Because such a high percentage of Jews continue on to college education, the inclusion of the age group 18–24, during which education is still being completed for many of them, might distort the comparison between Jews and the rest of the white population. However, as the second part of Table 2.1 shows, proportions change very little when we consider only the population 25 and over. This enables us to use comparative data published for the 18 and over population only, as in Table 2.2, without risking undue distortion of the conclusions.

Their relatively high level of education is reflected in the degrees earned by the American Jews. Not all Jewish sons get to fulfill the stereotypical mother's dream of becoming doctors or lawyers but most of them finish college. Over 60 percent of the Jewish men have at least a B.A., and over 30 percent have achieved some graduate or professional degree (14 percent have M.D.s, and 14 percent have law degrees; Table 2.2).

Over half of the American Jewish women have at least a B.A. and over 25 percent, a graduate or professional degree. Most (84 percent) of the graduate degrees they earned are M.A.s; 6 percent earned Ph.D.s, 6 percent, law degrees; and 4 percent, M.D.s.

TABLE 2.2
Highest Academic Degree, by Sex, U.S. Jewish and Total White Population, 18 and over, 1990

Highest Degree Earned	U.S. Jewish			U.S. White		
	Males	Females	Total	Males	Females	Total
None	4.8	3.0	3.7	19.2	19.5	19.4
High school diploma	29.6	40.3	34.9	52.7	55.7	54.3[a]
Vocational, Associate of arts	4.3	5.2	4.7	6.4	7.8	7.2
Bachelor of arts	31.3	28.9	30.1	14.1	12.0	13.0
Master of arts	16.2	19.1	17.6	4.7	4.0	4.4
Ph.D.	5.3	1.2	3.3	1.0	0.3	0.6
First professional degrees[b]	9.1	2.3	5.7	1.9	0.3	1.2
Total (%)	100.0	100.0	100.0	100.0	100.0	100.0
(N in thousands)	(1,867)	(1,814)	(3,582)	(75,262)	(81,123)	(156,385)

[a]For U.S. whites, this includes those who went to college but received no degree or certificate.
[b]This includes dental, medical, law degrees for U.S. Jews; for U.S. white population, this includes in addition chiropracty, optometry, osteopathy, pharmacy, podiatry, theology, and veterinary medicine.

Source: NJPS, 1990; National Center for Education Statistics (NCES), 1993, Table 11.

In contrast, almost a fifth of the general white population had no diploma or degree; less than 20 percent have more than a high school diploma; and only 6 percent have gone on to get graduate or first-pro- fessional degrees (Table 2.2). Less than 20 percent of the men in the wider U.S. white population have at least a B.A.—less than one-third of the proportion among the Jewish men—and only 7 percent have graduate or professional degrees—less than a quarter of the proportion of Jewish men. More than three-quarters have no post-secondary degree, more than double the proportion among Jewish men.

Similar differences are found between Jewish women and the wider white population of women. Among white women in the United States, only 17 percent have a B.A. or higher degree, compared to nearly three times that proportion among Jewish women, and less than 5 percent have some graduate degree, less than a quarter of the proportion among Jewish women.

Both Jewish men and women are considerably more educated than their counterparts in the wider population of American whites. The dif- ferences between the two sets of men are similar to that between the two sets of women and are reflected in the different distributions of years of education and degrees achieved of the total population in each group.

The Gender Gap in Educational Attainment of American Jews

Even though both Jewish men and women are considerably more edu- cated than their counterparts in the wider population, we still find tradi- tional types of differences in the educational levels of Jewish men and women. Jewish men are more educated than Jewish women. They have an average of 1.1 more years of education, which reflects a higher percentage of men continuing on to 16 or more years of education and almost twice as many women as men stopping their education at high school. This may be result of there being a higher proportion of the elderly among women than men (since women live longer on the average than men) and a bigger gender gap among the elderly, given the remaining effect of immigration and the lower socioeconomic status that followed it. (We will control for age in a later section.)

The gender gap increases with each year of higher education—more than twice the proportion of men as women completed 20 or more years of schooling (18 vs. 8 percent, respectively). Apparently the gender gap in education has not been erased but may have been moved to a higher level of education.

Unlike the Jews, the median years of schooling of men and women in the general white population in the United States is nearly the same: the men have only .1 year more education on the average than the women. As among the Jews, more women than men stop their education at high school, but the proportions are closer for men and women in the wider population. More men than women complete 16 or more years of education, and the gender gap among those having 16 or more years of education is somewhat greater than among the Jews.

A similar picture can be seen when we compare the academic degrees of men and women. Overall, Jewish women are more likely to have only high school diplomas than men; and although two-thirds of the men have some college degree, just over half of the women do. A much higher proportion of women who did earn graduate degrees earned M.A. degrees than of men, and higher proportions of men earned doctorates, law, dental, or medical degrees (Table 2.3). "My son the doctor" is, in reality, "my son" and not "my daughter": of all the medical degrees held by Jews in the 1990 population, only 14 percent belonged to women; of all the law degrees held by Jews, 27 percent belonged to women. As we shall see later, this is changing gradually but is still the dominant pattern among Jewish men and women.

Among the general American white population, the degrees earned are quite similar between men and women. Seventy-four percent of the men and 78 percent of the women have a high school diploma or less, and only 7 percent of the men and 4 percent of the women have graduate degrees.

Among those who have graduate degrees, 59 percent of the men and 84 percent of the women have M.A. degrees, quite similar to what is found for American Jewish men and women. American women had earned 15 percent of the medical or dental degrees in the wider population and 13 percent of the law degrees in 1987 (Kominski and Adams, 1992, Table 3). Although the proportion of women with medical or dental

TABLE 2.3
Graduate Degrees Earned, by Sex, U.S. Jews, 25 and over, 1990

Graduate Degree	*Males*	*Females*
M.A.	52.8	84.5
Ph.D.	17.4	5.5
D.D.S.	2.1	0
M.D.	14.2	3.8
Law	13.5	6.2
Total (%) earning graduate degrees	100.0	100.0
(N in thousands)	(563)	(405)

Source: NJPS, 1990.

degrees is similar in the wider population and among American Jews, the proportion of law degrees going to women is greater among the Jews than in the wider population.

The Relative Efficiency of Years Invested in Schooling for Jewish Men and Women

One reason for the disparity in educational attainment may be that men and women invest different numbers of years to reach academic degrees. If men are really more professionally oriented in their education, they may go directly to a degree, whereas women may spend more years in school without getting a marketable credential.

In fact, however, there is very little difference between Jewish men and women in terms of the years they have spent in school for each academic degree, and except for medical and law degrees, women have invested somewhat fewer years for each degree (Table 2.4). Women have invested about a year more schooling on the average to earn an M.D., and about half a year more to earn a law degree. These degrees, which take on the average 19–21 years to complete, would bring students to a minimum age of 25 if they learned straight through from first grade at age 6. By that age, most Jewish women have married and are well on their way to having children (average age at first child is 26); increased family roles may slow down women's progress. Included among those women who go on for medical and law degrees are also women who have switched to these fields mid-career or after having taken a break to raise families, since the medical and law fields have only recently opened up widely to women

TABLE 2.4

Mean Years of Education for an Academic Degree, by Sex,
U.S. Jews, 25 and over, 1990

Academic Degree	Males	N in (Thousands)	Females	N in (Thousands)
None	10.2	(78)	10.1	(54)
High school diploma	13.0	(452)	12.6	(644)
Associate, R.N.	14.4	(74)	14.3	(84)
B.A.	16.2	(534)	16.1	(482)
M.A.	17.9	(301)	17.3	(344)
Ph.D., professional	19.8	(208)	20.2	(52)
Ph.D.	21.4	(78)	21.4	(20)
D.D.S.	19.9	(8)	—	—
M.D.	20.3	(61)	21.3	(10)
Law	18.9	(61)	19.5	(22)

Source: NJPS, 1990.

(Jacobs, 1989); this may also add a year or two to their training. All in all, however, it is difficult to attribute the differences in educational attainment to a lack of efficiency on the part of women.

To determine whether the slight differences in the number of years it takes for men and women to get academic degrees was significant, we compared the results of multiple regression analyses predicting the academic degree achieved of men and women, respectively, by years of study (and controlling for age, to minimize any changes that might have been introduced by changes in the years needed to get a B.A., M.A., or other degree over time).[9] The nonstandardized regression coefficients[10] were virtually identical for men and women ($B = .364$ and $B = .359$, respectively); that is, a year of study is worth the same increment in degree for women as for men.[11] This reinforces the conclusion that the efficiency of their educational investment is virtually the same for American Jewish men and women.

Among the general American population, women seem to get their degrees slightly faster than men (National Center for Education Statistics [NCES], 1991b, Table 2:6-1, p. 124): 49.4 percent of the women who earned college degrees took only four years or less after high school graduation to receive a B.A., compared to 41.4 percent of the men; on the other hand, 27.1 percent of the men took six years or more after high school graduation to get a B.A., compared to 26.8 percent of the women. But the difference between men and women has decreased in recent years, suggesting that it is an American pattern that the efficiency of men's and women's years invested in schooling is very similar in terms of degree earned. Schooling may have once been less credential-oriented for women but it seems no different from men's today. If anything, women seem to get their credentials in fewer years (at least B.A.s), perhaps to finish their education before family roles might interfere.

COHORT DIFFERENCES IN EDUCATIONAL ATTAINMENT

Given the changes that have taken place in availability of higher education in the United States and especially in the education offered to American women following World War II and later Title IX of the Education Amendments Act in 1972, younger cohorts—especially women—have considerably increased their educational attainment. Changes in social norms about whether women should receive higher education and to what purpose reinforce these legal and structural changes. American Jews have also increased their education over time, as higher education has become more available and accessible. As we have discussed previously, the further American Jews get from the mass immigrant experience, they have also risen in social status, which facilitates the achievement of higher education. All of these make it important to look at the differences between cohorts when looking at educational attainment.

In this and the subsequent chapters both *cohort* and *age* are measured by the same variable, year of birth. The two concepts are used to indicate two different aspects measured by this same indicator: when we use *age*, we focus on differences and patterns that vary by life cycle stage; when we use *cohort*, we focus on historical changes indicated by different timings of birth and growth. To separate these two aspects fully, we would need panel data (to follow the same people through different stages of the life cycle) or time series data (which collects the same data at different points in history). As neither are available to us, we derive crude indications of each from the same variable, which lends itself to both interpretations.

When we consider cohort differences in the present analysis, we are, of course, limited by the nature of our cross-sectional data, which may involve a selectivity both in terms of who survives to reconstruct the past and the reliance on memory to reconstruct the past.[12] In the case of education, memory is not likely to distort the facts; however, we are limited by not knowing how much of the education was achieved during adult years. Nevertheless, we are able to interpret some of the differences between birth cohorts as changes over time. In doing so, the appropriate reservations must be kept in mind.

In the present section we look at the differences between cohorts to see how gender differences have changed over time for American Jews. As we show, younger cohorts of both men and women have considerably higher levels of education than older cohorts. The mean education of Jewish men has risen from 14.1 years among the cohort now 65 or older, to a peak of 17.0 years in the cohort now 40–44, an increase of about 17 percent (Table 2.5 and Figure 2.2). The mean level of education in younger cohorts is lower because it has not yet been completed. This is an example of the confounding effects of age and cohort. We cannot conclude from the fact that men in the age group 18–24 or 25–29 have less education than older men, that the educational level of men is declining. Rather, because it takes a minimum of 22 years of age to have completed 16 years of education and many men continue beyond this, many have not completed their education until their late twenties or early thirties. Therefore, we confine our analysis to 25 and above but still take caution in interpreting the results of the younger cohorts. In the general American population there has been a leveling off of men's educational attainment since the 1980s,[13] but there is little indication of a similar trend among American Jewish men.

Although older cohorts had less education, on the average even those 60–64 completed four years of college; only in the oldest cohort (65+) is

TABLE 2.5
Mean Years of Education, by Sex and Age,
U.S. Jewish and Total White Population, 1990

	U.S. Jews		U.S. Whites	
Age	Males	Females	Males	Females
25–29	16.1	15.6	12.9	12.9
30–34	16.4	15.8	12.9	13.0
35–39	16.8	16.2	13.4	12.9
40–44	17.0	16.7	13.8	12.8
45–49	16.8	14.9	12.9	12.6
50–54	16.1	15.3	12.8	12.5
55–59	16.5	14.3	12.7	12.5
60–64	16.2	14.3	12.6	12.4
65+	14.1	13.3	12.2	12.2
(N in thousands)	(1,871)	(1,815)	(74,830)	(88,393)

Source: NJPS, 1990; Kominski and Adams, 1991, Table 1.

FIGURE 2.2
Mean Years of Education, by Age and Sex,
U.S. Jewish and Total White Population, 1990

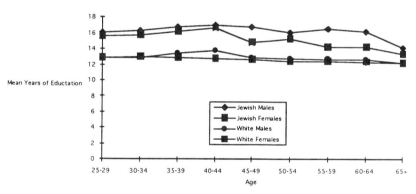

Sources: NJPS, 1990; Kominski and Adams (1991), Table 1.

men's education considerably lower than in the other age groups. A slightly higher proportion of foreign-born and -educated among this oldest age group may contribute to the lower education in this cohort,[14] but it also reflects cohort changes common to the wider American population.

The educational level of Jewish men averages three–four years higher than that of all American white men at all ages except the very oldest (65+), when not as many Jewish men went on to graduate education as they do today (so the difference between Jewish and all white men is less in this age group). As among Jewish men, the changes in the educational level of American white men have been relatively minor, with the difference between the least educated cohort (65+) and the most educated cohort (40–44) representing an increase of about 13 percent. The high education of the cohort 40–44 stands out even more than it did among the Jewish men, suggesting that the level did reach a peak in the generation educated right after World War II and that it has leveled off at a somewhat lower level.

Changes have been even more dramatic for Jewish women than for the men. There are almost three years difference between the average education of the oldest cohort of women and that of the 35–39-year-old cohort. Some women have returned to school at a later age: 35 percent of the women attending college in 1990 were 35 or over (compared to only 15 percent of the men). Nevertheless, older cohorts have less education on the average than do younger cohorts, especially those born between the two world wars, whose higher education would have been right around World War II. Unlike men, who benefited from the GI bill following World War II, women's education was neglected until the 1960s, when women began to catch up to men (McLaughlin et al., 1988). There has been a noticeable increase in women's college enrollment and completion since the 1970s, partly due to increases in part-time attendance and enrollment in two-year colleges (Bianchi and Spain, 1986). The higher level of Jewish women's attainment suggests that it does not come from part-time attendance at two-year colleges, but from full-time attendance at four-year colleges or universities and continuing on to at least partial graduate school.

Comparing Cohort Changes in Education Among
American Jews and the Wider American Population

The changes in the mean level of education of the wider white population of American women have been much more gradual. Between the oldest cohort (65+) and the cohort with the highest education (30–34), there is only a 7 percent increase, from 12.2 to 13.0 years, whereas the increase for the Jewish women represented a gain of 20 percent. The highest education is in the age group 30–34, indicating that some women do not complete their education until then. This is at an earlier age than among the Jewish women, who stay in school for more years. In general, the variance in education is much lower than among the Jewish women, because the more recent gains in women's education have been in college and graduate education, of which Jewish women took advantage. In the wider population, most women do not continue much beyond high school, which was accessible to men and women alike from the early part of the century.

Because women's education has changed more than men's, younger cohorts have a smaller gender gap in education. The gap between Jewish men's and women's education has narrowed especially in the cohorts under 45. There are indications that gender equality in education will be achieved in the near future, as the great majority of both young men and women finish at least a B.A. and many continue on to graduate degrees. To some extent the narrowing of the gap among these most highly educated cohorts is a result of a ceiling in the achievement of men. Few men or women are in school for more than 22 years even for an advanced degree. As more women approach this level of education, men do not keep learning more—they have already achieved the highest level of education. Unless a new degree is invented, the gap will close because men's level will remain stable while women catch up.

The gender gap among Jews is much greater in the older cohorts than it is among their counterparts in the wider population, because in the wider population for the most part neither men nor women have completed college or graduate education, where the gender gap is greatest. Higher education beyond partial college may compete with the time and energy put into starting a family, especially for women at these ages. It has taken changes in social norms about women's nonfamilial roles and delayed marriage and childbearing to make it acceptable—and even attractive - for women to invest in education to the same extent as men have.

Except for a brief period in which men's education is somewhat higher (going up to 13.8 years among those 40–44), men's and women's education in the wider population has been practically equal, averaging between 12 and 13 years.

Cohort Changes and the Gender Gap in
Degrees Attained Among American Jews

The gap in years of education is paralleled by the gap in degrees earned. In the age group 25–44 the proportion of women who have college degrees is about 93 percent that of men. But among the age group 45–54, the proportion of Jewish women who received graduate degrees is only 68 percent that of men. Most striking is the age group 55–64, when men were twice as likely as women to get any college degree, and four times as likely as women to receive a Ph.D. Although men in the oldest age group (65+) were nearly four times as likely as women to receive Ph.D.s, overall the differences are less dramatic because fewer men went on for college degrees in general. And, in the oldest age group, the proportion of women who got graduate degrees is less than half that of men (Table 2.6).

In terms of first professional degrees, the gender gap is also narrowing: 43 percent of the 30–34 year-old Jews who received medical degrees were female, compared to 7 percent of the 50–59 year-olds (Table 2.7). The proportions of Jewish women who received law degrees have also grown in recent cohorts: 40 percent of the 30–34 year-olds and 32 percent of the 35–44 year-olds. The proportion of Jewish 30–34 year-olds receiving law degrees who are female is even higher than the proportion of 25–29 year-olds. One reason for this is reentry into school later in the life cycle among women (which we have already noted), a pattern that has become more common in recent years among the general population as well as among Jews (Jacobs, 1989).

These changes in degrees attained by American Jews reflect in part the changes in degrees attained by cohort for the general white population in the United States. For instance, women made up 13.1 percent of the American lawyers in 1985 in contrast to 2.5 percent in 1951, and of lawyers under age 29 in 1985, 24.4 percent were women (Jacobs, 1989). By 1983, women represented over one-third of those accepted to law school. The proportions of Jewish women out of all Jewish lawyers today is even higher than the general percentage of women in the law profession.

In the medical profession, there were relatively low rates of medical school applications by women in general until recent years (Cole,1986), partly because parents were reluctant to pay for medical education for

TABLE 2.6
Highest Academic Degree, by Sex And Age, U.S. Jews, 1990

Degree	25–34 M	25–34 F	35–44 M	35–44 F	45–54 M	45–54 F	55–64 M	55–64 F	65+ M	65+ F
High school	20.4	26.4	19.2	23.7	27.8	40.6	25.5	55.1	56.2	71.9
A.A./R.N	7.1	5.5	4.6	6.6	4.9	7.4	5.0	4.8	8.5	2.4
B.A.	43.1	46.2	35.4	32.1	31.7	27.3	31.3	19.5	21.9	16.2
M.A.	16.2	15.0	18.7	28.0	17.4	19.9	17.3	15.7	7.6	5.8
Ph.D., profes-sional[a]	13.2	6.9	22.0	9.7	18.2	4.8	20.9	4.9	13.4	3.7
Total (%)	100.0	100.0	100.0	100.0	100.0	100.0	100.0	100.0	100.0	100.0
(N in thousands)	(310)	(319)	(361)	(359)	(233)	(218)	(192)	(203)	(340)	(392)

[a]This includes dental, medical, and law degrees.

Source: NJPS, 1990.

daughters, banks were unwilling to extend educational loans to women medical school students, guidance counselors discouraged women from applying to medical school, and internships and residencies for female medical school graduates were difficult to obtain (Morantz-Sanchez, 1985; Phillips, 1981; Walsh, 1977). Nevertheless, female medical school students increased after World War II and then again after 1972, when Title IX ensured legal gender equality in education. We saw the effects of these periods among American Jews: the cohort that was 60–69 in 1990 was born between 1921 and 1930 and were in their twenties during World War II. Of this cohort, 18 percent of those who went into medicine were women—a relatively high percentage. A similarly high percentage of women earning medical degrees is found among the cohort aged 30–34 in 1990, the first cohort affected by Title IX provisions.

Therefore, American Jews differ from the more general white population in the United States in terms of levels of educational attainment among both men and women. A gender gap in education is seen mainly at the higher educational levels, so Jews have a higher gender gap than the wider population, since more Jewish men and women continue on to

TABLE 2.7
Percent of Women of Total U.S. Jews In Each Age and Degree Group, 1990,
(*N* in thousands)

Age	*Ph.D.*	*D.D.*	*M.D.*	*Law*
25–29	100.0	0	21.1	31.9
	(.6)	(0)	(6.2)	(8.1)
30–34	13.7	0	42.5	40.0
	(6.7)	(1.8)	(9.7)	(16.4)
35–39	25.2	0	13.5	26.1
	(16.0)	(1.7)	(9.1)	(16.8)
40–49	17.1	0	0	32.9
	(28.1)	(1.8)	(15.9)	(23.4)
50–59	25.9	0	6.8	6.7
	(21.6)	(0)	(9.6)	(6.5)
60–69	19.5	0	17.9	0
	(13.4)	(5.3)	(13.2)	(3.3)
70+	19.4	0	0	0
	(9.7)	(2.3)	(7.1)	(8.0)
Total	20.8	0	13.7	26.3
	(979.5)	(8.2)	(70.6)	(82.5)

Note: Under age 25, too few Jewish men or women earned these degrees to include them in this table.

Source: NJPS, 1990.

higher education. The remaining differences between Jewish men and women seem well on their way to disappearing, even before the gender gap in higher education disappears in the wider population (which has a longer way to go to achieve parity). Factors that affected gender equality among the wider population, such as expanded opportunities of education at the turn of the century, expanded opportunities following World War II, and greater gender equity after the passage of the Title IX amendment to the Educational Act of 1972, have also affected American Jews.

FAMILY ROLES AND EDUCATION

As we have suggested previously, family roles can both influence the level of education achieved and be influenced in their timing and extent by the level of education achieved. Higher education is an investment in nonfamilial roles that usually prepares the student for an occupational career. The strong association between level of education and labor force participation among women suggests that it is seen as an investment in nonfamilial roles for women as well as men. But nonfamilial roles conflict with familial roles because of the time and energy resources involved in each, which decreases the possibility of performing them simultaneously. Accommodations for the married and parenting student or worker—such as childcare facilities on campus or at places of work, tuition breaks for married students, and tax breaks for working parents—are rare, at least in most institutions of higher learning and places of employment in the United States. This conflict is greatest for women, who are expected to be the primary caregivers for children and provide a proper family environment (at the least, clean and nutritiously satisfying).

To reduce this conflict, family roles may be postponed while nonfamilial roles are established (higher education, the foundations of a career, etc.). But this in itself may affect further investment in family roles.

> The higher a woman's educational attainment, the more likely she is to remain childless or to have few children. The negative correlation between education and fertility has several explanations. The economic value of a college-educated woman's time is greater than that of a high school graduate's time, and thus years out of the labor force spent in childbearing have greater economic costs to highly educated women. Foregone income is greater the more highly educated a woman is.
>
> Schooling can also alter preferences for children and attitudes toward desired family size. The more educated the couple, the more likely they are to use effective contraception, and highly educated couples use contraception earlier in their marriages. (Bianchi and Spain, 1986, pp. 126–127)

This reflects not only the practical incompatibilities but the social norms regarding the combination of family and educational roles.

Entrance into nonfamilial roles (whether higher education or economic roles) may be postponed while investing in family roles. However, this, too, has an effect on subsequent nonfamilial role involvement. When men marry, implied is an assumption of financial responsibility for a household, which usually necessitates a full-time job, unless parental assistance, academic stipends, or other sources of income are available. This financial responsibility is often shared by the wife, which may preclude further schooling on her part because her nonfamilial time must be spent earning money. She may also be called upon to support her husband finishing higher education, which will also interrupt her own higher education. When marriage occurs at an early age, it may therefore reduce the level of education attained for both men and women. On the other hand, low-achieving students often opt for earlier marriage as a validating adult role when they perceive other avenues of adult achievement blocked (Cusick, 1987). Therefore, early marriage appears to be both a cause and an effect of low educational achievement.[15]

Because women marry earlier on the average than men and their familial roles as wives and mothers tend to be more demanding or time consuming then men's (cf. Berk, 1985), the role conflict between higher education and noneducational roles is likely to affect their higher educational attainment more than it does men. This probably explains why more women in higher education are part-time students than men and why it takes them somewhat longer to achieve advanced degrees on the average.

Similarly, the earlier childbearing occurs, the less likely high levels of education will be achieved.[16] Higher schooling usually becomes a possibility only after the children have grown and household savings or the husband's career provides enough income to allow the wife to return to school at an advanced age. For men, the financial responsibilities of supporting a household usually lock them into a career pattern that is rarely interrupted for academic purposes (unless it is a job-sponsored and -paid training program), but the responsibilities of providing well for a family, the later age at marriage of men, and the different responsibilities within the family held by men ensure higher educational achievement before a career is even begun.

Here we will consider these relationships between education and the timing and extent of family roles among American Jews. Given their relatively late ages of marriage and childbearing, it is possible that entrance into family roles among Jews is not related to educational attainment. However, lower educational attainment may be associated with earlier and more family roles. With our cross-sectional sample, it will be difficult to sort out the direction of effect. However, we will discern the extent of the relationship.

Marriage and Education Among American Jews

The first relationship we look at is between marital status and education. On the average married Jews have had more years of schooling than unmarried Jews. But, because many of the unmarried Jews are young and single and may not have completed their education yet or are older and widowed and have less education because of their age, without controlling for age we do not know how much of the relationship between marital status and education is spurious. Family roles often have a different meaning for men and women, especially in terms of whether they compete with nonfamilial roles such as higher education, so we also need to control for gender to see more clearly the relationship between marital status and education. To do so we performed a multiple regression analysis, in which years of schooling was the dependent variable and marital status, age, and gender, the independent variables (Table 2.8). Both gender and age had significant negative relationships with years of schooling, reflecting what we have seen earlier, that women have less education than men and that older cohorts have less education than younger cohorts.

After controlling for gender and age, being married has a positive relationship both with years of schooling and degree achieved. In addition, two interactions also have significant effects on both years of schooling and degree achieved: the interaction of age and marital status, which reflects the greater impact of being married among older cohorts; and the interaction of gender and marital status, which indicates that marital status does not have the same relationship to schooling for men and women.

As Table 2.9 shows, most men and women have gone on to college except among the widowed, who are mostly older. The main differences

TABLE 2.8
Percent with Four Years of College, by Marital Status and Sex,
U.S. Jewish and Total White Population, 25 and over, 1990

Marital Status	U.S. Jews		U.S. Whites	
	M	F	M	F
Never married	67.7	74.3	28.2	36.7
Married	64.6	52.5	26.4	19.8
Separated	59.1	52.5	17.6	10.8
Divorced	51.3	48.4	18.9	16.8
Widowed	37.9	25.2	11.9	8.2
(N in thousands)	(1,698)	(1,664)	(64,834)	(70,371)

Sources: NJPS, 1990; U.S. Bureau of Labor Statistics, 1991, Table 3.

in education can be seen in the percent who have completed four years of college or more.

Among men, nearly twice as many married and never married men have completed four years of college than widowed men. Fewer of the separated and divorced men have completed 4 years of college than married and never married men. It is possible that this is one of the causes of marital difficulties: men with less education may have more difficulty supporting the family, therefore have trouble in their marriages, and wind up separated or divorced. (It is less reasonable to think that the lower education was a result of divorce or separation, because education is usually established by the time couples marry or shortly thereafter.)

Comparing the Relationship of Marriage and Education Among Jews to the Wider American Population

These differences are very similar to what is found in the wider American population of whites, even though the level of education is much lower on the average. Married and never married men are the most likely to have completed four years of college or more; widowed men are the least likely (probably because of their older age on the average); and separated and divorced men have lower proportions who completed four years of college than married or never married men.

Among Jewish women (like men), widowed women have much less education than the other women, undoubtedly related to their higher age on the average. However, even more noticeable is the high education of

TABLE 2.9
Multiple Regression Analysis of Years of Education on Sex, Age, and Marital Status, U.S. Jews, 25 and over, 1990

Independent Variable	Unstandardized Coefficient	Standardized Coefficient	Significance
Sex (male)	−.575	−.091	.012
Age	−.044	−.225	.000
Being married	2.689	.382	.000
Interaction between age and being married	−.016	−.128	.043
Interaction between sex and being married	−.774	−.193	.004
R .333			
R^2 .111			
(Unweighted n) (2567)			

Source: NJPS, 1990.

the never married in comparison to the other women. Even though some of this may be due to cohort differences, it also reflects the tendency for women with higher education to postpone or even opt out of marriage, so that a higher percentage of them are not (yet) married. Unlike men, there is little difference among women who are married, divorced, or separated.

The higher education of the never married is even more dramatic in the wider American population of women. Nearly twice the proportion of never married women have completed four years of college as opposed to married women. One's first inclination is to think that this might be because of the younger age of the never married women, but even among women 25–34 years old, there is a large difference, although it is not as large as among the total (37 percent of the never married and 24 percent of the married aged 25–34 have completed four years of college or more; Kominski and Adams, 1992, Table 3). Unlike the Jews, separated and divorced women have less education than the married women in the wider population. In general, differences in educational level between Jewish women of different marital statuses are not as exaggerated as in the wider population.

In both the Jewish and the wider American white population, women have more education than men among the never married, reinforcing the interpretation that women with higher education are less likely to marry. In the other groups, men have more education than women (as in the total). Among Jews, the biggest gender gap is among the widowed, which is probably due to being from an older cohort. But among the other groups, the married have the largest gender gap, reflecting the different relationship between having marital roles and education for men and women. For men being married does not imply getting or having less education, although for women it does, either because marriage interferes with getting higher education, because women choose between marriage and nonfamilial roles, which men do not, or because highly educated women have less desire or opportunity to find a suitable marriage mate.

In the wider population, the gender gap is largest for the separated, which may be an indication of why the marriage did not work.[17] The gender gap among the married is even larger than among the Jewish population (the proportion of women completing four or more years of college is 75 percent that of men in the wider population and 81 percent that of men among the Jews). More generally, the gender gap among all categories of marital status of the general white population is greater in all groups than among comparable groups of Jews. Even among the never married, the gender gap (in the reverse direction) is greater for the general white population than the Jews. This may be related to the overall higher educational achievement of Jews and therefore less variation in achievement. It may also be related to the lower fertility of American Jews, which reduces the family responsibilities that would interfere with educational achievement.

Age at Marriage and Education

We have mentioned the timing of marriage in relationship to educational achievement in at least two ways. We suggested that earlier marriage may interfere with educational achievement for both men, who are forced into the labor force at an earlier age, and women, whose family responsibilities preclude continuing to higher education. We have also suggested that highly educated women postpone marriage and sometimes do not marry at all (either because they delayed too long to find a suitable partner or because they choose to devote their energies to nonfamilial roles).

We consider the impact of age at marriage on educational achievement in multiple regression models predicting years of schooling and highest degree achieved of men and women (Table 2.10). Because of the differential impact of being married for men and women, we have separated the models for men and women. Because older cohorts married earlier, we have also controlled for age in each model.

For men, age at marriage has no significant relationship with years of education, which reflects the lack of difference between married and unmarried men we saw earlier. However, the earlier Jewish women

TABLE 2.10
Multiple Regression Analysis of Years of Education on Age
and Age at Marriage, U.S. Jews, 25 and over, 1990

Independent Variable		Unstandardized Coefficient	Standardized Coefficient	Significance
Men:				
Age		−0.058	−0.257	0.000
Age at Marriage		−0.012	−0.021	0.512
R	.261			
R²	.068			
(Unweighted *n*)	(1369)			
Women:				
Age		−0.060	−0.301	0.000
Age at Marriage		0.086	0.145	0.000
R	.331			
R²	.109			
(Unweighted *n*)	(1300)			

Source: NJPS, 1990.

marry, the fewer years of education achieved; conversely, the later Jewish women marry, the higher their academic achievement.

As Table 2.11 shows, both Jewish men and women who married before age 19 have less education than men and women who married later. They are much less likely to have completed high school education and even less likely to have completed four years of college or more than those who married later. Men and women who married between 19 and 21 are also less likely to have completed four or more years of college, although the proportion completing high school is no lower. For men, those who marry between the ages of 22 and 34 are the most likely to complete four or more years of college, but those who marry later have slightly fewer college graduates. This curvilinear relationship explains why the regression coefficient is not significant in the multiple regression analysis. It suggests that Jewish men with less education may have difficulty finding a mate if they do not marry young. Among women there is no such curvilinear relationship, and the regression coefficient is significant, as we saw in Table 2.10.

In comparison, fewer than 4 percent of the women in the general population who had married in their teens had finished four or more years of college; only 7 percent of teenaged grooms had a college degree; although persons who married after age 21 had much higher college completion rates (Bianchi and Spain, 1986). Those who married at age 24 or 25 had the highest completion rates among women, and men who married in their late twenties were the most likely to be college graduates. Among Jews, the level of achievement is much higher, even among those who marry in their teens, and those who marry after age 22 show no effects of age at marriage. The highest proportion of women completing college is among those who married between 25 and 29. Postponing mar-

TABLE 2.11
Years of Education by Age at Marriage and Sex, U.S. Married Jews, 1990

Age at Marriage	4 years high school or more (%)		4 years college or more (%)		(N in thousands)	
	M	F	M	F	M	F
Under 19	78.1	79.1	25.3	20.3	(27)	(128)
19–21	93.1	97.6	54.0	44.7	(150)	(457)
22–24	97.3	96.0	66.9	57.0	(419)	(447)
25–29	95.6	94.8	65.3	59.5	(468)	(279)
30–34	95.8	90.3	67.5	53.0	(199)	(82)
35+	92.8	100.0	57.9	54.9	(99)	(70)

Source: NJPS, 1990.

riage until the thirties is related to completing advanced degrees, but not completing college (which is usually accomplished by the mid-twenties).

Age at Marriage and Degree Attainment

Jews who married younger are also less likely to attain higher educational degrees. Nearly 75 percent of the women and 63 percent of the men who married at 18 or younger attained no higher than a high school diploma, compared to 43 percent of the total female Jewish population over 25 and 32 percent of the total male Jewish population. On the other hand, women who married later (ages 30 and above), were more likely to have a Ph.D. or professional degree. Unlike women, doctoral and professional degrees are more common for men who married between the ages of 25 and 34. Apparently, although late marriage for women is associated with higher education; for men, the absence of a wife and family to support them during graduate school may hinder their educational attainment (or Jewish men who do not go on to graduate school have more difficulty finding spouses).

Among American Jews, there is less gender difference in educational achievement among those who marry late (age 35+) or early (up to age 18), the latter having low educational attainment among both genders; the former having higher for women but lower for men compared to men who married between the ages of 19 and 34, bringing about greater gender equality. There is a similar convergence of men and women who married late in terms of attaining doctorate or professional degrees .

Again, this is similar to the patterns in the general U.S. population. Alexander and Reilly report that "women realize a significant increment to schooling for every year they defer marriage, and conclude that if women married at the same age as men (that is, about 2.5 years later), they would obtain almost a third of a year more schooling on the average than they currently do. Delayed marriage for women could reduce the postmarriage educational gap between men and women by as much as three-quarters" (cited in Bianchi and Spain, 1986, pp. 124–126).

Age at Birth of First Child and Education

Marital roles include both a spousal role and a parenting role. Among Jewish women, the parenting role interferes or competes with higher education, rather than the spousal role. When we add age at birth of first child into the regression model predicting academic achievement for married women, the effect of age at marriage becomes nonsignificant whereas age at birth of first child is significant, which means that it is not entrance into marital roles that interferes with higher education but becoming a mother (Table 2.12). The age at having one's first child does not vary

TABLE 2.12
Multiple Regression of Years of Education on Age at Marriage, Age at Birth
of First Child, and Age, U.S. Married Jewish Women, 25 and over, 1990

Independent Variable	Unstandardized Coefficient	Standardized Coefficient	Significance
Age	–0.028	–0.303	0.000
Age at marriage	0.001	0.004	0.935
Age at birth of first child	0.078	0.262	0.000
R .410			
R^2 .168			
(Unweighted n) (951)			

Source: NJPS, 1990.

clearly by age (among women 65 and over, entrance into motherhood occurred at an average age of 26.3; whereas among women 45–54, the average age at birth of the first child was 23.5; among women 35–44, 27.1; and among women 25–34, 25.4), so that we should not expect that this is a spurious relationship resulting from the relationship between age and education, and indeed the relationship is significant even though age is controlled in the regression.

The effect of age at motherhood is illustrated in Figure 2.3, which shows that the younger the age of having children, the less likely were the

FIGURE 2.3
Mean Years of Education, by Age at Birth of First Child,
U.S. Jewish Married Women, 1990

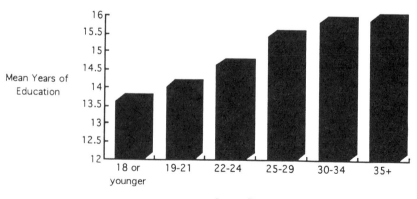

Source: NJPS, 1990.

women to complete high school or to go beyond high school education. One-fifth of the women who had children before they turned 20 did not complete high school, compared to 3–7 percent among the rest of the women; 57 percent of those having children before they turned 20 did not go beyond high school, compared to only 14 percent of those who began childbearing after the age of 34). As Figure 2.3 shows, the later the woman becomes a mother, the higher is her educational achievement.

Similarly, the older the age at which a woman has her first child, the more likely the women were to complete four or more years of college and the more likely they were to have obtained more than a high school diploma. Women who had no children until they were 35 or older were more than *seven times as likely* to have completed doctorates or professional degrees than women who had children before the age of 21 (Table 2.13). Among those who had their first children in their teens, only 25 percent got more than a high school diploma (compared to 55 percent in the total).

As we have explained, this may be because women who go on for higher education postpone childbearing. Nearly 80 percent of the women who earned Ph.D.s had their first child after 25 and 43 percent after age 29 (more than double the 16 percent in the total). On the other hand, among the women who received no diploma, 27 percent had their first child in their teens (compared to 6.6 percent in the total). The direction of effect is, again, not clear from our data. It may be that women who have children earlier stop their education in order to devote themselves to childrearing and, later, support of the family. Whether or not these

TABLE 2.13
Age at Birth of First Child, by Highest Academic Degree,
U.S. Married Jewish Women, 25 and over, 1990

Highest Academic Degree	19 or Younger	20–21	22–24	25–29	30–34	35+
None	27.4	8.9	9.1	3.9	1.1	0.0
High school diploma	3.9	20.0	24.7	6.8	5.9	3.7
Vocational/A.A.	11.3	28.1	25.1	25.1	25.7	16.7
B.A.	36.9	31.0	32.2	49.3	43.9	35.7
M.A.	16.2	8.9	1.9	9.8	16.5	20.3
Ph.D./ Professional[a]	4.2	3.1	7.0	5.2	6.9	23.7
Total (%)	100.0	100.0	100.0	100.0	100.0	100.0
(N in thousands)	(87)	(163)	(318)	(478)	(136)	(69)

[a]This includes dental, medical, and law degrees.

Source: NJPS, 1990.

women will return to school at a later age will depend on how many children they have and whether the family can afford for them to do so.

Although we lack directly comparable data for the wider population, this relationship appears to be similar to more general American trends. Teenage births generally appear to deter future academic achievement and lower educational aspirations (Rindfuss, Bumpass and St. John, 1980, cited in Bianchi and Spain, 1986, p. 128; Waite and Moore, 1978); whereas more educated women tend to postpone childbirth (Bianchi and Spain, 1986). What is interesting is that even at the high levels of educational achievement, the age of parenthood continues to have a strong effect on how much education is attained.

Number of Children and Education

The more children a woman has, the less likely she is to have higher education: 63 percent of the Jewish women with no children have 16 or more years of education compared to 34 percent of the women with four or more children, almost twice the proportion; on the other hand, 43 percent of the women with four or more children have high school or lower education, compared to 16 percent of the women with no children, less than half the proportion (Table 2.14). Similarly, among women who have no children, a higher proportion have at least a B.A. or an M.A. Women who have more children are less likely to have more than a high school diploma (Figure 2.4).

Of course, the relationship can be seen in the other direction as well: the more education a woman has, the less likely she is to have four or more children and the more likely she is to have no children. Women with Ph.D.s are no more likely to be childless than women with some college degree, but they are less likely to have more than two children than women with lower degrees. And women with less than a B.A. are somewhat more likely to have four or more children. Women with high school diplomas or less, are less likely to be childless (Table 2.15).

That women who have less education have more children is true for the general American population as well. Women who have less than a high school education have more than double the number of children as women who completed 17 or more years of education. What is interesting is the comparison of the mean number of children at each educational level between the wider population and Jews: Jews have more children on the average at each level of education (Figure 2.5). The lower average number of children among Jewish families is because a higher proportion of the mothers have more education, but not because Jewish women at the higher level of education have fewer children than other highly educated women.

TABLE 2.14
Education by Number of Children,
U.S. Jewish Married Women, 25 and over, 1990

	Number of Children					
	0	1	2	3	4+	Total
Years of education:						
11 or less	(1.2)	(3.9)	6.8	(2.7)	(8.1)	4.7
12	15.0	17.2	27.6	30.0	35.0	24.9
13–15	20.9	25.7	19.3	24.6	23.0	22.0
16	32.3	30.3	26.2	26.7	20.0	27.5
17+	30.5	23.0	20.1	15.9	14.0	20.9
Highest academic degree:						
None	(1.3)	(2.9)	5.0	(2.4)	(6.1)	3.6
High school diploma	27.8	34.4	42.2	51.3	50.8	41.1
Vocational, A.A.	5.5	6.4	4.4	3.7	8.1	5.1
B.A.	33.3	32.9	25.7	24.1	16.2	27.1
M.A.	28.5	18.1	18.9	17.7	18.0	20.0
Ph.D., Professional[a]	3.7	5.4	3.7	0.8	0.8	3.2
Total (%)	100.0	100.0	100.0	100.0	100.0	100.0
(*N* in thousands)	(240)	(256)	(579)	(306)	(115)	(1495)

Note: Percentages in parentheses indicate unweighted *n* < 10.
[a]This includes dental, medical, and law degrees.

Source: NJPS, 1990.

Family roles have changed historically, younger cohorts tend to delay marriage and childbearing and have smaller families (Bianchi and Spain, 1986). American Jews were among the first to exhibit these trends (Goldscheider and Zuckerman, 1984). As Table 2.16 shows, both the average age at marriage and at childbearing has fluctuated over the years without a clear relationship to cohort (age at first child was over 26 in the oldest cohort as well as the age group 35–44). Even though the number of children was higher for older cohorts and has declined, it should be remembered that fertility may not yet be complete in the two youngest age groups (25–44). To control for any variation which might be introduced by age or cohort, age is controlled in the regression analysis in Table 2.17, which considers the relationship between the various indicators of family roles and education.

Among Jewish women, the age of becoming a mother is much more strongly related to educational achievement than how many children the woman has. When number of children is added to the multiple regression

FIGURE 2.4
Highest Academic Degree, by Number of Children,
U.S. Jewish Married Women, 1990

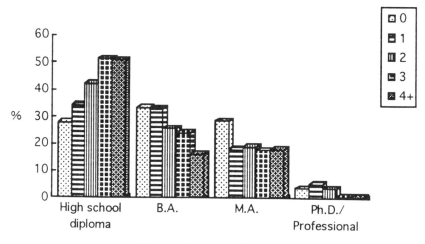

Source: NJPS, 1990.

model predicting academic achievement, controlling for age, age at marriage, and age at birth of first child, we can see that how many children a woman has is not significantly related to either years of education or highest academic degree. Because women who start having children early have more children, there is a relationship between number of children and academic achievement, but it is actually a spurious relationship (Table 2.17). The real factor involved is the age at which the parenting responsibilities begin, whether they are before or after higher education has been completed.

SUMMARY AND DISCUSSION

We have seen in this chapter that both American Jewish men and women have higher education than their counterparts in the wider American population. However, despite their high achievements, a traditional gender gap in educational achievement is found among American Jews: more Jewish men than women go on to graduate school, and the gender gap increases with each year of schooling. Jewish women still have a long way to go to catch up to Jewish men. In the wider population, the gender

TABLE 2.15
Number of Children by Education,
U.S. Jewish Married Women, 25 and over, 1990

	Number of Children						
	0	1	2	3	4+	Total % (N in thousands)	Mean Number of Children
Years of education:							
11 or less	(4.1)	(14.1)	56.5	(12.0)	(13.3)	100.0 (70)	3.3
12	9.7	11.8	42.9	24.7	10.8	100.0 (372)	2.3
13–15	15.2	19.9	34.0	22.9	8.0	100.0 (329)	2.0
16	18.8	18.8	36.9	19.9	5.6	100.0 (411)	1.8
17+	23.4	18.8	37.2	15.5	5.2	100.0 (482)	1.7
Highest academic degree:							
None	(5.8)	(13.7)	54.0	(13.5)	(12.9)	100.0 (54)	3.1
High school diploma	10.9	14.3	39.8	25.5	9.5	100.0 (614)	2.2
Vocational, A.A.	17.3	21.6	33.8	14.9	12.3	100.0 (76)	1.8
B.A.	19.7	20.7	36.8	18.2	4.6	100.0 (405)	1.7
M.A.	22.8	15.4	36.7	18.1	6.9	100.0 (298)	1.8
Ph.D., professional[a]	18.7	28.7	45.4	5.2	2.0	100.0 (48)	1.5

Note: Percentages in parentheses indicate unweighted $n < 10$.
[a]This includes dental, medical, and law degrees.

Source: NJPS, 1990.

gap in education is less noticeable because there is more concentration of educational attainment at the high school level, which is compulsory and free for both men and women, and at this level fewer gender differences are found, at least among the white population, which is most comparable to the Jews.

It is clear that American Jews are influenced by trends in the wider American society. Just as the wider population of men benefited from the GI bill after World War II, just as the wider population of women benefited from the Title IX amendment reinforcing gender equality in the schools, so have American Jews. The recent trends of narrowing the gender gap in educational attainment since the 1970s can be found among American Jews, and as in the wider population changes in men's education have been less dramatic than the increases in women's education in

FIGURE 2.5
Mean Number of Children, by Years of Education, for U.S. Jewish (1990)
and Total U.S. Women (1987)

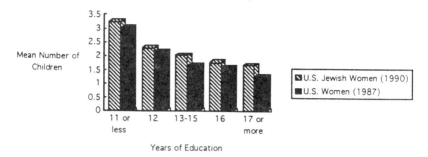

Sources: NJPS, 1990; Chadwick and Heaton (1992): Table D1-8.

TABLE 2.16
Age at Marriage, Age at Birth of First Child, Number of Children, and Age of
Youngest Child, by Age, U.S. Jewish Married Women, 25 and over, 1990

Age	Mean Age at Marriage	Mean Age at First Childbirth	Mean Number of Children	Mean Age Youngest Child	(N in thousands)
25–34	23.7	25.4	1.1	2.9	(221)
35–44	25.0	27.1	1.8	8.8	(321)
45–54	22.1	23.5	2.2	20.7	(209)
55–64	21.7	24.4	2.4	29.2	(202)
65+	24.8	26.3	2.2	39.2	(202)

Source: NJPS, 1990.

recent cohorts. Among Jews, the narrowing of the gap may be even faster
than in the wider population, as Jewish women catch up to Jewish men in
terms of the numbers of professional and graduate degrees rewarded
them.

Although family roles are generally related to the education of American Jewish men and women in ways similar to the wider population,
there is less variation by marital status and age at marriage among the
Jews than in the wider population. This may be due to later ages at marriage, which occur on the average after even a four-year college education
can be completed.

For Jewish women the specific family role that interferes more with
educational attainment seems to be the parenting role. The earlier is the

TABLE 2.17
Multiple Regression Analysis of Highest Academic Degree on Family Variables,
U.S. Jewish Married Women, 25 and over, 1990

Independent Variable	Unstandardized Coefficient	Standardized Coefficient	(Standard Error)
Age at marriage	−.011	−.040	(.010)
Age at birth of first child	.080	0.268*	(.012)
Number of children	.035	0.026	(.045)
Age (cohort)	−.031	−.338*	(.003)
Constant	1.995	.000*	(.331)
(Unweighted *n*)	(951)		

*α < .001.

Source: NJPS, 1990.

first birth, the lower the educational achievement—and the higher is the educational achievement, the later the first birth (the direction of effect cannot be determined from this data). Even though there is a relationship between level of education and number of children, the age at which the first child is born is more strongly related to educational achievement than how many children the woman has.[18]

CHAPTER 3

The Labor Force Participation of American Jewish Men and Women

Labor force participation patterns are known to vary over the life cycle and by gender for a number of reasons. Both men and women do not usually start to work full-time in the labor force until they have finished their education, so that entrance to the labor force usually occurs sometime between the ages of 18 and 30, depending on the level of education achieved. Because men are expected to provide for themselves and their families (if they marry), they are socialized to enter into the labor force when they finish school. Women, on the other hand, have the option to choose when and even if they will enter the paid labor force. As children at home, neither boys nor girls are expected to support themselves. They are, however, expected to support themselves once they finish their education, and often concurrently with the pursuit of higher education. Women, however, may be supported by their husbands; although presumably wives provide unpaid labor for the family, the assumption of economic support is not explicitly in exchange for such services (and women who earn money from paid labor provide similar domestic services as well).

Norms about women's economic dependence are changing, influenced by and influencing the high rates of divorce in the United States and the realities that many women wind up supporting themselves even if they did not intend to, and there is an increasing expectation for women to plan careers as men do. More and more young men and women expect wives and mothers to be employed (Moen, 1992). Nevertheless, there is persisting concern about the effects on children (Moen, 1992), and many potential husbands and wives prefer mothers not to work when their children are young. Further, family roles are still seen as competitors to women's availability and flexibility in the labor force, whereas men are less likely to perceive a conflict between their work and family roles (Greenhaus and Beutell, 1985; Voydanoff and Kelly, 1984, 1985). There are identifiable junctures in women's lives at which they make decisions to pursue labor force involvement—or not to (Gerson, 1985; Waite and Stolzenberg, 1976). Further, there are different stages in the life cycle at which domestic roles impinge more heavily on women's nonfamilial role involvement, such as when the first child is born (Cramer, 1980; Hout, 1978).

How these patterns vary, however, differs by social norms and institutional arrangement of household and public economic roles. In a pioneering paper on the subject, Weller (1969) showed how social norms about the compatibility of economic and domestic roles influence the rate of married women's labor force participation. Changes in gender role norms have been linked as both cause and effect of changes in married women's and mothers' labor force activity (Moen, 1992). Increasing interest in variation among minority groups within the United States has related the equality of men's and women's labor force participation not only to social norms about appropriate gender roles but also the minority group's place in the wider class structure (Almquist, 1987; Dugger, 1991; Goldsmith, 1989, Section V).

To put American Jews' labor force participation patterns in context, it is relevant to consider Jewish values about labor force participation in general and how they differ when applied to men and women; differential norms about roles that might conflict with labor force participation, such as family roles; and the effect of the American Jews' place in the wider society.

Among Jews, labor force participation is valued not as an end in itself but as a means for supporting the family. In some religious traditions, such as early Protestantism (the "Protestant ethic"), work itself has a sacred value, perceived as contributing to ultimate salvation; the Jewish heritage, however, does not have a background of making participation in the labor force a sacred value. Nevertheless, it is accepted as a central part of life. Contributing to the family economy is seen as a duty of both men and women, and there is a long tradition of women's contribution to the household economy by activities both within the home and in public arenas (Baskin, 1991; Wegner, 1988). Judaism is characterized by a lack of ideological opposition to women's participation in public economic roles.

However, the central arena for women's activity is the family, and traditionally economic roles could be curtailed to appropriately manage roles relating to the family (Wegner, 1988). At some times in Jewish history, including among American Jews from the turn of the century, domestic roles were conceived as all-encompassing, and it was deemed preferable for wives and mothers to remain in the home. This was also a status symbol in the wider society, a sign that wives no longer needed to contribute to the household economy because husbands were so successful that a second income was not needed (Baum, Hyman, and Michel, 1976). This belief characterized not only Jewish women, but the upwardly mobile American middle class in general (Fishman, 1993).

Only with the changing norms about women's labor force participation and an increasing perception that a single income is no longer adequate to maintain an upper-middle-class lifestyle, did labor force participation by American Jewish women begin to increase, following the trends in the wider society.

Because of the proportions of Jews continuing on to higher education, their entrance into the labor force may be delayed (especially in comparison with the wider American population, who have a lower level of education on the average). Because men continue on to more advanced degrees than women (as we have seen in the previous chapter), we would expect a gender difference when men are continuing their graduate studies and more women have already completed their (initial)[1] education. The gender gap would be in the opposite direction to the "normal"—in this case, women will be expected to be employed in the paid labor force when more men of the same age are still in school.

Whatever advantage this might offer women by giving them a head start is likely to be reversed when they marry. Wives are more apt to take on time-consuming domestic roles, whereas men are apt to take their provider role seriously. For the Jewish homemaker, such domestic roles may have increased valence as her major role in the continuity of the religion (depending, of course, on how traditional she is),[2] requiring time and both physical and creative energy.

As the couple begin to have children (as 70 percent of the women in our sample did), role differentiation between mothers and fathers is probably at its peak. Egalitarian ideologies notwithstanding, the predominant pattern is still for mothers to do the majority of childcare when children are young, while fathers do the most consistent providing. Female "coproviders" (Lewis, 1992) must still deal with the responsibility of childcare, young children requiring intensive attention that takes up most of the hours of the day. Even though mothers may substitute some of the required hours with hired help or share some of the responsibilities with their spouses, the more they value their own contribution to their children's development, the less likely will they be to give up these roles. Previous research has suggested that Jewish women prefer to stay at home themselves with their young children and curtail their hours and weeks of employment if not to take a complete break (Chiswick, 1986).[3] It is not clear whether this pattern will persist in the younger generation (see the discussion in Fishman, 1993), particularly as the pattern of combining labor force participation with motherhood (rather than "sequencing" one and then the other) becomes the norm in the wider American society (Moen, 1992). Given the importance of children in the Jewish tradition and the centrality of "properly" raising them, sharing or relinquishing the childcare role with mother substitutes involves perhaps somewhat more role conflict (and soul-searching) for Jewish women than for women from less familistic traditions.

As children spend more and more time outside the home, first in school and later in college or supporting themselves, relatively highly educated women are likely to return to the labor force. But the career damage resulting from interruptions and part-time work reduce their worth on the labor market (Hewlett, 1987), and the continuing family roles of wives and mothers of children "returning" to the nest (whether on a long-term or intermittent basis) are expected to maintain some gender gap in labor force participation. Married women, particularly married mothers, will not act completely like men in the labor force, even after their children are grown.

Because of women's socialization to employment as a choice rather than a duty and the tendency to follow the husband's lifestyle (and since most husbands are older, this means retiring when the husband does, which is earlier for the younger wife, as we shall see in Chapter 5), women are also likely to retire from the labor force earlier than do men. The high education of Jewish women is expected to reduce the gender gap in labor force participation at older ages, but not eliminate it.

Our indication of life cycle stage is age. However, age in our sample is also an indicator of cohort, which confounds our interpretation of age as a life cycle stage. Cohorts have changed with regards to the norms of labor force behavior, especially for women.

> What has changed so dramatically is *not* women's roles but their duration and sequence. Today a majority of American women engage in employment and child rearing *simultaneously* . . .
>
> In contrast to their mothers or grandmothers, American women now in their 20s and 30s are better educated, have fewer children, and bear them later in life. They are postponing marriage and are less likely to marry or to stay married. And they are more likely than ever to be employed, regardless of their family responsibilities. Decisions about marriage and divorce, the number and timing of children, and personal aspirations all influence and are influenced by whether or not women are employed. (Moen, 1992, pp. 3–6)

It will be difficult with our cross-sectional sample to separate out whether patterns we see in the younger cohort differ from the older cohort because of different family responsibilities, different physical and mental stamina, or different expectations of role performance. We do our best to control for obvious differences, such as the level of education and the number of young children at home, but our single indicator will still confound the two influences of life cycle stage and cohort. We will try to be attentive to these confounding influences as we try to sort out the contemporary patterns of labor force behavior among American Jewish men and women.

THE GENERAL PICTURE: THE LABOR FORCE PARTICIPATION
OF AMERICAN JEWISH MEN AND WOMEN

Among American Jews, 71.5 percent of the men 18 and over, and 56.7 percent of the women 18 and over were working in the paid labor force in 1990 (Table 3.1). As in most populations, the men participate more than the women; women's participation rate being about 80 percent that of men, reflecting the traditional gender role division.

Jewish men and women are somewhat more similar than are men and women in the wider white population in the United States, mainly because the labor force participation rate of Jewish men is somewhat lower than that of all white men (76.4 percent).[4] As we shall see later, the lower participation rate of Jewish men can be attributed to later entrance to the labor force, because of higher educational levels; the population of American Jewish men is also older than the wider population and therefore the overall rate of Jewish men includes a higher proportion of retirees. The overall rate of Jewish women is similar to that of all white women (57.3 percent). The lower participation of younger Jewish women,

TABLE 3.1
Percent in Paid Labor Force, by Sex and Age,
U.S. Jewish and Total White Population, 1990

Age	U.S. Jews			U.S. Whites		
	Males	Females	Female Rate/ Male Rate	Males	Females	Female Rate/ Male Rate
18–24	38.0	35.0	92.2	79.4	69.3	87.3
25–29	78.0	77.3	99.2	94.5	74.7	79.0
30–34	92.3	76.4	82.8	95.5	74.2	77.7
35–39	95.7	74.4	77.7	95.7	74.9	78.2
40–44	94.7	75.3	79.5	94.8	78.4	82.7
45–49	91.8	81.8	89.1	93.2	75.6	81.1
50–54	87.6	73.6	84.1	89.4	67.6	75.6
55–59	87.0	68.7	78.9	82.9	56.0	67.6
60–64	72.1	45.4	63.1	56.6	36.3	64.1
65+	29.4	11.3	38.4	16.0	8.3	51.9
Total	71.5	57.7	79.2	76.4	57.3	75.0
(N in thousands)	(1,871)	(1,815)		(74,691)	(81,006)	

Source: NJPS, 1990; U.S. Bureau of Labor Statistics, 1991, Table A-4.

because of their longer years of education, are offset by higher labor force participation rates throughout almost all the other stages of the life cycle, especially the older ages (as we shall discuss). If we confine the comparison to the main working ages of 25–64, the overall rates of labor force participation of Jews and the wider white population are very similar: 88.8 percent and 90.1 percent for Jewish and all white men, respectively; and 68.3 percent and 68.5 percent for Jewish and all white women, respectively.

GETTING INTO THE LABOR FORCE

As we saw in the previous chapter, most Jewish men (83 percent) and women (74 percent) continue their education after high school. At 18, only 18 percent of the men and 28 percent of the women have completed their education;[5] at age 25, 71 percent of the men and 82 percent of the women have completed their education. It is not until age 32 that almost all of them have completed their education. As a result, the full entrance into the labor force of Jewish men and women is delayed to a relatively late age.

At 18, less than 25 percent of the men work in the paid labor force. Through the twenties, there is a slow increase in percent participating, so that, by age 25, two-thirds are working in the labor force; but it is not until age 29 that more than 90 percent have entered the labor force (Figure 3.1).[6] Labor force participation continues to rise through age 34 for men, when it reaches 96.8 percent.

Jewish women finish their schooling earlier than Jewish men: using our crude index, 95 percent of the women have completed their education by age 27, while it takes men until 30 for a similar percentage to finish. As a result, on the average, they enter the labor force somewhat earlier than men. At 18, even fewer women than men are employed in the paid labor force, but by age 25 their labor force participation is the same as men's (68 percent) and for a few years they have an even higher participation rate than men, as higher proportions of men finish their education. However, in the late twenties, men's labor force participation rate again rises above that of the women, and it remains so until retirement. Between ages 25 and 29, nearly 80 percent of the women are in the labor force on the average, but after age 30 the percent participating begins to fall, and by age 34 less than three-fourths of the women are in the labor force.

In other words, the entrance of both Jewish men and women is delayed by higher education, and their labor force participation is very similar up until their late twenties. Only in their late twenties do men overtake women's rate of participation, as men increasingly enter the labor force

FIGURE 3.1
Percent in Paid Labor Force, by Sex and Age, U.S. Jews Ages 18–34, 1990

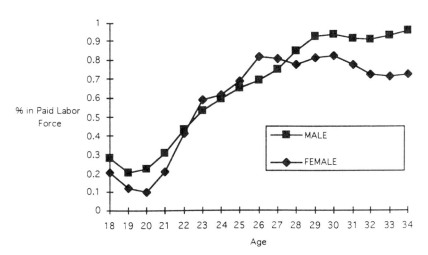

Source: NJPS, 1990.

until over 95 percent are working, while not more than about 80 percent of the women are working at any age and the percent of women in the labor force starts to decline in their late twenties and early thirties.

As mentioned previously, the entrance patterns of Jewish men and women are later than for the total population. This can be at least partially attributed to the higher proportion of American Jews continuing on to higher education than among the wider white population (56 percent of the men and 52 percent of the women, compared to over 74 percent of the Jewish women and 83 percent of the Jewish men). Only 9 percent of the 25–29 years-olds are still in school,[7] compared to 25 percent of the Jewish men and 29 percent of the Jewish women aged 25–29.

The labor force participation rate of Jewish men 18–24 is considerably lower than the comparable age group in the general white population (Table 3.1, Figure 3.2). Fewer Jewish men are in the labor force until their mid-thirties, when virtually all education is completed.

Like Jewish men, a high proportion of Jewish women are also in school through the age of 24, and their labor force participation rate is nearly half of the labor force participation rate of the general white population of women between 18 and 24. By ages 25–29, the two groups are quite comparable.

In the wider population, gender role differentiation is apparent even from the age of 18, and by age 25 the familiar gap[8] of men's and women's

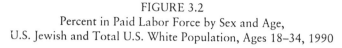

FIGURE 3.2
Percent in Paid Labor Force by Sex and Age,
U.S. Jewish and Total U.S. White Population, Ages 18–34, 1990

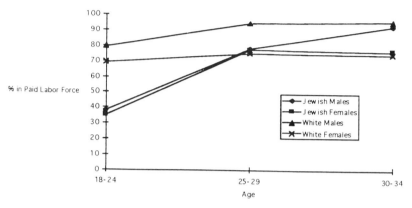

Source: NJPS, 1990; unpublished tabulations of the 1990 Current Population Survey, U.S. Bureau of Labor Statistics.

labor force participation is nearly at its peak. Among Jewish men and women the peak of their difference comes later, in their mid-thirties, probably because of the different timing of family roles. Jewish women have fewer children and begin childbearing at later ages (cf. Goldstein, 1992), which suggests that domestic responsibilities that conflict with labor force participation come later than in the wider population (we will explore this in more detail later). The later timing of family roles for Jewish women and their higher educational levels and the lower participation of young Jewish men who are involved full-time in higher education decrease the gender gap in labor force participation among Jews until their mid-thirties, when the Jewish gender gap begins to resemble that of the wider population.

A second indicator of entrance into the labor force is the extent of full-time work in the labor force. As many of the entrances into the labor force are not into full-time jobs (especially for students) the hours of work per week also show patterns of labor force entrance at this age.

As Jewish men enter the labor force, they start out with about 35 hours of work per week on the average and gradually increase the average number of hours (Figure 3.3). By age 25 the average hours of work are about 40, but by age 30 their hours have increased to over 42. During the ages 30–34 their average hours of work are over 45 per week. This reflects, of course, the high proportion of Jewish men in the professions or self-employed, each of which implies long working hours and a high degree of career commitment.

FIGURE 3.3
Mean Hours of Work, by Sex and Age, U.S. Jews, 1990

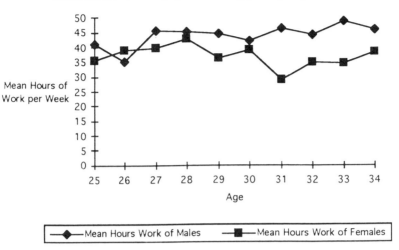

Source: NJPS, 1990.

The extent of women's labor force participation, however, follows a different pattern. Starting out with about the same number of hours per week as men, women and men continue to have similar hours of work until about the age of 30. Before 30, women sometimes work more hours per week than men, and men sometimes work more hours per week than women, but the differences are slight. In the early thirties, however, women's hours of work drop to about three-fourths that of men (an average of 35 hours per week), the same ages at which labor force participation rates drop.[9]

The relatively late entrance of men into full-time jobs is not, however, very different than in the wider American population. Among all U.S. men up to age 24, 25.7 percent[10] were working part-time (35 hours or less) compared to only 20.3 percent of the Jewish men of this age. Among young women in the United States, 34.2 percent work part-time compared to only 25.0 percent among the Jewish women. When Jewish women of this age work, they are more likely to have full-time jobs. This is probably because of their relatively higher education, the later age of childbearing, and the types of occupations they enter.

The labor force participation patterns of Jewish men and women before age 34 seem to be related to the effect of three main factors and their interactions: higher education, getting married, and (for women) having children. These factors do not simply affect labor force participation directly during these ages: they have opposing effects at different ages during this period, sometimes the same factor affects men and women differently, and there is some interaction among the factors at these ages that also affect labor force participation. This makes it difficult to adequately untangle the factors that explain the pattern of entrance to the labor force in this kind of cross-sectional survey.

At this young age, for instance, participation in the paid labor force competes with participation in the educational system, creating a negative relationship between education and labor force participation. Generally, however, higher educational attainment reflects more valuable human resources that enable finding a better paying and more interesting job. For women, especially, education plays a major part in their option of whether or not to participate in the labor force. This consideration may decide, for instance, whether it is worthwhile for a woman to hire substitutes for her household labor and childcare roles. Higher education also widens the occupational opportunities so that the highly educated who do not work forego more interesting jobs and have more to lose if they do not use their training (England and Farkas, 1986).

Because men are expected to fill the "good provider" role no matter what their level of education, the same considerations may apply, but education is more important in determining *what* they do, more than *whether* they participate in the labor force. The education achieved during this period influences the long-term patterns of labor force participation for both men and women.

We see that, at this period of entrance into the labor force, education works in the opposite way until it is completed. Finishing school opens up wider opportunities in the labor force and increases the cost of staying out of the labor force for both men and women, although the timing and level of education achieved prolongs and intensifies the effect for men.

During these same ages, most Jewish men and women get married, the average age of marriage being 23.3 for women and 26.0 for men. Getting married has somewhat different implications for men and women, as we shall show. On the one hand, it implies additional domestic roles, but on the other, it implies additional financial obligations. The financial obligations are particularly salient for men, who usually take on the main provider role. More and more women share in this role as coproviders. But the domestic roles usually are disproportionately allocated to wives (even in so-called egalitarian marriages), and these may infringe on the time and energy available for participation in the paid labor force. Although we see no drop in labor force participation among women in their mid-twenties, we do see a slight drop in number of hours worked and a halt to the increase in average number of hours worked, which took place prior to that age. At this age women no longer work longer hours than men, as they did for a short while in their early twenties.

Among men, on the other hand, we see an increase in number of hours worked following their average age of marriage (26), as well as a continuing increase in how many men are working. This is the beginning of a differential effect of marriage on men and women working in the paid labor force, and we shall follow it through the life cycle in the next section.

Having children increases the mother's domestic roles in addition to other marital roles, although many women return to the labor force after a short period. We can see that, shortly after the average age at which women have their first child (26), fewer women work in the labor force and the average number of hours worked drops down to three-fourths that of men.

We will deal with the effect of these family roles in a more precise way in the following sections.

GETTING MARRIED AND WORKING
IN THE PAID LABOR FORCE

With the considerable attention given to the rising divorce rate and the below-replacement fertility of Jews, we sometimes overlook that, during these same years we have been talking about, most Jewish men and women get married. Among those 30 and over in our sample, over 90 percent had married, and 85 percent of these marriages had lasted until the time of the survey. Although only 3 percent of the men and 11 percent of the women 18–24 are married, two-thirds of the men and three-fourths of the women are married by ages 30–34.

Being married has a long-range effect on the labor force participation patterns of both men and women, increasing the participation and the work hours of men and decreasing the participation and work hours of women (as we shall show). Being married indicates the effect of the current marital status. *Age at marriage*[11] is more of a long-term indicator that shows the effect of orientations during the earlier part of life cycle, the priority of family roles (indicated by marrying early) or nonfamilial roles (indicated by postponing marriage). Of course, such choices may not have been voluntary and are influenced by the person's standing on the marriage market and the marriage market available to him or her; nevertheless they influence the options for action available at any point in the life cycle.

As we have discussed in the previous chapter, early marriage may interrupt education. The later the age at marriage is, the higher the education that can be completed and the greater the investment that can be made in a career before marriage. Especially for women, delayed marriage has been associated with greater career involvement (again, either because the unmarried woman has more time to devote to a career, whether this was her preference or not; or because the women who are committed to a career are the same women who are ambivalent about marriage and postpone entrance into it).

The longer the span between the end of education and the age of marriage is, the greater the likelihood that a woman will need to support herself and thus gain some work experience. Later age at marriage would again imply a greater investment in the labor force for practical reasons if for none other, and a likelihood to continue this pattern of labor force participation. Early experience in the labor force is still the best predictor of later patterns of labor force participation (Desai and Waite, 1991). Like the education acquired during these same years, we expected that the timing of marriage would be more directly related to the education acquired (as shown in the previous chapter), but more indirectly related through a long-term effect to labor force participation.

It was thus with some surprise that we found that age of marriage has no effect on current labor force participation patterns of Jewish men and women (Figure 3.4). Earlier marriage does not result in significantly lower participation rates; and postponing marriage does not result in a different pattern of labor force participation throughout the life cycle. It does not seem to allow women, for instance, to establish a labor force participation pattern to which they then are committed, whatever their

FIGURE 3.4
Percent in Paid Labor Force by Age at Marriage and Sex, U.S. Jews, 1990

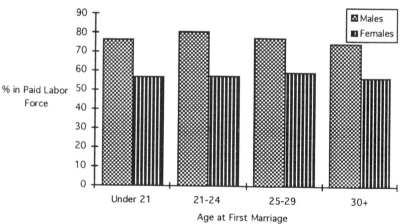

Source: NJPS, 1990.

marital status. The findings are equally true for men and women. The lack of effect is not due to differential education or age composition of those who marry at particular ages: when age and education are controlled in a multivariate analysis (shown later in Table 3.19), the age at marriage still has no significant effect. The obligations associated with being married influence the labor force patterns but not the age at which one enters the marital state.

BEING MARRIED AND WORKING
IN THE PAID LABOR FORCE

Marriage used to signify the end of a working woman's career, and Jewish women were no exception to this pattern, as Ritterband (1990) and Condran and Kramarow (1991) have shown. It still contributes to the lower labor force participation of women as compared to men, because most often women shoulder the main housekeeping and mothering roles and there is limited time and energy to fulfill extensive family roles at the same time as full-time labor force roles. Nevertheless, in the last few decades, although the labor force participation of married women has not reached that of men, more and more married women and mothers joined the labor force, the combination of family and labor force roles has become much more variable, and there are multiple ways in which these roles are combined (Gerson, 1985; Hochschild, 1989; Moen, 1992). Family and employment roles interact, affecting each other in different ways at different points in the life cycle. Some women follow a pattern of rising employment aspirations, accompanied by ambivalence toward motherhood, which often is expressed in delayed childbearing and even delayed marriage. Still others, once they begin to get involved in their jobs, change toward greater career commitment, even if it means curtailing some of the family roles they had aspired to at an earlier age. Early investment in an occupation increases the cost of leaving it later on. Other women follow a "traditional model" of female development, in which domestic roles are emphasized over any others; early childbearing of many children will delay investment in a full-time career (unless the mother can afford a lot of hired help and does not mind leaving her children in someone else's care). However, even women following this traditional model may find that they need to work for economic reasons; they may work only part-time, in order to accommodate multiple demands, or "sequence" employment and childrearing, returning to work only after their children are grown. Other women start out with a strong career commitment but may not succeed at work or for other reasons may not get support for their career orientations, and they turn to the domestic roles for greater fulfillment. Both early aspirations and later experiences shape how much marital and labor force roles are combined over the life course (Gerson, 1985; Moen, 1992; Waite, Haggstrom, and Kanouse, 1985; Waite and Stolzenberg, 1976).

Because men are expected to fill a provider role for their families, an association is also expected between labor force activity and family roles among men, but in the opposite direction from women. Married men are more likely to feel a responsibility to succeed at work, which may entail longer work hours to get appropriate promotions, and a pressure for more steady employment so the family will not be deprived of its major income. Men are known to postpone marriage until they feel they can provide an adequate income, and many of the frustrations of young couples stem from the financial pressures that demand long hours of work commitment at the same time that the family is growing and needing attention. Whereas women may be pulled into more domestic roles at this stage in the life cycle (between getting married and sending the children off to school), men may be driven away from family roles and into more extensive economic roles in order to work harder and make more money for the family. This would lead us to expect the most gendered division of labor at the same time that family roles are at their peak, which explains the growing and large gap in labor force participation patterns we saw for American Jews in their early thirties.

But part of the socialization to the masculine role is to succeed in a career, regardless of family obligations. From this point of view, all men are expected to participate to a similar extent in the labor force. A relationship between marital status and labor force commitment may be related to some prior characteristic—for instance, the same men who are motivated to succeed at work may also be motivated to get married because of some inner drive to achieve in every realm; men who do not succeed at work may not marry because they find it difficult to accept responsibility in any situation.

It is difficult to untangle the causal relationships between the work and family commitment even using a life course or longitudinal perspective; in a cross-sectional sample such as ours, it is practically impossible. At first we will discuss the simple relationship between marital roles and labor force participation, then we will attempt to control for some of these other influences to unravel the net effect of family roles on labor force participation and the possible interaction among them.

To study the relationship between family roles and labor force participation, we first look at how *being married* is related to labor force participation. Does marriage per se still make it more difficult for women to participate in the paid labor force or have social norms and household conveniences made it easier to combine the two? Do the financial obligations implied in providing for a family express themselves in married men participating more in the labor force or does the family provide enough support that it frees men to be more committed to their careers? Or, as more and more married women and mothers participate in the labor force, we know there is some impact on men's domestic roles (e.g., Hochschild, 1989): are fathers drawn into domestic roles to ensure proper care of their children?

Marriage and the Labor Force Participation of American Jewish Men

As we expected, married Jewish men are considerably more likely to be in the labor force than unmarried men (Table 3.2). Divorced and separated men have similar rates of labor force participation as married men, because many of them also have families to support. Single men are less likely to be in the labor force and widowed men even less.

Single men are concentrated in the early stages of the life cycle, at the same period of time that education is being completed and entrance into the labor force just beginning. Widowed men, on the other hand, are concentrated in the older stages, when retirement from the labor force is more common. However, even in the main labor force stages (25–55), there is a consistent difference between married and unmarried men,[12] which shows that the difference between married and unmarried men is not simply an artifact of age (Figure 3.5).

The difference between married and unmarried men, however, is especially apparent among the younger and the older men. Jewish men in

TABLE 3.2
Percent in Paid Labor Force, by Marital Status and Age,
U.S. Jewish Men, 1990

Age	Married, spouse present	Single	Divorced, Separated	Widowed
18–24	(67.4)	37.0	(100.0)	—
25–34	94.5	76.7	86.2	—
35–44	97.7	91.2	84.4	(100.0)
45–54	94.9	30.7	86.4	(100.0)
55–64	81.3	73.6	77.5	(0.0)
65+	30.1	(13.7)	30.0	28.6
Total	76.2	61.2	79.0	45.2
(N in thousands)	(1,236)	(480)	(119)	(61)

Note: Percentages in parentheses indicate unweighted *n* < 10.

Source: NJPS, 1990.

FIGURE 3.5
Percent in Paid Labor Force, by Age[a] and Marital Status,
U.S. Jewish Men, 1990

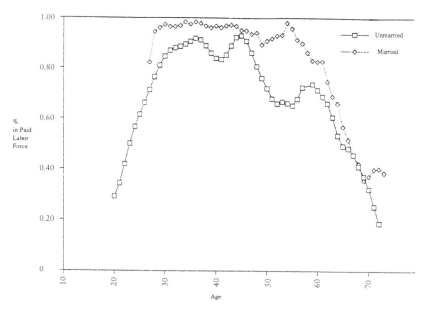

Source: NJPS, 1990.

[a]For ages 65 and older the graph has been smoothed out, as the relatively small number of cases caused random variation from age to age.

their twenties and early thirties apparently can prolong their student and carefree days a bit longer when they are not married—or perhaps some postpone marrying because they are not ready to be saddled with the varied responsibilities of a family. In the oldest age group the difference between married and unmarried men is also quite large: apparently family obligations prevent married men from retiring as early as unmarried men. However, we can see the effect of being married at every stage of the life cycle: married Jewish men work more than their unmarried counterparts.

In addition to participating more in the labor force, married men in the labor force work longer hours per week than unmarried men[13] (as shown in Figure 3.6). Unmarried men work on the average more than 40 hours a week throughout the life cycle, but married men work more than 45 hours a week from ages 25 to 54. This reflects both the stronger motivation to succeed in providing for the family and the support a family

FIGURE 3.6
Mean Hours of Work, by Age, Sex, and Marital Status, for U.S. Jews, 1990

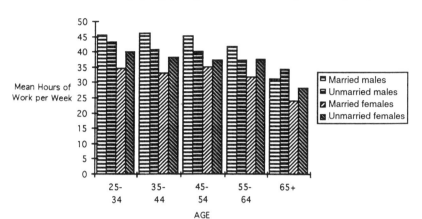

Source: NJPS, 1990.

offers, which enables men to spend this amount of time at work. The difference between married and unmarried men is consistent across all age groups, except the very oldest, among whom non-married (primarily widowed) men work slightly longer hours than the married men. It is possible that for older men the labor force participation of younger wives allows married men to cut down their hours more than the unmarried can (we will explore this further in the chapter on couples).

Comparing the Relationship Between Marital Status Among Jewish Men to the Wider American Population

Differences between the married and unmarried can be seen among the general white population as well (Table 3.3), but the difference is somewhat greater among Jewish men than the wider white population. The higher participation of married Jewish men is particularly noticeable in the younger age group, when married Jewish men either interrupt education[14] (over 80 percent of the Jewish men who are still in college during these ages are not married) or start to work right after completing school or even during school (a higher proportion of married men attending college attend only part-time—79 percent compared to 21 percent among the unmarried, and 85 percent of the married combine their college attendance with work in the labor force, compared to 68 percent of the unmarried). Because less of the total white population (married or not) is still involved with education at this age, differences between the married and

TABLE 3.3
Percent in Paid Labor Force, by Age, Sex, and Marital Status,
U.S. Jewish and Total White Population, 1990

| | U.S. Jews | | | | U.S. Whites | | | |
Age	All Men	Married Men	All Women	Married Women	All Men	Married Men	All Women	Married Women
Total	75.0	78.7	58.9	58.7	77.4	75.0	55.9	55.4
25–34	84.9	94.6	76.8	74.5	95.2	93.6	74.2	66.4
35–44	95.2	97.3	74.9	71.7	95.3	94.3	76.6	71.0
45–54	90.0	94.1	78.4	72.3	91.6	91.1	71.4	66.4
55–64	79.6	83.6	57.2	54.7	68.7	67.3	45.5	40.6
65+	29.4	34.3	11.3	10.6	16.8	18.2	8.6	8.2
(N in thou sands)	(1,869)	(1,223)	(1,813)	(1,149)	(64,281)	(45,630)	(70,356)	(44,738)

Sources: NJPS, 1990; unpublished tabulations from the 1990 Current Population Survey, U.S. Department of Labor Statistics.

unmarried in the wider population are less outstanding.

Differences are also more notable for Jewish men over 65: because a relatively high proportion of Jewish men continue to work over age 65 compared to the wider population (which is related to their higher education and higher proportions in self-employed occupations), we see the difference between married and unmarried Jewish men more than among the wider population.

Marriage and the Labor Force Participation of American Jewish Women

The relationship between age, education, and marital status is somewhat more complicated among women than among men. Because men marry at about the same time as they finish education and both finishing education and getting married are related to greater labor force participation, their labor force entrance is relatively easy to explain. As most women marry between 18 and 24 (average age of marriage 23.3) and during the same period most women are in the process of finishing their education, the various processes are entangled, especially for this age group. Women in this age group who have not yet married are mostly still in school and therefore work less than married women. Getting married may indicate an end to education, but does not necessarily imply stopping work except when children are young (as we shall see), given the financial incentives of building the new life together. So in this age group we find almost double the proportion in the labor force among married women than among the unmarried. As most of the unmarried finish their education during these ages, we see a jump in labor force participation between 18–24 and 25–34 for the unmarried, from 32 to nearly 80 percent. From the late twenties there is a consistent pattern of Jewish married women working less than Jewish single, divorced/separated, or widowed women (Table 3.4). Single women in the age group 25–34 work somewhat less than divorced/separated women in this age group, perhaps because the single women are anticipating marriage, while the divorced or separated women are anticipating or experiencing the need to be financially independent. Otherwise the unmarried women of various kinds tend to behave similarly, except in the oldest age group, when divorced or separated women appear to participate more than the other groups, again anticipating their need to provide for their own old age. In comparison with the married women, all types of unmarried women participate more at each life cycle stage, and due to the small numbers we have combined them into married and unmarried for further analyses (Figure 3.7).

The difference between married and unmarried women is particularly large for those in their fifties, when unmarried women (especially the singles) are extremely active in the labor force: 92 percent of the single women participate in the age group 45–54, 88 percent of the divorced or separated, and 72 percent of the married women participate. The labor force behavior of unmarried women in this age group is practically the same as men's and reflects both the inadequacy of financial support from other sources and the lower role conflict with domestic roles. However,

TABLE 3.4
Percent in Paid Labor Force, by Marital Status and Age,
U.S. Jewish Women, 1990

Age	Married, Spouse Present	Single	Divorced, Separated	Widowed
Total	59.0	57.6	78.6	24.8
18–24	51.4	32.6	(100.0)	—
25–34	76.1	76.8	88.7	(0.0)
35–44	71.4	86.4	83.7	(100.0)
45–54	73.8	94.6	90.0	(100.0)
55–64	54.5	73.4	(69.1)	63.1
65+	10.6	(23.1)	23.8	10.9
(*N* in thousands)	(1,173)	(326)	(156)	(201)

Note: Percentages in parentheses indicate unweighted *n* < 10.

Source: NJPS, 1990.

80 GENDERED PATTERNS OF SECULAR ACHIEVEMENT

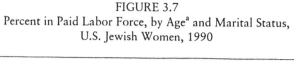

FIGURE 3.7
Percent in Paid Labor Force, by Age[a] and Marital Status,
U.S. Jewish Women, 1990

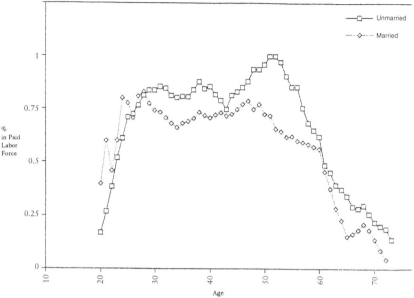

[a]For ages 65 and older the graph has been smoothed out, as the relatively small number of cases caused random variation from age to age.

Source: NJPS, 1990.

the difference between unmarried women in this age group and the previous may also reflect a cohort difference. Because the numbers are fairly small, it is difficult to go into more detailed analysis here.

In addition to having a lower labor force participation rate, Jewish married women who are in the paid labor force also work significantly fewer hours per week than unmarried women[15] (Figure 3.6). The fewer work hours of married women is consistent over the life cycle, reflecting the effect of domestic roles on married women's availability for longer work hours in the labor force, no matter what age. It is somewhat greater in the younger age groups, when married women have more extensive mothering roles that curtail their hours in the labor force.[16]

Married Jewish women have consistently higher rates of participation in the paid labor force than married women in the wider white U.S. population at all ages (Table 3.3), probably related to their higher educational level and fewer children (which we will explore in greater detail). Unmarried Jewish women also have higher rates of participation than their counterparts. Being married appears to have a similar effect on Jewish women and the wider U.S. population, slightly decreasing the amount of participation, especially during the prime childbearing and childrearing years (25–44).

Marriage and the Gender Gap in Jewish Labor Force Participation

We have seen that being married is related differently to the labor force participation of Jewish men and women, which is one of the reasons for the larger difference that develops between men and women after their mid-twenties and during their early thirties. Whereas married men are more likely to participate in the labor force than other men and to work longer hours per week, married women are less likely to participate in the labor force than other women and work shorter hours. The resulting gender gap expresses the differentiation in social roles of married men and women. Differences between married men and women are particularly large up to age 45, during the most intensive years of childbearing and childrearing. As in most modern industrialized countries, at ages 45–54 we see something of a resurgence in the hours worked by married women, as their children get older and leave the house and they return to the labor force (Roos, 1985). This is reflected in a two-peaked participation curve for women, the first peak prior to the childbearing and childrearing ages and the second peak after children have grown up. However, among American Jewish women, the second peak comes somewhat later than in the wider white U.S. population and is somewhat less pronounced. After age 54, women, like men, begin to disengage from the labor force in hours as well as participation, and marital status makes less of a difference in their labor force behavior.

    Unmarried men and unmarried women are more similar in their labor force participation patterns than married men and women, unmarried men participating less and working fewer hours than married men, and unmarried women participating more and working more hours than married women. Unmarried men and women diverge mainly after age 65, as women cut down their working hours more than men (see more in the section on retirement patterns).

Comparing the Relationship of Marriage and the Gender Gap in Labor Force Participation Among Jews and the Wider Population

When we compare Jews to the wider white population in the United States, marriage seems to have little overall effect on the gender gap of men and women in the labor force among both Jews and the wider white population (Table 3.3). But when we look at age groups, different patterns of Jews and the wider population are apparent. Because childbearing starts earlier in the wider population, the wider gender gap characteristic of married men and women begins already for the 25–34 year-olds in the wider American population, but among the Jewish population we do not see a differentiation of married men and women until the next age group, 35–44. Marriage also differentiates more the gender roles of Jews 45–64 than in the wider population. In this age group, unmarried men and women among Jews are more similar in labor force behavior than the unmarried in the wider population; therefore, although the married Jewish men and women in this age group differ to a similar extent as in the wider population, marriage appears to differentiate the roles more than in the wider population. Jewish husbands (like Jewish men in general) have a much higher proportion working in the labor force after age 65 than husbands in the wider population (34 percent compared to 18 percent); while Jewish wives (like Jewish women in general) also work more than the wider female population of this age, the difference is much smaller (11 percent of the Jewish wives 65 and over work, compared to 8 percent of the total white American wives). Therefore, the gender gap among the 65 and over group among both married and total population is greater among Jews.

It seems again that the higher education of the Jewish population influences their labor force participation patterns, in this case how marriage influences these patterns in comparison to how it affects the labor force participation of the wider American population. The higher education of both Jewish men and women postpones the entrance of Jewish men to the labor force (making them more similar to women at this earlier age) and in turn delays the age of childbearing, so that time-consuming domestic roles are postponed; the higher education of the unmarried in the 45–64 year-old age group makes unmarried women act more similar to men, while married men and women in this age group retain the patterns characteristic of earlier age groups.

EDUCATION AND LABOR FORCE PARTICIPATION
OF MEN AND WOMEN

We have been referring to the effect of the higher education of Jewish men and women on their labor force participation patterns throughout this chapter. In this section, we assess the relationship between education and labor force participation patterns of men and women and how education affects the gender gap in this behavior.

Because work in the paid labor force is considered more of an option than a duty for women as compared to men, education usually has more of an effect on whether women work in the paid labor force than for men. As we have mentioned, the higher the education is, the higher the costs of staying out of the labor force, because of the better job opportunities in terms of pay, interest, and challenge. "An economic interpretation of the association between education and labor force activity is that the 'cost' of staying home is greater for a college-educated woman than for a woman with a high school diploma, because more highly educated women are usually paid higher wages. It could also be argued that a woman with higher education usually has more occupational choices and thus may be more likely to seek work. The process of receiving a college degree can also widen a woman's aspirations to include more than work in the home, just as higher education may influence her preference for family size" (Bianchi and Spain, 1986, p. 130).

Because of the pay and better access to information that accompanies higher education, the better is the access to high-quality child care (Desai and Waite, 1991). As discussed in the previous chapter, higher education also increases the commitment to achievement-related activities and in this way is also expected to reduce the gap in expectations about appropriate roles for men and women, and therefore more educated men and women should also behave more similarly.

However, more educated women have been found to be as likely to stay home with their children as less educated, at least for a short period (Desai and Waite, 1991; Leibowitz, 1974), possibly because they are more likely to breastfeed their children (Haaga, 1989). This interruption in labor force behavior may reduce their advantage vis-à-vis less educated women in the labor force, particularly since less educated women have invested in fewer skills and hence suffer less from their depreciation when they are not being used in the labor force (Desai and Waite, 1991).

Education and the Labor Force Participation of American Jewish Men and Women

As a group, American Jewish women are particularly highly educated compared to the wider population. Most studies of the effect of education find especially large effects of college education, and a very high proportion of Jewish women have some college education, especially in the most recent cohorts. Equal proportions of Jewish men and women have some college education, although more men than women have completed college degrees, and the gender gap increases with number of years of education. It is expected that the equality in those going beyond high school should make the gender gap in labor force participation among Jews smaller than in the wider population, but it is not clear what the effect of the persisting gap in educational attainment has on labor force participation.

We confine the presentation here to those 25 and over to minimize the negative effect of education caused by young people who are still completing their schooling. As expected, the more years of education, the higher is the participation of both men and women (Figure 3.8), but the effect of education is weakened at higher levels, especially for men. The major effect of education for men is between those with no college education, and those with some college education. After 17 or more years of education, the increase in participation is very mild. Among women, education has a steadier effect, except among those few women with less than high school education, who work as much as women with high school education only.

However, the gender gap in labor force participation narrows only slightly with education: women with partial college education work at 80 percent the rate of men, whereas women with 20 or more years of education work at 90 percent the rate of men. Although education brings

FIGURE 3.8
Percent in Paid Labor Force, by Years of Education and Sex, U.S. Jews, 1990

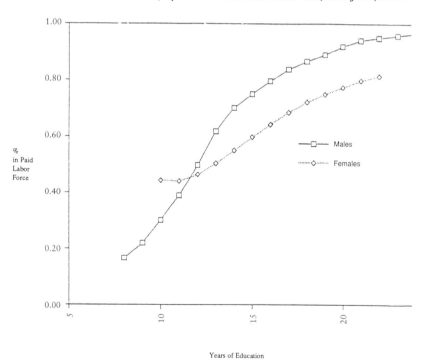

Source: NJPS, 1990.

men and women a little closer, it does not erase the effect of other factors bringing about differentiation between men and women. As we shall see, even though education has a significant effect on women's labor force participation, it does not eliminate the negative effects of being married or being older in reducing the labor force participation of women.

It was expected that higher education would also increase the investment in hours worked per week because of the greater job commitment and interest made possible by the range of occupational opportunities available to those with higher education. For those who are working in the labor force, higher education is associated with more hours of work per week for both men and women. Men's hours of work go from an average of 38.7 in the least educated group (high school or less) to 47.2 among those with 20 or more years of education. Women's hours range from 33.7 to 39.4. Education does not, however, appear to reduce the gender gap in hours worked: women work 75–80 percent of men's hours on the average at each level of education. Apparently, factors other than education suppress the hours that women work per week (such as domestic responsibilities that compete for their time or the nature of most of the occupations in which women are employed, which may—as for teachers—entail a lower number of formal hours per week even for a full-time job).

The effect of education can be seen even more clearly by looking at the highest academic degree earned (Table 3.5). Men with no academic degree are much less likely to participate in the labor force (only 26 percent participate); men with high school degrees participate nearly three times as much (61 percent); and between 80 and 90 percent of the men with some college degree are in the labor force. Because most of the men without even a high school diploma are older, and these men are less likely to be working, the effect of education is somewhat exaggerated here. When we control for age, the biggest differences for men are found in the older age groups: men 45–54 with a B.A. or higher degree participate more in the labor force; among men 55–64, men with Ph.D.s participate more than other men. But among the oldest age group of men (65+) that education has the steadiest effect, with labor force participation increasing with each additional degree, apparently having a decisive effect on whether the post-retirement-age man continues to work or not. This is at least in part because retirement is later for those in professional and academic occupations, since these occupations tend to be more intrinsically satisfying and the higher earnings associated with these occupations make retirement more costly (Pavalko, 1988).

Academic degree is related to the labor force participation of women in much the same way (Table 3.5). Only 23 percent of the women with no academic degree are working in the paid labor force, 43 percent of those with a high school diploma, and 84 percent of those with doctoral or

TABLE 3.5
Percent in Paid Labor Force and Mean Hours of Work,
by Highest Academic Degree, Sex, and Age, U.S. Jews, 1990

Sex and Age	High School or Less	Undergraduate College	M.A.	Ph.D., Professional[a]	(N in thousands)
Percent in Paid Labor Force:					
Male (total)	55.7	82.5	83.2	89.6	(1,704)
25–34	77.4	86.9	83.5	92.0	(372)
35–44	91.8	94.9	96.2	99.2	(428)
45–54	79.6	91.2	95.1	98.3	(273)
55–64	74.7	79.4	72.9	96.8	(250)
65+	23.1	33.4	43.4	51.3	(381)
Female (total)	41.6	66.7	77.8	84.3	(1,669)
25–34	61.4	79.5	84.3	92.0	(351)
35–44	67.7	70.6	81.6	99.2	(419)
45–54	69.6	76.5	95.5	98.3	(272)
55–64	50.7	61.1	69.7	96.8	(260)
65+	10.3	10.4	20.6	51.3	(368)
Mean Hours in Labor Force per Week:					
Male (total)	38.5	42.9	42.7	46.1	(1,284)
25–34	41.7	43.9	44.8	49.0	(553)
35–44	42.8	42.9	40.9	50.9	(408)
45–54	37.3	44.9	44.8	46.3	(246)
55–64	38.1	42.3	43.0	42.6	(199)
65+	30.7	31.3	36.1	29.2	(114)
Female (total)	33.4	33.7	37.4	42.9	(987)
25–34	37.6	35.6	38.0	48.1	(269)
35–44	34.9	33.0	37.4	37.8	(228)
45–54	32.8	32.7	40.0	44.9	(214)
55–64	33.1	32.0	31.7	45.9	(149)
65+	24.8	26.9	34.1	41.7	(42)

[a]This includes dental, medical, and law degrees.

Source: NJPS, 1990.

professional degrees. When we control for age, the differences are somewhat less dramatic; yet within each of the age groups, education continues to have a strong effect on labor force participation. Each of the college degrees adds to the likelihood that the woman is working. This fits the rationale presented previously, that the greater is the investment in education, the higher the cost of staying out of the labor force and the greater the labor force attachment.

Some, but not all, of the gender gap in labor force participation is explained by level of education. Given the same degree attained as men, women are less likely than men to be working in the paid labor force at each degree. However, the gender gap narrows considerably among men and women with graduate degrees, leaving little difference between them, and most of this difference occurs in the main ages of childrearing, ages 35–44, or after age 55, when women's earlier pension entitlement leads to earlier retirement than among men. The larger differences we saw between men and women are partly because of the differences in educational attainment, which we saw in the previous chapter, since few women attain the highest graduate degrees. Even at this highest educational level, however, women participate to a somewhat lower extent, related to their domestic roles (as we shall see).

In addition to participating more in the labor force, working men and women with higher academic degrees spend more hours per week at their jobs (Table 3.5). For men, there is a break between those with college degrees and those without: men who have high school diplomas or none at all work on the average less than 40 hours a week, especially men 45 or older, while men with any college degree work on the average 43–46 hours a week. Younger men with Ph.D.s or professional degrees put in especially long hours of work, reflecting the nature of the occupations they are in.

For women, the main difference is between those who have earned a doctorate or professional degree, who work on the average 42 hours a week, and the other women, who work on the average 34 hours a week. Among the most educated women, hours of work are close to that of men (more than 40 hours a week), except during the main childrearing ages of 35–44; in the other groups, women usually work closer to three-fourths the hours of men at all ages.

How Education Is Related to Differences in the Labor Force Participation of American Jews and the Wider Population

As we have seen, the labor force participation rates of Jewish men and women in the main stages of the working life (25–64) are very similar to the overall rates of the wider American population. Given the higher education of the Jewish population, this is actually somewhat surprising, because education is associated with higher labor force participation, especially among women. As the comparison to the wider American population by level of education shows (Table 3.6), both Jewish men and women participate to a somewhat lesser extent than the wider population at each level of education, except the lowest. Older Jewish men and women, who are the most likely to have this low level of education, tend

TABLE 3.6
Percent in Paid Labor Force, by Years of Education and Sex,
U.S. Jewish and Total U.S. Population, Ages 25–64, 1990

	Less than 4 years of High School	4 Years of High School Only	1–3 Years of College	4 Years of College or More	(N in thousands)
U.S. Jewish:					
Males	81.3	84.6	85.6	92.5	(1,568)
Females	65.2	55.5	70.3	76.5	(1,629)
U.S. Total:					
Males	78.3	90.7	92.4	94.8	(61,664)
Females	47.1	68.5	75.0	81.0	(65,058)

Source: NJPS, 1990; U.S. Dept. of Labor, Bureau of Labor Statistics, unpublished tabulations from the Current Population Survey, 1990 annual averages.

to retire later than the wider population, as we have seen, and this is reflected in the higher rates of participation of this educational level. The lower participation of the other groups of Jews may be related to differential age composition (Jews tending to be older and hence show more early retirees), education that continues into the thirties for some, a higher proportion of unmarried men among the Jews, or a stronger effect of marriage on Jewish women. However, we lack the data for more detailed comparison at this point.

MULTIVARIATE ANALYSES OF THE LABOR FORCE PARTICIPATION OF AMERICAN JEWISH MEN AND WOMEN

Up to now we have dealt with the effects of basically three variables—age, marital status, and educational attainment—on the labor force participation of men and women. However, as suggested at a number of points, these three factors do not necessarily affect labor force independently. For instance, as we have seen in the previous chapter on education, married men have somewhat more education than unmarried men[17] (except in the younger ages, when single men are still in school); whereas married women have somewhat less education than unmarried women[18] (especially in the younger ages, when single women go on for higher graduate degrees). Being educated increases labor force participation both in the sense of participating more in the labor force, especially for women, and increasing the number of hours worked when one does participate, as we have just seen. The question arises as to whether the difference we see between married and unmarried men and women is a spurious result, rather than an actual relationship between marital status and labor force participation.

Because the sample size precludes breaking down into too many subgroups to get a better understanding of how these factors relate to labor force participation, we used a multivariate analysis that provided us with the independent effect of each of these factors while controlling for the effects of each of the other factors on labor force participation and interaction effects as well.

We used a stepwise multiple regression model with work in the paid labor force[19] being the dependent variable. In the model, we controlled for age, because, as we saw, labor force participation varies over the life cycle. But age has no simple linear relationship with labor force participation, because it usually increases or remains stable until retirement is neared, when labor force participation drops quite sharply. To improve the linearity between age and labor force participation, we broke up the age indicator into two variables: "before retirement age" which indicated whether or not the individual had reached retirement age (0 = yes; 1 = no; ages 65 for men and 60 for women), dividing the sample into those whose age is prior to the peak of labor force participation and those who are after it; and "age," a continuous variable indicating the variation resulting from age itself. We included being married and highest academic degree[20] as independent variables.[21]

As we have done all along in this chapter, we separated the analysis for men and women because of the different patterns of relationship between labor force behavior and each of the main factors. However, as much as possible, we kept the models comparable for the two sexes, even if for each sex we could have somewhat improved the model. For example, for men, years of education is a better predictor of labor force participation than is highest academic degree and improved the model's fit. However, for women, degree is a much better predictor and makes a bigger difference than using years of education does for men. It was therefore optimal to use degree achieved for both men and women to be able to compare the models.[22]

Table 3.7 presents the results of the analysis. For men, the model fits labor force participation with a multiple correlation (R) of .633, the square of which (R^2) is .400; that is, 40 percent of the variance in men's labor force participation could be explained by these independent variables. The fit for women is not as good, $R = .527$, with only 28 percent of the variance explained. This indicates that our set of explanatory variables is more adequate for men. Apparently, to explain better women's labor force behavior, we would need to include additional factors not included

TABLE 3.7
Multiple Regression Analysis of Paid Labor Force Participation,
U.S. Jewish Men and Women, 1990

	Males				Females			
	Step 1	Step 2	Step 3	Final Model	Step 1	Step 2	Step 3	Final Model
Highest academic degree	.075** (.132)	.075** (.131)	.062** (.108)	.061** (.108)	.108** (.163)	.095** (.266)	.096** (.285)	.095** (.292)
Below retirement age	1.135** (.552)	.927** (.450)	.859** (.417)	.822** (.399)	.827** (.425)	.519** (.266)	.556** (.285)	.561** (.292)
Age		−.007** (−.131)	−.011** (−.210)	−.005* (−.104)		−.011** (−.197)	−.011** (−.188)	−.014** (−.242)
Marital status			.316** (.167)	.713** (.377)			−.205** (−.105)	−.490** (−.250)
Interaction of age and marital status				−.009** (−.278)				.006* (.161)
R	.603	.609	.629	.633	.503	.514	.525	.527
R²	.364	.371	.395	.401	.253	.265	.276	.278
(Un- weighted n	(1369)				(1300)			

Note: Standardized regression coefficients are in parentheses, others are unstandardized.
*α < .05.
**α < .001.

Source: NJPS, 1990.

in this model; some of these will be considered later.

In the first step of the regression, two basic variables were included: education and retirement age. With these two factors alone, 36 percent of the variance in men's labor force participation is explained. Being younger than the age of retirement (for men, age 65) has the stronger relationship to labor force participation, having a standardized regression coefficient four times that of academic degree achieved. The higher the academic degree is, the greater the labor force participation (as we have shown already).

When we add age to the model, age has a negative effect on being in the labor force, reflecting early retirement or disengagement from the labor force, and it reduces some of the strong effect of reaching retirement age. However, retirement age continues to have the stronger effect. The effect of education is independent of the ages of those who attained different levels of education. Since the effect of education does not change when age is controlled, it is not because those who attain lower education are older and those who attain higher education are younger that education has an effect on labor force participation.

Married men are more active in the labor force, even after age and education are controlled. The positive relationship between being a married man and working more in the labor force is not explained by education or age differences between the married and unmarried. Even though its effect is weaker than the age indicators, it is stronger than the effect of education on whether or not a man participates in the labor force.

When marital status is controlled, the effect of education declines, because part of the positive effect of education reflects the fact that the more educated are more likely to be married. Controlling for marital status, on the other hand, results in a stronger effect of age, reflecting that part of the negative effect of age is suppressed by older people being more likely to be married than younger people.

When in the final step of the model we enter the interaction between age and marital status, it has a significant effect on labor force participation, reflecting the differential effect of marital status at the different ages. This could reflect the importance of marital status at different life cycle stages. As we saw earlier, marital status makes a larger difference among the young and the old: among the young, married men work more while unmarried men go to school; among the older, married men work more while unmarried men retire earlier.[23] When the interaction term is included, the effect of age becomes much weaker (although still significant), because some of its effect is due to its interaction with marital status.

For women, being younger than retirement and having a higher academic degree explain 25 percent of the variance in women's labor force participation, being younger than retirement having an effect about 2½ times stronger than that of education. Having a higher academic degree reduces the effect of retirement only slightly, reflecting the slight tendency for more educated women to retire later.

Controlling for age adds to the model, reducing the effect of retirement by about 40 percent, because disengagement from the labor force begins earlier than age 60 for some women. The effect of education changes very little when age is controlled, indicating that the positive effect is not due to the lower education of older women and the higher education of younger women.

Marital status adds to the model, showing that the effect of being married is not a spurious result for women either—married women participate less in the paid labor force, even after we control for age and education. However, unlike men, being married has a weaker effect than age or education.

In the final step we include the interaction of age and marital status. As for men, it clarifies and strengthens the effect of marital status, because being married has stronger effects at particular stages of the life cycle (as we saw). Alternatively, it could be indicating the greater effect of marriage among the older cohorts, which we saw earlier and which we expect, given the changing norms about married women's participation in the labor force. Including the interaction term also strengthens the negative effect of age, because some of the younger women do not work because of their marital roles and when this is controlled the net negative effect of age is more apparent.

Comparing the models predicting labor force participation of men and of women shows us different patterns of effects. For both, being younger than the average age of retirement and being married have the strongest effects on labor force participation, but for women the effect of age is spread throughout the life cycle rather than concentrated at the age of retirement, perhaps because of the earlier retirement patterns for women (which we will discuss later).

Comparing the unstandardized regression coefficients of each variable for men and women shows us that retirement age has a stronger effect on the labor force participation of men than women. This is because the effect of age begins earlier than retirement for women and is spread between the retirement age variable and the continuous age variable, which is less important for men.

Also, marital status, in addition to having a different direction of effect for men and for women, affects men's participation more than it does women's. This is probably because it is less marriage per se that affects women's employment than the domestic roles that accompany having and caring for children, which are partially indicated by the marital status and partially by age. In the next section we will concentrate on the effect of children on women's labor force participation. It may also be because women, although they refrain from participating because of their marital domestic roles, are also pushed to participate, as men are, because of the financial demands of family life.

Education has a somewhat stronger effect on the labor force participation of women than of men, reflecting the greater latitude accorded women for choosing not to work unless it is financially worthwhile or interesting.

The dependent variable of these regressions was extent of labor force participation, which was coded 0 for not participating, 1 for part-time participation (less than 35 hours a week), and 2 for full-time participation. For a cleaner measure of participation, we dichotomized the variable into those who were in the labor force and those who were not and used a logistic regression model. The results reinforced our findings (not presented here).[24]

For those who are working in the labor force, we studied extent of labor force participation with a multiple regression model in which the dependent variable was hours of work per week. As in the participation models, the independent variables were age, retirement age, highest academic degree attained, and being married.[25] No interactions were included in the model, because they were not significant. The results are presented in Table 3.8. The model explains hours of work more weakly than it did labor force participation, the multiple correlation (R) being .314 for men and .240 for women.

In the first step we see that for men the effect of education on hours worked is much stronger than that of being younger than retirement.

TABLE 3.8
Multiple Regression Analysis of Hours of Work per Week,
U.S. Jewish Men and Women in the Paid Labor Force, 1990

	Males			Females		
	Step 1	*Step 2*	*Final Model*	*Step 1*	*Step 2*	*Final Model*
Highest academic degree	12.315** (.115)	8.753** (.174)	7.646** (.152)	1.114* (.101)	1.031* (.2094)	1.044* (.079)
Below retirement age	1.183** (.115)	1.193** (.116)	1.065** (.104)	5.407* (.117)	2.841 (.061)	3.659 (.095)
Age		-.124* (-.113)	-.098 (-.088)		-.108** (-.088)	-.079 (-.065)
Marital status			7.896* (.240)			-4.941** (-.158)
R	.283	.296	.314	.168	.181	.240
R²	.080	.088	.099	.028	.033	.057
(Unweighted N)	(1115)			(951)		

Note: Standardized regression coefficients are in parentheses, others are unstandardized.
*$\alpha < .05$.
**$\alpha < .001$.

Source: NJPS, 1990.

When age enters the model, the effect of education is weakened, since some of its effect is because older men are less educated.

Of these variables, education continues to have the strongest relationship with hours worked until marital status is entered. The effect of being married on hours worked that we saw previously (married men work more hours than unmarried men) is significant, even when age and education are controlled. Marriage itself is apparently a motivator and a facilitator to spend more hours in the labor force—the family needs the additional income and supports the provider with services that enable him to concentrate his time more fully on his work.

Once marital status, education, and retirement age are controlled, age ceases to have a significant effect on hours worked. Some of its relationship comes from married men, especially younger married men, working more hours in the labor force.

Although the model explains only 5.7 percent of the variance in the hours women work, we can see how these factors affect women's hours in the labor force. Reaching retirement age has a much stronger for women than for men. In the first step of the model its effect is four times as large as it was for men. On the other hand, education has a much smaller effect than retirement age and a much smaller effect than it did for the number of hours men work.

When age is entered, the effect of being at retirement age becomes nonsignificant. The effect of getting older, or being in an older cohort, influences how many hours a woman spends at her job and not just whether or not she has reached age 60.

When marital status is entered, we see that being married lowers the hours worked, even when age and education are controlled, and it has the strongest effect of the independent variables. This analysis confirms what we saw in simpler analyses—being married affects men and women significantly but in opposite directions both in terms of whether they participate in the labor force and, when they do, how many hours they work per week.

In terms of hours worked, the age variable does not adequately capture the fluctuations in women's labor force patterns, which depend more on the extent of domestic roles than age and therefore do not vary linearly with age. Once marital status is controlled, the effect of age becomes insignificant. Only marital status and education retain significant effects.

In conclusion, the multiple regression analyses show us that being married is one of the most important predictors of both labor force participation and hours of work even when age and education are controlled. Moreover, the effect of being married is in an opposite direction for men and women and affects the labor force participation of each differently at different ages. Second, they show that age affects negatively whether men and women are in the labor force, regardless of education and marital status, and especially important is whether they have reached retirement age or not. How many hours they work is affected less by age, especially for women, once domestic responsibilities are controlled by marital status. Education has a weak but positive effect on both labor force participation and hours of work for both men and women, which is independent of age and marital status.

CHILDREN AND THE LABOR FORCE PARTICIPATION OF WOMEN

The negative impact of marital status on women's labor force participation and its greater impact in older cohorts led us to explore further some of the domestic responsibilities implied in marriage and their impact on whether or not women are in the paid labor force. More and more mothers of young children are participating in the labor force in the United States as in most industrialized countries. But the Jewish values about raising children call into question the extent to which Jewish mothers follow this trend. Although higher education, characteristic of Jewish women, is associated with higher rates of labor force participation, it is not clear whether more educated women return more quickly to the labor force after birth than other mothers. We explore here how strong the effect of children is on Jewish women's labor force participation.

Some indicators about children indicate the short-term responsibilities implied in childcare, such as the age of the youngest child and whether or not there is a small child or a school-age child to take care of. If getting married implies additional domestic roles for women and additional financial obligations for men, having children implies even more of the same. More children mean more responsibilities of parenthood at any age, although each additional child may not make as much of a difference as the first transition to parenthood. Recent research suggests that at the time of the first birth fertility has the strongest impact on labor force participation (Desai and Waite, 1991).

Other indicators reflect more a familistic orientation rather than the immediate impact of childcare duties, such as when the mother had her first child or how many children she had (whether or not they are still young). The high value placed on children among Jews is expressed in a high investment in developing and nurturing children. Some research has shown that in comparison to non-Jewish women, Jewish women are more likely to stop working when they have a child. The younger the age at which this occurs, the earlier a woman's career is interrupted, and she will be at a greater disadvantage if and when she wants to return to the labor force. Hewlett (1987) has discussed the detrimental effects of interrupting a career, especially at its formative stages, in terms of later occupational achievement and wage returns.

We are interested in the extent to which the everyday responsibilities of childcare, as well as the more long-term indicators of how familistic the woman is, influence her labor force participation.

We confine our analysis in this section to married women, because we do not have enough cases of women with children who are not currently married[26] to analyze separately, and the factors affecting married and unmarried mothers, especially regarding labor force participation, are different and would confound the results.

Short-Term Factors of Childcare Among American Jews

As expected, women with children participate in the paid labor force less than women with no children—68 percent and 85 percent, respectively. Women with no children participate nearly as much as men (85 percent compared to men's 89 percent). Having one child does not make much difference. But with two or three children (the modal number of children for American Jewish women with children), participation goes down about 15 percent, and with four or more children it goes down another 30 percent.[27]

Having many children can reflect both a practical limitation on participation in the labor force, and a lifestyle preference—to be a "family" person rather than a "career" person. If it reflects mainly a lifestyle preference, we would expect women of all ages who have children, especially many children, to participate much less in the labor force than women with fewer children. If it reflects primarily a practical role conflict, we would expect the effect of having children to be stronger when children are younger; that is, among younger mothers. The effect of children may also have changed over cohorts, affecting older cohorts more than the younger ones because of the change in norms about mothers working (see discussion in Fishman, 1993, pp. 88–94), the advent of conveniences making childcare easier (e.g., disposable diapers, ready-made food and formula—what Bergmann, 1986, has called the *industrialization of childcare*), and the change in number of children mothers have.

Older cohorts had more children, and even though the younger cohorts have not completed their fertility, they both have and intend to have fewer children than the older cohorts.

> [T]here are sweeping changes in childbearing patterns among large segments of the Jewish population. . . . Changes in marriage patterns have affected both the timing and the size of today's families. In 1990,

93 percent of Jewish women aged eighteen to twenty-four had not yet had children. More than half (55 percent) of those aged twenty-five to thirty-four had no children. Among Jewish women aged thirty-five to forty-four one out of four had no children. While almost all Jewish women aged forty-five or over reported having children, either biological or adopted, it is not clear that all or even most of the 24 percent of childless women in the thirty-five-to-forty-four age group will in fact achieve the status of motherhood. As a result of delayed marriage and childbirth, the societal preference for smaller families, and unwanted infertility, most demographers now estimate the completed size of the contemporary Jewish family to average fewer than two children per married household. (Fishman, 1993, p. 49)

When we control for age, we see that among American Jewish women aged 25–34 (prime childbearing and childrearing ages), women with no children participate in the paid labor force 18 percent more than women with children—in fact they work nearly as much as men of these ages (whose labor force participation rate is 84.9 percent; Table 3.9). Having one child makes little difference in labor force participation rates, but in this age group labor force participation declines with each successive child more than in the total sample. Less than 20 percent of the women of this age who have four or more children are in the labor force.

TABLE 3.9
Percent in Paid Labor Force, by Number of Children and Age of Mother,
U.S. Jewish Married Women, 1990 (*N* in thousands)

		Age of Mother			
Number of Children	*Total*	*25–34*	*35–44*	*45–54*	*55–64*
With no children	84.9	82.2	90.8	89.6	63.5
	(366)	(203)	(103)	(466)	(134)
With children	67.9	69.4	69.7	76.4	56.8
	(935)	(146)	(317)	(226)	(245)
With one child	78.1	79.7	82.1	82.2	59.7
	(209)	(67)	(89)	(24)	(30)
With two children	67.5	70.5	65.6	77.4	57.8
	(411)	(52)	(165)	(106)	(89)
With three children	66.5	50.1	76.6	75.3	57.8
	(234)	(21)	(43)	(79)	(91)
With four or more children	46.8	19.9	35.4	66.9	49.3
	(80)	(7)	(21)	(17)	(35)

Source: NJPS, 1990.

Some of this may be attributed to the younger ages of the children of mothers in this age group, as we will discuss later.

Like their younger counterparts, women ages 35–44 with no children participate in the labor force at nearly the same rate as men (90.8 percent compared to 95.2 percent of the men of this age). This is about 30 percent more than women with children. Women of this age with only one child participate almost as much as women with no children, and slightly more than younger women with one child. Although women of this age group who have three or four children participate much more than younger women with the same number of children, they participate less than other women of their age. Only about one-third of the women with four or more children are in the labor force.

Having children affects labor force participation less in the older cohorts, even though older cohorts had more children, suggesting that the effect is more a practical effect of role conflict and the respective time and energy required for each role than a reflection of women who have chosen different lifestyles. It seems that the number of children is less critical than the number of young children, because women in younger cohorts are more likely to have younger children than women in older cohorts (see later discussion of the effect of age of youngest child). It also goes in a direction opposed to the changing norms which are more accepting of mothers working in the paid labor force. Especially notable is that two-thirds of the women aged 45–54 who have four or more children are in the labor force. Among women 55–64, women with no children participate only 11 percent more than women with children and nearly half of the women with four or more children are employed.

Here we also see another of the difficulties of separating out the effect of age and cohort. The labor force participation rates of women ages 55–64 are lower than for younger women, partly because women have begun to retire by this age and partly because the norms about women working in this cohort were different and such women did not develop patterns of participation in the labor force like their younger counterparts. There is also some indication that women with many children (four or more) chose a different kind of lifestyle, as even when these children are no longer young their mothers participate less in the labor force than other women of their age. Having children who are older (as they are when their mothers are older) may also indicate other possible sources of financial support, which may be another reason for the lower participation rates among older women with many children.

Among Jewish women who work, the number of hours at work during the week is also influenced by number of children (Table 3.10).[28] The main difference is between women who have no children and women who have children. Women who have no children, at all ages, work more

TABLE 3.10
Mean Hours Worked per Week in Paid Labor Force,
by Number of Children and Age of Mother,
U.S. Jewish Married Women Employed in the Labor Force, 1990
(*N* in thousands)

		Age of Mother			
Number of Children	*Total*	*25–34*	*35–44*	*45–54*	*55–64*
0	40.6	40.4	41.1	40.6	(41.3)
	(311)	(167)	(103)	(42)	(9)
1	33.3	32.5	34.9	34.3	(27.4)
	(163)	(53)	(733)	(14)	(18)
2	30.5	27.6	29.8	33.6	30.3
	(278)	(36)	(108)	(82)	(51)
3 or more	32.1	(32.7)	30.6	35.0	32.3
	(193)	(12)	(40)	(71)	(70)

Note: Means in parentheses indicate unweighted *n* < 10.

Source: NJPS, 1990.

than 40 hours a week on the average, that is, have full-time jobs, like men of these ages. On the other hand, women with children, at every age, work less than 35 hours a week on the average. Whether there are one, two or three children seems to make little difference.

We had expected the number of children to make more of a difference in the younger age groups than in the older (just as number of children made more of a difference in labor force participation for younger women), but we found little variation over age among women with the same number of children. Having children may start women into a pattern of part-time labor force participation or into certain types of occupations that are characterized by a lower average number of hours per week, and this pattern may persist throughout the life cycle. Thus having children may have a long-term effect on patterns of labor force activity, even if it has little long-term effect on whether or not a woman works in the paid labor force.

Age of Youngest Child and Labor Force Participation of American Jewish Women

How many children a woman has does not tell us very precisely how demanding her mothering roles are today. We learn more about this from the age of the youngest child, because younger children are more dependent and require more constant attention.

As expected, the younger the youngest child is, the fewer women participate in the labor force (Table 3.11). It seems that fewer mothers of 2 and 3 year-olds are in the labor force than mothers of infants, showing that the effect of young children continues through the preschool years and not only in the first years of life. Once the youngest child is in school, the mothers are more likely to return or enter the labor force, and this increases as the youngest child gets older, until by the time the youngest child is high school age (14–17) nearly three-fourths of the mothers are working in the labor force.

The effect of the age of the youngest child on labor force participation is strong in all the main fertility ages (25–39): having a child age 3 or under in the household cuts down the labor force participation of mothers of all ages (Table 3.12). Among women 25–29, 68.3 percent of the mothers of children age 3 or under are in the paid labor force compared to 94.3 percent of the women with no child under 18; among women ages 30–34, 53.1 percent of the mothers of children age 3 or under participate compared to 78.9 percent of the women with no child under 18; among women ages 35–39, 54.9 percent of the mothers of children age 3 or under participate compared to 92.8 percent women with no children under 18.

Because of their higher education, we would expect Jewish women with young children to be working in the labor force more than the general population. However, the value placed on bringing up children properly and the mother role raises questions about whether Jewish women continue to work when they have young children. Chiswick (1988) found that Jewish women are more likely to stay out of the labor force when they have children than non-Jewish women. When we compare our sam-

TABLE 3.11
Percent in Paid Labor Force, by Age of Youngest Child,
U.S. Jewish and Total White Married Women, Spouse Present, 1990

Age of Youngest Child	U.S. Jews	U.S. Whites
0–1	54.8	53.3
2	43.5	60.3
3	53.3	62.3
4	66.7	63.2
5	63.2	62.0
6–13	71.8	72.6
14–17	72.7	74.9
(N in thousands)	(1,173)	(30,500)

Sources: NJPS, 1990; U.S. Bureau of the Census, 1992, Table 621.

ple of American Jews to the wider white population of married women in the United States, we see that at most ages of youngest child, the labor force participation rate of Jewish women is quite comparable to the labor force participation rate of the wider white population. However, Jewish women are much more likely to be out of the labor force when their children are age 2 or 3 than is the wider population. The comparison suggests that Jewish women are more likely to stay out of the labor force longer with their children than the wider population. As children enter school and get older, Jewish women's labor force participation returns to the level of the wider population. As a result, the effect of having young children appears to be greater for Jewish women than for the wider population.

Another indication of the effect of children on patterns of labor force participation is the number of hours worked in a typical week for women in the paid labor force. Here again we see a greater and longer effect of children on Jewish women's labor force participation than in the wider population. Jewish women with young children are less likely to work full-time than are mothers in the wider population (Table 3.13).[29] Differences are especially large for mothers of children age 3–5 and school-age children (6–17). Among Jewish women with children of these ages less than half are employed full-time in the labor force; among the wider pop-

TABLE 3.12
Percent in Paid Labor Force, by Age of Youngest Child and Age of Mother,
U.S. Jewish Married Women, 1990
(*N* in thousands)

Age of Youngest Child	Age of Mother			
	25–29	30–34	35–39	40+
3 or under	68.3	53.1	54.9	37.9
	(14)	(37)	(24)	(16)
4–5	65.3	77.2	72.7	50.5
	(19)	(56)	(55)	(128)
6–17	x	(86.1)	61.3	75.0
		(9)	(43)	(99)
None under 18	94.4	78.9	92.8	49.6
	(55)	(30)	(19)	(549)

x = based on 1 case or less from the unweighted sample.
Percentages in parentheses indicate cells with 10 cases or less in the unweighted sample.

Source: NJPS, 1990.

TABLE 3.13
Percent of Workers Employed Full-Time, by Age of Youngest Child,
Married U.S. Jewish and Total White Women, 1990
(N in thousands)

Age of Youngest Child	U.S. Jews	U.S. Whites
Under 3	58.0 (79)	61.1 (6,667)
3–5	43.2 (62)	60.9 (2,617)
6–17	46.5 (174)	67.1 (8,066)
None under 18	67.7 (656)	74.8 (13,072)

Sources: NJPS, 1990; unpublished tabulations from the 1990 Current Population
Survey, U.S. Bureau of Labor Statistics.

ulation, over 60 percent of the mothers of children age 3–5 and over
two-thirds (67.1 percent) of the mothers of children age 6–17 are
employed full-time. These differences may reflect a socioeconomic status
that allows a greater proportion of Jewish women not to work full-time in
the labor force, a different choice of occupations for Jewish women
(which we will consider in the next chapter), and a greater value put on
spending more time with children.

CHILDREN AND THE EDUCATION OF THE MOTHER:
INFLUENCES ON LABOR FORCE PARTICIPATION

There are a number of reasons to think that having children will affect differently women of different levels of education. As we have seen, more
educated women are more likely to participate in the labor force. The reasons for this are partly economic and partly a result of different values
and lifestyle orientations. The orientation to work commitment and
attachment in the early years is related to reduced and delayed childbearing (Waite and Stolzenberg, 1976) and to spending less time out of
the labor force when children are born (Jones, 1981; Taeuber, 1991).

Educated women are also more likely to be married to educated men
(in general, and, as we shall see, in the case of American Jews), whose
earnings are higher, and therefore they are better able to afford satisfac-
tory substitutes for childcare than other families, which would ease the
combination of labor force activity with having children. Educated men
are also more likely to have nontraditional sex role attitudes and therefore
be more likely to accept their wife's participation in the labor force even
when they have children. For these reasons, we expected children to have
less of an effect on labor force participation among more educated women
than less educated women.

However, more educated women might be able to afford not to work, if a second family income is not needed, which would lead us to expect a greater effect of children on the labor force participation of educated mothers.

Children, Education, and the Labor Force Participation of American Jewish Women

No matter how many children, more educated women are more likely to be in the labor force than less educated women. Even among mothers with three or more children, 67.8 percent (over two-thirds) of the women with 17 or more years of education are in the paid labor force (Table 3.14). The effect of education seems to be greatest among women with two children, and least among women with three or more children; but since less educated women are older, it is possible that the low level of participation among less educated women with two children is due to age rather than the effect of children.

At the same time, having children has less impact on the labor force participation of more educated women. Among women with 12 or fewer years of education, having children lowers the labor force participation by 28 percent; among women with 17 or more years of education, having children lowers the labor force participation by only 20 percent.

TABLE 3.14
Percent in Paid Labor Force, by Number of Children and Years of Education,
U.S. Jewish Married Women, 1990
(*N* in thousands)

Number of Children	Years of Education			
	12 or less	*13–15*	*16*	*17+*
No children	48.7 (39)	66.7 (63)	81.4 (113)	90.5 (84)
With children	35.0 (300)	45.6 (237)	62.3 (256)	72.1 (193)
1	39.5 (43)	64.2 (53)	63.9 (61)	77.3 (44)
2	27.9 (143)	34.7 (95)	62.5 (136)	72.3 (94)
3 or more	42.1 (114)	46.1 (89)	60.1 (59)	67.8 (55)

Source: NJPS, 1990.

More educated women are also more likely to continue working when they have a young child at home than less educated women (Table 3.15). There is greater difference between women with 12 years of education or fewer and women with at least some college education (13 years of education or more) than between women with different amounts of college education; that is, education does not seem to have a linear relationship with the labor force participation of women with small children. Among women with school-age children, there is a difference between college educated and non-college educated women, but among the college educated women there is no clear effect of education.

Among the most educated women, nearly as many women with preschoolers at home work as those with school-age children at home, but at other educational levels, women appear to enter or return to work as their children get older. The especially low participation of less educated women with no children under 18 may be due to their older age.

Because younger women have higher education, it is hard to answer more complicated questions with this simple analysis, such as how much of what we see is an effect of cohort or age or how much being educated reduces the effect of having children. To determine the relative importance of the presence of children and young children on the labor force participation of women, we again turned to a multiple regression model, which gives us the net effect of each variable independent of the other variables. The independent variables were age, retirement age,[30] highest academic degree attained, number of children, having a preschooler (youngest child under age 6), having a school-age child (youngest child age 6–17). The stepwise regression model, presented in Table 3.16, has a

TABLE 3.15
Percent in Paid Labor Force, by Age of Youngest Child and Years of Education,
U.S. Jewish Married Women, 1990

Age of Youngest Child	Total (N in thousands)	Years of Education			
		12 years or less	13–15	16	17 or more
Under 6	60.8 (273)	41.9	60.7	62.1	70.4
6–17	70.6 (126)	54.1	74.1	78.4	71.1
No child under 18	55.1 (523)	35.6	50.8	64.6	80.2

Source: NJPS, 1990.

multiple correlation of .527 with labor force participation, explaining 27.7 percent of the variance.

In the first step, age alone explains 17 percent of the variance in labor force participation, older women working less than younger women. A good part of this influence can be explained by whether the woman has reached 60, as we see when the retirement age variable is entered: the effect[31] of age is reduced by more than 50 percent, but maintains a smaller but significant negative effect on labor force participation. Some of the relationship with age is also explained by education: when highest degree is entered into the model, the effect of age is reduced even more, but still continues to be statistically significant.

More educated women work in the labor force more than less educated women, but the age of the woman is more important than her education. This may reflect the changing norms about married women participating in the labor force: in the younger cohorts, more and more married women work in the paid labor force, but in the older cohorts,

TABLE 3.16

Multiple Regression Analysis of Paid Labor Force Participation on Age, Education, Number and Ages of Children, U.S. Jewish Married Women, 1990
(Standardized Regression Coefficients)

Independent Variable	Step 1	Step 2	Step 3	Step 4	Step 5	Final Model
Age	−.412*	−.197*	−.166**	−.099***	−.282*	−.348*
Below retirement age		.265***	.250***	.290***	.208***	.207***
Highest academic degree			.129***	.108***	.126***	.129***
Number of children				−.165***	.120***	−.094*
Preschooler					−.224***	−.284***
School-age child						−.115*
R	.412	.440	.456	.483	.517	.526
R²	.170	.194	.208	.233	.268	.277
(Unweighted *n*)	(951)					

*$\alpha < .05$
**$\alpha < .01$
***$\alpha < .001$

Source: NJPS, 1990.

fewer married women worked (especially after they had children). Because education has increased dramatically in recent cohorts (as we already saw), much of what we see as an effect of education is actually a reflection of different cohorts, their norms, and educational composition.

When number of children are entered into the model, the effect of age drops even lower, since part of it reflects the effect of older women having more children. Having more children is related to less labor force participation (although the causal direction of the effect is not so clear-cut, as we have suggested in the earlier discussion).

Even more important than the number of children, however, is the negative effect of having a preschooler, which has a standardized regression coefficient nearly twice the size of having children.

When having a preschooler enters the model, the effect of age again becomes much larger, and this is because age also reflects life cycle stage: when children are young, labor force participation is lower; these are the younger ages, so that part of the negative effect of age was suppressed by indicating that life cycle stage when children are young. When we control directly for that factor, the negative effect of age becomes even clearer.

Having a school-age child also affects labor force participation negatively, but not nearly to the extent that having a preschooler does. Its standardized regression coefficient is less than half that of having a preschooler. However, having children under 17, whether preschoolers or school-age children, is more restrictive in terms of labor force participation than having many children not of these ages.

In the final model, getting older still has the strongest relationship with labor force participation, but having a preschooler has nearly as much effect and having a preschooler is more important in terms of labor force participation than having a school-age child, many children, or high education. For women childcare responsibilities compete with labor force participation, but they are a temporary competition for time and energy, and once the most demanding stage of parenthood has passed, women return to the labor force, especially when they have higher education and have not yet reached the age of retirement.

Childcare responsibilities also help us to understand how many hours are worked per week by women in the labor force. Among married women, only 1 percent of the variance in hours worked is explained by age and education—education adding hardly anything to the explanation (Table 3.17). Once variables relating to the day-to-day responsibilities of childcare are included in the model—having a preschooler, having a school-age child, and the number of children—the variance explained increases by 6 percent. The most important effect on hours worked is having a preschooler at home, with a beta coefficient of $-.214$. Although

TABLE 3.17
Multiple Regression Analysis of Hours of Work per Week,
U.S. Jewish Married Women in the Paid Labor Force, 1990
(Standardized Regression Coefficients)

Independent Variable	Step 1	Step 2
Age	-.089*	-.157*
Highest academic degree	.060	.060
Number of children		-.108*
Preschooler		-.214**
School-age child		-.135*
R	.116	.270
R²	.014	.073
(Unweighted n)		(951)

*α < .05.
**α < .001.

Source: NJPS, 1990.

it has a small but significant negative effect on hours worked, how many children is less important than whether there is a preschooler or a school-age child to care for. How many children is also less important than how old the woman is.

As we found when we analyzed the model predicting the labor force participation of married women, the effect of age is clarified and made stronger when the presence of young children is controlled. Because younger women have the younger children, and this makes them work fewer hours in the labor force, the negative effect of age is suppressed unless the presence of young children is controlled. Once the presence of young children enters the model, the negative effect of age nearly doubles (from -.089 to -.157).

When we predicted these hours worked for the total sample of women, age did not have a significant effect. Apparently the effect of marital status and education combined to camouflage the effect of age: once we could break down the elements of being married that affect hours worked, the net effect of age appears and is significant. Once the responsibilities of childcare and age are controlled, education has no significant effect on hours worked.

*Long-Term Effects of Having Children
for American Jewish Women*

We expected that the earlier a woman began having children to indicate an early familistic orientation or preference for family roles. Because this is often seen as competing with work commitment outside the home, we also expected that women who had children at an early age would invest less in labor force activity at that time. As a result, they would have less advantage in the labor force in later years and would be less likely to continue in labor force activity later on.

We find this true for women who had their first child before the age of 20 (Table 3.18), but here we also see the confounding effect of cohort on our findings: most of the Jewish women who had children in their teens were born before the 1930s and are less likely to participate in the labor force because of their current age rather than the age at which they started having children.

If the first child was born when the mother was at ages 20 or 21, the mother's labor force participation rate is higher than the other groups; and if she had her first child after age 34, she was even less likely to be working at the time of the survey. The latter is actually a surprising finding, because it is usually women who have invested in careers and seek to minimize their time out of the labor force who delay their first birth until their late thirties (Jones, 1981). In the wider American population, it has been found that women who have their first child after the age of 30 are less likely to quit their jobs or to take unpaid leave and more likely to take no breaks whatsoever (O'Connell and Bachu, 1992). These are, for the most part, planned and long awaited births, however, and it is possible that late parenthood is related to greater investment in the child.

Because we know that younger cohorts are delaying childbearing, and that more educated women delay childbearing (as shown in Chapter 2), there was a question as to whether the age of the first child would have an effect once we controlled for age (or cohort) and education. Further, since women who begin having children early usually have more

TABLE 3.18
Percent in Paid Labor Force, by Age at Birth of First Child,
U.S. Jewish Married Women, 1990

Age at Birth of First Child	Percent in Paid Labor Force	(N in thousands)
18–19	46.8	(87)
20–21	58.4	(163)
22–24	53.2	(318)
25–29	53.5	(478)
30–34	53.6	(136)
35+	43.3	(69)

Source: NJPS, 1990.

children (the Pearson correlation between the mother's age at the birth of the first child and number of children is –.751, the lower her age at the first birth, the more children), the mother's age at first childbirth is expected to have a long-term effect on labor force participation because of having more children.

In the multivariate regression model presented in Table 3.19, we see that the mother's age at her first childbirth has an effect on labor force participation independent of how many children the woman has, and vice versa—having many children has an effect independent of when she started to have children. Both these effects overshadow the effect of education but are less important than the effect of being under retirement age.[32]

It is also clear from the model in Table 3.19, that the age at which marital roles begin is not an important influence on labor force participation: parenting roles present the significant role conflict with roles in the outside economy.

LABOR FORCE PARTICIPATION IN OLDER AGES

If the roles associated with raising young and school-age children are so influential in reducing women's labor force participation and the gap in men's and women's labor force participation is bigger during these ages, it would be expected that, after children are grown and no longer as

TABLE 3.19
Multiple Regression Analysis of Paid Labor Force Participation on Age,
Education, Number of Children, Age at Birth of First Child,
and Age at Marriage, U.S. Jewish Married Women, 1990
(Standardized Regression Coefficients)

Independent Variable	Model 1	Model 2
Below retirement age	.378**	.374**
Years of education	.082*	.086*
Number of children	–.107*	–.112*
Age at birth of first child	–.105*	–.120*
Age at marriage		–.045
R	.479	.480
R^2	.229	.231
(Unweighted n)	(951)	(951)

*$\alpha < .05$.
**$\alpha < .001$.

Source: 1990 NJPS.

dependent on their parents, mothers would be more likely to be working in the paid labor force and the gender gap would narrow. More educated women (like the American Jewish women) are also known to be much more likely to stay in the labor force past age 55 than other women (Hayward, Grady, and McLaughlin, 1988; Herz, 1988). Also, there is a trend for men, but not necessarily women, to retire earlier in recent cohorts (Hatch, 1992), and this trend toward earlier retirement has been found among Jewish men as well (Goldstein, 1992). Some of the reasons for this earlier retirement (Kleemeier, 1961) are particularly applicable to the Jewish population: the self-employed are more likely to stay in the labor force later in life, yet there has been a general decline in self-employment, found among Jews as well (Chiswick, 1992a); higher income allows for earlier retirement, and the increasing occupational achievement of American Jews has elevated the income level of many older Jews (Goldstein, 1992); and the increasing importance of large firms, which are more likely to be characterized by age discrimination in hiring and compulsory retirement policies and which employ an increasing number of American Jews (Kuznets, 1972). Although trends toward earlier retirement among women are expected in the future (R. L. Clark, 1988) and women's retirement patterns have become more similar to men's in recent years (Allen and Brotman, 1981; Hayward et al., 1988; Soldo and Agree, 1988), the trends toward earlier retirement among women are less easily observed because of the diversity in women's labor force participation patterns and the general increase in women's labor force participation at all ages. All of this leads us to expect a narrowing gender gap in older ages.

Labor Force Participation Among
Older American Jewish Men and Women

From about the age of 50, both men and women begin to disengage from the labor force, both by stopping work (retiring) and by cutting down their number of hours. As we saw in Table 2.16 and again in Figure 3.9, the gender gap narrows between the ages of 45–54, but never reaches the similarity that men and women under 30 shared, and after age 55 the gap again widens, as men retire from the labor force somewhat later than women. Nearly three-fourths of the men 60–64 and 30 percent of the men 65 and over are still in the labor force, and over 25 percent are still working in their mid-seventies (Figure 3.9). In contrast only 11 percent of the women 65+ are in the paid labor force, and after age 70 hardly any women work.

Both Jewish men and women remain in the labor force for longer years than the wider population. More Jewish men 55 and over work

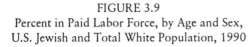

FIGURE 3.9
Percent in Paid Labor Force, by Age and Sex,
U.S. Jewish and Total White Population, 1990

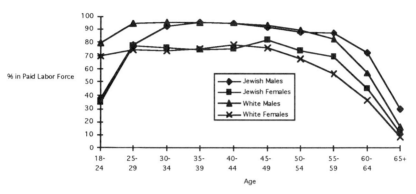

Source: NJPS, 1990; U.S. Bureau of Labor Statistics, 1991, Table A-4.

than their counterparts in the wider population, and more Jewish women work than their counterparts from about the age of 45, when children are grown and mothers return to or enter the labor force. But because Jewish men are especially likely to remain in the labor force past age 65, but Jewish women are only slightly more likely than the wider white population to remain in the labor force past age 65, the gender gap among American Jews over age 65 is particularly wide in comparison to the total white population and does not narrow until after the age of 80 when hardly any women work and fewer and fewer men do (at age 80 about 20 percent of the men still report employment!).

Among those who are working in older ages, women work considerably fewer hours than men (Figure 3.10). There is a relatively steep drop in hours worked after age 60 for both men and women, but by age 65 most women who are in the paid labor force are working less than 26 hours a week; men who stay in the labor force do not reach this low level of participation until well into their seventies.[33]

Both men and women are more likely to retire earlier from low status, low earning jobs that lack seniority protection (Hatch, 1992) and are less likely to be self-employment. Because such jobs are more common among those with lower education, we expect these retirement patterns to vary considerably by level of education.

As expected from these findings from other populations, more educated American Jews are much more likely to be working in the labor force beyond the age of 50 than are the less educated men and women (Figure 3.11). Only a quarter of the men and women with less than 12

FIGURE 3.10
Mean Hours of Work, by Age and Sex, U.S. Jews, Ages 50 and Over,[a] 1990

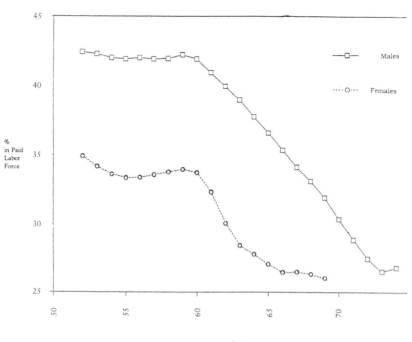

[a]For ages 65 and older the graph has been smoothed out, as the relatively small number of cases caused random variation from age to age.

Source: NJPS, 1990.

years of education are still in the labor force. For men the proportion in the labor force increases steadily with education, until 84 percent of those with 20 or more years of education are still working after age 50. Among women, the increase in proportion working by years of education is more gradual: only a quarter of the women with 12 years of education are working and little more than a third of those with partial college education. As a result the gender gap among American Jews is much greater among those with less education than those with more education (except for those who did not complete high school, since only a quarter of the men at this level are working). Among men and women with 16 or more years of education, the proportion of women in the labor force is 90 percent that of men.

There is a tendency for married men and women to retire earlier than the unmarried. Some couples "synchronize" their retirement

FIGURE 3.11
Percent in Paid Labor Force, by Years of Education and Sex,
U.S. Jews, 50 and Over, 1990

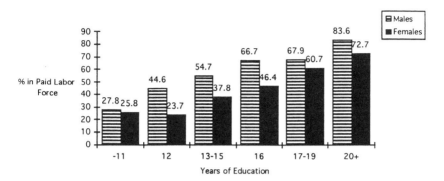

Source: NJPS, 1990.

(Brubaker, 1985), and this affects women more than men, because typically husbands are older than wives and therefore wives retire earlier than they otherwise would to share the same lifestyle as their husbands. Women who are single, widowed, divorced, or separated have been found more likely to retire late because of economic need (Atchley and Miller, 1983; Silverman, 1987).

As we have seen, among American Jews, marital status also affects continued employment in later ages, but it has a stronger effect on men than on women, and it is not in the direction suggested in the literature. Married men stay in the labor force longer than unmarried men, apparently because they need to support their family and a pension is not enough. Married women are less likely to stay in the labor force, but the difference between married and unmarried women becomes negligible after age 60. The difference is that married women do not increase their participation as much as unmarried women during their fifties, and therefore their decline in labor force participation between age 50 and 60 is much less steep than among unmarried women. In these ages, the cushion of a husband's income or pension reduces the economic need for married women to work, and the push for synchronized retirement with their husband leads more married women to retire earlier.

SUMMARY

In sum, the patterns of gender difference in the labor force participation of Jewish men and women appear to be influenced distinctively by two main factors throughout the life cycle: their relatively high educational level compared to the wider American population and the time devoted to raising young children on the part of Jewish women. The process of attaining high education by both genders postpones their entrance into the labor force, compared to their counterparts in the wider population, and it does so for men more than women. As a result, for a short time, during their twenties, Jewish women participate in the labor force more than men. However, as they marry and especially as they begin to have children, the labor force participation of married Jewish women falls below the level of married Jewish men, even though it remains much above their female counterparts in the wider population because of their educational level. Many Jewish women stay home with their preschoolers, even longer than mothers in the wider population, but because they do not have large families and plan the birth intervals, as a group their labor force participation rates remain relatively high even during the childbearing years. They are more likely to work at older ages than are other American women—a result, apparently, of their higher educational level and the consequent types of occupations they enter; Jewish men also remain in the labor force longer than their counterparts in the wider population. As a result, the gender gap at older ages is not much different than it is for the wider population, but is at a higher level of employment for both men and women.

CHAPTER 4

Occupational Achievement of American Jewish Men and Women

American Jews are recognized as high occupational achievers, along with their high educational achievements. "Community studies in every decade since the 1950's, as well as the NJPS-1970/71, have shown Jews to be heavily concentrated in the upper ranks of the occupational hierarchy. Moreover, comparative data over the last four decades point to a continuing increase in the proportion of Jews engaged in white-collar work . . ." (Goldstein, 1992, p. 114).

In this chapter we consider whether this high occupational achievement characterizes Jewish men and women alike in the 1990s or whether this high achievement means more gender difference among Jews. We also attempt to understand whether the explanations of high occupational achievement are similar for Jewish men and women. For instance, with nearly as much educational attainment as men (as we have seen already), do Jewish women have as high occupational returns as men to their educational investment?

Generally, the differences in men's and women's occupational achievement have received much attention in the last two decades, as researchers attempt to explain why women are in different occupations than men, and why so many of the women are in less well-paying, boring, stressful, insecure, and dead-end occupations that require little (on-the-job) training and whose incumbents are perceived as easily replaced (Bergmann, 1986; Dexter, 1985; Renzetti and Curran, 1992). Explanations range from the biological to the cultural, from individual attributes to the class structure of society (see excellent reviews in Jacobs, 1989; Marini and Brinton, 1984; Reskin, 1993). Explanations that focus on the differential abilities of males and females are less than conclusive,[1] particularly in linking differences to overall ability (Blake, 1989) or later performance in jobs (Jacobs, 1989).

From a human capital perspective, gender differences in occupational achievement stem from the lower education, labor market experience, and time available for women to invest in labor-related activities because of women's competing familial obligations and socialization to appropriate gender roles (England and Farkas, 1986: Roos, 1985). Jewish women are an interesting case when we consider the human capital approach, for although their educational attainment is not as high as that of Jewish men and differences remain in the types of academic degrees earned, Jewish women still have a much higher educational achievement than the general white U.S. female population. Moreover, Jewish women have higher rates of labor force participation at most ages and stay longer in the labor force than most of the general white population of U.S. women.

There is some evidence that American Jewish women have somewhat different human capital to offer on the labor market than the men: as we have seen in Chapter 2, men and women get different types of degrees (e.g., men are more likely to get professional or doctoral degrees, while women are more likely to get general academic degrees and usually on a lower level; men are more likely to specialize in medicine or law than women).

Today's Jewish culture does not carry over from its past limits on the type of women's economic activity. Even historically in the Jewish tradition, women have been employed in a variety of occupations. From the biblical "woman of valor" (Proverbs 31) to the business and commercial pursuits of the European Renaissance woman to the factory workers and seamstresses of turn-of-the-century immigrants in America (Fishman, 1993; Glenn, 1990), Jewish women have engaged in multiple nonfamilial economic pursuits, and few injunctions against type of appropriate work seem to have been invoked.

On the other hand, the traditional emphasis on women's family roles increases to some extent the role conflict between family and paid work, as discussed in the previous chapter. It is expected that this role conflict between family and labor force roles would vary by occupation; following Rosenfeld and Spenner (1992), and Glass and Camarigg (1992), some occupations are more compatible with family roles than others. Among Jews, however, conflict between family and labor force activity is minimized by the average small family size and the timing of births, as we have shown and as suggested by Goldscheider (1986). Therefore, it is not clear how much the family roles of Jewish women affect which occupations they are in or their occupational achievement.

Beyond the effect of human capital qualities and family obligations is the presence of gender discrimination in the labor market, which has long been noted (e.g., Bergmann, 1986; Reskin, 1993), and even if it may have decreased in recent years, it has been too long established to disappear overnight. Discrimination has been inferred or documented in such diverse occupations as banking, book editing, crafts, law, insurance, medicine, and management (Reskin and Hartmann, 1986; Reskin and Roos, 1990), so that it seems to involve occupations of both more and less educated workers. Even though the direct study of such discrimination is beyond the scope of this endeavor, it seems unlikely that it is different for Jewish women than for other white American women with comparable qualifications.

We thus have a number of questions about the gender differences in occupations among American Jews. First, we consider whether gender differences in occupations are greater among the Jews than in the wider American population, given the high occupational achievements of American men. We consider the extent to which Jewish women's higher human capital relative to other women and the lack of cultural restrictions on their economic activity helps American Jewish women reach occupational equity with their male peers. On the other hand, we consider the extent to which the traditional familial and maternal role orientation of American Jewish women hinders their occupational achievement or channels them into particular occupational roles.

We look at two dependent variables in this chapter: occupational type and occupational achievement, indicated by occupational prestige. Occupations are grouped into occupational categories, which are combined to achieve maximum comparability to the wider American population. Respondents reported the current occupations of themselves and other household members or the occupations held at last employment, for those who were not currently working in the paid labor force. Thus the numbers of those reporting an occupation is somewhat larger than the number of people in the sample who were actually employed at the time of the survey.

Occupational prestige is an indicator of social esteem accorded the incumbent of a particular occupation, a social status that "carries with it social recognition, respect, admiration and some degree of deference" (Theodorson and Theodorson, 1969, p. 312). In other words, it is a reward of social standing directly emanating from occupational involvement.[2] Although we are unable to distinguish whether particular incumbents in an occupation would be evaluated with different prestige scores, research indicates that prestige is a characteristic of an occupation rather than an incumbent (Reszke, 1984), be that incumbent a male or female, and it is correct to discuss the average prestige scores of men and women using a common scale of prestige (see Hartman, Kraus and Hartman, 1989; Hodge, 1981).

We use the occupational prestige scores determined in 1989 by a national sample of over 1,500 persons (see Nakao and Treas, 1990, for more details on the computation of these scores). As in the previous chapter on labor force participation, we restricted our analysis of occupation to those 25 and over, to minimize the effect of part-time or temporary jobs taken while finishing school.

The first part of the chapter presents the occupational distributions of American Jewish men and women and some of the factors associated with their different occupational roles. In the second part of the chapter we concentrate on the occupational rewards for these roles, by comparing the occupational prestige of Jewish men and women and the role of the different factors related to achieving this prestige.

THE OCCUPATIONS OF
AMERICAN JEWISH MEN AND WOMEN

The distinctiveness of American Jewish occupations that was seen in previous decades continues in 1990, even if it has decreased somewhat as the general labor force moves in the direction of white-collar employment (Goldstein,1992; Kuznets, 1972). Nearly 90 percent are in white-collar occupations compared to 58 percent of the general white population—34 percent are in professional occupations (including the stereotypical "Jewish lawyers and doctors"), compared to 15 percent of the general white population (Table 4.1). The proportion employed in academic, managerial and administrative, sales and clerical occupations is slightly higher for

TABLE 4.1
Occupation by Sex,
U.S. Jewish and Total White Population, 1990

Occupation	U.S. Jews			U.S. Whites		
	Total	Males	Females	Total	Males	Females
Professional, academic	34.4	38.9	29.8	13.2	14.3	11.8
Technical	5.4	3.2	7.9	3.2	3.1	3.4
Managerial, administrative	17.6	19.8	15.1	13.2	14.3	11.8
Sales	14.1	17.2	10.9	12.8	12.1	13.7
Clerical	17.6	6.5	29.4	15.4	5.4	27.6
Crafts	4.3	6.9	1.6	11.8	19.8	2.2
Operatives, laborers	2.8	4.3	1.2	14.3	19.6	7.8
Services	3.7	3.2	4.2	12.3	8.9	16.5
Total %	100.0	100.0	100.0	100.0	100.0	100.0
(N in thousands)	(3,264)	(1,666)	(1,598)	(101,505)	(55,781)	(45,721)

Sources: NJPS, 1990; U.S. Bureau of Labor Statistics, 1991, Table A-23.

Jews than the general white population. But more significantly, less than 11 percent were in blue-collar and service occupations, compared to over 41 percent of the general white population. When Jews are employed in blue-collar and service occupations, there is some concentration in the protective services (like policing and guarding), food serving (waiters), hairdressing and cosmetology, electric repair, and crafts, such as jewelers and watchmakers. As the dissimilarities in Table 4.2 show, 30 percent of the Jewish population in the labor force would have to change occupations to have the same occupational distribution as the general white population in the United States.[3]

The highest dissimilarity coefficient (36.9) is between the occupations of Jewish men and the general white male population. Nearly 40 percent of the Jewish men are in professional occupations, compared to 13 percent of the general white population; similarly, higher proportions of Jewish men are employed in managerial and sales occupations than the general white population of men, although the differences are not as great. This probably reflects the long-standing resistance to Jews in corporate America, which has only recently shown signs of changing (Korman, 1988; Slavin and Pradt, 1982). On the other hand, Jewish men have considerably lower proportions in blue-collar and service occupations, mainly because of their higher educational level.

Even though Jewish women also differ from the general white population of women, the differences between the two groups of females is not as great: less than a quarter of the women would have to change occupa-

TABLE 4.2
Dissimilarity Coefficients[a] of Occupational Distributions, by Sex,
U.S. Jewish and Total White Population, 1990

	U.S. Jews			U.S. Whites		
	Total	Male	Female	Total	Male	Female
Jews Total						
Male	13.85					
Female	14.70	28.55				
Whites Total	30.18	35.81	34.31			
Male	40.46	36.91	45.10	15.54		
Female	29.70	40.41	21.59	19.10	34.62	

[a]The coefficient of dissimilarity is defined as $D = \frac{1}{2} \sum [P_{ai} - P_{bi}]$, where P_{ai} and P_{bi} are the percentages of workers in occupation i from the first in a pair of distributions (a) and the second in a pair of distributions (b), respectively.

Sources: NJPS, 1990; U.S. Bureau of Labor Statistics, 1991.

tions to have identical occupational distributions (the dissimilarity coefficient being 21.6). Like Jewish men, Jewish women have a much higher proportion in professional occupations than the general white population of women (30 vs. 17 percent), have higher proportions in managerial and technical occupations, and markedly fewer in blue-collar and service occupations (7 percent compared to 28 percent of the general white female labor force). These differences are expected, given the different educational achievements of Jewish women and the wider American female population, but they are smaller than the differences between male distributions. Hence, the differences between Jewish occupations and those in the general white population is attributable more to differences between the male occupational distributions than the female.

The Concentration of Jewish Women and Men into Separate Occupations

There is a greater similarity in the occupational distributions of Jewish women and the general white population of women because both are under the same discriminating constraints that result in a concentration of both sets of women into relatively few occupational categories compared to men. For instance, in both groups, nearly 30 percent of the women are concentrated in clerical occupations. The ten leading occupations of Jewish women bear strong resemblance to the ten leading occupations of all American women (Taeuber, 1991: Table B5-7) and especially to the ten leading occupations of women with five or more years of college education (Renzetti and Curran, 1992). The two populations share the common female occupations of social worker, teacher, and the related administrative positions in education; other common occupations of educated Jewish and non-Jewish women are managers and administrators, lawyers, and physicians.

Looking at the detailed three-digit classification of occupations, it takes only ten occupations to employ 50 percent of the Jewish women, including the well-known "female" occupations of teacher, social worker, secretary, bookkeeper, as well as the more "desegregated" occupations of manager and administration and office manager (Table 4.3). On the other hand, the top ten occupations of Jewish men employ 43 percent of the men, and it takes another four to employ 50 percent of the men. Further indication of the greater concentration of women in the labor force is that Jewish men are spread over 197 of 246[4] detailed occupations, but women are found in only 155 of the 246 occupations.

Because of the concentration of men and women into different occupations, the occupational distribution of men is different than of women, in the general population as well as in the Jewish population. Men are more likely to be in higher paying jobs, jobs that allow for some inde-

TABLE 4.3
The Ten Leading Occupations of U.S. Jewish Men and Women,
25 and Over, 1990

Men		*Women*	
Occupation	*% of All Employed Jewish Men*	*Occupation*	*% of All Employed Jewish Women*
Managers, administrators	10.8	Teachers	7.8
Sales clerks	8.4	Clerical workers	7.6
Physicians	4.1	Secretaries	7.3
Lawyers	4.0	Sales clerks	7.0
Accountants	3.5	Managers, administrators	6.8
Engineers	3.3	Bookkeepers	4.8
Advertising agents	2.8	Social workers	3.2
Teachers	2.7	Registered nurses	2.4
Insurance agents	2.0	Real estate agents	2.0
Real estate agents	1.7	Office managers	1.8
Consultants	1.7	Accountants	1.8

Source: NJPS, 1990.

pendence of action and authority, that have fewer boring duties, and that lead to still better jobs (Bergmann, 1986, p. 87; Coser and Rokoff, 1971). Some research has suggested that women's occupations are more stressful, requiring completion of tasks under time pressure with minimal errors (Reskin and Hartmann, 1986). However, because of the higher educational and occupational achievement of American Jews, occupational differences between Jewish men and women were expected to be less pronounced than in the wider population.

Indeed, as we learn from the dissimilarity coefficients, the dissimilarity between the occupations of Jewish men and women is somewhat smaller than among the general white population's occupations (28.5 compared to 34.6, respectively);[5] that is, there is greater equality of occupational distribution among Jewish men and women than among men and women in the greater population. The extent to which the remaining differences in occupations are due to the differences in educational attainment that exist among Jews, which we have seen already, will be explored.

The differences between Jewish men and women are in the same direction as in the wider population but of smaller magnitude: a higher proportion of men are in professional occupations, whereas a higher proportion of women are in the technical occupations. A higher proportion of men than women are in sales, whereas women are much more likely to be employed as clerical workers. Although the proportions are small for both genders, more men are employed in blue-collar occupations and more women are in the service occupations.

Comparing the "top ten" occupations of men and women (Table 4.3), we find both for men and for women the white-collar occupations of managers and administrators, sales clerks, teachers, accountants, and real estate agents; but among men's top ten occupations are such professional occupations as physician, lawyer, and engineer, and the independent occupations of advertising agents, insurance workers, and consultants; women's more common occupations differ from men's in that they include clerical occupations like secretary, bookkeeper, and office manager, and such semi-professional occupations (nurturing but relatively low paying) as social workers and registered nurses.

Occupational Segregation of Jewish Men and Women

As in the general population, these different concentrations of men and women into occupations are related to gender segregation in the occupations of Jewish women and men: in close to 50 of the occupations in which Jewish women are employed, 90 percent or more of the workers are women (from among the Jewish population only), and there are close to 100 occupations in which Jewish are employed that are 90 percent or more male (from among the Jewish population only).

This is hardly unique to Jewish men and women. In 1985, over two-thirds of the women in the U.S. civilian labor force worked in occupations that were 70 percent or more female (Jacobs, 1989); in 1980, nearly half of the women worked in fields in which 80 percent or more of the workers were women (Rytina and Bianchi, 1984). Among male employees, 71 percent worked in occupations where 80 percent of the workers were men (Rytina and Bianchi, 1984), indicating high occupational segregation between the sexes.

EDUCATION AND OCCUPATION

Investment in education is obviously related to the occupations attained. On average, Jewish men in the labor force have a year more education than the Jewish women in the labor force (Table 4.4). Within single-digit occupational categories, men also have higher education on the average than do the women in the comparable occupation. The differences are biggest for professional occupations where men average over 18 years of education, compared to women's 16.5; clerical occupations; and skilled crafts (men presumably having more vocational education). Part of these

TABLE 4.4
Mean Years of Education, by Occupation and Sex,
U.S. Jews, 25 and over, 1990

Occupation	Men	Women
Professional	18.1	16.6
Technical	17.1	16.6
Academic	15.4	16.5
Managerial	14.5	13.5
Sales	12.8	13.0
Clerical	14.4	12.8
Blue collar	12.3	11.1
Services	14.2	13.5
Total	16.0	15.0
(N in thousands)	(1,656)	(1,590)

Source: NJPS, 1990.

big differences are technical, related to the occupational classification; looking at more detailed occupations, the largest differences between men's and women's average education are in occupational groups that have a wide range of occupations in them (among teachers, where men are more likely to be the university and college teachers and women the teachers at lower levels; among medical workers where men are the podiatrists and veterinarians and women are the dieticians and registered nurses). In a few occupations women are more educated on the average than men, but they tend to be smaller occupations (less than 1 percent of the labor force). Reflected in these differences are norms about appropriate jobs for women, as well as differences in educational levels. The generally higher qualifications of men raise the question as to how much education explains the differential occupational distributions of men and women.

Looking at the total population of Jews, we see that occupational distribution is strongly related to educational level. Being in a professional occupation, for example, is twice as likely for Jews with 17 or more years of education than for those with 16 years of education only and five times as likely than for those with 13–15 years of education to be in a professional occupation. Persons with 12 years or less education are three times as likely as those with 16 or more years of education to be in clerical work, four times as likely to be in blue collar work, and three times as likely to be in service occupations (Table 4.5).

The first question we have to ask, then, is whether the differences in men's and women's occupations are explained by their differences in educational achievement, which we already have seen. Table 4.6 sum-

TABLE 4.5
Occupation, by Years of Education and Sex, U.S. Jews, 25 and over, 1990

Years of Education	Sex	Occupation									
		Professional	Academic	Technical	Managerial	Sales	Clerical	Blue Collar	Services	Total	(N in thousands)
–12	Total	3.7	4.8	1.8	14.5	14.8	35.8	17.1	7.6	100.0	(715)
	Male	6.1	5.9	1.5	17.8	17.2	10.2	32.3	8.8	100.0	(289)
	Female	2.1	4.0	2.0	12.2	13.1	53.3	6.7	6.7	100.0	(426)
13–15	Total	6.2	8.0	5.9	22.5	17.0	25.9	10.0	4.4	100.0	(653)
	Male	7.9	7.5	2.2	27.9	24.0	7.8	18.8	4.0	100.0	(309)
	Female	4.6	8.4	9.3	17.8	10.6	42.2	2.1	4.9	100.0	(344)
16	Total	19.2	22.3	5.5	18.6	16.0	11.6	4.1	2.7	100.0	(985)
	Male	25.9	14.8	1.8	23.0	19.7	7.1	5.5	2.2	100.0	(521)
	Female	11.7	30.7	9.7	13.6	11.8	16.7	2.6	3.3	100.0	(464)
17+	Total	34.4	29.6	6.2	15.9	7.7	3.9	1.3	1.1	100.0	(893)
	Male	43.2	22.0	5.7	16.0	8.2	1.5	2.1	1.4	100.0	(537)
	Female	21.1	41.0	7.0	15.7	6.9	7.6	0	.8	100.0	(356)

Source: NJPS, 1990.

marizes the differences between the occupational distributions of men and women with different levels of education, which we saw in Table 4.5. The dissimilarity coefficients show that there is a decreasing difference between men and women as education increases.

Therefore, among those with 12 years of education or less, 42 percent of the men would have to switch their occupations to have the same occupational distribution as women (Table 4.6). For those with 13–15 years of education, the percent who would have to change is 40.6. But among those with 16 years of education, the dissimilarity coefficient is 35, and among those with 17 or more years of education, it drops to 30.5, showing that men and women's occupations become more similar with higher educational attainment. Higher education for both men and women narrows the range of occupations in which they are found and with this narrows the gap between them.

Even though they decrease with education, however, gender differences persist.[6] As we saw in Table 4.5, over half of the women with 12 years of education or less are in the clerical occupations, but men with similar years of education are spread much more widely throughout the labor force: 17.8 percent in managerial and administrative occupations, 17.2 percent in sales, 32.3 percent in blue-collar work. Women with 13–15 years of education are more likely than men to be in technical and academic occupations or clerical ones. In general, women who have gone to college are more likely to be in clerical occupations than men: over 40 percent of those with 13–15 years of education, 16.7 percent of those with 16 years of education; and 7.6 percent of those with 17 or more years of education, as opposed to 7.8, 7.1, and 1.5 percent of the men, respectively. Women with 16 or more years of education are more likely to have technical or academic occupations, but men with the same education are more likely to have professional or managerial occupations.

The meaning of these occupational differences in terms of occupational prestige awarded will be discussed later. However, it is clear that men and women with similar education get to different types of occupational slots, occupational slots considered appropriate for men and women. For the most part, as we shall see, this works to the advantage of men; sometimes, at least in terms of occupational prestige, it works to the advantage of women.

How Education Affects the Differences Between the Occupations of American Jewish Men and Women and the Wider American Population

Controlling for education reduces some of the differences between American Jews and the wider white population but not all. As can be seen in

TABLE 4.6
Dissimilarity Coefficients[a] for Occupational Distributions, by Years of Education and Sex, U.S. Jews, 25 and over, 1990

Years of Education	Sex	-12 Total	-12 Male	-12 Female	13–15 Total	13–15 Male	13–15 Female	16 Total	16 Male	16 Female	17+ Total	17+ Male	17+ Female
-12	Total												
	Male	25.0											
	Female	17.4	42.3										
13–15	Total	19.0	28.0	28.1									
	Male	29.2	19.0	46.6	23.2								
	Female	26.7	40.2	19.5	17.4	40.6							
16	Total	40.4	35.5	46.6	23.9	30.7	31.1						
	Male	44.0	35.3	50.5	25.0	22.4	37.2	16.0					
	Female	40.4	44.5	42.3	29.1	42.8	29.9	19.0	35.0				
17+	Total	61.5	58.0	64.8	43.5	52.1	47.8	25.3	29.7	26.5			
	Male	61.6	58.0	64.8	49.3	52.2	47.8	27.6	29.8	36.7	11.8		
	Female	61.4	57.8	64.6	49.7	47.6	52.0	25.2	35.0	21.4	18.8	30.5	

[a]For dissimilarity calculations, see note to Table 4.2. Based on distributions in Table 4.5.

Source: NJPS, 1990.

Table 4.7, occupational differences between Jews and the wider population of men and women who have 16 or more years of education are practically nonexistent: the dissimilarity coefficients between the occupational distributions of men at this level of education is 5.8 and of women, 5.7. However, the dissimilarity is greater at lower levels of education for both men and women, indicating that the occupations of less educated Jews are more similar to more educated Jews than they are to the wider population of less educated white Americans. Less educated Jews have higher proportions of managers, professionals, and other white-collar occupations; and smaller proportions of blue-collar and, among women, service occupations than the wider population. Therefore, not all of the difference between Jews and the wider population can be attributed to their educational attainment. There are, apparently, certain norms of Jewish employment, either out of differential preferences of Jews or differential preferences of employers of Jews, which result in less educated Jews acting more like more educated Jews than their counterparts in the wider population.

Although this is true for both Jewish men and women, there is less dissimilarity between Jewish women and the wider female population than there is between men at each level of education; this difference is especially notable among the less educated. This is probably related to the greater constraints on women's occupations no matter what their level of education (as mentioned previously).

Because Jews with less education are disproportionately employed in white-collar occupations and less in typically male blue-collar occupations, the gender dissimilarity of Jews with less education is somewhat smaller than among the wider population.[7] Among the more highly educated, however, the gender dissimilarity is somewhat higher than in the wider population, which is probably a reflection of the wider range in educational attainment among Jews than in the wider population; because higher proportions of Jewish men in particular have gone on to graduate and professional degrees, they are qualified to enter into different occupations than Jewish women, fewer of whom have completed the same degree of education. Among the wider American population, the educational attainment of men and women with 16 or more years of education is more similar, because fewer men have continued on to higher education than among Jews.

The lower gender dissimilarity in occupational distributions among American Jews is, therefore, related to their higher educational level, because a higher proportion of them have 16 or more years of education, which brings about greater overall occupational similarity between the sexes. Although considerably narrowed, gender dissimilarity is not completely eliminated even at this high level of education, however.

TABLE 4.7

Occupation, by Years of Education and Sex, U.S. Jewish and Total White Population, 1990

Years of Education	Sex	Occupation				Total %	(N in thousands)	Gender Dissimilarity[a]
		Managerial, Professional	Technical, Sales, Administrative	Service	Blue Collar			
U.S. Jews:								
12 or less	Male	29.8	29.0	8.8	32.2	100.0	(28.9)	39.2
	Female	18.3	68.3	6.7	6.7	100.0	(42.6)	
13–15	Male	43.2	34.0	4.0	18.8	100.0	(30.9)	26.1
	Female	30.8	62.2	4.9	2.1	100.0	(34.4)	
16 or more	Male	72.6	21.9	1.7	3.8	100.0	(105.8)	9.5
	Female	65.5	30.9	2.2	1.4	100.0	(82.0)	
U.S. whites:								
12 or less	Male	10.8	15.1	9.1	64.9	100.0	(23,972)	41.7
	Female	12.4	47.9	21.6	18.4	100.0	(19,807)	
13–15	Male	26.0	28.3	8.9	36.7	100.0	(9451)	31.0
	Female	29.8	53.3	11.2	5.8	100.0	(8274)	
16 or more	Male	66.7	21.9	2.7	8.7	100.0	(14,047)	6.5
	Female	69.2	25.2	3.4	2.1	100.0	(9,497)	

(continued on next page)

TABLE 4.7 (continued)

| Years of Education | Sex | Occupation | | | | Total % | (N in thousands) | Gender Dissimilarity[a] |
		Managerial, Professional	Technical, Sales, Administrative	Service	Blue Collar			
Dissimilarity between Jews and total white population:								
12 or less	Male	31.9						
	Female	26.7						
13–15	Male	21.9						
	Female	14.7						
16 or more	Male	5.8						
	Female	5.7						

[a]For dissimilarity calculations, see note to Table 4.2.

Sources: NJPS, 1990; U.S. whites estimated as average of U.S. Bureau of the Census (1990), Table 656, and U.S. Bureau of the Census (1992), Table 631.

EXTENT OF LABOR FORCE PARTICIPATION
AND OCCUPATION

Another question that may be raised is whether investment in the labor force in terms of hours worked explains gender differences in occupation attained. This investment is generally measured as accumulated work experience, of which we do not have a direct measure, and hours of work per week. As we have seen in the previous chapter, more women are engaged in part-time work than men. Twenty-one percent of the Jewish labor force works part-time (less than 35 hours)—32 percent of the women, and 13 percent of the men in the labor force (Table 4.8).

The percentage of part-timers varies by occupation: among Jews, managers and blue-collar workers are less likely than those in other occupations to work part-time, and academic and technical workers are more likely to work part-time than those in other occupations.

In many of the occupational groups, the percentage of women working part-time is more than double the percentage of men working part-time.[8] The largest gender differences are in the technical occupations, where men as engineering and science technicians are more likely to work full-time than women as health technicians: five times the proportion of women work part-time than men. A large difference is also found in the clerical occupations, where women are considerably more likely than men to have part-time, temporary jobs. Smaller gender differences are found in the academic and blue-collar occupations (in the academic occupations because a relatively high proportion of men work part-time like women).

TABLE 4.8
Percent of Part-Time Workers, by Occupation and Sex, U.S. Jews, 1990

Occupation	Total	Males	Females	Female/Male Ratio
Professional	14.2	11.0	22.5	2.0
Academic	29.7	24.2	34.2	1.4
Technical	29.5	8.4	42.2	5.0
Managerial	13.5	7.1	23.6	3.3
Sales	26.2	16.9	45.0	2.7
Clerical	26.4	6.8	32.2	4.7
Blue collar	16.5	15.4	23.2	1.5
Services	21.7	5.9	35.0	5.9
Total	21.3	13.1	32.0	2.4
(N in thousands)	(2,232)	(1,259)	(973)	

Source: NJPS, 1990.

Given the gender differences in percent part-time in general and in the various occupations, we consider the extent to which the differences in Jewish men's and women's occupations are explained by the hours invested in the labor force per week. Among both full-time and part-time workers, however, most of the traditional gender differences are found: men are more likely to be in professional, sales and blue-collar occupations; women are more likely to be in clerical occupations. There are some differences between full-time and part-time workers: among full-time workers, women are more likely to be in academic occupations than are men, a gender difference that is not found among those working part-time, where about a quarter of both men and women are academic workers. A higher percentage of part-time women workers are in managerial occupations than are part-time men workers, but among full-time workers, more men are in managerial occupations than women. All in all, however, the dissimilarity of men's and women's occupations is about the same among part-time and full-time workers as it is in the total (Table 4.9): among part-time workers, 32 percent of the men would have to change occupations to have the same occupational distribution as the women; among full-time workers, 30 percent of the men would have to change occupations to have the same occupational distribution as the women. Therefore, different hours of work does not explain the different occupational distributions of Jewish men and women.

TABLE 4.9
Occupations of Full- and Part-Time Workers, by Sex, U.S. Jews, 1990

Occupation	Full-Time Workers[a]		Part-Time Workers[b]	
	Male	*Female*	*Male*	*Female*
Professional	28.0	15.5	23.0	9.6
Academic	12.6	22.2	26.6	24.6
Technical	3.8	6.7	2.3	10.3
Managerial	21.4	18.5	10.8	12.1
Sales	15.8	8.6	21.3	14.9
Clerical	5.4	22.0	2.6	22.2
Blue collar	10.1	2.5	12.1	1.6
Service	2.9	4.0	1.2	4.6
Total	100.0	100.0	100.0	100.0
(*N* in thousands)	(1,094)	(662)	(165)	(311)

[a]Worked 35 or more hours a week.

[b]Worked less than 35 hours a week.

Source: NJPS, 1990.

FAMILY ROLES AND OCCUPATIONS

Another explanation for differences between men's and women's occupations that has been suggested are the family obligations of women, which take time and energy away from the labor force and career development.

> [M]arriage and childbearing responsibilities are expected to operate negatively to affect the differences in occupational distribution and attainment of ever-married women, relative to those of never-married women: (1) by reducing their total amount of on-the-job experience, and hence their seniority, because of labor-force interruptions due to childbearing and -rearing; (2) by reducing their incentive to invest in additional education or on-the-job training for purposes of occupational attainment; (3) by limiting the number of hours, time and energy they can commit to the work force because of familial constraints on their time; (4) by encouraging them to maximize job characteristics other than status or earnings (for example, better working hours, convenient job location); and (5) by limiting their geographic mobility (Hudis, 1976). (Roos, 1985, p. 120)

Rosenfeld and Spenner (1992) suggest that certain occupations are especially compatible with the familial responsibilities characteristic of married mothers and therefore are more attractive to women; such occupations offer more flexible hours and less demanding work (Glass and Camarigg, 1992). This suggests that women with family obligations might select different occupations than women with fewer family responsibilities or than men, whose family responsibilities differ (or that women might pursue different family patterns once they have chosen an occupation, in order to maintain compatibility with their chosen career).

Marital Status and the Occupations of Jewish Men and Women

Among American Jews, the occupations differ in the proportion married among their workers (Table 4.10). Among American Jewish men, unmarried men are more likely to be in clerical occupations, where younger men often find part-time temporary employment until they move on to more permanent career-oriented occupations; the highest percentage of married men are found in professional and managerial occupations, followed by sales. There are probably two reasons for this difference. These occupations generate higher paying jobs, which would be sought by men with family obligations; further, professional and managerial occupations at least are enhanced by family support, which usually alleviates some of the tasks the incumbent must fulfill himself (such as cooking, laundry, entertainment), leaving the working husband more time and

TABLE 4.10
Family Characteristics of Occupations, by Sex, U.S. Jews, 1990

Occupation	% Married		Mean Age at Marriage		Mean Age at Birth of First Child	Mean Number of Children	(N in thousands)	
	Male	Female	Male	Female			Male	Female
Professional	80.4	70.9	26.7	24.2	26.3	1.4	(344)	(133)
Technical, academic	67.4	72.7	26.3	24.0	26.2	1.5	(227)	(300)
Managerial	78.3	69.8	26.2	22.7	25.3	1.8	(252)	(160)
Sales	75.0	66.9	25.6	23.6	24.4	1.8	(208)	(103)
Clerical	51.1	70.6	25.9	23.3	24.7	1.9	(63)	(215)
Blue collar	69.6	68.6	28.0	23.2	24.6	1.8	(131)	(22)
Service	67.4	61.5	27.7	22.4	24.8	1.9	(34)	(44)

Source: NJPS, 1990.

energy to devote to his career.⁹ The higher up the occupational ladder, the greater is the "backstage wealth," at least for men, that enhances the husband's career and allows him to devote himself to his career and accordingly progress (Hochschild, 1989).

Among Jewish women, unmarried women are more likely to be in services, where a number of younger women work, often part-time, until they finish their education and move on to more secure occupations—or marry and drop out of the labor force altogether; the highest percentage of married women are in professional, technical, and clerical occupations. To some extent this is related to social class, as we shall see in the chapter on households: women in professional and technical occupations are more likely to be married to men in professional and technical occupations, and between the two, they are likely to be able to afford the kind of household help and childcare that make possible dual-career families. Clerical positions are often part-time, which make them more easily adapted to family schedules and can be entered and reentered relatively easily even when interrupted for having and rearing children.

It is obvious that understanding the relationship between marital status and occupations is related to the household structure, which we discuss in greater detail in the chapter on Jewish couples. At this point, it seems clear that marital status is part of the reason for the gender differences in occupational roles, because married women are more likely to be in occupations compatible with part-time employment, leaving time for family roles, unless they can afford substitute help for their family obligations.

Marital Status and Gender Differentiation in Jewish Occupations

Given the familial roles implied by being married, the human capital approach leads one to expect that women who are not married are more similar in labor force behavior to men than are married women, because unmarried women will have more time and energy to invest in the labor market than married women whose familial roles compete for their attention. We have seen already that this is true when it comes to labor force participation and hours of work per week. The rising labor force participation of married women in the past few decades, however, and the increasing preponderance of dual-earner families, raises the question of how different in occupational attainment married women are in comparison to unmarried women and whether this difference overrides the strong gender differentiation that pervades the occupational structure. In her comparative study of workers in twelve industrialized countries, Roos (1985) compared the occupational distributions of married and unmarried men and women. She concluded that never-married women were more like men in labor force behavior and occupational commitment, but because they continued to prefer to work in "female" professions, gender dissimilarity in occupational distributions was greater for the unmarried than the married. However, gender dissimilarity continued to be much larger than the dissimilarity of either married and unmarried men or married and unmarried women, respectively. She therefore concluded that women's disadvantage in occupational attainment could not be explained only by marital responsibilities.

Calculating the dissimilarity in occupational distributions between Jewish men and women who are married or not, we find that marital status makes a greater difference for men than it does for women: the dissimilarity between married and unmarried men's occupations is 15.7, compared to a dissimilarity coefficient of 4.5 between married and unmarried women's occupations. The greater similarity of women's occupations reflects the limits imposed on women's occupations, which narrows their variation. It also reflects the greater difference that marital status per se makes for men than for women, similar to the greater effect of marital status on the labor force activity of men, which we saw in the previous chapter.

Both differences in marital status are much smaller than the dissimilarity coefficients between men and women within each marital status: there is a dissimilarity of 24.4 between unmarried men and women and of 29.9 between married men and women. The dissimilarity is somewhat larger between married men and women than among the unmarried, probably because married men are more likely to be in professional and managerial occupations in which women are less highly represented.

These results are in line with Roos's (1985) findings that marital status differences are notably smaller than gender differences, but we find that married men and women differ more than unmarried men and women. Our finding is that expected by human capital theory, which reasons that women with familial commitments cannot invest as much toward occupational attainment (e.g., higher education, labor force experience), and hence they achieve less in the labor force. However, our data suggest that this is not the explanation; in fact, there is hardly any difference between the occupational distributions of married and unmarried women. Rather, the difference between married and unmarried men's occupations explains the greater dissimilarity of the married, because married men are more likely to be in professional and managerial occupations than are unmarried men. This may reflect the support a family lends to men in such occupations as well as the greater motivation of a man with a family to support to attain higher occupational achievement. It also reflects the tendency of married American Jewish women to participate and achieve in the labor force in patterns similar to unmarried women, probably because of their high educational level and relatively small family sizes.

Unlike Roos (1985), who concluded that the occupational distributions of married men and women are more similar because never-married women prefer typically "female" occupations, we find that the occupational distributions of the unmarried are more similar because of the positive support the Jewish family gives to men's careers.

Age at Marriage and Jewish Men's and Women's Occupations

For men, there is a slight relationship between age at marriage and occupational roles, in that men in blue-collar and service occupations have married later, and men in sales and clerical occupations have married earlier.[10] A partial explanation for this relationship may be that sales and clerical occupations require less investment in education, so that the men in these occupations can marry and start supporting a family earlier than men who stay in school longer and go on to academic, technical, or professional occupations. But this does not explain the older age at marriage for blue collar and service workers—perhaps they could not afford to marry earlier, or they are in occupations not common for the Jewish population and found it more difficult to find a spouse. Further, higher education among men does not seem to result in postponed marriage as much as it does for women, because it is more common for women to help support the family while men are completing a graduate degree so that men's education need not be interrupted.

Among women, professionals marry later, which is as expected; professional women tend to invest more in a career and training for a career, and a number of studies have suggested that they postpone marriage to do so. It may, of course, also be that, because these women did not marry (out of choice or lack of opportunity), they decided to continue their studies and then made appropriate use of their education in the labor force. The youngest age at marriage is found among women with service occupations and then women in blue-collar occupations—the least educated. Age at marriage gradually increases through clerical, sales, and technical or academic occupations, with the exception of managers, whose age at marriage is more like the women in service occupations. Because women are usually in lower level managerial positions, this may reflect the lower level of their occupations. We shall see later the extent to which educational level explains these relationships.

Age at Birth of First Child and Jewish Women's Occupations

Women in the professional, technical, and academic occupations not only marry later but are also older when they have their first child than women in sales, clerical, blue-collar, or service occupations. Women employed in the latter are less likely to be career-oriented and are more likely to be part-time or temporary workers. As Rosenfeld and Spenner (1992) have shown, this kind of employment is more compatible with investment in family roles indicated by having children at a younger age.

Number of Children and Jewish Women's Occupations

Having more children is also indicative of time, energy, and attitudinal investment in family roles, and therefore it is not surprising to find an association between the total number of children and women's occupations:[11] women in the professions have the least children on the average (1.4), women in technical and academic occupations follow closely with an average 1.5; and there are an increasing average number of children with managerial or administrative, sales, and clerical occupations (in that order). Women in service occupations have 1.9 children, like women in clerical occupations. These occupations may be particularly compatible with greater family roles, since they are often part-time and can be reentered more easily if one has dropped out of the labor force while the children are young. Therefore women who have invested in more family roles and at an earlier age may choose different occupations or women who have chosen particular occupations may find more family roles to be incompatible with their career. Women in blue-collar occupations have fewer children than women in clerical occupations.

However, because women in blue-collar and professional or managerial occupations tend to be relatively younger, some of the lower fertility in these groups may be a result of the women being at varying stages of reproduction. Further, even though the variation is interesting, it should be noted that, in all occupation groups, fertility is relatively low, so that there is little deviation from the overall Jewish pattern of having few children in any occupation.

In summary, family roles do seem to be somewhat related to types of occupations that both American Jewish women and men enter, but in different ways: men in professional, technical, academic, and managerial occupations are more likely to be married, but they will have married at an older age, presumably after completing higher education. Although being married is not related to the occupations women are in, the age at which family roles have been entered is. Women in professional, technical, academic, and managerial occupations had children later, and have fewer children than women in clerical, sales, blue-collar, and service occupations. This lends support to the human capital theory, which suggests that women who have invested more in family roles would have less time and resources to invest in the labor force and hence would attain different occupations than women who invest more in the labor force and relatively less in family roles. Unlike women, men's human capital may be raised by being married because of the support provided by the family, and therefore married men are also more successful in the labor force.

COHORTS AND OCCUPATIONS

Some occupational milestones require a certain number of years of experience before they can be achieved. Workers rarely become managers directly out of school, but often spend some years working themselves up the career ladder (although the professionalization of managers has decreased this avenue into managerial positions, as we will see evidence of). There are also changes in the occupations entered by a cohort due to changes in the occupational structure as new occupations are created and demand for different skills becomes common. Therefore we would expect fewer workers in their sixties to be involved in computer positions, because they were less common when they trained for and became active in the labor force. Generally, there has been a move away from blue-collar jobs and toward white-collar managerial and clerical jobs as we become a "postindustrial" economy, and this is reflected in some of the changes in occupational distribution over cohort.

In addition, as educational opportunities have opened up and more and more young people continue on to college and graduate school, the occupations for which a cohort are qualified change toward professional and managerial and away from clerical and blue-collar occupations. As we shall see, this is especially apparent in the occupational changes among women, whose educational attainment has changed dramatically over the last few decades and therefore broadened the kinds of occupations for which they qualify.

American Jewish Cohorts and Occupational Change

Clearly both life cycle and cohort effects are reflected in the occupational differences of age groups among American Jews. In Table 4.11, we present the dissimilarity coefficients between the occupational distributions of the different cohorts for the total Jewish population, men and women. Recall that the dissimilarity coefficient tells us what proportion of one population subgroup would have to change occupations to have the same occupational distribution as the second population subgroup. The higher the coefficient is, the more dissimilarity between the age-cohort groups. In the total Jewish population, there is little difference between the two youngest cohorts (only 4.3), but between the oldest two cohorts there is more difference (15.2), and between the youngest and the oldest cohorts there is considerable difference (23.4). That is, 23.4 percent of the youngest cohort would have to change their occupations, to have the same occupational distribution as the oldest cohort.

These dissimilarities result from a number of gradual changes over the cohorts, as shown in Table 4.12. Despite being at an earlier stage in their career, those now in their twenties and early thirties are more likely to be professionals than their older counterparts, indicating a cohort change that is supported by the gradual increase in percent professional among the younger. There is a similar increase in the proportion in technical and academic occupations among the younger (the proportion of 25–34 year-olds is double that of those 65+ in the technical occupations, for instance).[12] Managers and administrators are most likely to be found among the 45–54 year olds, which reflects the need to reach a certain seniority in the labor force to be promoted to such a career position, as well as the growing tendency for younger cohorts to be in professional, technical and academic occupations. The 55 and over are more likely to be in sales, the 65 and over in clerical work.[13] (Few of any cohort are in the blue-collar and service occupations.)

The changes in the occupations of the various cohorts are reflected in the average age of Jews employed in the various occupations: the average age of professionals, technicians, and academics is about 46 years of age, and the average age of those employed in craft occupations is 54. The younger average age of blue-collar workers should not be taken to mean that the younger generation is moving toward employment in these occupations, as this is not supported by our knowledge about changes in the labor market; rather, a life cycle explanation is more plausible, that is,

TABLE 4.11

Dissimilarity Coefficients[a] of Occupational Distributions,
by Age and Sex, U.S. Jews, 1990

Sex	Age	Total				Male				Female			
		25–34	35–44	45–64	65+	25–34	35–44	45–64	65+	25–34	35–44	45–64	65+
Total	25–34												
	35–44	4.3											
	45–64	9.6	11.7										
	65+	23.4	24.6	15.2									
Male	25–34	13.8	12.7	13.0	24.1								
	35–44	19.0	17.5	20.1	23.6	9.3							
	45–64	17.6	16.1	15.5	25.1	3.9	9.4						
	65+	26.9	25.5	21.8	23.9	18.4	19.2	15.7					
Female	25–34	15.2	16.6	17.2	26.3	28.9	34.1	32.7	44.0				
	35–44	19.7	18.0	20.4	26.1	30.6	35.5	34.1	35.1	11.6			
	45–64	19.6	21.1	16.2	15.0	23.1	33.4	31.7	38.0	19.7	18.3		
	65+	41.2	37.6	28.5	25.6	45.4	45.6	46.9	49.5	31.3	35.2	20.8	

[a]Based on distributions in Table 4.12. For dissimilarity calculations, see note to Table 4.2.

Source: NJPS, 1990.

TABLE 4.12
Occupation, by Age and Sex, U.S. Jews, 1990

Sex	Age	Professional	Technical	Academic	Managerial	Sales	Clerical	Blue Collar	Service	Total % (N in thousands)
Total	25–34	19.7	7.0	20.1	15.8	13.3	13.3	5.6	5.1	100.0 (532)
	35–44	19.8	7.3	20.9	17.9	11.5	12.0	6.7	3.9	100.0 (660)
	45–64	16.4	4.2	17.7	19.0	15.6	18.5	5.5	3.1	100.0 (840)
	65+	10.4	3.7	11.5	16.6	15.9	27.4	11.6	3.0	100.0 (541)
Male	25–34	25.0	2.9	17.1	18.9	16.1	7.5	8.2	4.3	100.0 (280)
	35–44	29.3	5.1	12.5	17.9	15.2	5.1	11.0	3.9	100.0 (335)
	45–64	26.1	3.0	15.6	20.5	17.2	6.8	8.2	2.6	100.0 (429)
	65+	16.7	1.4	11.0	22.1	20.6	6.8	18.9	2.5	100.0 (281)

(continued on next page)

TABLE 4.12 (continued)

| | | Occupational Group | | | | | | | | |
Sex	Age	Professional	Technical	Academic	Managerial	Sales	Clerical	Blue Collar	Service	Total % (N in thousands)
Female	25–34	13.9	11.5	23.4	12.3	10.3	19.8	2.8	6.0	100.0 (252)
	35–44	10.2	9.5	29.5	17.8	7.7	19.1	2.2	4.0	100.0 (325)
	45–64	6.3	5.4	20.0	17.5	13.9	30.7	2.7	3.6	100.0 (411)
	65+	3.5	6.2	11.9	10.8	10.8	49.6	3.8	3.5	100.0 (260)
Mean age:										
Total										
	Male	49.1	47.3	47.0	50.0	50.6	48.7	53.8	45.2	
	Female	49.1	42.9	45.4	47.8	50.8	54.6	53.8	46.6	

Source: NJPS, 1990.

these occupations are engaged in mainly as temporary rather than as end careers; as we shall see later, this is true for both men and women.

There is a greater difference between cohorts among Jewish women than among Jewish men, reflecting the increasing opportunities for women in the labor force as well as changing norms about appropriate roles for women and how much they should engage in career-oriented occupations. The dissimilarity coefficients show bigger differences between the occupational distributions of different cohorts of women than of men (Table 4.11). Among men, for instance, only 3.9 percent of the 25–34 year-olds would have to change occupations to be similar to the 45–64 year-old men; among women 30.6 percent of the 25–34 year-olds would have to change to be like the 45–64 year-old women. This reflects the changes in actual proportions in certain occupations: for instance, 26 percent of the 45–64 year-old men were professionals, very close to 25 percent of the 25–35 year-olds and 29 percent of the 35–44 year-olds. Only among the men 65 and over is there a lower percentage, 16.7 percent. Among women, however, only 6 percent of the 45–64 or older group had professional occupations, compared to 14 percent of the 25–34 year-olds—an increase of more than double. Similar changes can be seen in the proportion of women in technical and academic occupations: the proportion of 25–34 year-old women who are academics is nearly double that of those 65 and over, for example.

On the other hand, the percentage of women who have clerical occupations has decreased by over half between the cohort 65 and older and the younger cohorts 25–44. Here, a very dramatic change can be seen between those 65 and older and those 45–64, and then again for those under 45. These signify very important changes in the opportunities open to women (46–64 is the war generation cohort; 25–44 are the baby boomers benefitting from the opening of opportunities and affirmative action following the Equal Opportunities Act in 1972) as well as decreasing family size, which made it easier for women to devote themselves full-time to more demanding careers.

Many of the changes in cohorts' occupational distributions can be attributed to the entrance of women into new occupations. As Rytina and Bianchi (1984) showed for the general American population, all moves toward occupational integration between 1970 and 1984 were due to shifts in female employment—not changes in men's occupations. Lengermann and Wallace (1985) show how women's occupations have shifted during this century dramatically, with a 35 percent increase in clerical and sales workers, a 19 percent increase in female professional, technical, and managerial workers (especially in elementary school teachers and registered nurses), and a 23 percent decrease in private household and service workers. Part of this is due to a postindustrial shift toward bureaucracy, opening up new positions of record-keeping, which are expressed in the increased white-collar work needed and available. Jewish women, being highly educated, demonstrate in particular the shift toward more professional, technical, and managerial workers.

It is clear that younger Jewish women are going into different occupations than have older women. One indication of this is the average age of women in the various occupational groups (Table 4.11): the average age of women in the professional occupations is younger by over 12 years than women in crafts and by 10 years than women in clerical occupations. However, the average age of women in blue-collar occupations is also younger, which may reflect that younger women are entering into traditionally male blue-collar occupations. From a life cycle perspective, it may be that younger women enter blue-collar occupations temporarily before moving on to better and more stable jobs later in the life cycle (as seems to be the case for men as well).

To be sure, men's occupations have also changed, with an increase in the proportion in professional, technical, and academic occupations, but the increase occurred earlier than it has for women: the shift is between the 65 and over cohorts, and the younger cohorts under age 65, but the percentage change is barely 33 percent. As will be seen, the main reason for the change among men is an increase in the number of educated men; among women, there is an added factor of increased occupational opportunities for the highly educated woman.

Men and women in the labor force are about the same age on the average, but some of the differences between men and women in more specific occupations are instructive. Women are considerably younger than men in the professional, technical, and academic occupations—especially in such specific occupations as engineers, physicians, and officials and administrators, for instance—suggesting that these are occupations women are "breaking into," younger women entering occupations in which men have been for many years. On the other hand, women are considerably older than men in clerical occupations (55 on the average, compared to the average age of men at 49), especially with regard to such occupations as secretary, bookkeeper, bank teller, real estate and stock and bond sales, suggesting that younger men are also breaking into traditionally female occupations or that men engage in these occupations at the beginning of a career as a stepping stone to higher positions, but women are more likely to stay in them without being promoted higher (see also Stewart, Prandy and Blackburn, 1980, on this point).

Some of the changes over cohorts can be attributed to the rising educational level of both men and women, as we have shown. Related to this are changes in the educational requirements of certain occupations. The increase in proportion of highly educated men and women who have become managers, for instance, indicates the increasing requirements and professionalization of the managerial occupations in recent years. It is accompanied by a decrease in the proportion of men and women with 16 years of education or less who have gone into these occupations. With regard to education, however, another interesting difference between men and women can be seen. When education is controlled for the four main cohorts (Table 4.13), we see that the proportion of men with 17 or more years of education who have gone into professional occupations has remained almost constant over the cohorts, with a slight decrease as more educated men have also moved into managerial positions. In other words, older educated men had as much chance to go into professional occupations as the younger cohort with the same education. Among women, however, a very different picture emerges. Among women with 17 years or more of education, the proportion going into professional positions has increased dramatically to the 27.8 percent in the youngest cohort. This indicates that professional opportunities for educated women have widened for the cohorts, enhancing the changes

TABLE 4.13
Occupation, by Age, Years of Education, and Sex,
U. S Jews, 1990

Age		Male				Female			
		0–12	13–15	16	17+	0–12	13–15	16	17+
25–34	% Professional	8.3	9.5	23.5	41.6	3.3	6.7	13.0	27.8
	% Managerial	25.0	16.7	16.9	22.1	10.0	13.3	10.6	16.7
	% Clerical	8.3	14.3	9.6	0.0	46.7	37.8	13.0	5.6
	% Blue collar	37.5	16.7	5.1	0.0	3.3	2.2	4.1	0.0
35–44	% Professional	22.7	9.8	17.7	45.9	0.0	4.5	9.3	17.7
	%Managerial	13.6	25.5	22.1	12.3	17.1	17.9	17.8	17.7
	% Clerical	4.5	9.8	8.0	1.4	57.1	28.4	17.8	3.5
	% Blue collar	36.4	21.6	9.7	4.8	5.7	4.5	1.9	0.0
45–64	% Professional	0.0	11.4	24.7	43.6	2.6	5.8	6.3	12.7
	%Managerial	16.7	20.0	28.8	16.7	16.5	24.3	15.2	13.9
	% Clerical	19.6	8.6	6.2	1.9	48.7	34.0	22.3	11.4
	% Blue collar	30.4	15.7	3.4	1.3	5.2	2.9	1.8	0.0
65+	% Professional	2.6	3.2	34.0	49.0	1.5	1.4	6.3	17.3
	%Managerial	18.4	37.1	22.0	11.8	10.0	12.5	12.5	8.7
	% Clerical	9.6	10.5	10.5	21.1	58.5	61.1	25.0	4.3
	% Blue collar	32.5	19.4	6.0	0.0	6.2	0.0	0.0	0.0
	(N in thousands)	(28.9)	(30.9)	(52.1)	(53.7)	(42.6)	(34.4)	(46.4	(35.6)

Source: NJPS, 1990.

that have come about as women attain higher levels of education. This change in the proportion of highly educated women entering professional occupations is accompanied by a decrease in the proportion of college-educated women (with 13–15 and 16 years of education) going into clerical occupations. Women with 16 years of education are more likely to enter professional or managerial occupations in the younger cohorts than in the older cohorts. Women with 13–15 years of education are more likely to be in managerial occupations in the younger cohorts than in the older cohorts. So even though the labor force needs more clerical workers, Jewish women with college education are no longer filling this niche in the labor market to the extent that they once were, and this reflects an opening up of other job opportunities for the younger cohorts.

Opportunities for men have changed much less. The decrease in the proportion of Jewish men going into blue-collar occupations is not because men with 12 years of education or less have wider opportunities today than they used to. Among men with 12 years of education or less, 33 percent of the 65 and over cohort and 38 percent of the younger than 35 cohort are in blue-collar occupations, practically the same proportion. The overall decrease in men in blue collar occupations is mainly because fewer and fewer men stop at 12 years of education in the younger cohorts. This shows that the main differences in the occupational distribution of Jewish men more likely reflect changes in their educational achievement rather than in the kinds of occupational opportunities open to men.

OCCUPATIONAL PRESTIGE OF
AMERICAN JEWISH MEN AND WOMEN

Up to now we have discussed occupational roles of American Jews in the labor force and the gender differences related to them. We now address the difference in rewards for these roles. The main indicator available is occupational prestige.[14] Each occupation was coded by the occupational prestige score accorded to it by a national sample of Americans, with 1 being the lowest potential score and 100 being the highest (see Nakao and Treas, 1990, for more detail).

Previous research has shown that occupational prestige is some ranking of the social "desirability" of an occupation, which is related to the ability and skills required for an occupation and the material and other rewards associated with the occupation (for a recent review of the literature on occupational prestige, see Wegener, 1992). Attaining occupations with high occupational prestige is therefore strongly related to the qualifications needed for the occupational position, which may include educational training, as well as prior investment in labor force activity (Reszke, 1984). The more specialized is the training or talent needed, the more prestige given to those who can fulfill the role. The human capital invested in the labor force includes such factors as the type and extent of training, the number of years of experience in the labor force, and the number of hours invested in the labor force each week.

As occupations are to some extent grouped with prestige in mind, there is a clear relationship between occupational group and occupational prestige, prestige being on the average higher for the professional end of the occupations, lower for the blue collar, and in the middle for the "pink-collar" clerical occupations (Table 4.14). However, within these relatively large occupational categories is considerable variation in the occupational prestige for individual occupations. Therefore, the prestige score for each individual occupation indicates the extent to which a person working in that occupation is rewarded with prestige for performing that occupational role. This is an average score for all persons working in that occupation, and variation within an occupation is not measured.[15]

Given the high proportion of American Jews in professional, academic, technical, and managerial occupations, it comes as no surprise that the occupational prestige attained by American Jews is also high compared to non-Jews in the United States. In the current sample, the mean occupational prestige was 49.9. Just to put this in contemporary perspective, the mean occupational prestige for a national sample of Americans in 1989 was 41.3 (Nakao and Treas, 1990), indicating that

TABLE 4.14
Mean Occupational Prestige for Occupations, by Sex,
U.S. Jews, 1990

Occupation	Total	Male	Female
Professional	70.3	71.6	67.0
Technical	57.9	56.0	58.8
Academic	53.0	55.0	51.6
Managerial	51.5	51.3	51.7
Sales	39.5	40.0	38.8
Clerical	39.8	36.5	40.5
Blue collar	35.6	35.8	34.6
Service	36.0	38.5	33.9
Total	49.9	52.0	47.7
(N in thousands)	(3,259)	(1,662)	(1,597)

Source: NJPS, 1990.

Jews continue to have relatively high occupational prestige compared to the wider population (see also Chiswick, 1993).

Our main interest is the gender difference in occupational prestige. However, to discuss the net effect of gender (after the other variables have been controlled), we first present the effects of other variables found to be related to occupational prestige; we then discuss the gender differences that remain after the other variables are controlled and the extent to which each of these other factors explains the original (raw) gender difference.

Among American Jews, level of occupational prestige achieved is also related to these main factors of human capital. More educated Jews have higher occupational prestige than less educated Jews (Table 4.15). Jews with 17 or more years of education have about 25 percent more prestige than those with 11 years of education or less. Prestige is even more strongly related to the credential earned. Those with doctoral or professional degrees are in occupations with an average prestige score of 71.3, compared to those with no academic degree, whose average prestige score is 40.2. Each successive degree is rewarded with additional prestige, but the biggest difference is between those with M.A. or lower degrees and those with doctoral or professional degrees—a jump of about 40

TABLE 4.15
Mean Occupational Prestige,[a] by Education, U.S. Jews, 1990

Education	Mean Occupational Prestige
Years of education:	
0–12	41.6
13–15	45.8
16	50.7
17+	58.7
Highest academic degree:	
None	40.0
High school diploma	42.5
A.A. or R.N.	49.0
B.A.	50.1
M.A.	53.0
Ph.D. or professional[b]	71.1
(*N* in thousands)	(3,241)

[a]See explanation of occupational prestige in text.
[b]This includes dental, medical, and law degrees.

Source: NJPS, 1990.

percent in average prestige score. It is also clear that years of study that do not result in a doctoral or professional degree are not as highly rewarded with occupational prestige as those resulting in a high academic degree.

Greater investment in the labor force is another factor associated with earning higher occupational prestige. Work experience and time devoted to labor force activities are among the prerequisites to promotions to many positions with higher prestige in labor force. Time in the labor force also is often a prerequisite to more central and important positions, occupational attributes associated with higher occupational prestige (Wegener, 1992).

This factor is related to the occupational prestige of American Jews. Jews who have a more stable pattern of employment, and are currently working, have higher occupational prestige (a mean score of 51.5) than those who are currently not working (a mean score of 46.1).[16] Hours of work invested in labor force activity are also rewarded by higher occupational prestige: the mean prestige score of full-time workers is 52.1, compared to 47.2 for those not employed full-time in the labor force.[17]

Age is a somewhat problematic indicator. As we have mentioned in previous chapters, age indicates two aspects—a life cycle aspect and a cohort aspect. Each of these is related to occupational prestige attainment, but the relationship is not always in the same direction for the two aspects.

In terms of the life cycle (and in the absence of a direct indicator of years of work experience), age can act as a proxy for work experience by indicating the number of possible years of working life, especially for men, whose labor force activity is rarely interrupted once they begin to work. This is primarily a positive effect—the older is the person, the longer he or she has spent in the labor force—and this accumulation of experience enables the person to attain a more prestigious occupational position. The life cycle effect also reflects different education—to the extent that the youngest cohort has not yet completed all of its education, its eligibility for prestigious occupations will be weakened. Life cycle stages also reflect different family roles, which may compete with the possible time spent in the labor force, especially for women.

For the most part, the life cycle effect is a positive one; however it does vary by age. Its positive effect is mainly between the ages of 35–55, when the accumulation of work experience leads to higher occupational prestige. Prior to this age, incomplete education and entrance into marital roles may exert a negative influence on prestige attainment. After age 55, as the retirement process of disengaging from the labor force sets in, occupational prestige may decline.

In addition to life cycle variation, age also indicates birth cohort. From the cohort perspective, the younger cohorts, who have the most up-to-date preparation, should have the highest occupational prestige; the older the cohort is, the less applicable is the training, which would limit their entrance into prestigious occupations. From a cohort perspective, age (up to about age 45) should be related positively to occupational prestige; and the older the cohort is (45–54, and even more so those 55 and over), the lower is the occupational prestige.

The correlation between age and occupational prestige is therefore an average of these two types of influences. As summarized in Table 4.16, there are ages at which the life cycle and cohort effects conflict with each other, and other ages at which they reinforce each other. Up to age 35, the life cycle effect exerts a negative influence on occupational prestige attainment, while the cohort effect exerts a positive influence. Between 35–44, both effects are positive. From 45–54, the life cycle effect remains positive until retirement begins, but the cohort effect is expected to be negative. After age 55, both effects are expected to be negative.

These two aspects of age are reflected in the relationship between age and occupational prestige. As can be seen in Figure 4.1, occupational prestige is highest for the cohort aged 35–44, when both factors reinforce each other with positive relationships between age and occupational prestige. Prestige is lower prior to this age, as the life cycle effect is negative, even though the cohort effect is positive. Prestige begins to decline after age 45, as the cohort effect becomes negative; by the age of 65, both factors have a negative relationship with occupational prestige, and prestige is at its lowest.

Competing roles from other institutions also affect occupational achievement, and we therefore expected married people to have lower occupational achievement because of competing familial obligations to career devotion. Such an effect on women's occupational achievement, at least, is well-established in the literature. However, it was with some surprise that we found being married is related positively to occupational prestige: the average prestige score of married Jews is 50.6 compared to that of unmarried Jews, 47.9—a small but statistically significant differ-

TABLE 4.16
Estimated Direction of Life Cycle and Cohort Effects on
Occupational Prestige at Different Ages

Age Group	Life Cycle Effect	Cohort Effect
Under 35	–	+
35–45	+	+
45–55	+	–
55 and over	–	–

Source: ???

FIGURE 4.1
Mean Occupational Prestige[a] by Age, U.S. Jews, 1990

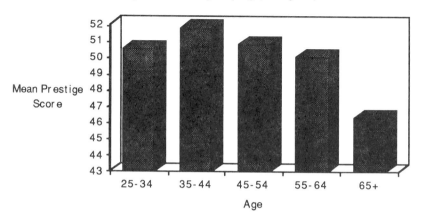

[a]See explanation of occupational prestige in text.

Source: NJPS, 1990.

ence.[18] Apparently both the support of the family and the motivation to achieve more for the family are expressed in the relationship between being married and achieving higher occupational prestige.

There is, obviously, a great deal of overlap between these factors. Family roles are related to the amount of time that can be invested in labor force activity, as we have seen in Chapter 3. The effect of these family roles varies, however, over the life cycle. The effect of education over the life cycle also varies, as we have mentioned. And labor force experience is different for men and women.

Therefore, to separate out the independent effects of each of these factors and to determine their relative importance for the attainment of occupational prestige among American Jews, we used a multiple regression analysis in which occupational prestige was the dependent variable. The independent variables included (1) both the number of years of formal schooling (a quantitative indicator of how much education) and the academic credential earned (a qualitative indicator of the type of education); (2) the number of hours invested in the labor force; (3) age and its interaction with education; (4) marital status; (5) gender; and the interaction of marital status and gender.[19] We turn first to the final step of the model, returning to the stepwise regression when we discuss gender differences later (Table 4.17).

As found in other populations, the most important contribution to occupational prestige achievement comes from education, in particular,

TABLE 4.17
Stepwise Multiple Regression Analysis of Occupational Prestige,[a]
U.S. Jews, 25 and over, 1990
(Standardized Regression Coefficients)

Independent Variable	Step 1	Step 2	Step 3	Step 4	Step 5	Step 6	Final Step
Sex	-.149*	-.056*	-.054*	-.042*	-.042*	-.043*	.017
Academic degree		.408*	.279*	.412*	.410*	.497*	.493*
Years of education		.134*	.128*	.136*	.133*	.135*	.136*
Age (natural log)			.051*	.067*	.059*	.105*	.094*
Hours of work per week				.045*	.044*	.042*	.036**
Marital status					.039*	.040*	.158*
Interaction of education and age						-.091**	-.090**
Interaction of sex and marital status							-.135*
Multiple R	.149	.536	.538	.539	.541	.541	.543
R²	.022	.287	.289	.291	.292	.293	.295
(Unweighted n)							(2669)

*Significant at α < .05.
**Significant at α < .10.
[a]See explanation of occupational prestige in text.

Source: NJPS, 1990.

the academic credential earned. With a standardized regression coefficient of .493, its effect on occupational prestige is more than three times higher than any of the other independent variables in our model. In addition to the academic credential earned, or the type of education, the number of years invested in formal schooling (the "quantity" of schooling) has an additional, independent contribution to the attainment of occupational prestige (β = .136).

Investing more in labor force related activities in terms of the number of hours worked per week also has an independent positive relationship, albeit a weak one, with the achievement of occupational prestige. The more hours invested in labor force activity, the higher is the occupational prestige earned. Its effect accrues not only because less educated and older persons work fewer hours in the labor force, as these variables have been controlled in the model. Its effect is weakened, however (as we shall see), by the lack of variation in hours worked per week among men, the relationship between time invested in labor force activities and occupational rewards being much stronger for women than for men.

Marital status has a significant, positive, independent effect on occupational prestige (β = .158). This is in addition to its relationship with hours of work invested in the labor force, which are influenced by the family roles of men and women, as we have shown in the previous chapter, and life cycle stage, as its effect persists after these have been controlled.

Cohort and Life Cycle Effects on Occupational Prestige

As we have discussed, age indicates both life cycle stage and birth cohort. To some extent it represents a life cycle effect by indicating investment in the labor force, in that it is a proxy of how many years the person has worked. At the same time, age indicates birth cohort, which has a different relationship to occupational prestige. As we have seen in Figure 4.1, if education is not controlled, occupational prestige is lower for the oldest cohort, and highest for the cohort aged 35–44, which has completed its education and is devoting itself full-time to career development. However, because of the different relationships of life cycle and cohort with occupational prestige, the overall correlation between age and occupational prestige is lowered.

Most of the life cycle effect relates to work experience, but most of the cohort effect is through differential education, which is more applicable to occupational achievement for younger cohorts. Because in our model education is better controlled, the effect of age (after education is controlled) is mainly one of life cycle variation (or work experience). Including educational level in the multiple regression model controls to some extent for the negative effect of cohort.

The significant interaction included in the model between age and education also indicates the differential effect of education for different birth cohorts. Because the education of younger cohorts is more relevant to the current labor force than the education of older cohorts (whose education was obtained on the average between thirty and forty years ago), the education of younger cohorts is more effective in achieving occupational prestige. In addition, education is more important for the younger cohorts because other factors, such as work experience, may not have accumulated enough importance to bring about considerable differences in prestige.

Therefore, the life cycle effect is the dominant age effect once education and its interaction with age has been controlled, and the relationship between age and occupational prestige is positive: the older the person is, the higher is the occupational attainment achieved. This effect is even stronger when we correct for the lack of linearity at the higher ages (when occupational prestige no longer increases) by taking the natural log of age.

Gender and Occupational Prestige

Women are known to be rewarded less for their labor force participation than men. Women receive on the average less income than men for the same amount of labor force participation (Taeuber and Valdisera, 1986) as well as nonwage benefits associated with occupational roles (Haberfeld and Shenhav, 1987). In terms of occupational prestige, the U.S. female labor force as a whole has less occupational prestige than the U.S. male labor force overall (Acker, 1980; Bose, 1973, 1985; Nilson, 1976).

Among American Jews, there is also a gender difference in occupational prestige. American Jewish men have a significantly higher mean occupational prestige than women, 51.9 compared to 47.8.[20] This fits what we have found already, that women are less likely to be in prestigious professional and managerial occupations than men.

Differences in occupational rewards of men and women have been attributed to three main factors, as we have mentioned earlier: (1) differences in the human capital of men and women, (2) differences in the distribution of men and women among different jobs, and (3) discrimination in the labor market (Taeuber and Valdisera, 1986). Similar explanations have been proposed for gender differences in occupational prestige in particular (England, 1979; Fox and Suschnigg, 1989; McLaughlin, 1978; Siegel, 1971). As differences in the human capital that men and women bring to the labor force decrease and as occupational opportunities for men and women become more equal because of changing norms about women's appropriate roles and capabilities, the gender gap in occupational rewards is expected to narrow.

Among American Jews, human capital differences between men and women explain some but not all of the gender differences in occupational prestige. As Table 4.18 shows, although men and women in the lowest education group have similar occupational prestige and women even have slightly higher prestige than men with 13–15 years of education, men with 16 or more years of education—especially 17 years or more—have higher occupational prestige than women. As a result it seems that higher education can bring about higher occupational prestige for men than for women.

Because more men with 17 and more years of education go on to attain Ph.D. or professional degrees, we wondered whether the credential earned would eliminate the difference in occupational prestige between men and women (Table 4.18). However, among men and women at each credential, men have somewhat higher occupational prestige than women. This difference continues at the highest credential level. Men with Ph.D.s or professional degrees have an average of 71.6 occupational prestige, but women have an average of 69.2.

TABLE 4.18

Mean Occupational Prestige,[a] by Education, Part- and Full-Time Employment, Marital Status, Age, and Sex, U.S. Jews, 1990

Education	Male	Female
Years of education:		
0–12	41.7	41.6
13–15	45.3	46.3
16	52.3	48.9
17+	61.4	54.7
Highest academic degree:		
None	41.2	38.2
High school diploma	42.4	42.6
A.A. or R.N.	45.7	51.9
B.A.	51.2	49.0
M.A.	54.7	51.6
Ph.D. or professional	71.6	69.2
Extent of employment:		
Part-time	48.9	46.3
Full-time	53.3	47.7
Marital status:		
Not married	48.7	47.2
Married	53.3	47.9
Age group:		
25–34	51.5	49.7
35–44	53.3	50.2
45–54	53.6	47.0
55–64	54.9	46.4
65+	48.2	44.1
(*N* in thousands)	(1,648)	(1,588)

[a]See explanation of occupational prestige in text.

Source: NJPS, 1990.

As we have seen in Chapter 3, women are more likely to work part-time than are men, and this part-time pattern is expected to result in lower occupational prestige. Part-time workers are less likely to receive on-the-job training (whether formal or informal), which results in fewer promotions, thus reducing the possibility of achieving occupational prestige (U.S. Bureau of Labor Statistics, 1994). Also, more prestigious occupations often require a high commitment to the labor force, even beyond the average full-time hours. Although our measure is of hours worked at only the most recent time in the labor force, there is some indication in other research that women tend to pursue a pattern of either full-time or part-time employment (Hartman and Hartman, 1990; Heuvel, 1989; Moen, 1985), so that the current measure may also indicate previous patterns of investment in labor force activities.

Men and women who work part-time are more similar in occupational prestige than those working full-time, but controlling for part-time employment does not eliminate the gender difference in occupational prestige. Part-time employment has a similar effect on prestige for both men and women, part-time workers having 8–9 percent less prestige than full-time workers in each gender.

Being married is related to occupational prestige differently for men and for women, having a much stronger positive relationship for men than for women, for whom family roles represent a competing claim on time and energy that might otherwise be devoted to preparation for the labor force and active involvement in it.

Age is also related to the occupational prestige of men and women differently. In the last few decades, women's status has changed considerably, as a result of changes in occupational and educational opportunities and patterns of behavior, reflected in changed attitudes about women's roles and status (Mason and Lu, 1988). Our sample represents Jewish women from different birth cohorts, which experienced different attitudes regarding women's status and possible achievements, had different educational backgrounds (as we saw in Chapter 2), and different labor force patterns (as we saw in Chapter 3). The environment surrounding gender roles made gender differences in roles and rewards much greater fifty years ago than today, and the possible rewards women could obtain over the life cycle were much further from men's than they are today. As a result, later cohorts are expected to have less gender difference in the achievement of occupational prestige than earlier cohorts.

As we can see in Table 4.18, without controlling for education or marital status, men's occupational prestige peaks during the ages 55–64, indicating that the longer they are in the labor force the higher the occupational prestige they achieve. The lower occupational prestige of men 65 and over may be due to a life cycle effect, change in occupation at this age (retiring from the main occupation and taking on a less prestigious job), or a cohort effect, because of the lower education of this birth cohort (which is tested in the multiple regression and we will discuss later), and the depreciated value of education obtained in the 1940s and 1950s (when the age group 65+ was in their twenties) compared to education obtained more recently.

Women's occupational prestige, however, is higher in the younger age groups (25–34 and 35–44), which seems to indicate a predominant cohort effect that reflects the increase in occupational opportunities and educational level of these younger cohorts, and the greater applicability of their more recent education.

Because of the different patterns of occupational prestige for men and women, the gap between men and women is somewhat larger for older cohorts and narrows for younger cohorts, although the gap does not disappear even among the 25–34 year-olds.

The Net Gender Difference in the Occupational Prestige of American Jewish Men and Women

To determine the net differences in occupational prestige between men and women once these various factors have been controlled, gender was included in the multiple regression model. In the following we will discuss the extent to which each of the factors discussed previously explain the gender differences in occupational prestige. To the extent that gender differences remain, they must be attributed to other factors, including discrimination in the labor force in the allocation of occupational prestige to Jewish men and women.

In the stepwise regression analysis (presented above in Table 4.17), gender has a significant relationship with occupational prestige before any of the other factors enter the regression equation, showing (as we have shown already) that Jewish men have significantly more occupational prestige than Jewish women.

One of the first questions we ask is how much the differences in occupational prestige between men and women may be explained by their differential education. In the multiple regression model, controlling for education alone (the second step in Table 4.17) does not eliminate the gender difference, although it does reduce the gender difference to nearly a third of its original magnitude (from a beta coefficient of -.149 to -.056, still significant at $a < .05$). Thus, educational differences explain some but not all of the gender differences in the occupational prestige of American Jews.

When we added hours of labor force participation to the multiple regression predicting occupational prestige as an indicator of investment in labor force activity, the effect of gender goes down by about 20 percent, from −.054 to −.042 (a statistically significant change), which indicates that the greater tendency for women to be employed part-time does explain some part of the gender differences in occupational prestige.

Our measure of cohort, age, does not allow us to separate the effect of birth cohort from life cycle differences between men's and women's achievement of occupational prestige. However, some of the life cycle differences are identifiable: marriage may interrupt women's educational achievement to a greater extent than men's (as we discussed in Chapter 2), resulting in lower occupational prestige; having small children at home may delay or interrupt women's labor force activity more than men's (as we discussed in Chapter 3), with resulting differences in prestige achievement. By controlling for education and marital status we control for the main life cycle differences between men and women (and we shall deal with the effects of children on women's achievement to a greater extent later), as well as cohort differences in the relevancy of educational background. In the regression model, controlling for age hardly changes the effect of gender—before age is entered into the regression model, the beta coefficient of sex is –.056; after age enters the regression model, the beta coefficient of sex is –.054. Apparently the cohort differences between men and women can be explained by their educational differences, so that controlling for age after education is in the model does not explain more of the gender differences. Similarly, the introduction of the interaction effect between age and education does not change the regression coefficient of sex significantly.

At this point in the regression equation, gender is significantly related to occupational prestige, even after education, age, and hours of work have been controlled; that is, beyond their differences in human capital (educational qualifications and investment in the labor force) and beyond cohort and life cycle differences, Jewish men have on the average higher occupational prestige than Jewish women. Although the educational differentials between the genders as well as their different labor force investment explain some of the gender difference, a significant difference remains.

In the next step of the regression analysis, marital status was introduced. As we have mentioned previously, being married is associated with higher occupational prestige (hence the positive beta coefficient of marital status in the regression model), but the effect of being married is not the same for men and women (being much stronger for men than for women). When we control for marital status in the multiple regression (step 5 in Table 4.17), the gender effect on occupational prestige is not changed. However, when the *differential* effect of marital status for men and women is controlled by the interaction effect of marital status and sex (in the final step of the model), the effect of sex changes from a significant negative effect to a positive but insignificant effect. In other words, the gender difference in occupational prestige is strongly related to the different implications of being married for men and women. For men, being married implies greater support so they can pursue career-related activities and also a motivation to achieve more for the family and fulfill their financial responsibilities as family providers. For women these same effects are countered by time and energy demands as a wife and, especially, as we shall see, mother.

The Different Ways in Which Men and Women
Attain Occupational Prestige

To clarify some of the differences in the ways men and women achieve occupational prestige, we present in the following section separate regression analyses of the occupational prestige of men and of women (Table 4.19). What we have seen already is that men and women attain different occupational prestige because of the different human capital each sex brings to the labor force and also because of the differential effect of family roles on the attainment of occupational prestige. In the following we compare the factors that result in occupational prestige for men and women.

One of the first things we notice in comparing the separate regressions is that the indicators in the regression model explain better men's occupational prestige than women's. With a multiple correlation of .597, over 35 percent of the variation in men's occupational prestige is explained by education, age, the interaction of age and education, hours

TABLE 4.19
Multiple Regression Analysis of Occupational Prestige[a]
for Men and Women Separately, U.S. Jews, 1990

Independent Variable	Men	Women
Highest academic degree	6.261	3.931
	(.595)	(.453)
Years of education	.518	.666
	(.109)	(.164)
Age (natural log)	5.131	3.944
	(.110)	(.109)
Interaction of age and education	−.019*	−.036
	(−.097)	(−.196)
Hours of work	−.001*	.052
	(−.001)	(.089)
Marital status	1.995	.348*
	(.057)	(.014)
Multiple R	.597	.436
R^2	.356	.190
(Unweighted n)	(1309)	(1238)

*$\alpha < .05$.
Note: Standardized regression coefficients are in parentheses, others are unstandardized.
[a]See explanation of occupational prestige in text.

Source: NJPS, 1990.

of work, and marital status. Only 19 percent of the variation in women's occupational prestige is explained with the same indicators. This is not unlike other populations in industrialized countries, where the attainment of men's occupational prestige seems to be enhanced by more factors than does women's (Roos, 1985).

In the next section we will explore some additional aspects of family roles of women and their impact on women's occupational prestige. However, the survey is limited in measuring changes over time, which is (as we have discussed) expected to have a considerable impact on the parameters of achievement for women. Similarly, little information is available on work experience and labor force patterns that occurred in the past, including interruptions and exits from the labor force, and these are expected to have a considerable influence on the occupational prestige achieved by women.

Occupational Prestige Returns to the Education of Jewish Men and Women

For both men and women, education is the major factor explaining the attainment of occupational prestige. The comparison of men and women shows clearly, however, that educational attainment explains more of the occupational prestige achieved by men than by women. A stepwise regression[21] (not presented here) showed us that academic degree and years of education alone explained more than a third (34.6 percent) of the variance in men's occupational prestige, but only 17.9 percent of the variance in women's occupational prestige. A comparison of the unstandardized regression coefficients shows that the degrees achieved by men have almost twice the impact on occupational prestige achieved than the degrees achieved by women on their occupational prestige (B for men = 6.261, compared to B = 3.931 for women). On the other hand, the number of years of education is somewhat more important for women than for men.[22]

Age and the Occupational Prestige of Men and Women

For both men and women, age has a significant positive effect. The cohort effect of age, which would be a negative effect, has been controlled to a great extent by educational achievement and by the interaction between age and education, which we discussed earlier. The remaining effect of age is primarily a life cycle effect for both men and women: the older one is, the longer he or she has worked in the labor force and has therefore had more time to achieve occupational status. However, as the comparison of the unstandardized regression coefficients shows, its effect is weaker for women than for men. This may be because age is a poorer proxy for work experience for women than for men, because of the variety of labor force patterns women might have. The life cycle effect of age is therefore weaker.

The interaction between education and age is not significant for men. However, when it is included, the effects of both academic degree achieved and age are strengthened, indicating that some of the independent effects of each were suppressed by the interaction between education and age (education being somewhat more effective for younger than older men because it is more updated and enables them to reach higher achievements).

For women, the interaction between age and education does have a significant negative effect, indicating that education has a different effect for the different cohorts, because more educated women have more opportunities among the young than the old, as well as the younger cohorts' education being more current. This also reflects the greater changes in women's roles over the cohorts, opening up opportunities for women to gain occupational prestige as time goes on.

Occupational Prestige Returns for Labor Force Activity of Men and Women

The hours of work that men put into the labor force was not found to be related significantly to their occupational prestige. This is because most men work full-time, except at the young ages when they are still in school or at the retirement ages when they gradually disengage from the labor force. These periods do not affect the main working life ages nor the attainment of prestige, which is accomplished during the main working period.

The number of hours women devote to labor force activity, on the other hand, does affect their occupational prestige significantly ($\beta = .088$), because it reflects dedication to a career; that is, the more investment in labor force activity, the higher is the return in terms of occupational prestige.

The Differential Effect of Marital Status on the Occupational Prestige of Men and Women

The addition of marital status brings the explained variance in men's occupational prestige up to 35.6 percent, with being married having a significant and positive relationship to the occupational prestige of men. The familial role of men is to provide, that is, to make a career and achieve as many rewards as possible, so that his family role coincides with his career role and dedication; in addition, being married enhances the pursuit of occupational prestige by providing "backstage support," in Hochschild's (1989) term.

In contrast to men, being married does not change the allocation of occupational prestige to women. The family does not act as a support to the pursuit of occupational advancement to the extent that it does for men nor is it a clear-cut motivator for the occupational advancement of women. On the contrary, it introduces family roles that compete for the time and energy of women. Entrance into family roles and particularly parenting roles may lower the starting point of women's career achievement or interrupt its development by introducing new demands on time and energy at a time when men, on the contrary, would be devoting their main time and energy to their career.

In the following we explore whether any family or child-related roles influence women's attainment of occupational prestige.

Family Roles and Jewish Women's Occupational Prestige

We probe further into the family roles of women with the multiple regression analysis presented for women in Table 4.20. It should be remembered that in less modern cultures women tend to fall into two major types, either family oriented, or career oriented, where the former tend to marry earlier, have larger families, and participate less in the paid labor force, but the latter women marry later, have fewer children, and are more active in the labor force.

As we have seen, most Jewish women participate in the labor force, and having children is not as much of a deterrent as would have been

TABLE 4.20
Multiple Regression Analysis of Occupational Prestige,[a]
U.S. Jewish Married Women, 1990

Independent Variable	Standardized Regression Coefficients
Highest academic degree	.289**
Years of education	.111*
Age (natural log)	−.002
Hours of work	.099*
Number of children	−.002
Age at birth of the first child	.077*
Multiple R	.441
R²	.195
(Unweighted n)	(892)

*α < .05
**α < .01
[a]See explanation of occupational prestige in text.

Source: NJPS, 1990.

expected in a different population. What we found about labor force participation was that it was not a familial orientation per se that interfered with labor force activity, but the timing of families, in particular the timing of the first child. Is it the same for occupational prestige?

In the regression model we included as independent variables the age at the birth of the first child and the number of children along with education, age, and extent of labor force involvement (hours of work) to see whether variation on the family-oriented variables would have an effect on attaining occupational prestige. Age at marriage and the number of children under 17 were not included in the model because they were found to have virtually no significant effect on occupational prestige.

We see that in terms of occupational prestige—as for labor force activity (which we saw in the previous chapter)—that it is not the number of children (i.e., the *quantity* of family roles) that competes with women's occupational achievement. The regression coefficient of number of children is not statistically significant.

What *does* have a significantly negative relationship with women's attainment of occupational prestige is the timing of parenthood—the younger is the mother at the entrance into parenthood, the lower is her occupational status; and on the contrary, the older the entrance into parenthood, the higher the occupational status. This effect is in addition to the negative effect of entering into parenthood on educational attainment and investment in labor force activity, which we saw in earlier chapters. When these family indicators are controlled, neither the beta coefficients of the education indicators nor of hours of work are changed significantly, suggesting that their main effect is a direct one. An early role of parenthood competes with investment toward occupational advancement and is not overcome at a later date. As we found that it is the timing of parenthood and not the number of children that affects occupational prestige, the data support the thesis that women who are concerned with getting ahead in their careers time their children to interfere minimally with their occupational advancement, but women who are less concerned with careers enter into parenthood earlier with less concern as to the effect of the birth on their occupational chances.

These additional indicators of family and parenting roles bring the variance explained of women's occupational prestige to 19.5 percent, still lower than for men. It is expected that more detailed information about women's family roles, their past labor force experience and the number and length of interruptions in their career development, and more information about changes in the wider social environment concerning women's roles would help us to understand even better the variation in women's occupational prestige.

CONCLUSIONS

The high occupational achievement of Jewish Americans appears to be shared by men and women alike, but is somewhat higher for Jewish men in part because of their higher education and in part because of the differential effect of family involvement on men and women. Comparisons to the wider American population indicate a somewhat greater gender equity among the American Jewish population in terms of occupational distributions. This suggests that the Jewish culture indeed facilitates an equality of occupational achievement. Nevertheless, gender differences in occupational roles between Jewish men and women persist, indicating that the reference group for Jewish women is Jewish men, rather than other women or the total population of American men.

The occupations of Jewish women are more similar to the wider population of American women than the occupations of Jewish men are to the wider population of American men. This reflects the norms constraining women's occupational roles, which are more restrictive than for men, among whom there is more occupational variation. It also reflects the greater concentration of Jewish men in high-level occupations compared to the wider population, whereas women tend to enter more traditional female occupations, albeit at the higher levels.

Education lowers the dissimilarity between men and women both among Jews and in the wider population, but dissimilarity persists, indicating the importance of norms governing women's occupational roles.

This occupational dissimilarity results in lower occupational prestige for women as compared to men, a gender gap partially explained by human capital differences (education and hours of work) but even more so by the differential effect of family roles on the prestige of men and women. It would seem that the importance both women and society place on women's family roles channels women into patterns of labor force behavior and occupational roles that are perceived as compatible with family roles but that are less rewarding in terms of prestige and even more so—as we know from other research—income. A critical difference that could not be adequately measured in the present data is the orientation to family roles—how important they are perceived to be, how central in relation to career goals, and how compatible family and career roles are perceived to be. The study allows us only to infer societal norms and discriminatory practices, which would also seem to be contributing to the occupational differences we found.

We were able to isolate some of the roles in the family that were most related to occupational achievement. Interestingly, it was not marital roles per se, nor the age at which marriage was entered, nor the number of children in the family. Rather, it was the age at which childbearing began, indicating that of critical importance is the timing of children and how they are combined with career development. The high achievement of Jewish women is apparently strongly related to an efficient planning of children to interfere minimally with their career development. Many Jewish women do interrupt their labor force activity to take care of their young children, as we have seen in the previous chapter, but are apparently able to time their children to present less role conflict between the family and their roles in the economy.

CHAPTER 5

Gender Equality
Within Jewish Couples

The patterns of gender inequality in terms of educational attainment, economic activity, and occupational achievement among American Jews have been discussed in the preceding chapters. As we have seen, these patterns have been changing over recent decades among American Jews as well as among the wider American population in the direction of greater equality. In general, as many women as men now continue on to higher education after high school and nearly as many receive advanced academic degrees. An increasing proportion of women are working in the paid labor force, and having children is less of a deterrent to participation in the paid labor force than it used to be. Although their occupations are not the same as men's, women are entering into an increasing number of occupations and achieving higher levels of occupational prestige than ever before.

As norms of gender inequality in public domains have been widely challenged, it is known that norms of gender inequality in private domains often persist. Just because men and women have more equal education does not mean that men still do not marry women who are less educated themselves. More gender equality in the labor force status of men and women does not necessarily mean that husbands and wives have more equal labor force status when both work. Patterns of mate selection may reinforce traditional status differences between husband and wife even when in the wider society differences between men and women are diminishing, and marital dynamics may preserve traditional differences. Class analysts have increasingly linked the reproduction of inequality in the wider society to the gendered domestic division of labor and power relations within the family, especially wives' economic dependence on their husbands (e.g., Wright et al., 1992).

According to exchange or resource theory, differences in education and occupational status are linked to power or leverage within family relationships. Spouses of equal education are more likely to divide household work equally, share more decision making, and make decisions in similar numbers of areas (Scanzoni, 1970). Wives who contribute to the household economy share more household power with their husbands, are less likely to experience domestic violence, and have access to better health care (Sørenson and McLanahan, 1987). Part of this stems from education and experience in the paid labor force being an investment in transferable rather than relationship-specific skills that enables a spouse to be less dependent on the current relationship for support (even if he or she is not currently employed; see discussion in England and Farkas, 1986, and findings in Sørenson and McLanahan, 1987). It is therefore important to assess the extent of equality between spouses, as the experience of gender equality in such an intimate setting has ramifications for the relative power and self-direction experienced in a broader setting.

In the current chapter we compare the age, education, labor force activity and occupational attainment of husbands and wives in Jewish couples. These inequalities (or equalities) serve as a background for expectations about power relations within the family, which are beyond the scope of this study, but certainly merit further research.

Spousal inequalities can be divided into two kinds: those resulting from the patterns of mate selection, and those resulting during the marriage and influenced by marital dynamics. Age is determined prior to marriage, and the comparative ages of spouses is a result of mate selection. Traditionally husbands have been older than their wives, and although age homogamy seems to be increasing in the wider American society (Atkinson and Glass, 1985), the mean age difference between husbands and wives was still 5.3 years in 1985 (Chadwick and Heaton, 1992, Table A2-3). Traditional age differences may result in differences in the education each spouse has managed to attain before marriage and thus may create or reinforce a difference in educational levels of husband and wife.

Because education is usually acquired before marriage, the similarity of husband's and wife's education is often a result of "assortative" mating also. Potential spouses are expected to select mates partially because they prefer similar lifestyles, and education is a major determinant of lifestyle. In addition, marriage selection is constrained by the marriage market to which potential spouses are exposed, and because more and more people are continuing on to higher education during their mate selection years, school is a common delimiter of marriage markets. This is especially true among the Jewish population, because such a high percentage continue on to college or university, as we have seen. Both factors encourage educational homogamy in mate selection, and it is generally accepted that there is such a tendency toward educational homogamy in spousal selection, especially in industrialized societies (e.g., Kalmijn, 1991a; Ultee and Luijkx, 1990).

As higher education becomes more common and more people continue on to graduate degrees, it is reasonable to expect that education will be finished during marriage, especially as age of marriage stabilizes or decreases as it seems to have done among American Jews (see later). It is not uncommon to hear of husbands finishing up their graduate or professional degrees while their wives work to support the family or that wives transfer colleges to finish their degree where their husband, already graduated, has started a new job. Increasing proportions of women return to school after their children are grown, an outgrowth of the rising level of education of women. Thus, educational similarity among spouses may become less directly a function of assortative mating (except insofar as educational aspirations are factors in selecting mates) and more a product of behaviors completed during marriage. To the extent that norms about spousal inequality are traditional, this may affect the relative educational attainment of husbands and wives.

Questions remain about whether a woman should be more intelligent than her mate and what effect this will have on his masculine ego. As reported in Faludi (1991), the American press relished a half-baked study of the deleterious effects on marriage odds of higher education for women, but was reluctant to clarify the findings once they were modified; Faludi suggests that this is an example of lingering traditional sex-role norms that still prefer patterns of male dominance.

Further, the high correlation of husbands' and wives' education, which is often used to show educational homogamy among spouses or homogamy within broad groups of education (e.g., Kalmijn, 1991a), does not preclude the possibility that husbands consistently have somewhat higher educational attainment than their wives. Therefore it is necessary to consider not only the correlation, but also the distribution of difference between husband and wife, its direction and meaning.

Spousal labor force participation and occupational attainment occur mainly during the marriage and generally have less direct relationship to mate selection. However, both labor force behavior and occupational attainment after marriage are related to some characteristics influencing mate selection, because both education and parents' status—strong effects on labor force behavior and occupational attainment—affect the marriage markets: further career plans and the expected domestic division of labor certainly are factors considered in spousal selection. Career patterns may and often have been established prior to marriage, particularly when the marriage occurs at an older age, but the decision of whether a spouse continues to work during marriage is nevertheless to a large extent a household decision and takes into consideration the need for income, the opportunities each spouse has for work, each spouse's age, family orientations (e.g., how many children the couples wants and the timing of their births) and attitudes (e.g., sex-role orientations; see Philliber and Vannoy-Hiller, 1990).

American attitudes about how much a wife's labor force behavior should take into account her husband and family have changed in the last two decades. In 1977, 63 percent of the Americans polled in the National Opinion Research Center General Social Surveys agreed that "It is much better for everyone if the man is the achiever and the woman takes care of the home and family." By 1985, the percentage supporting this statement had dropped to 47 percent (Mason and Lu, 1988). Nevertheless, a sizable proportion of the sample continued to link marital considerations and wive's labor force behavior, and research has shown that a wife's actual labor force behavior is influenced by her husband's characteristics (Geerken and Gove, 1983; Mocanachie, 1989). The parallel influence on a husband's labor force behavior by his wife's characteristics is not yet widely relevant and is unlikely to be as long as the labor force is organized along a "masculine prototype" (see Hertz, 1991).

Occupational achievements of both husband and wife are also affected by spousal characteristics (Hout, 1982). The labor force patterns that develop during marriage often result in differential occupational attainment (although certainly this is not the only factor influencing occupational attainment). Once it was considered functional for wives to facilitate their husband's careers, but not vice versa. American norms about the unequal pursuit of occupational objectives, however, have changed in the last two decades: in 1977, 61 percent agreed that "It is more important for a wife to help her husband's career than to have one herself." By 1985 the percent agreeing had decreased but was still 38 percent (Mason and Lu, 1988). The norm of letting the husband's career take precedence influences the extent to which women interrupt their careers, as when the husband is given a promotion that necessitates relocation. As the literature on dual-career couples has shown, women are more apt to make changes in their careers to accomodate their husbands' career needs, including relocating when the husband receives a promotion (Skinner, 1984), and are more likely to decline promotions of their own or other career changes out of consideration of their family (Bielby and Bielby, 1992; Izraeli, 1992) than are men in similar positions. On the other hand, women may benefit from their husband's being in a similar occupation as their own (Bryson et al., 1978), and husband's occupational attainment may also benefit from his wife's activity in the labor force (Hartman and Hartman, 1985).

EXPECTATIONS ABOUT GENDER EQUALITY WITHIN AMERICAN JEWISH COUPLES

What are our expectations about American Jews in this respect? There would appear to be three special influences on American Jewish couples with regard to the equality between spouses. Because both Jewish men and women are relatively highly educated, as we have seen, the variation in education within the Jewish population is relatively low and the range of possible differences between the spouses is restricted; hence, more equality between the spouses in terms of educational attainment was expected than among the wider American population. Because mate selection among the higher educated often takes place while they are at college and the age range of college students is limited, the age differences among Jewish couples are also expected to be lower than the wider American population.

Following the expected low difference in education of the spouses, it was expected that both the labor force behavior and occupational achievements of Jewish spouses would be similar. The strong support of Jewish women for women's equality via the feminist movement (cf. Fishman, 1993) reinforces our expectation that the achievement of Jewish wives would match that of their husbands (i.e., that they would push for equality within their marriages as they had in the public domain).

Jewish tradition has never opposed wives' contributing to the economic well-being of the family. On the contrary, traditionally wives were expected to contribute to the household economy and even to assume primary responsibility for maintaining it when the husband was a religious scholar (Fishman, 1993; Wegner, 1988), and throughout history we have examples of successful Jewish businesswomen (Baskin, 1991). Early immigrant families to the United States followed the same tradition of having the wife contribute to the household economy (Baum et al., 1976; Glenn, 1990; Weinberg, 1988).

At the same time, as we also have discussed, Jewish tradition places great importance on children and family life, the responsibility for which lays primarily with the mother and housewife. Family roles have been juxtaposed in contemporary modern industrial societies to career commitment, and women often feel pressured to make a choice between the two. In the Jewish heritage, the family took priority, but this did not mean the women did not engage in economic activity. However, their occupations were valued less as an expression of a wife's self-actualization than in terms of their contribution to the family's well-being. In the Mishnah, women's expected economic duties are lightened when they have young children to attend to (Wegner, 1988). Among contemporary American Jewry, the responsiveness of Jewish women's labor force behavior to the presence of children that we have seen previously (and earlier, in Chiswick, 1986)[1] reflects the priority put on family roles. Many Jewish women want both careers and families, in contrast to the feminist ethos that pressures them to put career first (Fishman, 1993).

The nature of the restrictions do not imply that Jewish women who do work in the labor force should worry about whether they are reaching higher positions than their husbands. Nothing in the Jewish tradition suggests that women should remain inferiors of their husbands in terms of secular education and occupational achievement. A set of rights and obligations establish the equivalence of husbands and wives as persons (Wegner, 1988) rather than inherently inferior and superior beings.[2] Wives' occupational achievement is accepted and even encouraged as long as it does not undermine the fulfillment of the highly valued family roles. Traditionally it was also accepted that the wife could bring in substitutes for her labor, but she did not relinquish responsibility for certain parts of the household economy, whoever would actually do the tasks. Rather than the traditional slogan of "a woman's *place* is in the home," the emphasis in the traditional Jewish community might better be understood as "a woman's *responsibility* is the home," and in many respects this emphasis has not changed.

The expectations therefore are along this compromise. The higher education of American Jewish women enables greater spousal equality, and elements of the Jewish heritage support such a major role for Jewish wives in contributing to the household economy. This support is limited by the expectation that career involvement will be for the benefit of the family and not at the expense of it. Among women with fewer family roles we expect no normative restrictions on labor force participation or occupational achievement, but on the contrary strong normative support of it. Dual earner families will more likely have fewer family obligations than families in which only the husband works, as in these families wives have probably stopped working to attend to their family roles. And the more Jewishly involved is the couple, the more they will be responsive to family obligations and curtail the wife's labor force participation while the children are young. This may or may not result in differential occupational achievement of husband and wife, but if it does it will be an indirect result rather than a direct result of Jewishness.

More specifically, we approached this subject with the following expectations:

1. Spousal inequality in education, paid labor force participation, and occupational achievement would occur within Jewish couples to a lesser extent than in the wider American population. One source of spousal inequality is assortative mating. Because of their generally high educational level, we expect Jewish couples to have relatively more spousal equality in education compared to the wider population, and this would bring about relatively more spousal equality in labor force participation and occupational achievement.

2. The expectation is that the direction of inequality that persists would be conventional; that is, husbands would be older than their wives, have more education, be more active in the paid labor force, and have higher occupational achievement.

3. A reason for the persisting spousal inequality is family role involvement, which affects husbands and wives differently. As a result, Jewish couples with more children would be more likely to have greater inequalities in labor force participation and occupational achievement. Partly because of this differential implication of family obligations, there will be more spousal inequality within Jewish couples than between Jewish men and women as a whole.

4. Because of the familistic orientation of the Jewish heritage, we expect couples who are more Jewishly involved to have more spousal inequality when familistic roles are present and that Jewishness will have less of an effect when family roles require less attention (i.e., when there are fewer or older children). Similarly, Orthodox couples will be more affected by family roles toward spousal inequality than Conservative couples; Reform couples will be affected the least. We will explore this issue in the next chapter.

In this chapter we will be discussing the inequalities between the spouses in the Jewish couples surveyed in terms of age, education, labor force participation, and occupational attainment; we will then consider the effect of spousal and family characteristics on each spouse's labor force activity and occupational attainment. As in our previous chapters we will be concerned with discerning a Jewish pattern, as distinguished from the wider American population.

POPULATION, SAMPLE, AND INDICATORS

The population to which this analysis applies is all currently married couples in which at least one of the partners is Jewish. To reach a sample of Jewish couples, we selected all currently married respondents in the survey. Because respondents were included as long as some member of their household was Jewish, we then had to eliminate any couples in which neither the respondent nor his or her spouse was Jewish. We also eliminated couples in which both partners were the same sex. The final sample included a total of 1,414 currently married heterosexual couples in which at least one partner is Jewish by the criteria defined on p. 19.[3] Because the population weights were developed for individuals rather than couples, the data presented in this chapter will not be weighted.

The dependent variables of spousal inequality on which we focus are education (both years completed and degree achieved), participation in the paid labor force, occupation, and occupational prestige. Differences in education are indicated as (1) *Eddif* (i.e., husband's education minus wife's education; negative values on this indicator result when wives have more education than their husbands); (2) *Edeq* (which indicates whether the husband's and wive's educational characteristics are equal, within one year of each other, or not); and (3) *Edconv* (how "conventional" the couple is). By *conventional* we mean that the husband is older, more educated, or has higher occupational prestige than the wife or has the same characteristics as she does. *Labor force differences* result in four types of couples: dual earners (in which both husband and wife participate in the paid labor force); male breadwinners (in which only the husband participates); female breadwinners (in which only the wife participates); and no earners (in which neither participates). Differences in occupational prestige result in *prsdif* (the husband's occupational prestige minus the wife's); *prseq* (when the husband and wife have the same occupational prestige score, within one point of each other); and *prsconv* (indicating that the differences are conventional: the husband has the same or more occupational prestige than his wife).

These indicators of spousal equality in achievement are related to (1) husband's age, which also serves as an indicator of *cohort*, wife's age, and *agedif* (husband's age minus wife's age); (2) *age at marriage* of husband and of wife; and (3) *number of children*.

AGE DIFFERENCES BETWEEN
JEWISH HUSBANDS AND WIVES

Because traditional norms of husbands being older than their wives lend themselves to traditional status differences between husbands and wives, it was important to establish the extent to which husbands and wives differed by age. Age patterns of Jewish husbands and wives do tend to be quite traditional (Table 5.1). The great majority (84 percent) of husbands are the same age or older than their wives; 27.6 percent are five or more years older than their wives; 9 percent are ten or more years older than their wives. In the 16 percent of the couples in which the wife is older than the husband, only in 3 percent of the couples are the wives five or more years older than their husbands.

Jews tend to be somewhat more traditional than the wider American population. More marriages have conventional age differences (husbands older than wife) and somewhat fewer have nonconventional age differences (wives older than husbands). This may be related to the relatively

TABLE 5.1
Age Differences of Husbands and Wives,
U.S. Jews (1990) and Total Population (1985, 1980)

	U.S. Jews	U.S. Total
Husband older than wife (total)	72.2	67.1[b]
Husband older (5+ years)	27.6	26.9[c]
Husband same age as wife[d]	11.5	10.8[b]
Wife older than husband (total)	16.3	22.1[b]
Wife older than husband (5+ years)	3.6	3.1[c]
Total	100.0	100.0
(Unweighted *n*)	(1,413)[a]	(40,155)

[a]*Source:* NJPS, 1990.
[b]*Source:* 1985 data reported in *Statistical Abstract of the U.S., 1990* (reproduced in Chadwick and Heaton, 1992, Table A2-3).
[c]*Source:* 1980 U.S. census data reported in Atkinson and Glass (1985): Table 2.
[d]Within one year of each other.

older age composition of the Jewish population (cf. Goldstein, 1992), because age homogamy between spouses has been increasing in recent cohorts in the wider American population (Atkinson and Glass, 1985) and in the American Jewish population as well. As Table 5.2 shows, the average difference between spouses was much greater for couples in which the husband is 65 or over and is increasingly smaller until in the youngest cohort (34 or younger), the average difference in age is less than one year.

This change in age differences results from a decline in average age at marriage of Jewish men, while the average age of Jewish women marrying has remained fairly stable (Table 5.3). (In Table 5.2 we have included the total population who married, rather than only the currently married,

TABLE 5.2
Age Differences of Husbands and Wives, by Husband's Age, U.S. Jews, 1990

Husband's Age	Mean Age Difference	(Unweighted n)
Under 35	.4	(277)
35–44	2.0	(449)
45–64	4.3	(430)
65+	5.1	(257)
Total	2.9	(1,413)

Source: NJPS, 1990.

TABLE 5.3
Mean Age at Marriage, by Age and Sex, U.S. Jews, 1990

Age	Men	(N in thousands)	Women	(N in thousands)
Under 35	25.8	(179)	23.5	(243)
35–44	26.2	(358)	24.7	(363)
45–64	26.2	(465)	22.0	(487)
65+	28.0	(361)	24.7	(346)
Total	26.6	(1,363)	23.6	(1,438)

Source: NJPS, 1990.

because this shows the trends in age at marriage regardless of current marital stability.)

Traditional age differences may reinforce traditional status differences by giving husbands an advantage in terms of educational attainment at time of marriage; further, if women are more likely to marry at an earlier age than men, they are more likely to interrupt their education when they marry, especially when they marry young. The traditional age difference also gives husbands a head-start in terms of occupational achievement (which is often reinforced by asymmetrical support of the husband's occupation by his spouse, as in the "two-person career" discussed by Papanek, 1973, and others). Therefore, couples with larger age differences are more likely to have greater educational and occupational dissimilarity as well.

The traditional age differences common to the Jewish population are thus likely to perpetuate traditional education and status differences, as we have suggested already. The increasing age homogamy of younger couples suggests that differences in education, and resulting differences in occupational achievement, will also be smaller in younger cohorts.

EDUCATION DIFFERENCES BETWEEN JEWISH HUSBANDS AND WIVES

Among American Jewish couples, the mean education of all wives is 14.9; of Jewish husbands is 15.6. As we saw in Chapter 2, married men and women have somewhat lower educational achievement than the never married, separated, or divorced. The differences are particularly large for women.

One reason that married men have somewhat less education on the average is due to their relatively older age. The mean age of married men is 51.7, compared to the mean age of all Jewish men, 49.0. Married women are younger than the population of all Jewish women, because although the unmarried Jewish women include the never married (generally younger), they include an even larger percentage of widows (who are older). However, more women are likely to marry at an age that interrupts their education. Even though few Jewish men or women dropped out of high school to marry, it is common to marry between the ages of 20 and 26, which could affect the completion of college or graduate school. Although less than 7 percent of Jewish men married under the age of 21, 30 percent of Jewish women did, and nearly 20 percent of the women married under the age of 20. Such ages at marriage are likely to reduce the number of women continuing on to graduate school or even completing college.

Nevertheless, the ratio of Jewish wives' and husbands' mean education is very similar to the ratio of years of education of all Jewish men and women. This suggests that assortative mating among Jews does not bring about greater educational inequality than is found among the wider Jewish population; otherwise there would be larger differences between all Jewish husbands and wives than between men and women in the general Jewish population.

On the contrary, Jewish spouses tend to have the same education. In nearly half (45.6 percent) of the couples husbands and wives have virtually the same number of years of education (within one year of each other). Furthermore, most of the heterogamous marriages are conventional: in over 80 percent of the Jewish couples husbands have the same or more education than their wives. Only in about a fifth of the couples (19.0 percent) do wives have more education than their husbands. Differences, however, are limited: only in 11.5 percent of the couples are differences more than five years in either direction (in 9 percent the husband has five or more years of education more than their wives; in 2.5 percent wives have five or more years of education more than their husbands). The extent of educational homogamy among Jewish couples is very similar to the wider American population, in which about half of the marriages are educationally homogamous (Kalmijn, 1991b; Kominski and Adams, 1992, Table 5).

The tendency to educational homogamy seems to be on the increase in the wider American population (Kalmijn, 1991b). Similarly, among Jewish couples, educational homogamy seems to be increasing. Among the youngest cohort of couples (husband's age less than 35), there is less than half a year difference between husband's and wife's education on the average; in contrast, among couples in which the husband is 45–64, the mean difference in years of education is more than a year. Among the oldest cohort (husband 65 and over), the difference is somewhat lower, because fewer men went on to graduate school than they do today (as we saw in Chapter 3). More than 36 percent of the couples in the youngest cohort have education within a year of each other, compared to 30 percent of the oldest cohort. The conventionality of the differences, however, has remained at a fairly stable 80 percent over the cohorts.

Contrary to our expectations, age differences are not related significantly to educational differences between the couples (the Pearson correlation between the spouses' age difference and their difference in years of education is –.003); that is, larger age differences between husbands and wives do not necessarily bring about larger differences in education. This may be more likely in populations whose range of educational level is greater than among American Jews and when early marriages (which interrupt education) are more common.

Because most higher education results in an academic degree in a similar way for both Jewish men and women (as we have seen in Chapter 2), differences of degree are similar to that of years of education. In nearly half of the couples, the husbands and wives have achieved the same academic degree; in about 80 percent of the couples, differences of degree are conventional (husbands have the same degree or higher than their wives); and in 20 percent of the couples the wives have higher degrees than their husbands (Table 5.4).

Husbands are more likely to have the same degree as their wives than would be expected randomly (see the diagonal in Table 5.4), and there is also a tendency for degree differences to be conventional; that is, husbands have higher degrees than their wives (the cells in boldface, mostly in the lower left corner of the table). On the other hand, we find fewer wives with nonacademic degrees marrying husbands with academic degrees than we would expect randomly (the italicized cells in the upper right corner of the table). So there is a tendency to educational homogamy, and when there are differences, for the differences to be conventional.

The magnitude of inequality between spouses also tends to be conventional, in that the inequality tends to be greater when the husband has a higher degree than his wife than when the wife has a higher degree than her husband. Among husbands with M.A.s, for instance, 23 percent of their wives have no college degree. Among wives with M.A.s, on the other hand, only 12 percent of their husbands have no college degree.

When we compare the degrees of Jewish spouses to the degrees of all Jewish men and women, we find hardly any difference: 13.7 percent of the Jewish wives would need higher degrees to have the same academic degrees as their husbands; 13.2 percent of all Jewish women would need higher degrees to have the same degrees as all Jewish men (Table 5.5). This reinforces the conclusion reached previously that gender dissimilarity in education between Jewish spouses is no greater than among the wider Jewish population.

TABLE 5.4
Husband's Academic Degree, by Wife's Academic Degree, U.S. Jewish Couples, 1990

Husband's Degree	Wife's Degree				
	Noncollege	B.A.	M.A.	Ph.D., Professional[a]	Total
Noncollege	31.0 (19.9)	6.1 (11.4)	3.0 (7.8)	.2 (1.3)	40.4
B.A.	11.0 (13.9)	11.5 (8.0)	5.3 (5.5)	.4 (.9)	28.3
M.A.	11.0 (8.1)	5.4 (4.6)	6.1 (3.2)	.6 (.5)	16.4
Ph.D., professional	2.7 (7.3)	5.2 (4.2)	4.9 (2.9)	2.1 (.5)	14.9
Total %	49.2	28.2	19.3	3.3	100.0
(Unweighted n)					(1,395)

Note: Total percentage is shown, with expected percentage in parentheses. Italics indicate observed percentage significantly less than expected; bold indicates observed percentage significantly more than expected.
[a]This includes medical, dental, and law degrees.

Source: NJPS, 1990.

TABLE 5.5
Highest Academic Degree of U.S. Jewish Husbands and Wives, and of All U.S. Jewish Men and Women, 1990

Highest Academic Degree	Jewish Husbands	Jewish Wives	All Jewish Men	All Jewish Women
None	4.3	2.8	4.5	3.0
High school	31.4	39.4	29.6	40.3
A.A., R.N.	4.7	7.0	4.3	5.2
B.A.	28.3	28.2	31.3	28.9
M.A.	16.4	19.3	16.2	19.1
Ph.D., professional[b]	14.9	3.3	14.4	3.5
Total	100.0	100.0	100.0	100.0
(N)[a]	(1,395)	(1,395)	(1,867)	(1,814)

[a]For couples, unweighted n; for total Jewish population, N in thousands, using population weights .
[b]This includes medical, dental, and law degrees.

Source: NJPS, 1990.

In sum, with regard to our hypotheses about educational inequality of Jewish spouses, we find that none of our hypotheses is validated: spousal inequality among Jewish couples differs little from the wider American population; there is no greater inequality within Jewish couples than within the wider Jewish population as a whole; and spousal educational inequality is not related to age differences of Jewish spouses.

PARTICIPATION IN THE PAID LABOR FORCE AMONG JEWISH COUPLES

Spousal participation in the paid labor force has increasingly come to be considered a household decision rather than a decision made without taking into account the family context. While the variation in wives' labor force participation is greater than of husbands', most Jewish women do participate in the labor force at some time in their lives as we have shown (98 percent of the wives in the couple sample had), even if at any given time a much smaller percentage are participating (60 percent were in the paid labor force at the time of the survey). Although men's labor force participation is more stable than women's over the life cycle, it is lower when men are students and later, when they retire. Therefore the couples could exhibit one of four patterns of labor force participation: the dual earner couple, in which both spouses are in the labor force; the male breadwinner couple, in which only the husband participates; the female breadwinner couple, in which only the wife participates; and the no earner couple, in which neither spouse participates. The recent increase in dual earning couples is reflected in a growing literature that relates the incidence and effects of dual earning to other aspects of married life and to the social context in which it develops (e.g., Lewis, Izraeli, and Hootsmans, 1992; Mocanachie, 1989). As we shall see, American Jewish couples are well integrated into this trend toward dual earning patterns.

Over half of the couples (55 percent) are dual earner couples. In 26 percent, the husband is employed outside the home but the wife is not. Of course, the case in which the wife is more active in the economic arena than the husband is rarer than the reverse, occurring in only 5 percent of the couples. In 14 percent neither is employed.

It should be noted that these figures are very similar to the wider American population. According to the U.S. Bureau of Labor Statistics (1990, Table 8), 52 percent of the married couples in 1989 were dual earners; in 27 percent, husbands were in the labor force but wives were not; in 4 percent, wives were in the labor force but husbands were not; and in 17 percent, neither was employed in the labor force.

This similarity of the Jewish couples to the wider American population is actually somewhat surprising, since the educational level of Jewish men and women is considerably higher than the general population and the Jewish population is considerably older than the American population. The more educated population would lead us to expect different labor force participation patterns from the general population for three reasons: (1) fewer spouses would be working up to ages 24 (or even 30), while one or both of the spouses are still in school; (2) more highly educated wives would increase the proportion of dual earner couples; and (3) more highly educated spouses would retire at a later age than other spouses. Among all American couples in which the husband or the wife had some college education (a subpopulation similar to the Jewish subpopulation in education), a higher percentage (60.9 percent) of the couples were dual earners in 1988 than among all couples (Chadwick and Heaton, 1992, Table G1-26); and in only 10 percent did neither the husband nor wife work in the paid labor force.

We have few couples who married before the age of 25 in our sample, but there is a slightly lower percentage of dual earners when husbands and wives are young, suggesting that one of the spouses are supporting the other while he or she finishes college (see Table 5.6). After the main ages of higher education (from age 25), and through the main ages of the working life cycle (up to 54), about two-thirds of the couples are dual earners; fewer than 30 percent of the couples have male breadwinners. This constant percentage of dual earners reflects the relatively high percentage of wives who continue to be in the labor force during the main childbearing and childrearing years, as is expected of a highly educated population. When the husband reaches retirement age, the wife (who is usually younger) may continue to work for a short while, so that there is a somewhat higher percentage of female breadwinner couples when husbands are 55–64 and even more when the husband is 65 or older. Because women tend to retire earlier than men, there is also an increase in the male breadwinner couples when the wife reaches 55. By the time the wife is 65 or older, in most couples both husband and wife are no longer in the paid labor force, and only 7 percent continue to be dual earners.

This change in couple's labor force patterns over the life cycle is similar to the wider American population (seen in Table 5.6). The percentage of dual earners is fairly constant in the main working life stages, 25–54, and begins to drop as wives and then husbands retire. What is different is the relatively lower percentage of dual earners among American Jews in couples where the husband is under 25, because of the longer education period of Jews who continue on in higher proportion to higher education. Also, the percentage of dual earners among American Jews is somewhat higher among older husbands, which can also be explained by the higher

TABLE 5.6
Types of Couples in Terms of Husband's and Wife's
Paid Labor Force Participation, by Husband's and Wife's Age,
U.S. Jewish and Total Couples, 1990

	No Earner	Female Breadwinner	Male Breadwinner	Dual Earner	Total % (Unweighted n)
U.S. Jews:					
Wife's age					
Under 25	8.3	8.3	36.0	47.2	100.0 (36)
25–34	1.5	4.2	27.9	66.4	100.0 (333)
25–44	1.3	3.7	27.4	67.5	100.0 (456)
45–54	5.3	4.0	24.8	65.9	100.0 (226)
55–64	22.2	11.9	30.3	35.7	100.0 (185)
65 and over	70.8	4.5	17.4	7.3	100.0 (178)
Total %	13.6	5.2	26.4	54.7	100.0 (1,414)
Husband's age					
Under 25	5.0	10.0	40.0	45.0	100.0 (20)
25–34	1.6	5.1	26.8	66.5	100.0 (257)
35–44	1.1	2.4	29.0	67.5	100.0 (449)
45–54	2.6	3.9	25.3	68.2	100.0 (233)
55–64	14.7	5.6	28.4	51.2	100.0 (197)
65 and over	57.6	10.5	19.8	12.1	100.0 (257)
Total %	13.7	5.2	26.4	54.8	100.0 (1,413)
U.S. Total:					
Husband's age					
Under 25	1.4	2.0	28.5	68.1	100.0 (1,721)
25–34	1.2	1.6	30.9	66.3	100.0 (11,551)
25–44	1.4	1.9	27.0	69.7	100.0 (12,449)
45–54	3.0	3.6	28.8	64.6	100.0 (9,079)
55–64	20.3	9.3	32.0	38.4	100.0 (8,247)
65 and over	73.2	9.3	12.0	5.4	100.0 (8,762)
Total %	16.8	4.6	26.5	52.1	100.0 (51,809)

Source: Jews, NJPS, 1990; all American couples, Chadwick and Heaton, 1992, Table G1-26.

education of both American Jewish husbands and wives. That these extended years of dual earner couples do not result in a higher overall percentage of American Jewish couples who are dual earners can be attributed to the older composition of the American Jewish population.

Most of the "no earner" couples consist of husbands and wives over 65. The female breadwinner couples are relatively uncommon in the main labor force participation ages of 25–64 and are more common in couples where the husband is 60 and presumably retired or when the husband is under 30 and presumably still in school.

The most common labor force types in the main stages of the working life cycle are therefore the dual earner couples and the male breadwinner couples. These two types of couples—the dual earners and male breadwinners—differ from each other in a number of aspects. As we have seen, dual earners tend to be younger couples than male breadwinners. As they get older, because women tend to retire earlier than men, many couples become male breadwinner types until the husband retires also. The couples differ both in terms of the mean age of the husband and of the wife.

Dual earner and male breadwinner couples do not differ much in terms of husband's and wife's years of education (although the difference in education between dual earner and male breadwinner wives is statistically significant, the difference is less than a year on the average). Dual earner husbands do not differ from male breadwinner husbands in degree earned either. What does differ considerably is that dual earner wives are more likely to have a college degree: 28 percent of the dual earner wives have M.A.s or higher degrees compared to 16.8 percent of the male breadwinner wives; 5 percent of the dual earner wives have Ph.D.s or professional degrees, compared to less than 1 percent of the male breadwinner types.

The large difference between dual earner and male breadwinner families in terms of how many children they have is not surprising, given the well-known negative link between female labor force participation and mothering. But a great deal of this difference can be explained by the cohort composition of the couples. We define cohorts here by the husband's age, the oldest cohort born around World War I, the second cohort born between the wars up until the end of World War II, the third cohort being baby boomers, the youngest cohort born after the baby boom. As we have shown, younger couples tend to be dual earners, and younger couples have fewer children than couples in older cohorts did (Table 5.7).

TABLE 5.7
Mean Number of Children, by Cohort, for Male Breadwinner
and Dual Earner Couples, U.S. Jews, 1990

	Oldest Cohort	Second Cohort	Third Cohort	Youngest Cohort
Male breadwinners	2.2	2.4	2.2	1.9
Dual earners	2.1	2.0	1.6	.9
(Unweighted *n*)	(257)	(330)	(449)	(277)

Source: NJPS, 1990.

However, even within cohorts, there is a difference in number of children between dual earners and male breadwinners, which is especially pronounced in the youngest cohorts (when children are younger). The differences in number of children among male breadwinner families changes little over the generations, but the number of children among dual-earners is significantly lower in younger cohorts.

We had expected to find that husbands in male breadwinner couples would show higher occupational achievement, since more family support might be available than when both spouses are working. In "two-person careers," advancement is strongly related to family support or "backstage wealth" (and this is generally greater for husbands than for wives because more wives have time and inclination to play these support roles; Fowlkes, 1987; Lopata, 1993; Papanek, 1973). However, the occupational prestige of dual earner husbands does not differ significantly from the prestige of male breadwinner husbands. Similarly, the occupations of the husbands in the male breadwinner families are very similar to those of the dual earner families (Table 5.8): only 6.4 percent of the husbands in the male breadwinner families would have to change their occupations to have the same distribution as the husbands in the dual earner families.

Given the significance of equal labor force participation for gender relations within the family, it is interesting to summarize how couples with more equal labor force participation differ. We noted that they are younger, which indicates that more egalitarian relationships within the family are on the increase; they have fewer children, which means that there are fewer family roles to invest in and allocate; and more of their wives have academic degrees, which suggests that higher education of wives brings about greater equality in division of economic roles in the marriage. Because women's education is increasing, this also reinforces the expectation that equal labor force participation patterns will become more and more common.

HUSBAND AND FAMILY CHARACTERISTICS
AS INFLUENCES ON WIFE'S LABOR FORCE
PARTICIPATION IN AMERICAN JEWISH COUPLES

One of the issues related to the equal labor force activity of the spouses is the extent to which husband's characteristics affect the wife's labor force behavior. Because of the importance of wife's labor force participation for equal status and power within the family, it is a mark of independence if the wife's labor force behavior is independent of her husband's characteristics or family obligations. Previous research has not been conclusive

TABLE 5.8
Occupations of Husbands in Dual Earner and Male Breadwinner Couples, U.S. Jews, 1990

	Professional, Technical	Academic	Managerial, Administrative	Clerical, Sales	Service, Blue Collar	Total %	(Unweighted n)	Coefficient of Dissimilarity[a]
Male Breadwinners	27.8	11.3	20.1	21.5	19.3	100.0	(363)	6.4
Dual earners	30.4	14.1	17.9	17.3	20.3	100.0	(738)	

[a]For dissimilarity calculations, see note to Table 4.2.

Source: NJPS, 1990.

with regard to how dependent wives' behavior is on familial and spousal considerations. Geerken and Gove (1983) in an American sample and Mocanachie (1989) in a South African sample found that husband's income did affect whether or not the wife was working, but differed in terms of the effect of husband's education and occupational prestige (Mocanachie found them influential, while Geerken and Gove did not). Wives' labor force participation has been shown to be related to her husband's occupation (and, in earlier studies, to social class, which was indicated primarily by the husband's occupation) in contradictory ways: when the husband's occupation is low, the couple feels a greater need for the additional income a wife's job can bring in; when the husband's occupation is high, even though the need for additional income may not be as great, leisure may be easier to come by and substitutes for the wife in the home (as mother, housewife, cook) easier to afford and wives may turn to the labor force for greater interest in their lives. There is thus a curvilinear relationship between social class, indicated by husband's occupation or income, and wife's labor force participation. Further, husbands with high occupations are more likely to marry a spouse of similar social class and educational background, who has appropriate training to make it worthwhile and interesting to work in the labor force. As women achieve higher and higher education, this latter effect becomes more common.

There has also been indication that wives who are more educated than their husbands may refrain from labor force participation to avoid stressful competition over relative occupational status (Hertz, 1986; Philliber and Hiller, 1983). We will include the interaction of husband and wife characteristics on wife's labor force participation to consider this aspect as well.

To study this, we fitted a logistic regression to the data predicting wives' labor force participation. What differs from our previous analysis of women's labor force participation is that here we include characteristics of the wife's husband in addition to family characteristics and the woman's own characteristics as influences on her participation.

Because the relationship between her participation and some of the husband's characteristics was not linear, the indicators of husband's age, education, and occupation were broken down into categories, each of which was defined as a variable (much like dummy variables), so that we could isolate at which levels the characteristic had an influence of the wife's behavior. As with dummy variables, not all categories could be included in the model, so the youngest cohort, lowest educational category, and lowest occupational category were eliminated.

The final model (presented in Table 5.9) correctly predicts the labor force participation of over 70 percent of the wives (980/1414). It shows that in addition to the wife's age, her academic degree, and how many

TABLE 5.9
Logistic Regression of Wife's Paid Labor Force Participation, U.S. Jews, 1990

Dependent Variable	Unstandardized Regression Coefficient	Significance
Wife's age	−.054	.000
Wife's degree	.141	.005
Number of children under 18	−.320	.000
Husband's degree		
High school diploma	.195	.597
A.A.	−.369	.095
B.A.	1.034	.084
M.A.	−.008	.975
Ph.D.	.224	.484
Cohort (Age)		
Husband 65+	5.090	.000
Husband 45–64	0.056	.229
Husband 35–44	−1.085	.247
Interaction of wife's education and husband's degree		
High school diploma	−.226	.093
A.A.	.127	.104
B.A.	−.022	.902
M.A.	−.029	.683
Ph.D.	−.047	.551
Interaction of number of children under 18 and		
Husband 65+	.243	.005
Husband 45–64	.083	.405
Husband 35–44	−.112	.237
Interaction of wife's age and		
Husband 65+	−.099	.000
Husband 45–64	.009	.574
Husband 35–44	.016	.489
Constant	3.538	.000
(Unweighted *n*)	(1,414)	

Source: NJPS, 1990.

children under 18 the couple has (influences on women's labor force participation we have already discussed in Chapter 4), husband's degree and husband's age also have significant contributions that improve the prediction. Because husband's occupation made no significant contribution to the explanation of the variance in wife's labor force participation, it was dropped from the model. We will concentrate here on the ways in which husband's characteristics affect the wife's labor force activity.

The husband's education affects his wife's participation only at certain levels of education. When husbands have no academic degree, their wives' labor force participation is independent of the husband's education—apparently related more to what kind of a job she can get (as indicated by her education) and how much it will cost her in terms of finding a substitute for her family roles (i.e., how many children she has). Only 15 percent of the wives in this group have college degrees, so the question of large status differences affects very few. At the other extreme, when husbands have M.A.s, Ph.D.s, or professional degrees, the wives' labor force participation is also independent of his education. In this group there can be little question of status problems, as the husband has a high status and there is less chance that the wife would attain higher status than he. However, in the middle ranges of education, the higher the husband's education is, the more the wife works. A full 85 percent of the wives of husbands with B.A.s work—even among women with a high school diploma only, 81 percent are working. In these families, both husband and wife share the ambition for upward mobility, which necessitates a dual income; they can afford the substitutes for household labor that enable the wife to work outside the home; and they have not yet reached a level where they can afford to have the wife not work and still maintain their economic status (as may happen in the highest educational levels of husbands).

The interaction between husband's and wife's education has a slight negative effect, and it appears only in the lowest categories of husband's education: in these groups, the wife would participate more if her husband had a higher educational level, especially women who have no academic degree. The question seems less one of status competition than of perceived labor force opportunities being lower when the husband's education is lower (otherwise, the effect would be greatest for women with much higher degrees than their husbands).

Our finding that there is an interaction between the husband's and wife's education only at some levels of education may also explain why husband's characteristics have more effect on wife's labor force participation in some populations than in others—it depends on the educational level of the husbands in the particular population. When the husband has a college degree, the wife's labor force participation is not affected by the comparison of her education to her husband's. At these levels, there is no evidence that wives who have more education than their husbands refrain from participating in the labor force because they fear status competition nor that they refrain from participating because they would have to enter a job at a much lower level than their husbands. We will discuss these status differences further when we discuss occupational combinations of husbands and wives. At this point we can conclude that the comparison of husband's and wife's education affects the wife's labor force participation only when the husband has lower education. Because most Jewish husbands have college educations, we find an effect of the interaction between husbands' and wives' education in relatively few couples, most of whom belong to an older cohort with lower education.

Husband's occupation and husband's occupational prestige have no effect on wife's labor force participation. The lack of effect of husband's occupational prestige does not support previous findings that if husbands have higher occupations, the family can afford for the wife not to bring in income; on the contrary, we find no evidence that in male breadwinner couples the husbands have higher occupations. Nor is there evidence that in dual earner families wives have to participate in the paid labor force because their husbands do not have high enough incomes to support the family.[4]

The cohort, indicated by husband's age group (as explained previously), does affect whether the wife is working. In fact, the effect of the husband's age (or cohort) explains more of the variance in the wife's labor force participation than her own age. The main effect is in the oldest cohort of the husband: the wife's labor force participation is especially low when her husband is 65 or older, even if she is at an age at which she would normally not yet retire. Apparently husband's retirement tends to bring about an earlier retirement for her. There is also an interaction effect of the husband's and wife's age, which again is explained by the effect of the husband being in the oldest cohort (65+) hastening the wife's retirement, especially when she herself is older.

The number of children under 18 the couple has is also related to whether the wife works—the more children, the more family roles conflict with participation in the labor force outside the home, as we have discussed more thoroughly in Chapter 4. The significant effect of children on the labor force participation of wives does seem to contradict our finding that the proportion of dual earner couples remains constant between the main childbearing and childrearing ages of 25 and 54. One explanation for this would be that the effect of having a child is relatively temporary (while the child is young) and Jewish families have on the average few children, at planned intervals, often spread over the fertility period. However, the planning of different families does not necessarily coincide; hence, not all women are affected at the same age by having young children not to work in the labor force, but rather the temporary effect is spread fairly evenly throughout the fertility period.

In summary, wife's labor force participation is influenced by both her husband's education and age, in addition to her own age, her own education, and how many children she has at home. Having an older husband and having husbands with certain levels of education restrict wives' labor force participation; but other levels of husband's education facilitate or encourage the wife's participation. In particular, more women are likely to participate when their husbands have B.A.s, probably because these are the couples with the most invested in upward mobility. Wives of husbands with lower education are less likely to participate than other women with the same educational qualifications, but the explanation seems to be less out of fear of status competition and more out of mutual perception of labor market opportunities. Wives are also influenced to retire earlier when their husband is older (65+) and himself retired. The evidence points to an influence of joint lifestyle on wife's labor force participation, rather than an imposed restriction on the independence of the wife's behavior.

OCCUPATIONS OF DUAL EARNER SPOUSES IN AMERICAN JEWISH COUPLES

In this section we compare the occupational achievement of husbands and wives who are currently in the labor force.[5] Philliber and Vannoy-Hiller (1990) show that a wife's occupational achievement is affected by her husband's occupational attainment: among wives of similar education, the payoff in terms of occupational achievement is greater for wives whose husbands have higher occupational attainment. Other studies have shown that the productivity of wives whose husbands are in the same occupation is greater than those whose husbands are in different occupations (Bryson, et. al., 1978).

A wife's characteristics also influence her husband's achievement. In an earlier study we showed how the husbands' occupational attainment is enhanced by his wife's labor force participation (Hartman and Hartman, 1985). Wives are often expected to fulfill certain supportive roles for their husband's occupation (Fowlkes, 1987); if they have their own careers, however, such roles may detract from their own career progress (Heckman, et. al., 1977). As the Rapoports (1978) suggested, dual career wives are simultaneously facilitated and exploited.

In the following we consider the extent to which the occupations of American Jewish husbands and wives are related and the extent to which characteristics of the spouses are related to the occupational achievement of their husbands or wives.

Husbands and wives have different occupations. More than a fifth of the wives (coefficient of dissimilarity = 21.2) would have to change occupations to have the same occupational distribution as their husbands. A large part of the dissimilarity between husbands and wives is, as in the wider population, that the husbands are more likely to be in professional, managerial, blue-collar, or service jobs than are the wives, while wives are more likely than men to be in either academic or clerical occupations (Table 5.10). The difference between husbands' and wives' occcupations is, however, very similar to the dissimilarity between occupations of all Jewish men and women (23.9). In other words, the difference in occupational achievement of Jewish husbands and wives is no greater than would be expected from the inequality between men and women in the wider Jewish population: assortative mating and processes of spousal differentiation do not increase inequalities in occupational achievement any more than they increase inequalities in age or education.

There is some tendency for spouses to marry spouses in the same occupational group, which brings about a statistically significant[6] association between husbands' and wives' occupations, but the relationship is not particularly strong[7] (Table 5.10). There is also a tendency for professional, academic, and managerial wives to marry professional husbands; and for wives with sales or clerical positions to marry husbands with blue-collar or service jobs. On the other hand, professional, academic, and managerial husbands are not likely to marry wives with sales, clerical, blue-collar, or service jobs; nor are professional, academic, or managerial wives likely to marry husbands with sales, clerical, blue-collar, or service jobs. In other words there is some congruence of occupations even when the occupational groups of husbands and wives are not identical, but there is also a certain randomness in occupational combinations of spouses.

Collapsing our occupational categories to upper/upper-middle class (professional, managerial,[8] and academic); middle class (sales, clerical); and lower/lower-middle class (blue collar, service), we find that 58.1 percent of the spouses are of a similar occupational class; that is, over 40 percent of the marriages are "cross-class," somewhat higher than has been found in other capitalist countries. Leiulfsrud and Woodward (1988) and Wright, et. al. (1992), in cross-national studies, found about one-third of the marriages to be cross-class. Some caution is in order in these comparisons, because the other research included a much higher percentage of working-class husbands and wives than is found among the Jewish population, and their occupational classifications are somewhat different from ours.

What is especially striking among the Jewish sample, however, is the direction of heterogeneity. Instead of more than two-thirds of the heterogeneous couples being in the direction that the husband has a higher class than his wife, as in the other studies, among the "cross-class" Jewish dual earners, two-thirds are in the opposite direction: the wife has a

TABLE 5.10

Occupations of Husbands, by Occupations of Wives, U.S. Jews, 1990

Husband's Occupation	Wife's Occupation					
	Professional, Technical	Academic	Managerial, Administrative	Sales, Clerical	Blue Collar, Service	Total %
Professional, technical	75	58	34	49	8	224
	(53.1)	(55.2)	(33.7)	(62.5)	(19.4)	(30.4)
	33.5	31.9	15.2	21.9	3.6	100.0
Academic	24	46	10	18	6	104
	(24.7)	(25.6)	(15.6)	(29.0)	(9.0)	(14.1)
	23.1	44.2	9.6	17.3	5.8	100.0
Managerial, administrative	28	31	32	32	9	132
	(31.3)	(32.6)	(19.9)	(36.8)	(11.4)	(17.9)
	21.2	23.5	24.2	24.2	6.8	100.0
Sales, clerical	25	22	16	57	8	128
	(30.4)	(31.6)	(19.3)	(35.7)	(11.1)	(17.3)
	19.5	17.2	12.5	44.5	6.3	100.0
Blue collar, service	23	25	19	50	33	150
	(35.6)	(37.0)	(22.6)	(41.9)	(13.0)	(20.3)
	15.3	16.7	12.7	33.3	22.0	100.0
Total %	175	182	111	206	206	738
	23.7	24.7	15.0	27.9	8.7	100.0

Note: Actual count, expected frequencies in parentheses, row percentages in italics.

Source: NJPS, 1990.

higher class than her husband. This is brought about by so many of the wives being academic (teachers) or clerical, but relatively more of the men are in sales or blue-collar jobs. Because fewer of the women are in blue-collar or service jobs than men, they could not all marry within the same occupational class and had no choice but to marry a woman in a higher occupational class. This suggests that the high education of Jewish wives undermines the expected traditional pattern of husbands having higher occupational class than their wives.

A different way of comparing occupational achievement is to compare the occupational prestige scores of husbands and wives. We find a relatively high percentage of wives who have the same or higher occupational prestige than their husbands (51 percent). Husbands have higher prestige than their wives in 49 percent of the couples.

As we have discussed already, there is indication that spousal characteristics are related to occupational achievement for a number of reasons: the extent of support available from the family, the mutual understanding of work demands, the allocation of familial and household roles that may take away from career advancement. To determine the effect of spousal and family characteristics on occupational achievement, we predicted each spouse's occupational prestige with a stepwise multiple regression (Table 5.11).

Predicting the wife's occupational prestige, we found a significant association between the husband's prestige and the wife's prestige—a beta coefficient of .262 ($\alpha < .000$). But when we added to that her education, the beta coefficient of husband's prestige is reduced to half (.131, still significant), and that coefficient is only a third of the effect of her own education on her prestige. In other words, her own education predicts her occupational achievement much better than her husband's prestige, but her occupational prestige is enhanced by her husband's, possibly because higher prestige indicates higher incomes and hence the ability to afford extra help to alleviate some of the dual roles working women assume. When we looked at the prediction of wife's occupational prestige for various age groups, the husband's prestige was significant only for the youngest cohort; that is, the cohort in which family roles most conflict with career demands. This supports the interpretation that at this age the added income indicated by her husband having a more prestigious job allows the couple to afford substitutes for domestic and childcare labor so the wife (who would otherwise carry more family roles) can devote more to maintaining a prestigious job.

Contrary to common expectations, the wife's occupational prestige is not affected by how many children she has nor the age at which she started having children. Because the variation in number of children is low and most families do not have more than two children and because of the

TABLE 5.11
Stepwise Multiple Regression Analyses of
Husband's and Wife's Occupational Prestige,[a] U.S. Jews, 1990

Step	Pearson Correlation[b]	Independent Variable	Standardized Regression Coefficient	Significance
Dependent variable: wife's occupational prestige				
Step 1	.262	Husband's occupational prestige	.262	.000
Step 2	.496	Husband's occupational prestige	.131	.004
		Wife's academic degree	.440	.000
Step 3	.519	Husband's occupational prestige	.089	.047
		Wife's academic degree	.465	.000
		Age at first child	.048	.336
		Number of children	.054	.240
Dependent variable: husband's occupational prestige				
Step 1	.262	Wife's occupational prestige	.262	.000
Step 2	.610	Wife's occupational prestige	.095	.004
		Husband's academic degree	.576	.000
(Unweighted n)				(1414)

[a]See explanation of occupational prestige in Chapter 4.
[b]Between dependent and independent variables.

Source: NJPS, 1990.

concentration of women in a few traditionally "female" occupations, apparently the role conflict introduced by having more children and at a younger age does not interfere with attaining prestige, especially when the husband's income allows the hiring of outside help.

Contrary to what might be expected, the wife's occupational achievement was not affected by her age. Apparently education differences of older and younger women are the main influence on occupational attainment and not the number of years in an occupation or career. This does not mean that the women in the younger cohort may not attain higher prestige during their careers—it means only that the comparison of older and younger women today does not show a significant difference in prestige when education is controlled.

Couple inequalities—differences in age and education—were also unrelated to the attainment of occupational prestige (for either wife or husband).

Similarly, the husband's occupational prestige is predicted mainly by his own education, although the wife's prestige has a secondary but significant effect. His age, the age difference between spouses, the difference in education of the spouses, and number of children do not contribute to the explanation of his prestige.

In summary, the attainment of occupational prestige on the part of both husbands and wives is mainly independent of their spouse's characteristics and related primarily to their own educational qualifications. That the findings are symmetrical for both husband and wife suggest an equality in the process of occupational attainment—Jewish wives are not unduly burdened by family roles or considerations of their husband's career in their occupational attainment. That a high percentage of Jewish wives have higher occupational prestige than their husbands also points in this direction—that Jewish wives are able to pursue occupational goals without being restrained by comparison to their husbands nor family obligations.

DISCUSSION

In this chapter we have looked at spousal inequality among Jewish couples. In general we found less interrelationship between the characteristics of husband and wife than we had expected. Of the five variables we considered—age, education, participation in the paid labor force, occupation, and occupational prestige—the two that mainly precede marriage through mate selection, age and education, had the strongest interrelationship; they were interrelated as strongly and as conventionally as the wider society—that is, in most Jewish marriages husbands are both older than their wives and more educated, despite the relatively high educational level of Jewish women.

Labor force behavior and occupational achievement were less closely interrelated. In over half of the Jewish couples, both the husbands and wifes participate in the paid labor force, but this was lower than we had expected given the relatively high education of Jewish wives. Further, the wife's labor force behavior was linked more to her own education and number of children than to any of her husband's characteristics. Occupational similarity was lower than was expected, and occupational prestige achieved was linked more to each spouse's own characteristics than to their partner's—although each spouse's characteristics had some significant effect on the other's achievement.

Some of the established findings concerning American couples—or more generally, couples in modern industrial societies—did not apply or applied only partially to the Jewish couples. For instance, decisions about wife's labor force participation are generally considered to take into account status comparisons between the husband and wife—but among the Jewish couples, the interaction of husband's and wife's education was not related to the wife's labor force behavior. Her labor force participation is often considered to be based on the husband's income and the consequent "need" for additional income, but neither husband's education nor occupation was related to whether the wife was in the labor force. Further research that includes data on the income of husbands and wives (not available in this survey) is needed to follow this up. Overall the wife's labor force participation was related more to her own characteristics than the spouse's. Some of this may be related to the restriction of range of education of both the husband and the wife, which results in a low level of education difference, on the one hand, and more equality between the spouses, on the other.

Conventionally wives are expected to have less occupational prestige than their husbands, but in over half of the Jewish couples the wife had the same or more occupational prestige than her husband. In contrast to other populations, heterogeneous marriages in terms of occupational class among the Jewish couples are even more likely to be between women of a higher class and men of a lower class than vice versa. Further research might follow up implications of these different patterns of occupational combinations in terms of power and dominance with the Jewish family. It may be that the sources of strength and dominance of the traditionally strong "Jewish mother" are changing but that the pattern itself is not.

Referring to the hypotheses presented in the introduction, we found that most of them were not supported: Jewish spouses are not more or less equal in age, education, or labor force behavior than the wider Jewish population. Their relatively high education does not seem to bring about more equality in labor force behavior than in the wider American population nor does it bring about greater equality in occupations. However, it is related to higher occupational achievements of Jewish wives, so that much of the inequality is in the direction of the wife achieving more than the husband. Their familistic orientation, indicated by number of children, has some limited effect on labor force behavior but, contrary to our expectations, did not affect occupational achievement among spouses who were employed.

PART 2

Are We One?
The Jewishness of
Gendered Patterns
of Secular Achievement

CHAPTER 6

Are We One?
How Jewish Involvement
Is Related to Gendered Patterns
of Secular Achievement

This chapter considers how much the patterns of gender equality in education and labor force activity are characteristic of all American Jews. In the previous chapters, we have placed American Jews in the context of the wider American society to highlight the ways in which the Jewish population is distinctive in its patterns. Here we shift our focus to differences among the Jews; we ask whether the Jews who are more involved in being Jewish differ in their patterns of gender equality from those who are less involved in being Jewish.

If the patterns we have seen earlier have their roots in Jewish orientations, then we would expect those who are more involved in being Jewish to show these patterns more clearly than those who are less involved in being Jewish. This contrasts with the expectations deriving from the secularization thesis that with modernization and its incumbent secularization, religion (in its entire complex of identity, belief, and practice) no longer has an influence on a wide range of social behaviors. Even though it is clear that religion is not dead—Americans are a very religious people if it is measured by belief in God and attending religious services (Roberts, 1990)—the impact of religion on wider aspects of social life is minimized, according to this secularization thesis.

In this chapter we return to our focus on individual Jews, except where noted otherwise. To explore the relationship between gender inequality and Jewish involvement, we had to develop a measure of Jewishness. The beginning part of this chapter describes our approach to this measure and the indices of Jewishness. We then relate these indices to the patterns of gender inequality we have described previously.

THE CONCEPT OF JEWISHNESS

Because Judaism prescribes *torat hayim*—a total way of life—the boundaries between secular and religious behavior have been less clearly distinguished than in religions more clearly "religious" in nature. Herberg (1956) drew a parallel between Judaism, Protestantism, and Catholicism in the United States, as religions, but he failed to "take into account the very great diversity of collective activities much beyond the purely religious field that developed from the religious congregational bases and that emphasized and articulated the collective, 'ethnic,' and even political components of Jewish identity . . ." (Eisenstadt, 1992, p. 130). Jewish activities, particularly in the United States, have not been restricted to religious institutions and behavior—and by the same token, Jewish religious institutions in the United States do not confine their activities to religious behavior.

> The synagogues and religious organizations that developed in the United States were not like those in the more traditional sectors of Jewish European society: a central focus, a traditional society, or a self-enclosed community with quite clearly structured boundaries. Nor, as in the case of the more diversified in patterns of Jewish life, in Eastern Europe, from about the last third of the nineteenth century, were they just one of many sectors or organizations, most of which no longer focused on religious life and organized mostly in the secular way, but oriented only to Jewish constituencies. Nor was the synagogue a purely religious organization in the modern Western European sense, which defined itself in a restricted religious sense, as distinct from ethnic or national ones, and which at most engaged in some religious education or philanthropic activities.
>
> The synagogue in the United States of course focused on religious activities, but such activities were not conceived as an all-encompassing, self-enclosed entity, but mainly as a basis for many other collective activities that no longer necessarily were religious. Nor was religion or religious activity the only manifestation of Jewish collective identity. (Eisenstadt, 1992, p. 130)

To separate "religious" activities from "secular" activities among the Jews is more difficult than with other religions, given the nature of the Jewish heritage—its all-encompassing nature—and later its institutionalization in the United States. As a result, involvement in being Jewish has often been studied not only as "religiosity" but as "Jewish identity" or as a combination of the two. Commenting on the distinction between ethnic or nationalistic identification and religiosity in Judaism, Herman (1977) notes that, "The two components are, however, so intertwined that they cannot be isolated without disturbing their essential character and distorting the nature of the Jewish identity" (p. 37). Although exclusively religious identification was more common in the nineteenth and early twentieth centuries, it "lost its attraction in the face of vehement racial antisemitism, the Holocaust, the achievements of the Zionist movement, and the establishment of the state of Israel. The destruction of Yiddish culture in Eastern Europe and the decline of its remnants in the West also undercut the foundations of a Jewish ethnic identity that could draw upon rich cultural resources with little regard to, or in opposition to, the religious heritage. Today, the ethnic or national component in Jewish identity may be the focal one for the majority of Jews in both the Diaspora and Israel, but it is expressed through symbols taken from the religious heritage" (Sharot, 1991, p. 257).

In their conceptualization of religious commitment, Glock and Stark (1965) arrived at five core dimensions of religiosity: the ritualistic, the ideological, the intellectual, the consequential, and the experiential. A review of various measures of Jewish identity (Philips, 1991) reveals a remarkable diversity of approaches among researchers as to how to operationalize this concept. Almost all include some measure of ritual observance (e.g., Cohen, 1983, 1988; Goldscheider, 1986). Others have included dimensions of knowledge or intellectual involvement; still others have attempted to measure "belief," what Himmelfarb (1982) designates as the "doctrinal" dimension of religiosity and Glock and Stark (1965) the ideological. Very little research has focused on the experiential (see Himmelfarb, 1982), which is apparently a less central element of the Jewish religion than of other religions. Most research has emphasized some element of communal affiliation or attachment—what might be considered expressions of the consequential dimension (that derivative of religiosity which affects the individual's relation to others rather than the individual's relation to God). However, in the Jewish religion, the emphasis on choseness and continuity of the Jewish people is an integral part of being Jewish, making it difficult to call communal affiliation and attachment a dimension deriving as a consequence of the other elements of religiosity. For some it is the central element of their Jewishness, and their ritualistic and intellectual contact may be a consequence of their communal affiliation rather than the other way around (see Phillips, 1991, on the direction of causality between these elements).

Measuring "Jewishness"

Convinced of its multidimensional nature, we consider involvement in the entire complex of commitments and behaviors that can be characterized as Jewish or "Jewishness." Rather than using a deductive approach to defining what the dimensions of that complex are—deciding on the dimensions a priori and selecting indicators appropriate for each dimension—we used an inductive approach, accepting the survey items as appropriate indicators and using factor analysis to develop the theory from the data; that is, to determine what dimensions of religiosity were apparent from the responses. Given the nature of this approach, the resulting factors could then be given a meaning by relating them to the theoretical precedents about Jewish religiosity and identity.[1]

Thirty items were included in an initial factor analysis, which suggested six factors of an acceptable eigenvalue (summarized in Appendix II); that is, six dimensions of statistical significance. Items that did not have high loading on any of the factors (i.e., were not well related to any of the dimensions) were eliminated. The actual factor scores, which measure the strength of Jewishness on each of the represented dimensions, were created at a second stage of factor analysis done separately for each factor, using the responses to the questions that had high loadings on the factor.[2]

It should be mentioned that many of the indicators come from the respondent's report of "household" practices, such as whether someone in the household lights Friday night candles or whether the Kashrut is observed in the household, rather than individual religiosity. However, we make an extension from the household characteristics to the individual's religious environment, and this is the basis for our analysis in this section. Since the questions asking about the individual's religious behavior (e.g., participation in Jewish organizations, attendance at synagogue) did not cluster in a factor different from the questions about the household practices, we feel justified in making this extension.[3]

Two types of ritual behavior were clearly differentiated by the factor analysis. That is, the statistical results of the factor analysis indicated a clear existence of two factors, and therefore these two aspects could not be combined.

The first factor (CEREMONY) reflects the more collective expressions of religious ritual and holiday celebrations, which typically take place in public or extended family settings. Having high loadings on this factor were attending synagogue services, belonging to a synagogue, attending a Passover seder, fasting on Yom Kippur, lighting Hanukkah candles, and contributing to some Jewish organization or cause.[4] These collective rituals and expressions of Jewish identity are practiced by the majority of American Jews. This factor explains more than 25 percent of the common variance of these Jewishness indicators, more than tripling the contribution of any other factor. As the most important factor among these indicators of Jewishness, it represents a dominant mode of expressing Jewishness among American Jews.

The second factor (RITUAL) reflected the more traditional type of religious ritual, based on halachic prescriptions. Having high loading on this factor were refraining from the use of money on Shabbat, fasting on the Fast of Esther (Ta'anit Esther, the day before Purim), keeping the dietary laws of Kashrut (buying kosher meat and using separate dishes for meat and dairy[5]), and lighting Shabbat candles. These indicators and this factor are characterized by what in Jewish tradition constitute rules about the individual's relationship to God and are performed primarily in abeyance to God's commandments (rather than as a symbol of collective identification). They are activities performed by the individual in a private context rather than a wider social environment.

This factor explained 6.8 percent of the common variance. Together with the first factor, nearly a third of the common variance is explained, which indicates that the expression of American Jewishness is dominated by some type of ritual practice, be it the more traditional observance of *mitzvoth* or the more collective celebration of Jewish identity.

The third most important factor indicated involvement in the more formally organized aspects of Jewish life (ASSOC): membership and volunteering in Jewish organizations, financial support of the organized Jewish community (contributions to the Jewish Federation or the United Jewish Appeal); subscribing to Jewish periodicals or newspapers; and celebrating Israel's Day of Independence (Yom haAtzma'ut). These are aspects of Jewish communal life that express identification with the American Jewish and worldwide Jewish collectivity. It also indicates that connection with worldwide Jewry is enhanced through membership in American Jewish formal associations. This factor explained 5.6 percent of the common variance.

It is interesting to note that synagogue membership and attendance have relatively high loadings on this factor. Going to synagogue fulfills a religious commandment, and the synagogue, especially in the United States, has come to be seen as a focus of collective activities and institutions that are not necessarily religious in nature and is closely related to the wider Jewish organizations and philanthropic activities linking American Jews to worldwide Jewry (as we have indicated). The multiple nature of synagogue life and its centrality to American Jews is reflected in the high loadings of these indicators on all three factors: CEREMONY, RITUAL, and ASSOC.

The fourth factor, explaining 4.9 percent of the shared variance, indicated denomination. Three variables were included in this factor (DENOM): the respondent's self-reported denomination, the denomination in which he or she was reared, and current household denomination. For this purpose, denominations were ordered by their closeness to Orthodox Judaism: respondents could designate denominational affiliation as Orthodox, Conservative, Reconstructionist, Reform, or nonaffiliated. That these indicators formed a separate factor shows that the other factors are not just indicators of a particular denomination, although there is a relationship between which denomination one identifies with and the scores on each of the factors, as we shall show.

The fifth factor indicated informal Jewish contact (FRATERNAL): having Jewish friends; living in a predominantly Jewish neighborhood; and valuing the importance of living in such a neighborhood. These indicators, explaining 4.5 percent of the shared variance, reflect the value put on Jewish solidarity and being involved in the informal networks and social circles of the Jewish community.

The final factor (explaining 4 percent of the common variance) reflected the amount and type of formal Jewish education the respondent had received, if any, and whether there had been any ritual celebration of Jewish status (Bar or Bat Mitzvah or Confirmation). That this ritual celebration had a high loading on this factor rather than on either of the ritual factors reflects the period of formal studies required before it and the contribution that it made to a stronger Jewish background or education (therefore we labeled the factor JED).

Even though these factors were extracted empirically from the data rather than superimposed from some a priori theoretical construct, they do resemble a number of the theoretical dimensions found in previous studies of religiosity and Jewish identity mentioned earlier.

The first two factors seem to express a ritualistic dimension (following Glock and Stark, 1965). They seem to divide into what Liebman and Cohen (1990), following Alexander (1987), distinguish as "ceremony" and "ritual"—*ceremony* referring to those rituals whose referent appears to be more a matter of "affirming membership in the social and cosmological order" (p. 124), and *ritual* expresses more a connection "to some transcendental presence" (p. 125). The fact that the data in this survey separate the ritual indicators into these two factors gives empirical reinforcement to this distinction.

It is interesting to point out that the ways in which the practices having a high loading on CEREMONY differ from the rituals having a high loading on RITUAL recall Sklare's (1971) discussion of the rituals most commonly observed in the United States: these are rituals that could effectively be redefined in modern, nonsupernatural terms;[6] they do not demand social isolation or a unique lifestyle (unlike, for instance, observing the dietary rules of kashrut); they are in accordance with the wider American religious culture, providing a "Jewish alternative" in a predominantly Christian culture—hence the centrality of lighting Hanukah candles, which has come to symbolize Jewish identification in a season of Christmas celebrations (Leibman and Cohen, 1990, pp. 15–16); they tend to be centered on children; and they occur annually or infrequently (as opposed to weekly lighting of Shabbat candles, daily keeping kosher).

This separation of two types of rituals among American Jews has not been apparent in all previous studies of Jewish religiosity. For example, in Israel, where the Diaspora environment is not present, no such differentiation was found in earlier research (Hartman, 1984; Kedem, 1991, after reviewing a number of other studies of religiosity in Israel, also concludes that all ritual items could be ordered in a one-dimensional scale of religiosity). Similarly, in traditional Judaism no distinction was made between different elements of Jewishness (Sharot, 1991). Cohen (1983) suggests that the American pattern reflects both a selectivity and an innovative tendency among American Jews who have "supplemented ancient forms of identification with an ever-changing array of new practices, forms of communal organizations, myths and symbols" (p. 176) to emphasize a "select group of activities, norms and values—derived from the traditional past and reshaped by the modern present—as the bare essentials of contemporary Jewish identification" (p. 176). Although no innovative rituals were asked about in this survey, the results suggest an innovative interpretation or reorganization in terms of emphasis of only some of the traditional rituals. For instance, Purim takes on disproportionate importance, because it fits into the child-centered, nonsupernatural orientation. Goldscheider (1986) suggests that "what remains . . . of traditional Judaism are forms of religious expression which do not conflict with the Americanization of the Jews" (pp. 151–152). The rituals more commonly observed are also less difficult and less demanding in terms of social isolation and knowledge. They may require a knowledgeable leader, such as the synagogue rabbi or the leader of the seder, but do not presume a great deal of knowledge on the part of the majority of the participants, fitting in with the "demise of intellect" (Neusner, 1987) characterizing the way most American Jews concern themselves with their Jewishness.

Leibman and Cohen (1990) add that the forms of religious experience chosen to be emphasized by American Jews reinforce what has come to define the American Jewish collective identity (more on this later, when it is contrasted to the Israeli Jewish identity). This would explain why the division of the rituals seems particular to the American setting, and why it differs from the more traditional Orthodox interpretation or emphases of the same rituals.

Two of the factors (ASSOC and FRATERNAL) seem to reflect formal and informal communal affiliation, which has been found to be a major component of Jewish identity in a number of studies (Phillips, 1991; Goldscheider, 1986; Cohen, 1983, 1988). The indicators separate themselves into the formal aspects of this affiliation—what Himmelfarb (1982) called the *associational* dimension; and the informal aspects of this affiliation, or what Himmelfarb (1982) called the *fraternal* dimension of religious involvement. According to Glock and Stark (1965) these would be part of the consequential dimension of religiosity, but as we have suggested already, we believe that in the Jewish case they should be considered an integral part of Jewish involvement and not a consequence of some "truer" religiosity.

The survey included no questions on the intensity of belief in principles of Judaism, but we believe identification with the various denominations serves as a proxy of the acceptance of belief or "doctrine" according to traditional Judaism (the ideological element of Glock and Stark). There is in addition an element of affiliation in these indicators, which is less a matter of ideological belief than of communal involvement.

We also had no direct indicators of Jewish knowledge in the survey, but some "intellectual" element is reflected in the JED factor—the closest indicator of religious knowledge we had—at least of a background that included exposure to Jewish learning.

Although not expressly designed to do so, these indicators of Jewish involvement thus empirically reinforced the idea that religious involvement is multidimensional and that the relevant dimensions include ritual, communal, ideological, and intellectual elements. Further the distinction of the two ritual and the two communal factors reinforced earlier findings about Jewish involvement. Each of the factors, by virtue of the method by which they were created, measure different and distinct aspects or dimensions of Jewishness, but they are related to each other in that they have as their center the focus on some type of involvement in being Jewish. For example, the Pearson correlation between ASSOC and CEREMONY is .6, which indicates an interrelationship, even though methodologically they form two distinct factors.[7]

DENOM has correlations of .4 or .5 with most of the other factors. However, this does not mean that the factors simply express denominational orientation, as the denomination factors loaded onto a separate, distinct factor. In Table 6.1 we show the mean scores on each of the other factors for persons indicating Orthodox, Conservative, Reform affiliation, or no affiliation.[8] They show that on all of the other factors except CEREMONY, the Orthodox have the highest scores: they are much more involved in the traditional rituals indicated by RITUAL (their mean score of .927 more than four times the score of the closest denomination, the Conservative); have stronger Jewish backgrounds, as indicated by JED (nearly three times the score of the Conservatives); are more likely to live in Jewish neighborhoods and have a Jewish social network (FRATERNAL); and are somewhat more involved in formal Jewish organizational life (ASSOC). Conservatives have the highest scores on CEREMONY, reflecting the dominant ritual observances among American Jews (as described earlier) and the major ritual mode through which Conservative Jews express themselves. The Reform have lower scores on all of the factors, being especially low on RITUAL, reflecting that keeping the traditional *mitzvoth*, which relate mainly to the relationship between

TABLE 6.1
Mean Score on Jewishness Factors, by Denomination and Sex, U.S. Jews, 1990

| Denomination | *Jewishness Factor*[a] | | | | |
	CEREMONY	RITUAL	ASSOC	FRATERNAL	JED
Total:					
(N in thousands = 2,749)					
Orthodox	.128	.927	.197	.308	.323
Conservative	.182	.028	.106	.113	.073
Reform	-.047	-.123	-.038	-.004	.032
Unaffiliated	-.377	-.035	-.377	-.106	-.026
Male (Total):					
(N in thousands = 1,357)	-.031	.048	-.021	.020	.072
Orthodox	.082	.957	.193	.394	.424
Conservative	.115	.037	.035	.059	.174
Reform	-.130	-.079	-.060	-.040	.123
Unaffiliated	-.369	-.135	-.355	-.158	.121
Female (Total):					
(N in thousands = 1,392)	.091	-.007	.044	.070	-.051
Orthodox	.190	.886	.202	.205	.182
Conservative	.247	.018	.175	.167	-.049
Reform	.034	-.165	-.017	.031	-.065
Unaffiliated	-.377	-.051	-.186	-.062	-.175

[a]For the meaning of factors and scores, see text.

Source: NJPS, 1990.

human and God, are not an integral part of the commandments they observe; they are also less likely to be closed in to predominantly Jewish social circles, less involved in the formal organizational life, observe the rituals indicated by CEREMONY less, and have weaker Jewish backgrounds. There may be other expressions of Jewishness through which the Reform are more likely to express themselves, but they were not measured here. The nonaffiliated are least involved on each of the factors, as might be expected. However, it must be remembered that these are mean scores on the factors and do not mean that denominational affiliation dictates to each affiliate how one will express one's Jewishness. That is one of the reasons that denominational affiliation forms a factor separate from the other five factors.

To visualize these relationships between the factors, we present a multidimensional scale in Figure 6.1. In this figure each one of the variables or factors is represented by a point in that space, and the distance

FIGURE 6.1
Monotonic Multidimensional Scaling of Jewishness Factors (one dimension),
U.S. Jews, 1990

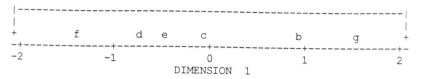

```
Coordinates in One Dimension

Variable    Plot    Dimension 1
_____    ____    _____


JED          b         0.98
DENOM        c        -0.05
ASSOC        d        -0.73
FRATERNAL    e        -0.46
CEREMONY     f        -1.32
RITUAL       g         1.59
```

Source: NJPS, 1990.

between the points represent how close they are in terms of a Pearson correlation. A higher correlation is represented by a shorter distance (see
Appendix III for a fuller explanation of the methodology). The idea is to
see the structure of the relationships among the factors in one graph. In
our case, the structure could be presented in one dimension (Figure 6.1);
in other words, they can be ordered along a straight line, where the distance between any two represents the correlation between them. Those far
apart are less related than those close together.

Two groups can be distinguished among the six factors: four of them
express Jewishness in a public, social setting (DENOM, FRATERNAL,
ASSOC, and CEREMONY) and two of them indicate more private
expressions of Jewishness (JED and RITUAL). RITUAL includes those
rituals performed as an expression of the individual's relationship to God
and are performed either individually (not using money on Shabbat) or
within the walls of one's own home (lighting Friday night candles, keeping
kosher). Jewish education is received in a social institution, and therefore
it is closer than RITUAL to the social aspects of Judaism, but like RITUAL,
it is mainly a contribution to personal Judaism. The more social aspects are

also ordered in terms of how much they reflect active involvement in Jewish social settings: the most active is CEREMONY, which involves active performance of rituals celebrated socially, such as attending a seder; participating in Jewish organizations or contributing money (ASSOC) may be more sporadic; FRATERNAL reflects one's immediate social surroundings but may not require as active a commitment or personal "sacrifice" as being involved in Jewish organizations or performing social rituals; denominational affiliation (DENOM) may simply be a label and reflect little active involvement. DENOM stands between the social and the more personal aspects because, on the one hand, it reflects closeness to Orthodoxy which emphasizes more than the other traditions rituals expressing the individual's relationship to God, but on the other hand, represents an institutional affiliation, which is a social aspect of Jewishness.

Jewishness and Gender, Age, and Marital Status

The question that concerns us in this section is who are the more Jewishly involved and how that might affect their secular achievements in education and labor force activity. Of particular interest to us is how being Jewishly involved is related to the achievement of men and women, and to understand this better, we must understand the different ways in which men and women are Jewishly involved. So in this section we consider what type of people are more Jewishly involved, whether the expression of Jewishness is different for men and women, how it is related to the life cycle stage of each. We emphasize that we are looking here at interrelationships rather than causal directions, since we cannot really answer the question of what causes someone to be more involved than another with answers such as we have to questions at one point in time; and in most cases cannot be sure which came first—the independent characteristic or their Jewish involvement.

Some research suggests that women tend to be more religious than men and tend to affiliate themselves with religion more than men (presented in Renzetti and Curran, 1992). However, subcultural variations have also been found, with little research done on Jews specifically. Weber (1963) suggested that women's religiosity and religion differs from men's, in that women have a more emotional, sentimental attachment than men and tend to be more otherworldly and millenarian in nature. This has been related to women's subjugation to men (McGuire, 1992), because subjugated people in general show a tendency to otherworldly, millenarian, emotional religion, which also varies by historical and cultural circumstances.

Studying elderly Jewish women in Jerusalem, Sered (1992) found that the women conceived of their religiosity in more interpersonal or contextual terms, whereas the religiosity of men was seen as more ritual-istic and abstract. Because traditionally Jewish women have not been bound religiously to the performance of the same religious *mitzvoth* as men, we might expect women to express their Jewishness by being involved in other aspects of Jewish life. Interpersonal relationships are usually more important to women than to men, so we would expect women to be more involved in social and collective aspects of Jewish life, especially on a familial basis, which is the primary context of the rit-uals they are expected to perform (e.g., lighting candles, keeping a kosher home), where their role was elevated, especially in the United States (Weinberg, 1988). Jewish women have also seen their volunteer work in Jewish organizations as "'their' Jewish activity, analogous in some ways to men's communal role in the synagogue" (Fishman, 1993, p. 72).

We therefore expected women to score higher on CEREMONY, ASSOC, and FRATERNAL, but lower on RITUAL. Because of tradi-tional differences in the religious education of Jewish men and women that have carried over to this day (see Schneider, 1985, Ch. 4) and the less common tradition of having girls' observe a Bat Mitzvah, until the last decade or so (Monson, 1992), we expected women to be less involved in JED as well. Denomination tends to be a family affair, so we did not expect differences on this factor.

As mentioned previously, there is an expectation that, with modern-ization, people will be less religious, be less inclined to use religious beliefs to explain the ultimate questions of life and death, be less inclined to allow their religious beliefs to influence their social behavior—the secu-larization thesis. This has led to the expectation that younger genera-tions will be less religious than older generations, although previous research has not substantiated the theory empirically (see, for example, Lyon, 1985; Sharot, 1991). There does seem to be, at least among Amer-ican Jews, a transformation in the way religiosity or Jewishness is expressed (Goldscheider, 1986), which suggests that the expression of Jewishness may vary by age. Religiosity, at least the observance of visible rituals, has also been found to vary by life cycle stage, people becoming more religious as they age (e.g., Sered, 1992, about women). We thus expected to find a relationship between age and Jewish involvement, with the younger being least involved and the older, most involved, at least in ritual observance.

Changes in the life cycle also come from being married and having children. Cohen and Ritterband (1988, cited in Leibman and Cohen, 1990) found that couples with children around the age of Bar Mitzvah are most likely to be affiliated with a synagogue and more observant, espe-cially of child-centered rituals and celebrations. The difficulties of the unmarried and childless to find a "place" in Jewish communal life (e.g.,

Diament, 1989; Schneider, 1984) reinforce the notion that Judaism is a "family" religion and way of life. We therefore expected to find the married more involved in the various aspects of Jewish life.

To determine the independent relationships of age, gender, and marital status with Jewishness, we used a multiple regression model with a Jewishness factor as the dependent variable and the other variables as the independent variables.[9]

Because changes in the life cycle may not have similar effects on the way men and women express their Jewishness, we also initially considered the various possible interaction effects. Generally, however, we did not find that any of the interaction effects contributed much to the explanation of Jewishness, so they were not included. This means that generally the relationship of age to religiosity is the same for each gender and that marital status has a similar effect on the religiosity of both men and women. That many of the indicators were of household rather than individual practices may have reduced the effect of the interactions, also.

The regression models for five Jewishness factors (excluding DENOM) are presented in Table 6.2. The table shows the regression coefficients for each independent variable in each of the models, respectively. The larger the regression coefficient is, the stronger the relationship between the independent variable and the Jewishness factor. By compar-

TABLE 6.2
Multiple Regression Analysis of Jewishness of Sex, Age,
and Marital Status for Each Jewishness Factor, U.S. Jews, 1990
(Standardized Regression Coefficients)

Independent Variable	Dependent Variable (Jewishness Factor)					
	CEREMONY	RITUAL	ASSOC	FRATERNAL	DENOM	JED
Being male	.069**	−.018	.046*	.023	.025	−.073**
Being married	.152***	.054**	.157**	.130**	.177**	.029**
Ages 25–34	−.070**	.078**	−.185**	−.099**	−.087**	.076**
Ages 35–44	−.019	.059**	−.083**	−.076**	−.067**	.085**
Ages 55–64	−.006	−.004	.022	−.025	−.002	−.018
Under retirement	.084**	−.099**	−.062*	−.094**	−.122**	.082**
R	.191	.098	.297	.224	.209	.166
R²	.036	.010	.088	.050	.044	.027
(Unweighted *n*)	(2,284)	(2,284)	(2,297)	(2,314)	(1,856)	(1,948)

*$\alpha < .05$.
**$\alpha < .01$.
***$\alpha < .001$.

Source: NJPS, 1990.

ing regression coefficients within each model, we also see the relative importance of each of the dependent variables.

The statistically significant positive regression coefficients of being male indicate those factors in which men are more involved than women; the statistically significant negative coefficients of being male indicate those Jewishness factors in which women are more involved than men. Women are significantly more active in Jewish organizations (ASSOC) and the collective rituals represented in CEREMONY. Although women tend to be more involved in informal Jewish circles when their raw factor scores are compared to men's (Table 6.3), the differences between men and women are a result of age and marital status differences between the genders. As we will see, older people are more involved in Jewish FRATER-NAL life, and as women live to be older than men, their higher score on this factor can be attributed to their age composition. Because husbands and wives usually live in the same neighborhood and have overlapping sets of friends, the gender variation in FRATERNAL is also reduced once marital status is controlled. Similarly, although the raw factor scores show that women are less observant of traditional rituals (RITUAL), once we control for the older ages of women, the difference between women and men becomes insignificant, because observance increases with age.

The results support our expectation that women express their Jewishness in more social ways, and men express their Jewishness through the observance of more traditional rituals, but some of these differences are a result of age and marital status. Once these are controlled, the main differences are the extent to which Jewish women are involved in collective ceremonial rituals and formal organizational life.

Age is related to the way Jewishness is expressed in that the older are more involved in formal organizational Jewish life and more involved in informal Jewish circles. The lower participation of the young in formal organizational life and informal Jewish circles may be a result of time available, as young people devote more time to their career and rearing young children. However, as children get older and as career demands weaken, participation in Jewish communal life becomes more common and more important. The informal social circles of the elderly are even more apt to have a Jewish character, and the elderly are active as volunteers in Jewish organizations and as philanthropists.

Age also indicates a cohort effect, not only a life cycle effect. For example, that the younger have had more formal Jewish education may be related to the increasing supply of Jewish education facilities and the higher socioeconomic status of younger Jewish generations, which enables them to afford formal religious training.

Being married has a significant positive relationship with Jewishness on each factor. In fact it has a stronger relationship with participation in

TABLE 6.3
Mean Score on Jewishness Factor, by Sex, Age,
and Marital Status, U.S. Jews, 1990

Sex	Age and Marital Status	Jewishness Factor				
		CEREMONY	RITUAL	ASSOC	FRATERNAL	JED
Male	Total	-.056	.030	-.046	-.006	.175
	(N in thousands = 1,480)					
	25–34	-.158	.095	-.406	-.182	.360
	35–44	.036	.115	-.124	-.089	.279
	45–54	.119	-.179	-.003	-.142	.202
	55–64	-.015	-.033	.227	.055	-.022
	65+	-.203	.066	.185	.316	-.048
	Married	.067	.058	.121	.106	.126
	Not married	-.386	-.044	-.493	-.322	.300
Female	Total	.075	-.008	.034	.057	-.043
	(N in thousands = 1,486)					
	25–34	-.073	-.038	-.387	-.266	.153
	35–44	.194	-.078	-.072	-.057	.138
	45–54	.181	-.159	.031	.061	.018
	55–64	.090	-.006	.347	.292	-.206
	65+	-.013	.158	.338	.338	-.495
	Married	.136	.052	.104	.107	.060
	Not married	-.059	-.138	-.118	-.058	-.297
Couples	(Unweighted n = 1414)[a]					
	With children	.00	.06	.05	.02	.10
	Without children	.09	-.05	-.03	-.13	.16

[a]The reason for presenting unweighted values of n for couples is discussed in Chapter 5.

Source: NJPS, 1990.

communal rituals, formal Jewish organizations, and informal Jewish circles than most of the other independent indicators (including gender). Because many of the religious rituals are centered in the household (lighting Sabbath candles, lighting Hanukah candles, having a Passover seder) or revolve around changes in the life status of children (circumcision, Bar and Bat Mitzvah), those who have set up their own household and are involved in passing Judaism on to their children may become more observant. The only exception to this is Jewish background, which varies more as a function of cohort.

The relationship between being married and being more Jewishly involved is not only a matter of having young children and wanting to involve them in Jewish life. Although couples who have children are more involved in the social and collective aspects of being Jewish (Table 6.3), those couples who have young children are not significantly more involved than those who do not in most aspects of Jewish life, and Jewish involvement does not vary by age of the oldest or the youngest child in any consistent way. We do not find that those who have children have stronger Jewish backgrounds nor that they are more observant of traditional rituals.

We had expected that the relationship of life cycle stage to Jewish involvement would be different for men and women, because at earlier stages of the life cycle, women's domestic roles may prevent them from participating as fully in community activities or ritual activities. Given the difference in the traditional obligations for men and women to perform certain *mitzvoth*, even the most observant women may be less active in Jewish activities when their domestic roles are more demanding. Child-rearing does not usually make the same demands on men, which is one reason we found opposite effects of being married on the labor force participation of Jewish men and women. Further, more men may find communal participation advantageous in terms of making connections that would be useful in their career. At older ages, more women than men are left on their own and may find communal religious activities a meaningful way to spend their time and make connections to other people. However, the lack of interaction between gender and age or marital status in these models does not support this expectation.

In summary, involvement in the formal social life and collective rituals of Jewish life is more characteristic of women than of men; and involvement in Jewish life in general varies by life cycle stage, both in terms of age and marital status. We consider in the following sections how Jewish involvement is related to the secular achievements in education and labor force activity of Jewish men and women and whether this involvement has the same implications for men and women alike. Because of the relationships between gender, marital status, age, and Jewish involvement and between these characteristics and secular achievement (as we have seen), we take into consideration these interrelationships in our analysis.

EDUCATIONAL ACCOMPLISHMENTS
OF MEN AND WOMEN AND THEIR JEWISHNESS

As American Jews' socioeconomic status has been transformed in the last few decades (as we have indicated with cross-sectional data in Chapter 4 and as Chiswick, 1993, and Goldscheider, 1986, document on a wider basis), we question whether this socioeconomic achievement actually reflects or expresses some predispositions to socioeconomic achievement inherent in the Jewish culture—or whether it has come about at the expense of traditional Jewish involvement, as a trade-off between "modernity" and traditional religion.

The minority thesis that has been advanced to explain the high educational achievements of American Jews suggests that the high educational ambitions are linked to their status as an immigrant minority. Implied in this thesis is that as their immigrant status and minority stigma dissipate, the strong impetus to educational attainment will decrease—and conversely, that as Jews attain higher education and socioeconomic success they will also become assimilated; that is, leave the distinctive features that make them Jewish, including involvement with the Jewish community, religious practices, associations with other Jews, and so forth. Therefore, according to this thesis, the high educational achievements of Jews are not an outgrowth of the Jewish culture per se but of a temporary status that passes with time and assimilation.

However, two empirical trends do not fit this thesis. Minority status has not been the impetus for educational achievement in all cases of minorities or immigrants, which has called into question this thesis in general or, at least, raised the need to specify the conditions under which minority status serves as an impetus for achievement. With this approach, Steinberg (1974, 1981) has suggested that American Jewish educational attainment was linked less to immigrant and minority status and more to "being in the right place at the right time," with the "right" socioeconomic background to take advantage of expanding educational opportunities. Immigrant status is found not to be a sufficient explanation for the high achievement of Jews. A second objection is that the high achievement of Jews has continued long beyond their immigration to the country. Could their numerical minority status be the sole explanation of their high achievement even after generations of establishment in institutions of higher learning and higher occupations?

The secularization thesis also implies a negative relationship between Jewishness and educational achievement, in positing that secular modernity and success (i.e., socioeconomic achievement) erodes the particularistic identification and religious involvement attendant on being Jewishly involved (e.g., Berger, 1967; O'Dea, 1966; Roberts, 1990; Stark and Bainbridge, 1985). This is a more general theory that sees secular modernity juxtaposed to traditional religious identification and involvement.

However, religious identification and involvement has not really declined with increased modernization. As Finke and Stark (1992) show for the United States, extent and type of religious affiliation and church attendance fluctuate not with modernization but with social needs and marketing of new (and old) religious movements; and religious affiliation and participation has certainly not disappeared as the United States has modernized. Refinement of the secularization thesis is in order.

An opposite relationship between Jewishness and educational achievement is posited by the cultural thesis that suggests that the Jewish orientation to education derives from a traditional cultural emphasis on learning and education (e.g., Zborowski and Herzog, 1962; see the previous discussion in Chapter 2). Goldscheider (1986) has suggested that the distinctive socioeconomic patterns of American Jews are not to be separated from their Jewishness and actually reflect new networks and patterns through which American Jews express and maintain their Jewishness (Goldscheider and Zuckerman, 1984).

Our interest in the present section is whether the level of educational attainment is related to Jewishness, whether it is related to all aspects of Jewishness in the same way or differently (as suggested in recent literature), and whether the relationships that we find are similar for men and for women.

However, there are serious deficiencies in the present survey for treating this particular topic. To determine a causal effect of Jewishness on education (what we would like to do ideally), we would have to correlate or show the Jewishness of the person and his or her parents at the time when education is acquired. In the survey, the indicators of Jewishness refer to 1990, the year of the survey. To adapt the data to our current purpose, we could have come to better results had one of two things been included in the survey: either detailed retrospective information on the religiosity of the parents and the family environment during the period of education or detailed inquiry and an adequate sample of families with children 17–30 today; that is, during the ages in which educational variation (how much higher education is pursued) is probable. Only about 20 percent of the sample had children in this age group, and this was not enough for studying the relationship between Jewish involvement and pursuit of higher education; nor were questions about educational plans and aspirations of the children asked. We only have limited retrospective information about how Jewish the environment was when the person was growing up (during the period during which he or she acquired education). Respondents were asked in what denomination they were brought up, whether they had a Bar or Bat Mitzvah or Confirmation, and the extent and kind of Jewish education they had (but not the age at which they had it), but no information was collected about how religious the parents were or which religious rituals were observed in the household nor how religious the respondent was during the formative years of education.

What we can and do analyze in the present chapter is the interrelationship between current involvement in Jewish life and acquired formal education (whenever it was acquired). Our assumption is that the relationship works in both directions. That is, acquired education affects to some extent how involved one is in Jewish life today; however, involvement in Jewish life may also affect one's motivation to be educated, and since today's involvement reflects to a great extent past involvement in Jewish life, the effect of Jewishness today will also reflect the effect of Jewishness in general on educational achievement. The regressions therefore have to be interpreted not as a prediction from present Jewishness to past education (which is illogical), but rather as a covariation between the two plus the effect of the Jewishness in the past as reflected in the effect of the present indicators of Jewishness on education. This assumption is reinforced by some of our findings (which we present later in Table 6.7) that, among younger cohorts, where the time gap between current Jewishness and acquired education is relatively smaller, there is a close relationship between the two.

In this sense, and following our earlier chapter on educational achievement, we will attempt to show that being "more Jewish" or involved in Jewish life is positively related to educational achievement, that this is as true for men as for women, and this does not decrease in the younger generations as they assimilate.

We have different expectations as to which aspects of Jewishness would be related to education based on the different theories about the Jewish experience in the United States. If the cultural thesis explains best the relationship between Jewishness and education—that is, something in the Jewish culture makes for more education—then all dimensions of Jewishness would be positively related to education.

On the other hand, there is reason to expect that the more social aspects of Jewishness would be more related, but negatively, to education, if the minority or assimilation theses more adequately explain the relationship. What makes a group a distinctive minority in the society is the social identification of its members as different and separate. According to these theses, the social aspects of religion (both formal and informal), more than private beliefs or rituals expressing an individual's relationship to God, would be more likely to be related inversely to educational attainment. These would be indicated by the factors of ASSOC (involvement in formal Jewish organizational life) and FRATERNAL (involvement in informal Jewish social circles).

Similarly, there will be a negative relationship between Jewishness and educational achievement if the secularization thesis is accurate. Here, we would expect that those factors indicating a more traditional expression of Jewishness, such as RITUAL and DENOM, would be most strongly related (negatively) to Jewishness.

We also had different expectations about the relationship between Jewishness and the educational attainment of men and women. Because of the traditional emphasis in Judaism on familial roles, especially for women, there is cause to expect that greater restrictions would be put on women's nonfamilial achievements (such as educational attainment) among the more religious or the more Jewish women. A negative relationship is not expected for males, because only among a minority of the extreme religious groups would it be expected that the religious man not engage in secular occupations and its attendant preparation through formal secular education. As a result, it is expected that the relationship of Jewishness to the secular education of men and women will differ, being more negatively related for women.

First, we establish the general relationship between Jewishness and education, and then consider its variation by gender. The pairwise correlations between the Jewishness factors and education are presented in Table 6.4. All but one of the Jewishness factors have a significant correlation with highest degree achieved.[10] Four of these relationships are positive, that is, the "more Jewish" in these aspects of Jewishness, the higher is the educational attainment. Two are negative—the closer to Orthodox denominational affiliation and the closer the ritual practices are to Orthodox *halachic* practices, the lower is the educational attainment. This suggests that the social definition of being Jewish is associated more with the attainment of secular education than the more traditionally religious dimensions of ritual observance. This is not in the direction expected by assimilation theory—collective or particularistic involvement and identification with Jews is associated positively, not negatively, with higher secular education. The more educated do not disso-

TABLE 6.4

Pairwise Pearson Correlation Coefficients Between
Jewishness Factors and Highest Academic Degree, U.S. Jews, 1990

Jewishness Factor	Pearson Correlation with Highest Academic Degree (unweighted n)
Ceremony	.111* (2,284)
Ritual	−.079* (2,284)
Assoc	.078* (2,297)
Fraternal	.015 (2,314)
Denom	−.100* (1,948)
Jed	.108* (1,856)

*$\alpha < .01$.

Source: NJPS, 1990.

ciate themselves from other Jews. But in partial support of the secularization thesis, the more highly educated are less religious in a traditional manner.

These general relationships show that there is an association between Jewishness and education but that not all of the aspects of Jewishness are related to education in the same way nor with the same strength. These relationships, however, are measured very crudely by these coefficients and may reflect spurious relationships with other variables. In Table 6.5 we consider the relationship between Jewishness and education when we control for gender and age. As mentioned earlier, we had expected Jewishness to be related differently to the education of men and women (positively for men, negatively for women). We also knew (from Chapter 2) that educational achievement varies by cohort, especially for women, and that this might be affecting the relationship between Jewishness and education. In Table 6.5 we compare the mean years of education of the most Jewishly involved and the least Jewishly involved[11] on five of the factors[12] for different age and sex groups.

On the factors of CEREMONY, ASSOC, and FRATERNAL, the more religious have more years of education. This relationship holds true for almost every age and gender group.[13]

Among older men (55+), the more ritually observant are less educated. The women who are more ritually observant are also less educated, perhaps because of a more traditional orientation to women's roles (which we will explore in greater detail later).

Within levels of Jewishness, the main educational difference among men is between the oldest men (65+) and the men under 65, but the women's education varies more by age, showing a later transition to higher education (as we saw in Chapter 2).

Level of Jewish involvement does not reduce the gender gap in education, but there tends to be a somewhat larger gap among the more Jewishly involved than among the less involved. This may be because the variation in men's education is greater and is seen in relatively higher achievements of more religious men. Women's education seems to vary somewhat less by Jewishnessy.

On some of the factors, the difference between the most and the least Jewishly involved seems to be greater among the younger cohorts, but on others the involvement seems to make a bigger difference among the older cohorts. To further explore these relationships, we turned to multiple regression, which portrays the net relationship between Jewishness and education (highest academic degree) when age, gender, and the interaction between age and Jewishness are held constant. This interaction factor indicates the different ways and intensities with which Jewishness is related to the education of the different age groups. In a preliminary anal-

TABLE 6.5
Mean Years of Education for the Most and Least Jewishly Involved
for Each Jewishness Factor, Age and Sex, U.S. Jews, 1990

Jewishness Factor	Jewish Involvement[a]			
	Least Involved		Most Involved	
	Male	Female	Male	Female
CEREMONY				
Age 25–34	15.8	15.2	17.3	16.5
35–44	16.7	15.3	17.2	16.2
45–54	15.9	15.1	17.5	15.4
55–64	16.7	13.9	17.0	14.8
65+	14.1	13.1	14.4	13.5
(N in thousands)	(472)	(388)	(557)	(586)
RITUAL				
Age 25–34	16.1	15.9	16.6	15.6
35–44	17.1	16.2	17.0	15.5
45–54	16.4	15.4	17.3	15.1
55–64	17.3	15.0	16.2	14.2
65+	14.8	13.3	13.5	13.3
(N in thousands)	(485)	(548)	(296)	(297)
ASSOC				
Age 25–34	15.7	15.4	17.3	16.2
35–44	16.4	15.7	17.6	16.2
45–54	15.5	14.7	17.7	15.5
55–64	15.9	13.9	17.0	15.2
65+	13.5	12.6	14.3	14.0
(N in thousands)	(574)	(426)	(438)	(429)
FRATERNAL				
Age 25–34	16.1	15.5	16.6	16.1
35–44	16.5	15.7	17.0	16.1
45–54	16.3	14.9	17.1	14.8
55–64	16.9	14.9	16.0	13.9
65+	14.3	14.0	14.0	13.1
(N in thousands)	(491)	(426)	(438)	(429)
JED				
Age 25–34	17.0	15.5	16.4	16.3
35–44	16.9	16.0	17.2	16.1
45–54	15.3	15.8	17.1	15.3
55–64	16.7	14.0	17.2	14.7
65+	13.0	13.2	13.8	13.2
(N in thousands)	(283)	(378)	(420)	(335)

[a]Based on a trichotomy of factor scores (most involved = highest third; least involved = lowest third).

Source: NJPS, 1990.

ysis, the interaction between Jewishness and gender was found not to be significant and not included in the model.

For each Jewishness factor a separate regression model was calculated. The unstandardized regression coefficients and their standard error and significance are presented in Table 6.6 for each of the Jewishness factors. Reinforcing what we have seen in Table 6.5, once age and gender are controlled, there is a significant positive relationship between Jewishness and education for four of the factors: CEREMONY, ASSOC, FRATERNAL, DENOM. The more involved in formal and informal Jewish social circles, the collective celebration of Jewish identity, and the closer to Orthodox affiliation, the higher is the educational achievement. The other two Jewishness factors—private ritual behavior and

TABLE 6.6
Multiple Regression Analysis of Highest Academic Degree
for Each Jewishness Factor, U.S. Jews, 1990

	Jewishness Factor					
Independent Variable	CEREMONY	RITUAL	ASSOC	FRATERNAL	DENOM	JED
Jewishness						
Unstandardized coefficient	.511*	−.088	.451*	.470*	.388*	−.057
(Standard error)	(.092)	(.089)	(.094)	(.091)	(.101)	(.104)
Standardized coefficient	.361	−.060	.321	.333	.271	−.040
Age						
Unstandardized Coefficient	−.028*	−.027*	−.029*	−.026*	−.025*	−.024*
(Standard Error)	(.002)	(.002)	(.002)	(.002)	(.002)	(.002)
Standardized coefficient	−.312	−.301	−.322	−.285	−.271	−.259
Sex						
Unstandardized Coefficient	−.512*	−.488*	−.512*	−.505*	−.526*	−.416*
(Standard error)	(.055)	(.056)	(.055)	(.055)	(.061)	(.062)
Standardized coefficient	−.180	−.172	−.182	−.179	−.185	−.149
Interaction between age and Jewishness						
Unstandardized Coefficient	−.007*	−.004	−.005*	−.008*	−.009*	−.003
(Standard error)	(.002)	(.002)	(.002)	(.002)	(.002)	(.002)
Standardized coefficient	−.257	−.135	−.164	−.304	−.332	−.093
Multiple R	.379	.362	.375	.353	.349	.313
(Unweighted N)	(2,284)	(2,284)	(2,297)	(2,314)	(1,948)	(1,856)

*$\alpha < .01$.

Source: NJPS, 1990.

Jewish educational background—are not related significantly to academic degree achieved when the other variables in the model are controlled. That is, the significant negative relationship between these factors and education that we saw represented in the multidimensional scale in Figure 6.1 and reflected in Table 6.5 becomes insignificant when age and gender are controlled. In other words, the crude relationship is a result of the age and gender composition of the more highly educated (who are more likely to be younger and male) and the more religious (who are more likely to be older and, for these aspects of Jewishness, male, as we have shown).

The lack of relationship between secular education and Jewish educational background is surprising, given that Jewish education and general education take place at about the same time so that there is a temporal closeness that is not true of the other factors and also because of the general orientation to learning reflected in both studying Judaism and general schooling. Because RITUAL reflects traditional rituals, its lack of relationship to higher education suggests that the more traditional orientation to religious education may not have been broadened to include secular education among these most observant Jews (as we suggested in Hartman and Hartman, 1989).

Not surprisingly we find that age and gender have significant regression coefficients in each of the models. The main effect of gender is negative, which expresses what we have seen above earlier—that women achieve lower academic degrees than men. Controlling for the Jewishness factors does not change this relationship. The effect of age is somewhat weaker, but it is also significant and negative, expressing the fact that younger cohorts have higher educational attainment than older cohorts (cf. also Chiswick, 1993).

The interaction of each Jewishness factor and age also has a significant and negative effect in each of the models, reflecting that Jewishness did not affect the education of the various cohorts in the same way. To further compare the relationship of Jewishness to educational attainment in different age groups, we analyzed separate regression models for different age groups (dropping age and the interaction between age and Jewishness in the regression models). This was instructive because it highlights how the relationship between education and Jewishness has changed over time. Table 6.7 presents the regression coefficients of Jewishness for the oldest and youngest age groups.

We found that the education of older cohorts was less related to the Jewishness factors of CEREMONY, ASSOC, FRATERNAL, and JED— that is, there was a weaker relationship between these Jewishness factors and education in the older cohorts. This would suggest that the rela-

TABLE 6.7
Multiple Regression Analysis of Highest Academic Degree for Each
Jewishness Factor, for Selected Age Groups, U.S. Jews, 1990

| | *Jewishness Factors* | | | | | | *Unweighted* |
	CEREMONY	RITUAL	ASSOC	FRATERNAL	DENOM	JED	n)
Ages 25–34:							
Jewishness	.262*	–.017	.244*	.146*	.011	.076	
	(.058)	(.049)	(.058)	(.054)	(.060)	(.058)	(461)
Sex	–.355*	–.320*	–.300*	–.287*	–.325*	–.120	
	(.106)	(.108)	(.106)	(.107)	(.124)	(.115)	
Ages 65+:							
Jewishness	.010	–.213*	.177*	–.108	–.272*	–.041	
	(.059)	(.069)	(.067)	(.067)	(.073)	(.087)	(508)
Sex	–.488*	–.483*	–.524*	–.542*	–.634*	–.628*	
	(.125)	(.124)	(.177)	(.126)	(.144)	(.163)	

*α < .01.
Note: Shown as unstandardized regression coefficients, with standard error in parentheses.

Source: NJPS, 1990.

tionship between these Jewishness factors, which include primarily the factors of collective identification and involvement as well as Jewish learning, and education is not an effect that is dying out but, on the contrary, is getting stronger.[14] On the other hand, the effects of RITUAL and DENOM are stronger in the older cohort and weaker in the youngest. The lack of effect of RITUAL in the younger cohort suggests that traditional Orthodox tendencies do not have the same negative relationship with education among the young as they did in the past. The young Orthodox in the United States are not necessarily closed in to a particularistic existence distanced from the modern world, but have found ways of bridging their Jewishness and participation in the modern secular world. "Even within Orthodox circles, in the last two decades there has been increasing participation in some of the 'general' arenas of life, such as higher education and political activities, which would have been anathema to the older Eastern European traditionalists" (Eisenstadt, 1992, p. 136; see also Leibman and Cohen, 1990). By redefining what had become part of Jewish custom and tradition in Eastern and Central Europe as "beyond the purview of the mandatory *halacha* (religious law)," modern Orthodoxy has "allowed modernity to fill the normative void created by the retreat of traditional law and custom" (Cohen, 1983, p. 30).

Apparently older cohorts observant in the Orthodox fashion had not completed the process of generalizing from the highly valued Jewish education to a value on education in general, including secular education; as a result there is a strong relationship between Jewish education and RITUAL in older cohorts, but not between secular education and RITUAL. As the generalized positive orientation to education becomes established, younger cohorts do make the transition and value secular education just as in the past they would value religious education.

Given the coding of the DENOM items, it, too, reflects a closeness to Orthodox tradition, and its lack of effect in the younger cohort also indicates that Orthodoxy no longer has a negative impact on acquiring secular education.

The DENOM factor gives us an indicator of closeness to Orthodox affiliation, but it does not tell us whether the different expressions of Jewishness measured by the factors have similar relationships with educational attainment in each of the major denominations. Because the Reform denomination was developed with the intent of making Judaism fully compatible with life in the modern, secular world, it might be expected that Jewish involvement would have little impact on achievement in a secular arena, such as secular education. Orthodoxy, on the other hand, accepts a more encompassing orientation to Judaism, as a way of life, although, as we have mentioned earlier, modern Orthodoxy also allows for more independent involvement in secular arenas. Conservative Judaism stands in between, accepting the traditional orientation to Judaism, but making modifications to accommodate between the religious and secular modern worlds. Given these differences, we would expect Jewishness generally to have the greatest impact on the academic achievement of Orthodox Jews and the least impact or relationship with the academic achievement of Reform Jews.

Separate regressions for the main denominations[15] are presented in Table 6.8, with highest academic degree achieved as the dependent variable. The relationship between gender, age, and academic achievement is similar in each of the denominations, in the same direction as for the total. Hence, this type of Jewish involvement (denominational affiliation) does not affect the relationship between gender and education or between age and education.

Comparing the unstandardized regression coefficients for each of the Jewishness factors results in some interesting variations. Generally, Jewishness is related more to the academic achievement of Conservative American Jews than to the achievement of either Orthodox or Reform Jews. This is true for Jewishness as expressed through CEREMONY, ASSOC, and FRATERNAL. In all three of these factors, Jewishness is associated positively with the academic achievement of Conservative Jews. Whether this is because their Jewish involvement pushed them to

TABLE 6.8
Multiple Regression Analysis of Highest Academic Degree,
for Main Denominations and Jewishness Factors, U.S. Jews, 1990
(Unstandardized Regression Coefficients)

Denomination	Independent Variable	Jewishness Factor				
		CEREMONY	RITUAL	ASSOC	FRATERNAL	JED
Orthodox	Sex	−.384*	−.358*	−.431*	−.339	−.460**
	Age	−.030**	−.034**	−.026**	−.041**	−.043**
	Jewishness	.379	−.077	.002	−.731**	−.613**
	Interaction between Jewishness and age	−.006	−.000	.170	.011	.008*
	Multiple R	.424	.424	.398	.415	.444
	(Unweighted n)	(163)	(163)	(151)	(153)	(139)
Conservative	Sex	−.521**	−.485**	−.515**	−.502**	−.400**
	Age	−.019**	−.020**	−.025**	−.019**	−.016**
	Jewishness	.629**	−.063	−.582**	.772**	.004
	Interaction between Jewishness and age	−.005*	.000	−.004**	−.012**	.003
	Multiple R	.381	.297	.393	.342	.274
	(Unweighted n)	(893)	(893)	(893)	(881)	(742)
Reform	Sex	−.420**	−.403**	−.436**	−.433**	−.351**
	Age	−.014**	−.015**	−.016**	−.015**	−.009**
	Jewishness	.099	−.003	.195	.510**	−.377**
	Interaction between Jewishness and age	.001	−.004	−.000	−.011**	.010**
	Multiple R	.250	.248	.255	.247	.213
	(Unweighted n)	(902)	(902)	(877)	(900)	(715)

*α < .05.
**α < .01.

Source: NJPS, 1990.

achieve more or their educational achievement makes it easier to integrate into the Jewish environment is difficult to determine with our data, but there is a definite interrelationship.

Among the Orthodox, only FRATERNAL and JED are related significantly to academic achievement, and these relationships are negative. The more that the Orthodox isolate themselves in predominantly Jewish social circles, the lower their secular education is; similarly, the more Jewish education they have had, the less secular education they attain. However, observance of rituals and participation in formal Jewish organizational life is not related to their academic achievement.

Among the Reform, involvement in Jewish social circles is related positively to academic achievement, as it is among the Conservative. This suggests that their Jewishness is reinforced by interaction among Jews, which stems from the college environment and continues in their professional contacts; such positive reinforcement of Jewishness through secular channels does not appear to be significant among the Orthodox.[16]

Among the Reform as among the Orthodox, more Jewish education is negatively related to secular academic achievement. This may be related to more involvement in Yeshivas among the Orthodox and perhaps rabbinical seminaries among the Reform. What is especially interesting in this case is the lack of relationship between Jewish education and secular education among the Conservatives. If we can assume that the Jewish education of Conservatives was through a Conservative institution, it would seem that the Conservatives have identified a method of Jewish instruction that does not interfere with or reinforce secular achievement. However, because we have not controlled for the type of Jewish education received in terms of denominational affiliation, this point is really speculative but merits further study.

Because of the different attitudes to family roles for men and women in Judaism, it would be expected that Jewishness would have a negative relationship with the education of women and a positive relationship with the education of men. However, the lack of interaction effect between gender and Jewishness means that the relationship between Jewishness and academic degree achieved is not significantly different for men and women. This is illustrated in Table 6.9, which presents the regression coefficients of Jewishness when regression models are calculated separately for men and women. As in the general model, four of the Jewishness factors have significant and positive relationships with education (the aspects emphasizing Jewish collective identity—CEREMONY, ASSOC, FRATERNAL, and DENOM) for both men and women.

It might also be noted that in all cases where Jewishness has a significant relationship with education, the unstandardized regression coefficient is somewhat larger for women than for men; that is, the relationship

TABLE 6.9
Multiple Regression Analysis of Highest Academic Degree on
Jewishness Factor and Age, for Men and Women Separately, U.S. Jews, 1990

| | *Jewishness Factor* | | | | | | *(Unweighted* |
	CEREMONY	ASSOC	FRATERNAL	DENOM	JED	RITUAL	*n)*
Males:							
Jewishness	.124*	.248**	.171**	.200**	.036	.035	
	(.067)	(.072)	(.069)	(.072)	(.079)	(.065)	(1093)
Age	–.029**	–.029**	–.028**	–.030**	–.026**	–.028**	
	(.001)	(.001)	(.001)	(.001)	(.002)	(.001)	
Interaction between age and							
Jewishness	–.001	–.003*	–.003	–.004**	–.001	–.002	
	(.001)	(.001)	(.001)	(.001)	(.002)	(.001)	
Females:							
Jewishness	.481**	.349**	.492**	.313*	.086	.030	
	(.129)	(.127)	(.123)	(.136)	(.139)	(.120)	(1131)
Age	–.032**	–.033**	–.031**	–.030**	–.032**	–.031**	
	(.002)	(.002)	(.002)	(.003)	(.003)	(.002)	
Interaction between age and							
Jewishness	–.007**	–.003	–.008**	–.008**	–.000	–.002	
	(.002)	(.002)	(.002)	(.003)	(.003)	(.002)	

* $\alpha = .05$.
** $\alpha = .01$.
Note: Standard error is in parentheses.

Source: NJPS, 1990.

between Jewishness and education is slightly stronger for women than for men (though the difference is not statistically significant, or the interaction effect would have significance).

To consider whether Jewishness had an impact on gender equality in educational attainment, we turned to our sample of Jewish couples. If the "patriarchal nature" of traditional Judaism[17] and the gender inequality in religious roles has a spillover effect on secular behavior, we would expect more involvement in Jewish life to be associated with greater inequality between the spouses. We would expect this to be especially apparent for the observance of traditional ritual (RITUAL) and closeness to Orthodoxy (DENOM).

When, however, we compare the patterns of spousal equality in education between the more and less Jewishly involved (derived from a dichotomy of the factor scores and presented in Table 6.10), we find no difference in the comparison of husband's and wife's years of education and no difference in how many couples show conventional differences in education (that the husband has the same or more years of education than the wife). Although Jewish religion does not accord men and women equal ritual roles, couples who observe traditional rituals are no more unequal in their secular education than couples who are less observant. Couples active in the more public or social rituals (CEREMONY) do not differ from couples who are less active, nor are couples with a stronger Jewish background compared to those with weaker backgrounds. Couples interacting in Jewish social circles do not show a distinct pattern of inequality in education.

TABLE 6.10
Spousal Inequality in Education, by Jewish Involvement
for Each Jewishness Factor, U.S. Jews, 1990

Jewishness Factor and Inequality Indicator	Jewish Involvement		
	More Involved	Less Involved	(Significance of t-test)
CEREMONY:			
% conventional education differences	74.1	73.1	(.72)
Mean difference in husband's and wife's years of education	.7	.8	(.41)
RITUAL:			
% conventional education differences	74.4	72.2	(.12)
Mean difference in husband's and wife's years of education	.7	.9	(.26)
ASSOC:			
% conventional education differences	74.9	72.5	(.40)
Mean difference in husband's and wife's years of education	.9	.6	(.26)
FRATERNAL:			
% conventional education differences	74.8	72.5	(.43)
Mean difference in husband's and wife's years of education	.8	.7	(.44)
JED:			
% conventional education differences	76.1	72.9	(.35)
Mean difference in husband's and wife's years of education	.9	.7	(.35)

Unweighted n = 1,414 couples.

Source: NJPS, 1990.

The elements in the Jewish religion that emphasize the reciprocal and equivalent nature of the husband and wife duties and obligations, which support an active economic role for wives, and the long tradition of secular achievement of both Jewish men and women counteract any spillover that might have been expected from the unequal ritual roles accorded to men and women in the Jewish religion.

Another comparison addressing this issue of how Jewishness related to spousal inequality involved Jews of different denominations. Comparing Orthodox, Conservative, Reconstructionist, Reform, and unaffiliated couples, we again found very little relationship between denomination and spousal inequality (Table 6.11). What seems clear is that, contrary to popular opinion, Orthodoxy is not associated with more spousal inequality: education differences are even smaller than among the Conservatives, Reforms, and Reconstructionists. This may be related to the tradition of very Orthodox wives supporting the family while the husband studied the religious books, so that some education was needed to prepare for these secular economic roles. Although this may be true for a small minority of American Jews today, the tradition of women being active in the labor force and needing, therefore, appropriate training for an occupation, has apparently continued through to the modern Orthodox.

LABOR FORCE PARTICIPATION
OF MEN AND WOMEN AND THEIR JEWISHNESS

We look now at the relationship between Jewishness and men's and women's participation in the paid labor force. As labor force participation

TABLE 6.11
Denomination, by Educational Characteristics of U.S. Jewish Couples, 1990

Couple Characteristic	Orthodox	Conservative	Reconstruc- tionist	Reform	Unaffiliated
% conventional education differences[a]	71.2	76.5	85.7	73.7	66.4
Mean difference between husband's and wife's years of education	.3	.9	1.7	.7	.4
(Unweighted *n*)	(60)	(303)	(78)	(358)	(153)

[a]Husband has same or more years of education than wife.

Source: NJPS, 1990.

is a continuation of activity leading toward secular achievement or "success," we can expect some of the perspectives discussed previously concerning the relationship between Jewishness and education to be applicable to the relationship between Jewishness and labor force participation as well. To the extent that an achievement orientation is part of the Jewish heritage, extended to achievement in secular arenas, we can expect a positive association between Jewishness and labor force participation. The achievement orientation could be derived from being a minority group on the American scene and become less apparent with generations and acceptance in the American secular scene. However, there is great variation in the achievement orientation of minority groups (see, for example, Lipset, 1995), and it would be doubtful if this offers the only explanation of the Jewish orientation to secular achievement. As already indicated, we are inclined to believe that the achievement orientation derives from the culture itself. It could derive from the cultural emphasis on goal-directed behavior and the absence of proscriptions on secular economic activity, even if it is not a "sacred" activity. Participation in the labor force does not have a sacred value in itself in Judaism, unlike that derived from the Protestant ethic, for instance; and unlike the value of learning, which seems to derive some sacred valence as an extension of religious study. Nevertheless, Jews derived values from their tradition that made them receptive to capitalism and its inherent work ethic (see Lipset, 1995: Chapter 6).

Further, labor force activity was accepted practically for both men and women as a means to support the family and make a living, as we have discussed in Chapter 3. Nevertheless, supporting the family was primarily seen as the husband's responsibility, especially in the first part of this century among Americans (see, for example, Baum et al., 1976; Weinberg, 1988). Further, it has been suggested that at certain times in the Jewish experience, women were more limited in their economic activities because of social norms. "Although the leading figures of the Hebrew Bible include an impressive number of forceful women, throughout medieval and postmedieval Jewish history women as a group were encouraged to remain modestly behind the scenes or to assume a subservient posture. . . . [C]ommunal leadership roles were deemed inappropriate for women—that is, at odds with requirements for feminine modesty. In general Jewish women were taught that their glory lay in the domestic realm; according to the biblical verse, 'the honor of the king's daughter is all within,' k-vodah bat-melech p-nimah (Psalms 45:14)" (Fishman, 1993, pp. 202–203).

However, the verse quoted refers mainly to the family and religious roles, which were centered in the domestic realm, justifying the limitations on women's religious requirements. It was not raised in Judaic tradition in connection with roles in the economy except when imposed from the outside culture, as among Jews in predominantly Moslem countries. On the contrary, few negative restrictions were placed on women's activities to make money for the family, and the proverbial "woman of valor" is praised for a range of economic activities. Women's work was valued no less than men's.

The family roles prescribed in Jewish tradition could, however, interfere with the labor force activities of women, as we have shown in Chapter 3. This would suggest that Jewishness has indirect relationships with labor force participation through its effect on family roles, especially among women, rather than a direct influence on labor force activity per se. We shall pursue this line of thinking in our analysis to follow.

We turn now to an analysis of the relationship between Jewishness and the labor force activity of men and women. Because we are measuring two sets of behavior that are current (Jewish involvement and labor force activity), some of the reservations we raised about the relationship between acquired education and current Jewishness can be relaxed.

In the simple relationships (Pearson correlations) between the Jewishness factors and labor force participation, practicing the collective Jewish rituals (CEREMONY), involvement with informal Jewish circles (FRATERNAL), and having a Jewish educational background (JED) all have significant positive correlations with labor force participation; whereas closeness to Orthodox denominational affiliation (DENOM), practice of traditional rituals (RITUAL), and involvement in the formally organized Jewish community (ASSOC) are related negatively to labor force participation. The significant positive correlations of CEREMONY, FRATERNAL, and JED are all in the same directions as the relationship between these factors and education; the negative correlations of RITUAL and DENOM are also in the same direction as the relationship between education and these factors noted earlier. Only the correlation of ASSOC and labor force participation is in a different direction; and as we shall see, this is a result of the negative relationship between ASSOC and women's labor force participation—the relationship between ASSOC and men's labor force participation is positive, similar to the relationship between ASSOC and education.

In Table 6.12, we compare the rates of labor force participation for the most and least Jewishly involved for the different age and gender groups. Here, we can see that the relationship between labor force participation and Jewishness is different for men and women. Men who are most involved in CEREMONY, ASSOC, FRATERNAL, and JED have higher rates of labor force participation. Even though men's rates of labor force participation tend to have little variation, regular patterns along these lines are apparent. Only among the more ritually observant is the

TABLE 6.12
Percent in Paid Labor Force, for the Most and Least Jewishly Involved, for Each Jewishness Factor, Age, and Sex, U.S. Jews, 1990

Jewishness Factor/Age	Jewish Involvement[a]			
	Least Involved		Most Involved	
	Male	Female	Male	Female
CEREMONY:				
Age 25–34	86.7	75.8	91.2	74.4
35–44	94.3	77.6	98.8	75.1
45–54	89.0	80.7	95.4	82.1
55–64	75.4	49.0	80.4	63.0
65+	22.6	10.0	38.5	15.6
(N in thousands)	(472)	(388)	(557)	(586)
RITUAL:				
Age 25–34	90.4	83.7	86.7	78.0
35–44	97.7	82.8	98.6	69.4
45–54	97.1	82.5	86.2	79.5
55–64	79.6	64.8	78.0	53.4
65+	48.4	22.3	25.3	11.8
(N in thousands)	(485)	(548)	(296)	(297)
ASSOC:				
Age 25–34	86.4	81.4	95.3	76.2
35–44	95.4	77.4	99.5	74.9
45–54	84.2	83.9	96.3	82.4
55–64	75.2	59.4	84.9	56.1
65+	38.0	15.6	30.5	13.4
(N in thousands)	(574)	(426)	(438)	(429)
FRATERNAL:				
Age 25–34	84.2	74.6	90.0	75.3
35–44	95.7	75.4	96.7	74.8
45–54	84.6	83.5	95.6	88.2
55–64	79.0	47.6	84.5	62.1
65+	35.0	10.5	25.7	12.3
(N in thousands)	(491)	(426)	(438)	(429)
JED:				
Age 25–34	88.7	74.2	85.3	67.9
35–44	97.7	87.1	97.1	71.9
45–54	92.3	78.3	89.2	84.7
55–64	83.8	52.1	83.3	55.4
65+	28.1	10.1	29.2	14.6
(N in thousands)	(283)	(378)	(420)	(335)

[a]Based on a trichotomy of factor scores (most involved = highest third, least involved = lowest third).

Source: NJPS, 1990.

relationship reversed, with the more observant having lower rates of labor force participation. Controlling for age enables us to see that these relationships are not because of the relationship between Jewishness and age.

Women who are more Jewishly involved, however, tend to participate less in the labor force or about the same as their less religious counterparts. Only older women (45+) with stronger Jewish background, more involvement in informal Jewish circles, and more involvement in public celebrations of Jewish identity (CEREMONY) tend to be more active in the labor force.

Because of these different relationships between gender, Jewishness, and labor force participation, the gender gap in participation seems to be wider among the more Jewishly involved.

Given the interrelationships of labor force participation, age, gender, and education (as we have shown) and the variations in Jewishness by age, gender, and education, we introduce a multivariate model to show the net relationships between Jewishness and labor force participation. A multiple regression model with extent of labor force participation as the dependent variable was used, with age and education as independent variables. Gender was controlled by repeating the model separately for each gender, because the patterns of labor force participation and their relationship to the other independent variables is very different for men and women.[18]

To determine the net relationship between labor force participation and Jewishness for men and women, we controlled for education, because the less educated are known to work less; further, because we have already seen that there are significant relationships between education and Jewishness, it was important to control for education to determine the net effect of Jewishness on labor force participation. Age was also controlled, because of the variation in both labor force participation and Jewishness over the life cycle. Table 6.13 presents the regression results of these analyses for men and women, for each Jewishness factor. For both of the genders, as expected, age has a consistently negative effect on extent of labor force participation (older people participate less in the labor force) and education has a consistently positive effect (more educated men and women participate more in the labor force).[19]

The Jewishness factors, however, have different effects for men and women, unlike the effect of Jewishness on education. Only two of the Jewishness factors had significant and positive relationships with men's labor force participation: CEREMONY, reflecting collective ritual behavior, and ASSOC, involvement in formal Jewish communal life. In these models, the magnitude of the relationship between Jewishness and labor force participation was the same as between education and labor force participation.

TABLE 6.13
Multiple Regression Analysis of Paid Labor Force Participation on Age, Education, and Jewishness, for Each Jewishness Factor and Sex, U.S. Jews, 1990

	CEREMONY	RITUAL	ASSOC	FRATERNAL	DENOM	JED
Males						
Jewishness						
Unstandardized						
Coefficient	.079**	−.036	.073**	.005	.012	−.004
(Standard error)	(.020)	(.021)	(.021)	(.021)	(.022)	(.024)
Standardized						
coefficient	.098	−.040	.088	.006	.014	−.005
Age						
Unstandardized						
coefficient	−.027**	−.027**	−.027**	−.026**	−.029**	−.024**
(Standard error)	(.001)	(.001)	(.001)	(.001)	(.001)	(.001)
Standardized						
coefficient	−.512	−.512	−.517	−.500	−.545	−.458
Degree						
Unstandardized						
coefficient	.078**	.488**	.079**	.505**	.526**	.416**
(Standard error)	(.015)	(.015)	(.015)	(.015)	(.015)	(.016)
Standardized						
coefficient	.135	.146	.136	.150	.148	.174
Multiple R	.575	.569	.555	.553	.596	.520
(Unweighted n)	(1,118)	(1,118)	(1,120)	(1,131)	(958)	(963)
Females:						
Jewishness						
Unstandardized						
coefficient	.013	−.106**	−.049*	−.029	−.015	−.054*
(Standard error)	(.024)	(.024)	(.025)	(.024)	(.027)	(.027)
Standardized						
coefficient	.015	−.117	−.055	−.032	−.017	−.063
Age						
Unstandardized						
coefficient	−.024**	−.024**	−.023**	−.023**	−.022**	−.024**
(Standard error)	(.002)	(.002)	(.002)	(.002)	(.002)	(.002)
Standardized						
coefficient	−.427	−.422	−.410	−.413	−.363	−.396
Degree						
Unstandardized						
coefficient	.089**	.085**	.093**	.095**	.082**	.084**
(Standard error)	(.019)	(.019)	(.019)	(.019)	(.021)	(.022)
Standardized						
coefficient	.135	.129	.140	.142	.124	.125
Multiple R	.493	.507	.491	.488	.427	.449
(Unweighted n)	(1,083)	(1,083)	(1,093)	(1,095)	(917)	(829)

*α = .05.
**α = .01.

Source: NJPS, 1990.

The other four Jewishness factors have no significant relationship with men's labor force participation. That Jewish educational background has no relationship with labor force activity does not tell us much about whether Jewishness has a relationship with labor force activity or not: having such a background tells us little about how much one actually knows about the Jewish heritage, which could depend on one's own intelligence or the quality of the training, or whether or not one has accepted what one has learned. So we cannot assume that it reflects a lack of relationship between Jewishness and labor force activity. Involvement in Jewish social circles is apparently not related to labor force activity per se, although it may be related to occupational achievement (which we will explore later). Observance of traditional rituals is not related to labor force activity, apparently because the more observant have found ways to be involved in the modern secular world, just like those who express their Jewishness in other ways. And closeness to Orthodox denomination is not related, either, probably for similar reasons. That the more privately expressed religiosity and closeness to Orthodox denomination are not related to labor force activity again provides partial support for the secularization thesis—that traditional religiosity no longer has connection to secular activities. We shall explore the meaning of the relationship (or lack of relationship) between Jewishness and labor force activity for each major denomination later, when we analyze results for each denomination separately.

For men, mainly the social, collective aspects of Jewishness are related to their labor force participation; that is, those more active in Jewish communal life and collective rituals (ASSOC and CEREMONY) are more active in the labor force. Or perhaps those more active in the labor force maintain closer Jewish networks which reinforce their collective expression of Jewishness. This supports Goldscheider's (1986) suggestion that American Judaism is to a great extent now maintained by networks that occur as much in secular settings of higher education and employment as in communal Jewish organizations (not necessarily religious in nature). This reinforces the idea that the American Jewish collectivity has been transformed from a strictly religious definition (as was suggested in Herberg's *Protestant, Catholic and Jew*, 1956) to a much more encompassing collective orientation, reinforced not only by religious frameworks but by common secular frameworks as well.

Among women, the effects of Jewishness are quite different. Those aspects of Jewishness that are significantly related to female labor force participation even after age and education are controlled (RITUAL, JED; and ASSOC), have negative effects; that is, those more Jewish have less participation in the labor force. Traditional Jewish religiosity (as indicated by RITUAL) is often associated with a stronger emphasis on familial roles, which might take time, energy, and effort away from labor force activity. Because more observant women are also more likely to have Jewish education, the same argument may be made about JED.

The negative relationship between ASSOC and labor force activity may also be because of the relationship between Jewishness and family roles, or it may be that the women involved in Jewish communal life (such as volunteer organizations) are less likely to be working in the paid labor force. For many years, volunteering was an acceptable activity for women, even if working in the paid labor force was not (Baum et al., 1976; Hyman, 1991). As a leisure-time activity, volunteering was seen as woman's domain, and the social-welfare and cultural activities they promoted were also seen as extensions of women's traditional roles (Elazar, 1976). In other words, all three indicate involvement in roles alternative to women's roles in the paid labor force. Recent changes in women's patterns of labor force participation have challenged the traditional organization of these volunteer associations, which are losing their supply of volunteers unless they reorganize to accommodate women who are also working for pay outside the home (Fishman, 1993). It might be summarized that all of these factors suggest involvement in roles alternative to or competing with women's roles in the paid labor force, which may underlie the negative relationship between Jewishness and female labor force participation.

At least at the present, labor force involvement does not seem to reinforce Jewish involvement for women nor does Jewish involvement reinforce labor force involvement. The networking that seems to maintain Jewish patterns of achievement for men does not seem to be applicable to Jewish women.

The lack of relationship between FRATERNAL and labor force activity can be explained, as it was for men: because no competition is involved, on the one hand; on the other hand, however, no enhancement of labor force activity comes from Jewish social associations either. The lack of relationship between CEREMONY and labor force activity also suggests that the rituals indicated by this factor are not very time consuming, occurring infrequently and usually at times that do not conflict with labor force activity (e.g., in the evening); because they are not very demanding, they do not compete with women's other roles. The lack of relationship also suggests that women do not make use of these occasions to further their labor force contacts, as men seem to do.

Comparing the relationship between Jewishness and labor force participation for men and women, we find that relationships are in opposite directions for the two genders: when Jewishness is significantly related to men's labor force participation it is in a positive direction—the more "Jewish" the man, the greater is the labor force activity; but for women, the more "Jewish" the woman, the less is the labor force activity. This contrasting direction of relationship is highlighted by the factor ASSOC, participation in Jewish organizational life: the more men participate in the Jewish organizations, the more active they are in the labor force as well (or, perhaps, as we have suggested, the more active in the labor force, the more money they have to contribute to Jewish organizations and the more contacts for participating in Jewish organizations); the more women participate in Jewish organizations, the less they participate in the labor force, as if one is an alternative to the other. Because these relationships are net of the relationship between Jewishness and education, we can understand that indirectly the relationship between Jewishness and education increases the positive relationship between Jewishness and labor force participation for men, but minimizes the negative relationship between Jewishness and labor force participation for women (because the relationship between Jewishness and education was positive for both genders).

As we have shown, family roles have opposite effects on the labor force participation of men and women, increasing men's participation in the labor force as they work to support their families and decreasing women's participation in the labor force as they juggle demanding family roles with labor force involvement. Because Jewishness is related to being married, we wondered whether the relationships between Jewishness and labor force activity could be explained by augmented family roles, as indicated by marital status.

We added the Jewishness factors to the regressions predicting the labor force participation of men and women (which were presented above in Chapter 3). The results for each factor are presented in Table 6.14. Controlling for marital status, age, and education does not change the relationship between Jewishness and labor force participation among men. The same two factors have significant positive relationships with labor force participation—CEREMONY and ASSOC—and the others do not. Participation in collective rituals and in formal Jewish organizational life is associated with intensified labor force participation (and vice versa), and this relationship is not explained by marital status. It is weakened somewhat but remains significant.

The inclusion of the Jewishness factors does change the strength of other factors' effect on men's labor force participation. The positive effect of being married is reduced by about a third: it remains positive and significant, but is somewhat smaller. The interaction between age and marital status also becomes smaller, although it also remains statistically significant. In summary, among men, the positive relationship between Jewishness and labor force participation is not explained by the marital status of the more Jewishly involved; however, part of the greater labor force participation of married men is explained by their tendency to be more Jewishly involved.

TABLE 6.14
Multiple Regression Analysis of Paid Labor Force Participation on Age, Education, Marital Status, and Jewishness, for Each Jewishness Factor and Sex, U.S. Jews, 1990

	CEREMONY	RITUAL	ASSOC	FRATERNAL	DENOM	JED
Males:						
Jewishness						
Unstandardized coefficient	.021*	−.035	.041*	−.004	.007	−.006
Standardized coefficient	.051	−.041	.050	−.004	.009	−.007
Under retirement age						
Unstandardized coefficient	.399**	.809**	.810**	.818**	.811**	.863**
Standardized coefficient	.394	.403	.397	.403	.410	.413
Age						
Unstandardized coefficient	−.003*	−.009**	−.009**	−.009**	−.010**	−.006*
Standardized coefficient	−.123	−.175	−.167	−.168	−.198	−.111
Being married						
Unstandardized coefficient	.219**	.527**	.544**	.515**	.526**	.629**
Standardized coefficient	.230	.278	.290	.273	.224	.347
Interaction between being married and age						
Unstandardized coefficient	−.002	−.006*	−.006*	−.005	−.005	−.007*
Standardized coefficient	−.151	−.179	−.199	−.167	−.132	−.230
Degree						
Unstandardized coefficient	.024**	.051**	.048**	.052**	.050**	.063**
Standardized coefficient	.084	.090	.083	.091	.090	.111
Multiple R	.589	.651	.636	.637	.670	.626
(Unweighted n)	(1,116)	(1,116)	(1,118)	(1,130)	(.958)	(962)

(continued on next page)

TABLE 6.14 *(continued)*

	CEREMONY	RITUAL	ASSOC	FRATERNAL	DENOM	JED
Females:						
Jewishness						
Unstandardized coefficient	.021	−.044**	−.036	.012	−.002	−.042
Standardized coefficient	.023	−.087	−.041	.024	−.002	−.049
Under retirement age						
Unstandardized coefficient	.602**	.359**	.634**	.373**	.587**	.622**
Standardized coefficient	.314	.337	.327	.347	.293	.306
Age						
Unstandardized coefficient	−.014**	−.005**	−.012**	−.005**	−.003	−.011**
Standardized coefficient	−.251	−.169	−.218	−.154	−.057	−.187
Being married						
Unstandardized coefficient	−.556**	−.103	−.502**	−.096	−.093	−.406**
Standardized coefficient	−.285	−.095	−.257	−.088	−.038	−.203
Interaction between being married and age						
Unstandardized coefficient	.006*	.001	.006*	.001	−.004	.001
Standardized coefficient	.197	.067	.171	.043	−.100	.101
Degree						
Unstandardized coefficient	.078**	.042**	.082**	.047**	.077**	.074**
Standardized coefficient	.118	.113	.123	.126	.116	.111
Multiple R	.532	.530	.531	.520	.470	.494
(Unweighted n)	(1,083)	(1,083)	(1,093)	(1,095)	(916)	(829)

*α = .05.
**α = .01.

Source: NJPS, 1990.

The effect of age, on the other hand, becomes somewhat greater, indicating that part of the negative effect of age and labor force participation was suppressed by the association between Jewishness and labor force participation: because older men tend to have higher scores on the Jewishness factors, and Jewishness has a positive effect on labor force participation, when Jewishness is controlled, the negative effect of age becomes clearer. The exception to this is the model including JED, because older men do not have more Jewish education than younger men.

Among women, in contrast, when we control for marital status the significant relationships between Jewishness and labor force participation disappear for all but one factor. That is, the negative relationship between Jewishness and labor force participation that we saw earlier is apparently a result of the family roles implied in being married, which are stronger for the more Jewishly involved (who are also more likely to be married). In other words, Jewishness itself has no direct relationship to the labor force participation of women, as we expected. It has an indirect effect through marital status, because married women are less likely to work in the paid labor force, and married women tend to be more Jewishly involved. The only exception to this is the significant negative relationship between RITUAL and labor force participation, which persists even when marital status is controlled.

When we discussed women's labor force participation earlier, it was not marital status itself as much as childrearing roles that were negatively related to women's labor force participation. Jewish involvement is related not only to being married but to having more children and being more involved in childrearing roles. Hartman (1984) showed that among Israeli women, being even slightly more observant of Jewish traditions was associated with more family roles (having more children and at an earlier age), and the greater the observance is, the stronger is the involvement in family roles. Among American Jewish women we study here, women who are more Jewishly involved, also have more children (Figure 6.2). Among the least religious or Jewish in terms of RITUAL, for instance, there is an average of 1.6 children per woman, compared with an average of 2.0 children per woman among those scoring highest on RITUAL.[20] We expected that the augmented childrearing roles of the more Jewishly involved would also explain the negative relationship between Jewishness and women's participation in the paid labor force.

The path analysis[21] illustrated in Figure 6.3 shows this more clearly. In it age, education, and Jewishness are considered three background factors (B), number of children indicates family roles (C), and labor force participation (LFP) is the dependent variable. Table 6.15 presents the path coefficients[22] for that model for each of the Jewishness factors. Each

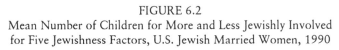

FIGURE 6.2
Mean Number of Children for More and Less Jewishly Involved
for Five Jewishness Factors, U.S. Jewish Married Women, 1990

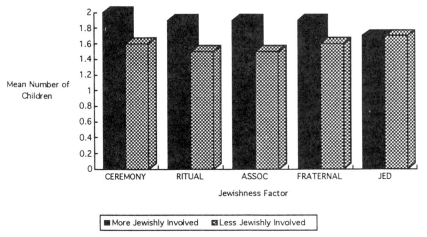

Source: NJPS, 1990.

column in Table 6.15 represents one path analysis using one indicator of Jewishness as a background variable. The upper part of the table presents the path coefficients of the various background variables predicting number of children; the middle part, the path coefficients of the same background variables predicting labor force participation; and the bottom part, the path coefficients resulting from a regression in which labor force participation is predicted by number of children.

The background variables age and education have the expected relationships with number of children and labor force participation: age is positively related to number of children (women in older cohorts had more children) and negatively related to labor force participation (older women participate less); education (academic degree achieved) is negatively related to number of children (more educated women have fewer children) and positively related to labor force participation (more educated women participate more). But our main interest was in the role of Jewishness in this model.

It is clear from the path coefficient of Jewishness to number of children (the first line in Table 6.15) that each Jewishness factor is significantly and positively related to number of children—the more "Jewishly involved" the woman is on each of these factors, the more children she has. Number of children clearly has a significant negative effect on labor force participation for each of the factors. This effect is not confined to observance of traditional Jewish rituals (RITUAL), but is found for the

FIGURE 6.3
Path Model of Labor Force Participation, U.S. Jewish Women, 1990

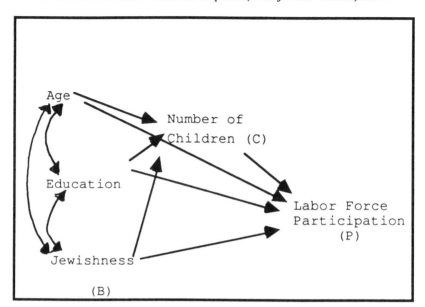

more collective and social expressions of Jewishness as well. Therefore, Jewishness, as reflected by all indicators, has an additional (negative) effect on the labor force participation of women, through augmented family roles (indicated here by number of children), an "indirect" effect through number of children. In addition, the path analysis shows that except for one indicator, the direct effect of Jewishness is also negative on labor force participation, but most of these direct effects are not statistically significant when number of children are controlled; only RITUAL, expressing a traditional orientation to Jewish ritual, continues to have a significant negative relationship with labor force participation; that is, only among the women with the most traditional or Orthodox orientation to religious practice is there a direct negative relationship between Jewishness and labor force activity.

Most of the relationship between Jewishness and female labor force participation can therefore be explained by the relationship between Jewishness and augmented family roles. As women invest more in familial roles, their time and energy for labor force activity is by necessity curtailed.

It is interesting to contrast this with the relationship between Jewishness and education. There a direct effect persists, reflecting the value of Jewishness on education; the lack of such direct effect on labor force

TABLE 6.15
Path Analysis of Paid Labor Force Participation, for Each Jewishness Factor,
U.S. Jewish Married Women, 1990
(Standardized Regression Coefficients)

Path	CEREMONY	RITUAL	ASSOC	FRATERNAL	DENOM	JED
			Jewishness Factor			
B → C						
Jewishness	.182*	.155*	.172*	.144*	.096*	.151*
Age	.285*	.280*	.240*	.251*	.244*	.337*
Degree	−.124*	−.095*	−.127*	−.112*	−.104*	−.102*
Multiple R	.384	.383	.372	.331	.377	.361
B → LFP						
Jewishness	.036	−.101**	−.034	−.016	−.007	−.042
Age	−.394**	−.396**	−.384**	−.385**	−.337**	−.351**
Degree	.116**	.116**	.121**	.125**	.107**	.105**
C → LFP						
Number of						
Children	−.124**	−.100*	−.119*	−.119*	−.118*	−.148*
Multiple R	.507	.515	.504	.501	.441	.470
(Unweighted						
n)	(1,133)	(1,133)	(1,143)	(1,148)	(963)	(863)

B → C = Background factors (age, education, Jewishness) predicting number of children.
B → LFP = Background factors predicting labor force participation.
C → LFP = Number of children predicting labor force participation.

*α < .05.
**α < .01.

Source: NJPS, 1990.

participation (for women) reflects the absence of proscriptions against women's participation in the labor force per se—only against its interference with family roles, which take precedence in Jewish values.

It should not be surprising that Jewishness is not related to the incidence of dual earner couples, given the weak relationship to both men's and women's labor force participation. There is hardly any difference between the more or less Jewishly involved couples on any factor in terms of how many are dual earners.

Similarly, when we compare the couples of different denominations, there is little difference in the percent dual earners. Fifty-two percent of the Orthodox are dual earners, 55 percent of the Conservative, 55 percent of the Reform, and 50 percent of the unaffiliated. What is clear again is that the inequality of religious roles found among the Orthodox does not spill over into the economic sphere. The slightly lower percentage of dual earners among the Orthodox could probably be explained by their larger families and more demanding family roles, which is related to fewer wives' participating in the paid labor force.

In summary, Jewishness strengthens the intensity of Jewish men's labor force participation, especially among married men, but only in terms of two expressions of Jewishness—observance of collective rituals (CEREMONY) and participation in formal Jewish life (ASSOC)—two aspects that themselves are reinforced by Jewish contacts in the secular arenas. For women, Jewishness is related to labor force participation mainly in an indirect way, through the augmented family roles of the more Jewishly involved. The mechanisms by which Jewish involvement is related to labor force participation differ for men and women and reflect the lack of Jewish value regarding labor force participation per se.

OCCUPATIONAL ACHIEVEMENT OF
MEN AND WOMEN AND THEIR JEWISHNESS

In this section we consider how the occupational achievements of Jewish men and women are related to their Jewish involvement. There are two foci here: how much occupational prestige is achieved and which specific occupations are entered.

Looking first at the occupational prestige achieved, a general relationship between occupational achievement and Jewishness could be approached from the earlier theses we introduced: Jewishness is expected to be associated with higher occupational achievement because of the general orientation to rationality and achievement in the Jewish heritage. The source of this achievement orientation may be in Jewish values themselves, although the previous section on labor force activity casts doubt on this. The achievement orientation may stem from either the specific circumstances of American Jews, that is, their minority status, or be mainly indirect through the Jewish values on education, the motivation to support the family well, or through the social network of Jews reinforced both in secular and religious frameworks. If the family motivation is intermediate between Jewishness and occupational achievement, marital status will attenuate whatever relationships we find. If the social networks provided by both secular and religious frameworks are the primary mechanism by which Jewishness is linked to occupational achievement, we should see a link only between those Jewishness factors indicating such networks (e.g., ASSOC). If, however, the main association is with education, there may only be an indirect relationship between Jewishness and occupational achievement.

There is no a priori reason to expect that Jewishness will result in differential occupational achievement for women than for men, except insofar as their unequal educational achievement or family roles have kept women from achieving as much as their male counterparts. As discussed earlier, the Jewish culture did not restrict women from engaging in a wide range of occupations, with the exception of particular religious roles that women were not allowed to perform. In American Judaism, many of these roles have also been opened to women through the Reform, the Reconstructionist, and later the Conservative movements, although these changes are not yet widely accepted and still meet with considerable resistance, especially among Conservatives and Orthodox.[23]

Four of the Jewishness factors have relatively weak but significant correlations with occupational prestige: CEREMONY, ASSOC, and JED have significant positive correlations (.066, .094, and .056 respectively), and DENOM has a significant negative correlation (−.070).[24] FRATERNAL and RITUAL have no significant correlations.

However, once gender, education, and age have been controlled, only ASSOC has an independent significant relationship with the occupational achievement of men. Men more active in formal Jewish life have higher occupational prestige. Because this is the only aspect of Jewishness with which occupational prestige retains a significant relationship once age and education are controlled, it suggests that the main relationship is again one of networking—men with higher occupational prestige are aided in their career development through the kinds of ties fostered in formal Jewish organizational life, and they are the ones contacted and recruited for leadership and philanthropic positions in Jewish organizations. This does not suggest an orientation to occupational achievement based on a value orientation in the Jewish heritage, because RITUAL and DENOM do not have significant relationships once age and education are held constant.

Participation in formal Jewish organizational life is not related to occupational prestige for women. This is probably because family responsibilities preclude women's involvement in Jewish organizations when they also have a career with high occupational prestige; also, because part of this factor reflects contributions to Jewish organizations, it may be that women's income is not considered independent of men's in determining a family's contribution to Jewish organizations, since it is usually the second income; the major relationship between contributions and occupation would seem to be mainly through the husband rather than the wife. Hence, the relationship between secular and religious networking frameworks is not the same for women, even when they have successful careers, probably because they have less time for organizational activities when they have a career and an income accompanying women's occupational achievements is not likely to be as high as men's nor is it likely to determine the household contributions to Jewish charities.

When we compare the occupational achievements of husbands and wives, we find virtually no relationship between degree of Jewish involvement on any of the factors, and spousal inequality in occupational achievement (Table 6.16). Jewishness does not hinder wives from achieving as much as their husbands, which may be one explanation that we earlier found so many Jewish wives who had achieved as much or more occupational prestige than their husbands.

The couples' denomination does not have a clear relationship with spousal inequality or equality in occupational achievement, either (Table 6.17). The Orthodox and the unaffiliated have the greatest similarity in

TABLE 6.16
Inequality in Spousal Occupational Achievement,
by Jewish Involvement, U.S. Jews, 1990

Jewishness Factor and Inequality Indicator	More Jewishly Involved	Less Jewishly Involved	(Significance of t)[a]
CEREMONY			
% conventional prestige differences	65.9	67.0	(.90)
Mean prestige differences	3.0	3.5	(.63)
RITUAL			
% conventional prestige differences	65.1	68.9	(.20)
Mean prestige differences	2.9	4.0	(.34)
ASSOC			
% conventional prestige differences	66.9	66.5	(.90)
Mean prestige differences	3.5	3.1	(.73)
FRATERNAL			
% conventional prestige differences	67.5	64.8	(.39)
Mean prestige differences	3.7	2.5	(.31)
JED			
% conventional prestige differences	69.9	68.4	(.06)
Mean prestige differences	4.5	2.3	(.13)
Unweighted n = 1,414 couples			

[a]Conventionally a statistically significant result has the value of .05 or less.

Source: NJPS, 1990.

occupational prestige, and the Reconstructionist and the Reform have the greatest dissimilarity. The Orthodox tradition of women contributing to the household economy, especially so that men can devote more time to religious study, may bring the spouses closer together in terms of occupational achievement. In any case, there is certainly no basis to claim that the inequality in religious roles spills over into occupational achievement.

Our second focus is on the actual occupations of Jewishly involved men and women. Two primary sources could serve as restraints to the occupations of Jewishly involved men and women. Observant Jews might find it difficult to succeed in careers that demand compromise with traditional ritual practices. Careers that entail extensive mealtime socializing, a conforming outward appearance, scheduling priorities that might interfere with Shabbat or holiday observance might present difficulties for the observant Jew and his or her employer (Mael, 1991). This has been a drawback for observant Jews to succeed in business, where corporate loyalty and commitment are measured by some of these same activities that an observant Jew practices. It has been suggested that "those few Jews who have succeeded in achieving high corporate status have generally done so at the expense of their Jewish identities, by eradicating any religious or ethnic indication of their heritage" (Mael, 1991, p. 345 citing Korman, 1988 and Slavin and Pradt, 1982). This would lead us to expect that the more Jewishly involved would be less likely to be in corporate management positions.

A second expectation stems from the patterns we saw above when we compared Jewish occupational patterns to the wider American popula-

TABLE 6.17
Spousal Occupational Inequality, by Denomination, U.S. Jews, 1990

Couple Characteristic	*Jewishness Denomination*				
	Orthodox	*Conservative*	*Reconstructionist*	*Reform*	*Unaffiliated*
% conventional prestige differences[a]	61.7	66.3	65.4	68.4	62.7
Mean prestige difference between husband and wife	2.8	3.1	4.6	3.6	2.1
Unweighted *n* =1,414 couples.					

[a]Husband has same or higher occupational prestige than wife.

Source: NJPS, 1990.

tion. What we presented reinforced the well-known overrepresentation of Jews in professional and managerial positions, and their underrepresentation in blue-collar and service occupations. While Jewish women like other American women are concentrated in typical "female" niches, they are over-represented in the semi-professional/technical occupations, and under-represented in blue collar and service occupations. If these reflect "Jewish" patterns, we might expect the more Jewishly involved to exhibit these patterns while the less Jewishly involved are more evenly distributed across the occupational categories.

In comparing the occupations of the more Jewishly involved to the less Jewishly involved on each Jewishness factor, we find no evidence to support the contention that observant Jews are less involved in corporate life. This may be because we are using a crude nine-group occupational classification, or it may be that this underrepresentation is confined to a minority of Orthodox Jews who are not represented well in this survey. Or it may be that this problem has passed, and Jews are now becoming well-represented in managerial positions as well. The more Jewishly involved men on each factor are more likely than the less involved to be found in professional and managerial occupations, while the less involved are more likely to be in the technical and semi-professional occupations or blue-collar or service jobs. This suggests that professional and managerial careers facilitate Jewish involvement, whereas the less successful in occupations are more alienated from Jewish life. Since a high proportion of professionals and managers are self-employed, it may also be that self-employment facilitates Jewish involvement or that the self-employed seek more Jewish contacts to further their business interests. The patterns that differentiate American Jews from the wider American population (a high proportion of professionals and managers and a high proportion of self-employed) also appear to differentiate the more Jewishly involved from the less Jewishly involved men.

Among women we find the more Jewishly involved tend to be in those occupational groups with typical female occupations—semi-professional and technical and clerical. The less involved are more likely to be blue-collar or service workers and, to a lesser extent, in professional occupations. The more Jewishly involved women appear to be more conventional in their occupations, perhaps because these occupations are easier to combine with the augmented family roles the more Jewishly involved have.

It would be interesting to determine whether this is particularly true of Jewish women, or of all women who are more involved in a religion; and whether it is an indirect effect of Jewishness through family roles as we found for labor force participation and occupational prestige. Unfortunately a more extensive sample would be needed for conclusive analysis. The findings do suggest that again the more demanding family roles of the Jewishly involved result in different occupational patterns.

The occupational dissimilarity between the Jewishly involved men and women is considerably higher than the occupational dissimilarity between the less involved Jewish men and women. (Table 6.18). Again, this may be because a higher proportion of the Jewishly involved are married, and there is greater differentiation between married men and women in their labor force patterns than among the unmarried (as we showed in Chapter 3). Nonetheless, it does show that there is greater gender differentiation in occupational roles among the more Jewishly involved than among those less involved, in every aspect.

SUMMARY

In this chapter we have asked whether the gender patterns of achievement described in earlier chapters were found among all types of American Jews or were more apparent among those more Jewishly involved in various aspects of American Jewish life. Jewish involvement did not change the relationship between education and gender nor was Jewishness related to educational achievement differently for men and women. Labor force activity, on the contrary, was related to Jewish involvement differently for men and women and enhanced by Jewishness for men but not for women. Apparently Jewish involvement, because of the Jewish familial orientation, increases the gender differentiation in the family, which in turn affects the

TABLE 6.18
Gender Dissimilarity in Occupational Distributions Among the More and Less
Jewishly Involved, for Each Jewishness Factor, U.S. Jews, 1990
(Dissimilarity Coefficients[a])

	Jewish Involvement	
Jewishness Factor	*More Involved*	*Less Involved*
CEREMONY	37.0	26.7
RITUAL	40.9	28.1
ASSOC	38.4	24.9
FRATERNAL	38.1	26.0
JED	32.9	30.1
Unweighted n = 2,278.		

[a]For dissimilarity calculations, see the note to Table 4.2.

Source: NJPS, 1990.

relationship between gender and labor force participation. This gender differentiation in turn affects occupational achievement. Jewishness, however, is not directly related to labor force participation or to occupational achievement; that is, there seem to be no proscriptions of women's secular involvement, only a positive value attached to family life, which has its own effect on secular achievement.

Contrary to our expectations, there was no evidence that Jewishness encouraged gender inequality between spouses; nor did spousal inequality vary consistently across the denominations. Despite the different orientations of the main American Jewish denominations to gender equality in terms of religious roles and stratification, we found no spillover in terms of secular achievement in the anticipated directions. On the contrary, some of the strongest evidence of gender equality within couples was found among the Orthodox, carrying a tradition evidenced historically in Jewish tradition.

CHAPTER 7

Are We One?
Gender Roles and Secular Achievement
Among Israeli and American Jews

Jews the world over share to some degree a Jewish heritage. As part of the greater Jewish civilization,[1] Jews share many common premises with which they approach the social construction of their reality and are influenced in their present behavior by many of the same forces. If Jews share a civilization, then the orientations to secular activities and achievements should be influenced by those civilizational premises. To the extent that the secular achievements of American Jews derive from aspects of the cultural heritage of Judaism, we expect these orientations to be shared by all Jews; similarly if the patterns of gender equality we have seen are "Jewish" in nature, they should be shared by all Jews. In this respect, in the previous chapter we have considered the extent to which American Jewish patterns of secular achievement are shared by men and women more and less Jewishly involved. To the extent that Israel represents a society in which the civilizational premises of Judaism have been institutionalized, "Jewish" patterns of behavior should be even more apparent among Israeli Jews. In this chapter we compare our findings about secular achievement of American Jewish men and women to patterns of secular achievement among Israeli Jewish men and women, in a further attempt to determine whether all Jews share the patterns we have observed among American Jews or whether the unique position of American Jews within the American setting has influenced their patterns of secular achievement and the way Jewishness is related to them.

American and Israeli Jews share certain similarities by virtue of their common heritage. In their comparison of American and Israeli Judaism, Liebman and Cohen (1990) summarize some of the similarities between the two:

> Jews in both countries observe many of the same holidays, rituals, and ceremonies, respond to many of the same symbols, retell many of the same myths. . . . Jews in both Israel and the United States (as well as in all other parts of the world) share a belief in their common people-

hood—the myth of common descent, common destiny, and a strong sense of mutual responsibility. . . . [B]oth Israeli and American Jews not only affirm a common past in nominal terms but continue to share much in that past. They share a set of symbols that are reflected in liturgy and ritual. . . . Israeli and American Jews are linked not only by their Jewish formulations and conceptions but by their enemies. . . . The two communities are also linked by ties of family. . . . Along with the continuing exchange of visitors and leaders between the two communities, these family ties mean that each side is at least vaguely aware of the new Jewish conceptions emerging in the other, and at least slightly influenced by them. (Liebman and Cohen, 1990, pp. 171–173)

As a civilization establishes itself in different historical contexts, however, the premises themselves may be altered or modified or different parameters emphasized at the neglect of others. Therefore, if there is an orientation to the secular achievement of Jewish men and women, we should find it for Jews the world over, unless there are historical contexts that interfere with or alter the realization of these premises.

All over the world, except in Israel, Jews live in a minority status with a more or less organized Jewish community life. Jews in the Diaspora are influenced by the wider social environment in which they are situated, both in terms of opportunities available to them (limited by extent of economic development, type of political regime, access granted to various arenas of social action governed by the wider society) and in terms of the wider cultural values to which they must accommodate. As a result, Jewish communities in the Diaspora often take on features obviously related to their wider social context. Leibman and Cohen (1990) have suggested that American Jews have reconstructed the tradition of Judaism through the prisms of personalism, voluntarism, universalism, and moralism—all value orientations compatible with the wider values of the American civil society. Personalism reflects the wider society's emphasis on individualism, which marks a radical difference from Israeli society's emphasis on collectivism (see also Eisenstadt, 1992, especially Chapter 8). Voluntarism reflects the lack of formal institutionalization characteristic of a subgroup within a society that provides wider institutions for all of its societal needs. Universalism reflects the American ethos of equality for all and an emphasis on Western liberal and humanistic orientations. Moralism enables the Jew to follow Jewish practices as an ethical rather than a particularistic or exclusive system, which would create tensions within the wider American society. "By defining Judaism as both centered on values and liberal in content, Jews maintain that their religion is highly compatible with Americanism. . . . For by emphasizing that Judaism is a system of shared values they deny the ethnocentricity of their heritage, by making Judaism accessible to those who share these values they universalize it, and by affirming the values as 'liberal' they moralize them" (Liebman and Cohen, 1990, p. 122).

Living within the American society, Jews are also influenced by the range of educational and economic opportunities available. As we have discussed with regard to educational achievement, part of the explanation for Jews' high educational attainment in the United States stems from the timing of the expansion of institutions of higher learning in the United States. This expansion coincided with a thirst for higher education created by the Jews' situation in Eastern Europe prior to their mass immigration and a drive to succeed in the new country in terms valued by their new American society. Without the availability of these institutions of higher learning and without the access guaranteed to all Americans by the basic American values of equality (and not to be taken for granted, since they were not always automatically given), American Jews would not have reached as high a level of educational attainment as they have today. The tension in the wider society over gender equality tapped the seeds of women's secular achievements among American Jews, which had been sown in earlier Jewish tradition but may have remained secondary, as they did among Jews living where the wider society was ruled by Moslems, for instance. The wider society thus can tap different emphases within the Jewish tradition, and provide different opportunities for Jews, which must be taken into account when two Diaspora communities of Jews are compared.

The comparison of Jews in two Diaspora communities differs from a comparison of Jews in a Diaspora community and in Israel. The former comparison, of two Diaspora communities, is somewhat easier, in that in both cases the wider social institutions, such as the economy and the political system, are for the most part external to the Jewish community. Interpretations of differences between the communities are somewhat more clear-cut, because it is easier to control for differences that relate to the surrounding environment and its relations to the Jewish community and thereby to isolate the influences of the Jewish environment itself.

Israeli Jews are unique in being a majority group both in the sense of numbers and dominance. When we try to compare Jewish behavior in a Diaspora community to Israel, we must take into account that the Jews themselves have set up and are responsible for the institutions of the wider Israeli society, such as the economy, the polity, and the educational system. It is to a great extent a self-sufficient society,[2] which for the most part cannot depend on other parts of the society to provide needed services. As the numerical majority in its country, Israeli Jews must fill nearly[3] the whole gamut of occupations in Israel, so that the Jewish population is much more varied socioeconomically than is the American Jewish population. Human resource needs in Israel include a demand for both highly educated and less skilled Jewish labor. Israel cannot afford that a majority of its Jews, like American Jews, be concentrated in the middle to upper-middle socioeconomic stratum of the population, as it cannot depend on the wider society to provide needed services. Although we try to control for some of these differences, the size of the samples used and some of the implications of being a whole society rather than a minority group are not controllable.

As a Jewish state, Israeli institutions reflect at least to some extent a Jewishness not found in the Diaspora.[4] In the words of the well-known Israeli writer, A. B. Yehoshua, "Everything that happens is our responsibility and reflects our Jewishness." This makes more difficult the comparison of the influence of Jewish involvement in a Diaspora community as opposed to in Israel. There are no easy indicators of "relations with the wider society" or external "values of the wider society" to compare to other Diaspora communities and from which to isolate the influences of the Jewish environment itself .

Rather than being plagued with problems of assimilation and trying to prove Jews' worth while preserving some sense of collective identity in a predominantly non-Jewish society, Israeli Jews grapple with setting up institutions to service a whole society and developing a sense of national collective identity. The nationalistic element of the Jewish heritage is developed to its fullest in Israel, whereas American Jews must juggle their nationalistic commitment to the United States with an ethnic-nationalistic-religious commitment to their Jewish heritage and people. The religious population in Israel tends to be more nationalistic than the rest of the population, but among Americans religiosity does not necessarily affect attitudes toward Israel or worldwide Jewish nationalism (see discussion in Liebman and Cohen, 1990, Ch. 6). Instead of emphasizing the rights of the minority and the individual in the wider society so that their rights as a Jewish minority and as Jewish individuals can be preserved, the Israeli culture emphasizes a common collective identity and background among its various Jews. Rather than adopting a universalism that will protect the individual's achievements whatever his or her particularistic characteristics (such as being a Jew in a predominantly non-Jewish society), Israel emphasizes the particularistic ties that bind the Jewish majority together, even though these Jews have immigrated from the world over. Instead of preserving the voluntaristic nature of Jewish institutions in the Diaspora, the Israeli state has institutionalized the traditional welfare and cultural functions of the Jewish volunteer organizations in the Diaspora. As a majority culture, Israelis have also institutionalized as part of their political culture certain Jewish practices and laws, such as the observance of Jewish religious holidays as national holidays; and marriage and divorce laws being governed by religious law (Jewish for Jews; Moslem for Moslems, etc.).

As a result nearly the whole Israeli Jewish population exhibits a degree of "Jewish involvement" just by being exposed to the Jewish heritage through institutions that have a Jewish basis. A recent study of religiosity among Israeli Jews shows that a majority, even those who define themselves as religiously "nonobservant," exhibit some component of Jewish identity or involvement (Levy, Levinsohn, and Katz, 1993).[5] Living in a Jewish neighborhood and having a majority of friends who are Jewish becomes a reality for most Israeli Jews, but one would have to try very hard to disengage oneself from such kinds of Jewish "involvement." Jewish holidays and heritage are taught to some extent in all schools, whether religious or secular. To the extent that there are values or orientations in the Jewish heritage that relate to gendered patterns of secular achievement, more Israeli Jews would be exposed to them than among American Jews, where the exposure and involvement is on a more voluntary basis.

On the other hand, some Jewish institutions that take on a much broader function for Jews in the Diaspora revert to being primarily religious institutions in Israel. The synagogue does not become a center for nonreligious activities for a Jewish and even nonJewish collectivity as it does in the United States, but becomes a predominantly religious center for the observant.

When we consider the effect of Jewish involvement on secular achievement, we are thus limited in the dimensions that can be compared between Israeli and American Jews, because of the different ways in which the populations are exposed to Jewish involvement. As we shall see, our comparison is reduced to how much ritual observance is related to secular achievement in each of the settings.

Patterns of secular achievement are restrained by this ceiling imposed by societal needs. When higher education and higher occupational positions are more scarce relative to the population in question, gender may be a basis for allocating scarce resources, resulting in greater inequality between men and women in their secular achievement. Therefore, we may expect greater gender inequality among Israeli Jews than among American Jews.

As a majority that must protect its claims to sovereignty in a sea of surrounding enemies, the state of Israel has had to develop a strong defense force, a military component that has had wide-range influence on the rest of the society. The value placed on the qualities needed to be a good soldier, the fact that official combat is reserved for men, that the strain of serving in the army is relieved by having a family to come home to—all serve to strengthen a gender role differentiation that permeates the society. That many[6] Israeli women serve in the army does not contradict this gender role differentiation, because within the army itself there is a high degree of gender differentiation. It stands in contradiction to the gender equality ideal of the Zionist socialist background that we describe. The institution of the army, in which men 18–21 and women 18–20 share compulsory service, has some latent functions for the society as well. For instance, it provides an institution that postpones the entrance of young people into the labor force. A high demand for higher education can be encouraged by a society needing a more skilled labor force or wishing to upgrade its human resources. It implies that the young population who continue on for higher education will not serve in the labor force until they finish their education, so that a society must be able to function without that labor supply. In a very young population, for instance, this would be difficult, because a smaller proportion of the population would be asked to support a larger number of dependents. In the United States, where unemployment is a veiled threat in any time of economic hardship, postponing the entrance of young people to the labor market is a blessing in disguise (or even an overt blessing) because it keeps more jobs open for the rest of the working-age population. In Israel, compulsory army service provides an alternative means for society to postpone the entrance of young people into the paid labor force. Further, constant economic expansion until the mid-1980s did not make unemployment a serious problem except in temporary adjustment to new waves of immigration. So that Israel had less pressure from the labor force to develop more extensive facilities for higher education.

A latent function of higher education in the United States is to prolong adolescence and provide an institutional setting while youth mature to a more adult level. In Israel, the army again provides an alternative institution for easing the transition from adolescence to adulthood. Those who pursue higher education are motivated primarily by a desire for an occupation requiring academic training rather than a desire to postpone adultlike decisions and responsibilities. Higher education becomes much more vocationally directed, B.A.s often providing adequate preparation to enter a profession, in contrast to the United States.

The army itself provides training for some occupations, which can then be followed up after the army. However, its influence is greater on the future careers of men than of women (Matras and Noam, 1987), due both to the differential positions open to men and women and the different orientations of men and women toward army opportunities.

In addition to being older and more professionally committed during their years of higher education, Israeli university students are for the most part economically independent, supporting themselves through the university years (by participating part- or full-time in the labor force) rather than relying on parental or governmental support. This adds to their more practical orientation and to the seriousness with which they weigh the worth of spending time in higher education. It might also result in different considerations for men and for women, because young couples may not be able to support two full-time students. Another difference between American and Israeli Jews is in the emphasis on "family values." Family life is strongly valued in Israeli society, and each child born merits some financial support by the National Insurance Institute. By the age of 40, 96 percent[7] of the Jewish population has married, and family size is on the average larger among Israeli than American Jews: the average number of children per woman among Israeli Jews is 2.7.[8] On the other hand, among American Jews, a higher proportion never marry—alternative lifestyles having achieved a degree of normative legitimation in American society—and among those who do, a higher proportion have no children or relatively small families (an average of 1.9). From a parent's point of view, having fewer children eases the financial burden of having children continue on to higher education. Delayed marriage, delayed childbearing, and having fewer children all reduce the conflict between familial roles and participating in nonfamilial roles such as higher education or paid labor force activity. The extent to which this affects the comparison between American and Israeli Jews will be explored.

A strong component of the historical background of Israel is Zionist socialism, which heralded equality among all Jews, no matter their ethnic background, gender, or other ascriptive characteristics. This movement, which spurred the founding of the early *kibbutzim* and laid the ideological foundations of the pre-state Yishuv society, introduced a premise of gender equality that remained an ideal if not a realized foundation of the Israeli society. Recent studies have debunked the myth of actual gender equality in the prestate society (Bernstein, 1990), be it in the *kibbutz* or in the military forces; but nevertheless the seeds of the ideology had been sown in the early history of Israel.

Such seeds of gender equality were reinforced by Golda Meir's ascendancy to the highest political office in the country, bringing about what some have termed the *Golda Meir syndrome* (Pogrebrin, 1991), a "myth" that if a woman could achieve this political office then equality of opportunity must be a reality. The institutionalized drafting of women into the army also gives the impression of gender equality, despite the de facto institutionalization of dissimilar gender roles in the military institution (Hazleton, 1977; Swirski and Safir, 1991). Whatever the reality, the ideal of gender equality had been sown (see also Shalvi, 1988).

Some of the Eastern European immigrants to the United States shared the same socialist background as the early immigrants to Israel, which in the United States was expressed in strong support of American unionism and was later generalized into the liberal political orientation that characterizes American Jewry. As a minority in both the American Jewish community and the wider American society, the socialist influence was much smaller than in Israel.

Another difference we will mention between Israeli and American Jews is their immigrant and ethnic background. The majority of Israelis are first or second generation immigrants, unlike the majority of Americans who are second and mainly third generation immigrants. This distance from the immigrant experience, as we have discussed already, has implications in terms of the motivation for upward mobility, which tends to be stronger among immigrants; in terms of the additional roles imposed on immigrant workers and, in particular, immigrant wives and mothers; in terms of the scarcity of resources available for investing in higher education because of the struggle to readjust after relocation. Such factors might make for greater gender differentiation in secular achievement for reasons that we have discussed above in relation to the American immigrant experience.

That so many of the Israeli population are first and second generation immigrants reinforces the need for nation building, emphasizing a collective identity and collective commitment that differs from the American Jewish emphasis on individualism and universalism.

A final difference is that the countries of origin of Israeli Jews also differ from that of American Jews. Most American Jews hail from Western and Eastern European origins. In contrast, about half of the Israeli Jews have immigrated or are descendents of immigrants from the Middle Eastern and North African Moslem countries, from which many Jews were expelled when the state of Israel was established. These countries generally were and are less modernized than the European countries. Coming from more traditional, less industrialized, and less urbanized countries, these immigrants came with a different background of secular education and occupational achievement. Even in the second generation their educational and occupational achievement lags behind Israelis of European-American background, and this is intertwined with a lower socioeconomic status. In many respects they fill the lower occupational slots, which in the United States are filled by non-Jews, as well as having less representation in positions of political and economic power.[9] Although fertility differences between the two ethnic groups have narrowed since the 1950s, there is still a much more traditional orientation to the roles of women in the family and in the labor force (see Hartman, 1983).

Because of their very different background and continuing differences in socioeconomic status, we have simplified our comparison by confining most of our analysis in this chapter to the Israeli Jews most similar in background to American Jews, the second generation of European and American immigrants (hereafter referred to as *EA*). This enables us to better isolate the influence of living as Jews in a majority status rather than a minority, as Jews are in the United States. Even though they are no longer a numerical majority among Israeli Jews, European-American descendants continue to enjoy a dominant status in Israel in terms of national culture, political power, and socioeconomic status. In addition, their similarity to American Jews in terms of orientations to secular achievement allows us to concentrate on the influence of the wider environment and Jewishness in the two settings.

The Israeli data for our comparison come from two main sources: published data of the Israeli Bureau of Statistics, based on comprehensive national samples, and a national survey of Israeli married women aged 22–39, in which a representative sample of urban Jewish women was interviewed in 1987–88 about fertility and labor force patterns, demographic characteristics, educational background, and family and personal religiosity.[10]

We consider (1) gender differences in secular achievement among Israeli as compared to American Jews, including educational attainment, labor force activity, and occupational roles; (2) patterns of gender inequality between spouses among American and Israeli Jews, including age, education, and labor force and occupational roles; (3) the relationship between Jewishness in each context and secular achievement. These comparisons will help to point out the uniqueness of American Jews and the extent to which the patterns seen in previous chapters are shared as "Jewish" orientations by Jews in the Jewish state.

GENDER DIFFERENCES IN SECULAR ACHIEVEMENT

The Education of Israeli and American Jews

In this section we consider to what extent the high educational level attained by American Jews is characteristic of Israeli Jews, whether the patterns of gender difference in education are shared by Israeli and American Jews, and the extent to which the Jewish influence is responsible for these patterns. This helps us to sort out the effect of the shared Jewish heritage and the effect of the immediate environment or historical circumstances on patterns of behavior of Jews in different settings. Because Israel is a Jewish state, all formal schooling in Israel includes some study of the Jewish heritage, be it through Jewish history, Bible study, or more detailed study of Jewish law and custom (especially in the religious schools).[11] Thus, any "Jewish" patterns should be even more pronounced in Israel than in the United States.

We do need to keep in mind that up until 1968 education was compulsory (and free) only through tenth grade in Israel, so that some of the older cohorts could not afford higher education—in this case, education past tenth grade. The generally lower socioeconomic status of Israeli Jews (as compared to American Jews) contributed to the difficulties in affording higher education, not only because of the direct expenses but because of the foregone earnings that would result.

Second, there are fewer institutions of higher education in Israel, so that, even if they wanted to, not all Israeli Jews could go on to college unless they went abroad, an unaffordable possibility for most Israeli youth. As a result fewer Israeli Jews are able to continue on to higher education in Israel each year than among Americans in general and American Jews in particular.[12] That there are fewer institutions of higher education in Israel than in the United States is both a function of supply and demand, as the recent growth in private "colleges" in Israel suggests. These colleges have sprung up to train students for specific occupations in which there is room for expansion or a shortage of personnel: teachers' colleges, law colleges, engineering colleges. There has also been less demand for higher education from the labor market, where job requirements are typically for a lower level of education than is found in the United States. Therefore, in the United States, there seems to be an inflation of educational requirements for some jobs that serves to narrow the pool of labor supply, on the one hand, and to fuel the demand for higher education, on the other.

One reason such an inflation of educational requirements has not occurred in Israel is that, as we have mentioned, the military institution limits the pool of labor supply of youth. The generally high demand for personnel in Israel (except during periods of mass immigrant absorption) as the young economy has undergone expansion and development has also reduced the need to restrict incoming labor supply. All these factors, plus others that we will bring out, color the comparison of the education of American and Israeli Jews.

As we have mentioned, American Jews are more highly educated than second generation Israeli Jews of European-American background (Table 7.1). Clearly the difference between the countries overrides any gender difference within the countries. Over 60 percent of the American Jewish men have 16 or more years of education; less than 30 percent of the second generation European-American Israeli men have reached a similar level.

The largest difference between Israeli and American Jews is in the proportion who did not go beyond high school. A much higher percentage of Israeli Jews than American Jews, especially among the men, stopped their education with high school or less: 47.2 percent of the second generation EA men, compared to 20 percent of the American Jewish men. Nearly half of the second generation EA women also stopped their

TABLE 7.1
Years of Education, by Sex, Second Generation European-American
Israeli Jews (1983) and U.S. Jews (1990), 25 and over

Years of Education	U.S. Jews		Israeli Jews	
	Male	Female	Male	Female
0–10	3.7	3.1	13.5	13.0
11–12	13.7	24.3	33.7	31.3
13–15	19.1	21.6	23.1	31.9
16+	63.4	51.1	29.7	23.7
Total	100.0	100.0	100.0	100.0
(N in thousands)	(1,710)	(1,672)	(125)	(128)

Sources: NJPS, 1990; Central Bureau of Statistics (1990), Table 2.

education at high school, almost double the percentage of American Jewish women who did. More American Jewish women stopped with high school than did American Jewish men, making the difference between American and Israeli Jewish women less than that between American and Israeli Jewish men. High school dropouts are practically nonexistent among American Jews, but 13 percent of the second generation EA have only 10 years or less education. Part of the reason for this, as mentioned, is that until 1968 education in Israel was free only through tenth grade.

Within each country, men have more education than women. The gender gap among second generation EA Israeli Jews is quite similar to that of the American Jews. The proportion of second generation EA Israeli women who have completed 16 or more years of education equals 80 percent that of the men of this background, similar to the 81 percent among American Jews.

Because second generation EA women are more likely to have gone on for 13–15 years of schooling, even more second generation EA women went beyond high school than did men (55.6 percent vs. 52.8 percent); among American Jews, men were more likely to have continued beyond high school than were women (82.5 percent vs. 72.6 percent).

Any tendencies we saw earlier toward gender equality in educational attainment are more pronounced among Israeli Jews than among American Jews. The extent to which this is a function of the higher educational level of American Jews, especially American Jewish men, remains to be determined only in the future, once the Israelis have raised their overall level of education and as American Jewish women take advantage of the educational opportunities that have recently opened to them.

Cohort Changes in Educational Attainment Among Israeli Jews

The gender difference is larger among older Jews in Israel, as in the United States. In Table 7.2 we see the proportion having 16 or more years of education by age in both populations. Because of the high proportion of Israelis whose higher education is delayed until they are out of the army, we begin our comparison from age 25. In the age group 25–34, there may still be some effect of incomplete education, which may contribute to the extremely large gap between American and Israeli Jews. The age group 35–44 is the first group that has probably completed education in both countries, and it has the highest proportion who completed 16 or more years of education in almost every subgroup. In this group the contrast between American and Israeli Jews is also very striking: more than twice as many American Jewish men and women went on for 16 or more years of education than second generation EA Israeli men and women, respectively. The difference between American and Israeli Jews is large in every cohort but is somewhat larger in the older cohorts than in the younger.

In both countries older cohorts are less educated, and age apparently is more related to educational attainment in Israel than in the United

Table 7.2
Percent with 16 or More Years of Education, by Sex and Age, Second
Generation European-American Israeli Jews (1983) and U.S. Jews (1990)
(*N* in thousands in parentheses)

Age	U.S. Jews		Israeli Jews	
	Male	*Female*	*Male*	*Female*
25–34	71.9	70.1	28.2	25.4
	(372)	(349)	(67)	(67)
35–44	75.9	67.2	32.8	25.0
	(428)	(419)	(34)	(35)
45–54	68.1	53.3	24.0	13.8
	(272)	(272)	(17)	(17)
55–64	70.0	38.5	13.4	6.7
	(251)	(259)	(5)	(5)
65+	33.6	21.9	10.8	5.1
	(381)	(366)	(2)	(3)
Total	60.6	49.5	21.6	18.2
	(1,871)	(1,815)	(176)	(175)

Sources: NJPS, 1990; Central Bureau of Statistics (1990), Table 1.

States. For U.S. Jewish men, as we saw, the main difference is between men 65 and older, and those under 65. Among Israelis, there is a gradual increase in each cohort, from 11 percent in the oldest cohort to triple that in the cohort 35–44 among second generation EA Israeli men.

Differences among the women have extended over a longer period of time, with constant increments of change, the proportion of highly educated increasing with each cohort. Among Americans, this means an increase from 22 percent in the oldest cohort to 70 percent in the 25–34 year-old cohort, when women achieve parity with men. For second generation EA Israelis, the increase is from 5 percent in the oldest cohort to nearly five times as many in the younger cohorts. As in the United States, because the increase is more dramatic for women, in the cohort of 25–34 year-olds there is near parity between men and women. Thus, the direction of change in the gender gap in education is similar in both countries, even though the level of achievement still differs.

Education and Family Roles

We saw in Chapter 2 that the education of American Jewish women was related to their family roles, particularly in that the earlier parenting begins, the lower is their educational attainment. When we compare this to Israeli Jews we have to keep in mind some differences between Israeli and American Jewish families. The family roles of Israeli Jews begin earlier and are more intense than those of American Jews on the average. Even though the median age of marriage is similar to American Jews (age 23.5 for women and 26.5 for men),[13] by age 30–34 over 90 percent of the Israeli Jewish women and 84 percent of the men have been married[14] (compared to 75 percent of the American Jewish women and 67 percent of the men). Israeli Jewish women have children at an earlier age: the mother's average age at birth of her first child was 25.0,[15] compared to 26.2 among American Jewish women. Israeli Jewish women have more children on the average than American Jewish women: 2.3 among second generation European-Americans,[16] compared to the 1.9 for American Jews.

In general, the relationship between family roles and education among Israeli women is similar to that of most populations, including American Jews. Recall from our discussion of education and family roles in Chapter 2 that early family roles may interrupt education, resulting in a strong relationship between early age at marriage and childbearing and lower education. On the other hand, investment in education may result in postponed marriage or childbearing, reinforcing the relationship. Among the Israelis these two directions of influence can be seen. Women with more schooling tend to marry later, delay their childbearing, and space their births at longer intervals, resulting in fewer children and fewer young children in the home at any one time (Peritz and Baras, 1992). And, on the other hand, women with lower education marry earlier, start having children earlier and have more children.

Looking at these two directions of influence between education and family roles, a number of issues are raised in the comparison of American and Israeli Jews. First, we consider the extent to which the lower education of Israeli Jewish women in comparison to American Jewish women can be explained by the earlier and more extensive family roles of Israeli Jews—in other words, does controlling for family roles eliminate the difference in educational attainment between the Americans and Israelis? Looking at the opposite direction of influence, we consider the extent to which the more extensive family roles of Israeli Jews reflect or result from their lower education—when we compare women of the same educational levels, are their family roles similar?

Looking first at the relationship between family roles and educational level, comparing Israeli women of European-American background to American Jewish women who had their first child at similar ages (Table 7.3), we see that their age at the birth of their first child is somewhat more related to the education attained of the Israeli group: the mean years of education increases by about one-third between women who had their first child before the age of 20 and women who had their first child after the age of 30 among American Jews, and by nearly 50 percent among the EA Israelis,[17] which means that more Israeli women either interrupted their studies to have children or plan on fewer children when they have higher education. Our interpretation of this relationship is that women in Israel, having more familistic tendencies, plan on more children, and these plans for more children interrupt their educational plans more than among American Jews. One result is that women in the two countries who have delayed childbearing until their thirties are more similar in the education they achieved than are women who had children before the age of 20.

But the earlier age of childbearing does not eliminate the difference in educational level of Israeli and American Jewish women. When we control for the mother's age at her first childbirth, the difference in education between the two sets of women is not eliminated. Even among women who postponed childbearing, there is a difference of nearly two years of education on the average. Most of the American Jewish women in these younger cohorts who postpone having children have gone on to graduate education; the Israeli women have stopped at partial undergraduate education, because of the different cultural norms and the lower standard of living, which precludes more women (and men, too) from affording higher education.

TABLE 7.3
Mean Years of Education, by Age at Birth of First Child and
Number of Children, for European-American Israeli Jews (1988)
and U.S. Jews (1990), Married Women, Ages 22–39

	U.S. Jews	Israeli Jews
Age at Birth of First Child		
Under 20	12.7	10.4
20–21	13.2	12.5
22–24	14.6	13.6
25–29	16.2	14.6
30+	17.1	15.3
Number of Children		
0	16.0	14.6
1	15.7	14.3
2	15.9	13.9
3	15.0	13.1
4+	14.1	12.6
(N)[a]	(1,229)	(897)

[a]For U.S. Jews, N in thousands, weighted with population weights; for Israelis, unweighted and not in thousands.

Source: NJPS, 1990; 1988 fertility survey (see text).

Women who had children between the ages of 20 and 24 are somewhat more similar in years of education than are women who had children either earlier or later, because earlier childbearing results in a greater educational differential among Israeli women (for many Israeli women, having children under 20 means that they do not even complete high school; among American Jews, even women who had children before they were 20 finished high school), while those who postpone childbearing reach higher levels of education (some graduate school on the average) in the United States than in Israel (rarely higher than a B.A.). So the effect of age at first child is milder for American Jews than for Israeli Jews.

The relationship between *number* of children and level of education is similar in the two settings (bottom half of Table 7.3): the more children a woman has by age 29, the lower is her level of education, and women aged 22–39 who have no children have the highest level of education. How many children Israeli women have as compared to the American Jews does not, however, explain the educational difference between the married women in the two countries. When we compare women who have the same number of children, a similar differential of about two years on the average appears in each group as it does in the total. Among women who have no children, American Jewish women have 16 years of education on the average, compared to 14.6 among the Israeli women. Even among women with four or more children, American Jewish women have 14.1 years of education on the average compare to 12.6 among the Israelis.

Educational level does not explain the big difference in fertility between the two countries, either. Even among young women with 16 or more years of education, Israeli women of European-American background have more than double the number of children on the average (2.2, compared to 1.0 of the American Jewish women of this age and level of education). American Jewish women who have more than 16 years of education postpone having their first child until after the age of 27. The Israeli women with higher education also postpone having children, but not as long; their average age at first childbirth is 25.7. This is probably because among the most highly educated American Jewish women, a higher proportion continue on for longer years of education than among the Israeli women, which results in a longer postponement of childbearing.

Participation in the Paid Labor Force

The labor force participation of second generation EA Israelis is very similar to that of American Jews (Table 7.4). As in other international

TABLE 7.4
Percent in Paid Labor Force, by Sex and Age,
Second Generation European-American Israeli and U.S. Jews, 1990

| Age | U.S. Jews | | Israeli Jews | |
	Male	Female	Male	Female
18–24	38.8	36.7	27.3[a]	41.7[a]
25–34	84.9	76.8	82.3	75.8
35–44	95.4	74.7	91.4	77.6
45–54	90.2	78.8	97.2	78.7
55–64	79.5	57.2	85.1	55.6
65+	29.8	11.5	31.9	11.4
Total	72.0	57.3	70.2	62.9
(N in thousands)	(1,568)	(1,629)	(153)	(136)

[a]This includes ages 15–24.

Sources: NJPS, 1990; Central Bureau of Statistics (1992a), Table 8.

comparisons (e.g., Hartman, 1971), the men in the two populations show more similarity than the women. Seventy percent of the second generation EA men are in the labor force, compared to 72 percent of the American Jewish men; and 63 percent of the second generation EA women participate in the labor force, a higher proportion than the 57 percent among American Jewish women.

Considering the main working ages of 35–54, the labor force participation of men is about the same in the two groups. At older ages, the second generation of EA men participate more than American Jewish men, suggesting that the trend toward earlier retirement is more prominent in the United States than in Israel. This may reflect better retirement arrangements in the United States and the generally lower socioeconomic situation of the Israeli environment. As for the early ages of labor force participation, 18–24, fewer Israeli men are in the labor force during these ages than are American Jewish men, probably because of army service and a resulting postponement of higher education.

Young Israeli women, on the other hand, have a higher labor force participation rate than young American Jewish women, probably because a higher proportion of American Jewish women of this age are still in school. In the rest of the age groups, second generation European-American women have about the same labor force participation rate as their American counterparts, indicating a slight increase in labor force participation between ages 25–54, as parenting responsibilities diminish, with a drop after age 55 and even steeper decline after age 65.

As expected, a higher proportion of men work in the paid labor force in both populations, and in both countries this gender difference is noticeable especially after age 25, when women begin to have childbearing and childrearing responsibilities; the gender difference is even greater after age 55, as women retire earlier than men. Overall the gender gap is lower for second generation EA Israelis, mostly due to the age group 18–24, during which a higher proportion of women are in the labor force than are men because of the extended army service, which affects the men in this group more than the women, and because fewer women continue on to higher education during these ages. Because army service hardly affects American Jewish men at all and more American women continue on to higher education during these ages, we do not find the same pattern among the American Jews.

As we have seen earlier, education is related to higher labor force participation rates, especially among women. Given the lower educational level of the Israeli men and women which we have shown previously, we were interested in how this was related to the labor force participation rates we have observed. Since the labor force participation rates are similar between American Jewish women and second generation

EA Israeli women, it would seem that Israeli women at each educational level would participate more than the Americans; otherwise, the overall rates would have been lower.

Education appears to affect Israeli men's participation less than it does American Jewish men. Second generation EA Israeli men with low education participate considerably more than American men of the same education, and the men with higher education have the same labor force participation rate as American Jewish men (Table 7.5).[18]

Among women, education affects labor force participation more in Israel than it does among American Jews. Second generation EA women with 11 or more years of education participate much more than American Jewish women at every level of education, including the highest. It seems that Israeli women's labor force participation is lowered mainly at extremely low levels of education, but is more common when women have average to high levels of education.

Among Israeli Jews, gender differences in participation in the labor force are strongly related to education. The largest differences between men and women are among those with less than 12 years of education; among those with 16 or more years of education, women have an even higher proportion participating in the paid labor force than men. Among the American Jews, gender differences do not disappear even at the highest levels of education.[19]

When we compared American Jews to the wider American population (in Chapter 3) we concluded that the pattern of gender difference at different educational levels was quite similar—among the wider population of Americans, gender differences do not disappear at the highest

TABLE 7.5

Percent in Paid Labor Force, by Years of Education and Sex,
Second Generation European-American Israeli Jews and U.S. Jews, 1990

Years of Education	U.S. Jews		Israeli Jews	
	Male	Female	Male	Female
0–10	28.5	39.6	65.7[a]	29.3[a]
11–12	54.2	38.4	62.4[b]	49.2[b]
13–15	61.3	49.7	75.4	71.1
16+	82.7	70.9	82.0	85.9
(N in thousands)	(1,568)	(1,629)	(153)	(136)

[a]5–8 years of education.
[b]9–12 years of education.

Sources: NJPS, 1990; Central Bureau of Statistics (1992a), Table 15.

level of education either, although gender differences in labor force participation narrow with education. A tendency toward gender equality in labor force participation is more strongly demonstrated by Israeli Jews, especially among highly qualified men and women.

Combining Family Roles and Paid Labor Force Participation

A high percentage of American Jewish women combine family and childrearing roles. The presence of small children, however, has a fairly strong influence on whether they are in the labor force, stronger than in the wider American population, an indication of the importance attached to mothering roles among American Jews. Israeli society appears to be considerably more familistic than the American. Although American Jews seem to be more familistic than the wider American society in terms of how their labor force participation responds to the presence of children and in terms of family stability and valuing high-quality input with children, they do not have as many children as their Israeli counterparts. In this section we compare how Israeli and American Jews combine family roles and labor force participation. We have seen that second generation Israeli women of EA background participate as much or more than their American Jewish counterparts during the main ages of childbearing and childrearing. Yet, we have also seen that they have more children on the average. This suggests that Israeli Jews may more easily combine family roles with labor force participation. We will in the following consider the different ways Israeli and American Jews combine the two.

Being Married and Working in the Paid Labor Force

Although being married made little difference in the labor force participation of American Jewish women, it made more of a difference in the labor force participation of American Jewish men. Married men were more likely to be working in the labor force. Among Israeli Jews, being married makes a significant positive difference for both men and women: married men and women participate more in the labor force (Table 7.6).

However, the difference between the married and unmarried women is actually a result of the age composition of the two groups. Controlling for age (Table 7.6) shows us that in the main ages of childbearing and childrearing (25–44), married women actually work less than unmarried women, but in the older ages marital status makes little difference. Because there are more older women (widows) among the unmarried, and older women's participation is lower, their overall participation is lower than the overall participation of the married women.

TABLE 7.6
Percent in Paid Labor Force, by Marital Status and Sex,
Israeli Jews and U.S. Jews, 25 and over, 1990

		U.S. Jews		Israeli Jews	
Marital Status	Age	Male	Female	Male	Female
Not married	Total	72.8	58.4	60.8	31.5
	25–34	77.3	78.1	74.2	79.4
	35–44	88.9	85.5	72.3	80.5
	45–54	72.6	93.3	69.1	65.1
	55–64	67.9	66.7	54.9	33.2
	65+	26.3	12.1	15.0	6.3
(N in thousands)		(484)	(527)	(133)	(178)
Married	Total	78.7	58.7	75.3	53.6
	25–34	94.5	76.1	84.2	64.5
	35–44	97.7	71.4	89.1	68.5
	45–54	94.9	73.8	91.2	61.0
	55–64	81.3	54.5	77.8	33.1
	65+	30.1	10.6	22.7	7.7
(N in thousands)		(1,223)	(1,149)	(835)	(793)

Sources: NJPS, 1990; Central Bureau of Statistics (1992a), Table 27.

Married Israeli men participate in the labor force more than the unmarried at all ages, reflecting the greater financial responsibility of the married (as among the American Jews).

The overall gender difference among Israelis seems larger for the unmarried than the married, but once age is controlled, the gender gap is similar in both groups. Among American Jews, the gender difference at most ages *is* larger for the married, because the gender role differentiation is greater after marriage.

Therefore when we consider the difference between the married and unmarried at different stages of the life cycle among Israeli Jews, we find that their patterns of behavior are actually quite similar to the American Jews. Among men, married men participate more in the labor force at every stage of the life cycle, as we found among American Jews (Figure 7.1). Among women, married women participate *less* than unmarried women except after age 65, when there is little difference between the married and the unmarried. Gender differences are reversed for the unmarried up to age 45 (unmarried women participating *more* than unmarried men); unmarried women participate more like married men at these ages. At older ages, the more traditional gender differences reappear

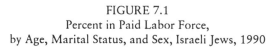

FIGURE 7.1
Percent in Paid Labor Force,
by Age, Marital Status, and Sex, Israeli Jews, 1990

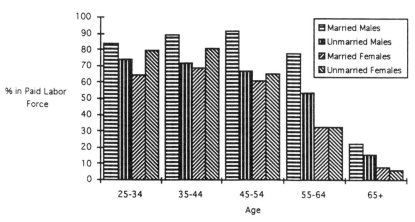

Source: Central Bureau of Statistics (1990), Table 27.

even among the unmarried. Because the majority of the unmarried are older, these are the dominant figures when age is not controlled.

Among the married, the gender differences are greatest up to age 45, as among the American Jews. Again, it is mainly because of the high participation of married men at these ages.

Children and Labor Force Participation
Among Israeli and American Jews

As Table 7.7 shows, the effect of children is somewhat different in the two countries. Women with no children participate in the labor force less than women with children in Israel, but this is because such a high proportion of these women are older.[21] Each successive child in Israel, however, affects women's labor force participation less than it does in the United States. A higher proportion of Israeli women work at every family size than American Jewish women.

Among Israeli women, labor force participation hardly changes between women with one–three children, declining somewhat when there are four or more children, but over half of these mothers still participate in the labor force. Among American Jewish women, labor force participation declines when there is more than one child, and drops to a lower level than among the Israelis with four or more children.

The greater tendency of Israeli women to continue to participate in the labor force when they have children may be related to the relatively

TABLE 7.7
Percent Participation in the Paid Labor Force, by Number of Children,
Second Generation European-American Israeli Ever-Married
and U.S. Jewish Married Women, 1990

Number of Children	U.S. Jews	Israeli Jews
None	84.9	65.2
1 or more	67.9	72.1
1 child	78.1	75.9
2 children	67.6	76.7
3 children	66.5	71.0
4 or more children	46.8	50.2
(N in thousands)	(2,233)	(998)

Sources: NJPS, 1990; Central Bureau of Statistics (1992a), Table 86.

lower socioeconomic status of Israeli Jews, and the consequential greater need for two incomes. It may also reflect an institutional and normative support for combining labor force and familial roles of women. One indication of this is the greater availability of child care in Israel and the greater normative use of child care: 75 percent of the 2 year-old, 96 percent of the 3 year-old, and 99 percent of the 4 year-old Israelis are in day-care or kindergarten (Central Bureau of Statistics, 1992b, Table 22.11). In the United States, only 55 percent of the 3–5 year-olds are enrolled in nursery or daycare (U.S. Bureau of the Census, 1990, Table 230). Daycare in the United States is overwhelmingly private and costly, but in Israel a much higher proportion is subsidized. Nursery school in Israel may be for only a portion of the working day, which is often a drawback, but it may also be more common for Israeli women to have help in the household, although we do not have comparative data available to show this.

Part of the reason that Israeli women's participation in the paid labor force is less affected by children than that of the American woman is the greater proportion of women working part-time, as can be seen in Table 7.8. This is true for both married and unmarried women. As among American Jews, among Israelis more married women than unmarried women work part-time, suggesting that part-time work is particularly important as a strategy for combining family and labor force roles, but it is a strategy used more by Israeli Jewish women than American. Lewin (1992) suggests that the prevalence of part-time employment in Israel reflects the continued importance of traditional familial roles in Israel (see also Shalvi, 1988) and the reluctance to give up these roles for more full-time career-oriented employment. That Israeli women can continue to combine both economic and familial roles reflects also the greater availability of part-time

TABLE 7.8
Percent of Part-Time Employment, by Marital Status,
Israeli (1988) and U.S. Jewish Employed Women (1990)

Marital Status	U.S. Jews	Israeli Jews
Married	39.0	43.2
	(647)	(425)
Not Married	24.7	35.6
	(330)	(111)
Total	34.1	41.6
	(977)	(535)

Note: N in thousands in parentheses.

Sources: NJPS, 1990; Israel, recalculated from Central Bureau of Statistics (1992a), Table 4.

opportunities in the Israeli labor market than in the American.

In summary, overall gender differences in labor force participation are quite similar for U.S. and Israeli Jews. Gender differences observed among Israeli Jews, in fact, demonstrate an even greater tendency to gender equality in labor force activity than among American Jews, continuing the direction of difference we found between American Jews and the wider population of American whites. Fewer gender differences in labor force participation are apparent among college educated Israeli Jews, although gender differences in the labor force participation of American Jews are apparent at all educational levels. The effect of children on the American Jewish women's labor force participation is especially great when there are four or more children. A higher proportion of Israeli women continue to work even when they have four or more children, reflecting either the normative and institutional support for combining family roles and labor force participation or the greater financial pressures on Israeli families to have two incomes. Data that allow us to control for husband's and wife's income would be especially helpful in further understanding this comparison.

Occupational Roles

Israeli Jewish women have a lower educational level than American Jewish women, together with more family roles. Nevertheless, they have higher labor force participation rates, although more of them are participating on a part-time basis. All of this leads us to expect that the occupational level of Israeli women will be lower than that of American Jewish women and that there will be a greater gender difference in the occupations of Israeli Jews than among American Jews. The occupations of second generation EA Israelis differ considerably from American Jews. More than a third (35.7 percent) of the second generation EA Israeli men would have to change their occupations to have the same occupations as American Jewish men (Table 7.9). American Jewish men are more likely to have scientific and academic occupations and managerial positions; Israeli men are more likely to be in technical and lower professional occupations and blue-collar work (Table 7.10). This is even though EA men have a similar position in relation to

TABLE 7.9
Dissimilarity Coefficients Between Occupational Distributions of
Second Generation European-American Israeli and U.S. Jewish Populations

	U.S. Jewish males	U.S. Jewish females	Israeli Jewish males	Israeli Jewish females
U.S. Jewish males				
U.S. Jewish females	28.6			
Israeli Jewish males	35.7	35.3		
Israeli Jewish females	59.8	33.7	40.1	

Note: Based on distributions presented in Table 7.10. For dissimilarity calculation, see note to Table 4.2.

TABLE 7.10
Occupations, by Sex, Second Generation
European-American Israeli and U.S. Jews, 1990

Occupation	U.S. Jews		Israeli Jews	
	Males	Females	Males	Females
Scientific, academic	38.9	29.8	16.5	14.3
Technical	3.2	7.9	17.3	35.3
Managerial, administrative	19.8	15.1	12.6	3.3
Sales	17.2	10.9	9.6	28.3
Clerical	6.5	29.4	10.7	5.5
Blue Collar	11.2	2.8	28.1	4.4
Service	3.2	4.2	5.3	9.0
	100.0	100.0	100.0	100.0
(N in thousands)	(1,656)	(1,590)	(150)	(127)

Source: NJPS, 1990; Central Bureau of Statistics (1992a), Table 56.

the total Israeli occupational distribution as American Jews do in relation to the total U.S. occupational distribution: a higher percentage of workers in the scientific, academic, professional, and managerial occupations and a lower percentage in blue-collar and service occupations.

A similar percentage of second generation EA women (33.7) would have to change their occupations to be like the American women. American Jewish women, like American Jewish men, are more likely to be in scientific and academic professions, whereas more of the Israeli women are in technical and other professional occupations; more of the American women are in managerial occupations than among the second generation EA Israeli women.

As we have seen, the dissimilarity between American Jewish men and women is 28.6,[22] the proportion of men in scientific and academic occupations is more than double that of women; women are more likely to be in technical and other professional occupations and clerical occupations than men. The dissimilarity between men and women in the total Israeli Jewish population is considerably greater than that of American Jews: 40.1, similar to the dissimilarity coefficients found in the total U.S. population and not unlike a number of other industrialized countries (cf. Roos, 1985). Although in Israel a similar percentage of men and women are in scientific and academic occupations, unlike American Jews, many more Israeli Jewish men are employed in blue-collar occupations than Israeli women, who tend to be found more in service and clerical occupations. Many fewer American Jews are in blue-collar occupations at all, and the gender gap is much smaller in these occupations.

To clarify this somewhat we controlled for education (Table 7.11).[23] In both populations, the dissimilarity between men and women diminishes with higher education. As we saw in Chapter 4 and see again in Table 7.12, among American Jews with 12 years of education or less the gender dissimilarity is 42.3; it decreases to 40.5 among those with 13–15 years of education and to 32.6 among American Jews with 16 or more years of education. Among Israeli Jews, the gender dissimilarity of the less educated group is somewhat higher than among the American Jews (50.3), but it decreases to 34.4 among those with 13–15 years of education and to 28.6 among the men and women with 16 or more years of education. Thus, with higher educational qualifications, Israeli Jewish men and women reach greater equality in occupations than American Jews do.

This is to a great degree because of the dissimilarity in occupational distributions of highly educated Israeli and American Jewish women. For example, the proportion of women in scientific and academic occupations is nearly three times as high among Israeli as American Jews at the highest educational level, and more American Jewish women with 16 or more years of education are in lower management, sales, and clerical

TABLE 7.11
Occupations, by Sex and Years of Education, Israeli Jews, 1990

Sex	Years of Education	Professional, Academic	Technical	Managerial, Administrative	Occupation Clerical	Sales	Blue Collar	Service	Total %	(N in thousands)
Total	0–12	.3	5.8	3.6	19.6	10.6	42.5	17.5	100.0	(951)
	13–15	6.6	42.4	7.6	16.2	6.6	12.9	7.7	100.0	(280)
	16+	43.0	28.6	8.9	8.2	4.5	4.3	2.5	100.0	(246)
Male	0–12	.3	4.3	4.9	10.0	11.3	57.9	11.3	100.0	(611)
	13–15	6.3	30.7	13.2	11.0	9.3	22.4	7.2	100.0	(134)
	16+	47.3	18.6	12.8	6.2	6.2	6.5	2.3	100.0	(141)
Female	0–12	.3	7.8	1.3	42.0	8.5	13.9	26.1	100.0	(371)
	13–15	6.9	53.4	2.4	21.1	4.3	3.7	8.1	100.0	(146)
	16+	37.3	41.9	3.7	11.1	2.3	1.0	2.6	100.0	(105)

Source: Central Bureau of Statistics (1991), Table 12.17.

TABLE 7.12

Dissimilarity Coefficients Between Occupational Distributions,
by Sex and Years of Education, of Israeli and U.S. Jews, 1990

Years of Education	Sex	U.S. Jews						Israeli Jews					
		0–12		13–15		16+		0–12		13–15		16+	
		M	F	M	F	M	F	M	F	M	F	M	F
U.S. Jews													
0–12	M												
	F	42.3											
13–15	M	19.0	46.5										
	F	40.2	19.5	40.5									
16+	M	45.4	55.6	37.1	39.3								
	F	47.8	52.2	45.2	36.0	32.6							
Israeli Jews													
0–12	M	51.4	56.9	55.4	60.9	69.8	65.9						
	F	29.6	58.5	34.0	63.2	65.1	68.7	50.3					
13–15	M	40.4	46.1	38.7	35.8	37.4	27.3	41.7	49.9				
	F	49.1	63.1	43.6	53.7	44.3	27.4	66.9	53.3	34.4			
16+	M	61.5	57.9	48.9	43.9	19.5	39.7	69.3	69.3	41.1	55.5		
	F	66.8	71.1	60.9	57.1	23.9	26.6	75.7	74.5	42.4	31.7	28.6	

Note: Based on NJPS (1990) and Israeli distributions presented in Table 7.11. For dissimilarity calculation, see note to Table 4.2.

occupations. Among women with 13–15 years of education, nearly 60 percent of the Israelis are in scientific, professional, technical, and academic occupations, whereas less than a fifth of the American Jewish women with this much education are.

Moreover, Israelis seem to utilize their education in the labor force more extensively than do American Jews. Nearly half of the Israeli males with 16 or more years of education are in professional and academic occupations, but only a third of the American Jews. Among the women, 37 percent of the Israelis with this education are in scientific and academic occupations compared to only 15 percent of the American Jewish women. On the other hand, over 30 percent of the American men with this education are in clerical, sales, or lower occupations, compared to 20 percent of the Israeli men. Among the women the comparable percentages are 35 percent among the Americans and 16 percent among the Israelis.

This may be related to the more practical career orientation of Israeli higher education, so that those who continue on to academic degrees are preparing for a specific, high-level career, whereas in the United States, higher education may be more general and less vocationally applicable.

The differences in occupational distribution between the two countries at this educational level may reflect the inflation in educational requirements in the United States such that having 16 or more years of education may not be a fine enough distinction to focus in on the highest professionals. As we saw in Chapter 4, the dissimilarity in occupational distributions did decline with education for American Jews, and was lowest for men and women with 17 or more years of education. In Israel, on the other hand, there are fewer people achieving 16 or more years of education, and therefore those who achieve it may have less competition getting into higher occupational roles.

The greater gender similarity at high educational levels among Israelis may also be related to the wider part-time opportunities available throughout the labor force in Israel as well as childcare facilities, making more occupations accessible to women even if they are combining a career with family obligations. Thus when women are qualified, they may be able to enter a greater variety of occupations without giving up competing roles.[24] Some have suggested that the institution of part-time employment hampers women's advancement, but this does not seem to be the case in Israel. More detailed occupational analysis undoubtedly would point out where the glass ceilings in Israel are, but it seems that, on the whole, with adequate education, Israeli women can get further ahead than American Jewish women. The long-time acceptance of women working in combination with whatever familial obligations they have may also allow women to get further ahead both from the family's point of view and from an employer's point of view. Therefore the American Jewish pattern, which shows that familism hampers women's occupational achievement, seems to be adapted to the American context. Familism is even more rooted among Jews in the Israeli context, yet Israeli women manage to get ahead in terms of occupational achievement together with these family roles.

Comparisons to the wider American population and the Israeli Jewish population indicate a somewhat greater gender equity among the American Jewish population in terms of occupational distributions, but closer examination of the Israelis shows that, among men and women with college educations, there is more gender similarity among the Israelis than the Americans and this is due mainly to the higher occupational achievements of Israeli Jewish women in comparison to American Jewish women. This suggests that the Jewish culture indeed facilitates an equality of occupational achievement and where the Jewish culture is institutionalized (as in Israel) it is more effective in bringing such equality about than where it is not, as in the United States, in spite of the high familism of Israeli society.

GENDER INEQUALITY BETWEEN SPOUSES

As suggested in Chapter 5, patterns of gender inequality may be maintained or reinforced by patterns of mate selection and marital dynamics that reinforce traditional gender differences even when changes occur in the wider society. In the case of American Jews, we found, however, that gender differences between spouses were no greater—and in terms of occupational achievement were actually more egalitarian—than in the wider Jewish population and especially more than in the wider American society. In this section we consider whether the patterns of gender inequality between Israeli Jewish spouses reinforces traditional or more egalitarian tendencies, and how they compare to patterns which we found among American Jews. Because of the stronger familism of Israeli Jews, coupled with the egalitarian patterns of labor force activity, differences between spouses may be an important clue to how such conflicting tendencies are resolved. Most of the results in this section are taken from the special survey of married women ages 22–39, selecting for wives of European-American background.[25]

Age Differences Between Israeli Spouses

The great majority of Israeli spouses have conventional age differences; that is, husbands are the same age or older than their wives (Table 7.13). About a quarter of the husbands are five or more years older than their wives. In less than 3 percent of the couples are wives older than their husbands by more than a year.

TABLE 7.13
Age, Education, and Labor Force Differences of
European-American Israeli (1988) and
U.S. Jewish (1990) Husbands and Wives (%s)

	U.S. Jews (Wife Under 45)	Israeli Jews (Wife Age 22–39)
Age differences:		
Husband older than wife (total)	72.2	67.0
Husband older 5+ years	27.6	23.9
Husband same age as wife (within one year)	11.5	29.9
Wife older than husband (total)	16.3	2.8
Wife older than husband 5+ years	16.3	.9
Education differences:		
Husband more educated than wife (total)	35.4	25.4
Husband more eeducated by 5+ years	9.0	5.6
Husband same education as wife (within one year)	45.6	51.3
Wife more educated than husband (total)	19.0	23.3
Wife more educated by 5+ years	2.5	2.9
Labor force differences:		
Dual Earners	66.7	49.9
Male Breadwinners	27.8	36.7
Female Breadwinners	4.1	5.7
No Earner	1.4	7.7
Total %	100.0	100.0
(Unweighted N)	(1,414)	(897)

Source: NJPS, 1990; 1988 special fertility survey (see text).

These results reflect somewhat greater age homogeneity among Israeli spouses than American spouses (29.9 percent of the spouses are within a year of each other, compared to 11.5 percent of the American Jewish spouses) and less nonconventional age heterogeneity; that is, fewer Israeli wives are older than their husbands. The greater homogeneity may result from the location of marriage markets during army service, when men and women of similar ages are in intensive contact with each other. It is not clear from the patterns of age difference whether traditional gender differences in status or secular achievement or more egalitarian patterns would be reinforced within Israeli couples.

Educational Differences Between Israeli Spouses

In terms of educational achievement, there is also a slightly higher tendency toward equality between Israeli spouses than between American spouses. Over half (51.3 percent) of the Israeli spouses have the same education, compared to 45.6 percent of the American Jewish spouses. There is also a somewhat higher proportion of Israeli wives who have more education than their husbands (Table 7.13).

Just as we found fewer educational differences between Israeli EA men and women than among American Jews, we find fewer educational differences between the Israeli spouses than among the Americans. This may be related to a smaller variation in education among both men and women in Israel and, especially, a smaller proportion of men achieving graduate and professional degrees, which caused the greatest difference between American Jewish men and their wives. Because many Israelis meet their potential spouses not in college, as is common among American Jews, but in the army or workplace, where educational level is less apparent and less salient, there is also a heterogeneity in both directions (i.e., about the same proportion of husbands and wives are more educated than their spouses). Among American Jews, more husbands have higher education than wives than vice versa, which tends to reinforce traditional or conventional patterns of gender inequality in education and its implications.

Spousal Inequality in Labor Force Activities

As among American Jews, a majority of couples are dual earners; that is, both the husband and wife participate in the labor force (Table 7.13). However a higher proportion of American Jewish couples at comparable ages are dual earners and a lower proportion are male breadwinner couples. This reflects the higher number of children among Israeli couples and the lower educational level of the EA Israeli women. Even though Israeli women with children tend to participate as much or more than American Jewish women with children, because they have more children and during these ages a higher proportion have young children, the actual proportion of wives in the labor force is lower. Also, although at similar levels of education labor force participation rates are very comparable, because a higher proportion of Israeli wives have less education than American Jewish wives, there is a lower percentage of dual earners.

In both populations, a higher proportion of single-earner families are male breadwinners rather than female breadwinners; that is, they follow a traditional pattern of inequality in labor force activity.

Among Israelis as among American Jews, male breadwinner families have more children on the average than dual earners (2.5 compared to

2.2), and husbands and wives are both significantly younger than among dual earners.[26] Unlike American Jews, however, there is also a significant difference both in the education of husbands and wives: dual earner husbands and wives each have higher education than male breadwinner husbands and wives.

Between dual earners and male breadwinners among American Jewish couples, we found practically no differences in occupational distribution of husbands, which indicated to us that husband's earnings were not the main determinant in whether wives worked (Table 7.14). Among Israeli couples, the dissimilarity in occupational distributions of dual earner and male breadwinner husbands is double that of American Jews, 13.7. That is, 13.7 percent of the dual earner husbands would have to change occupations to be the same as the male breadwinner husbands. However, as among American Jews, the differences do not point in the direction of being male breadwinner couples because they can afford that the wife not work. On the contrary, dual earning husbands are more likely to be in scientific and professional occupations, whereas male breadwinner husbands are more likely to be in lower white-collar (sales and clerical) or blue-collar and service occupations. It is more likely that when the husband is in a professional or scientific occupation, the family can afford substitute help to facilitate the combination of family and economic roles. The smaller number of children in these families also reduces the role conflict between mothering and labor force activity; and their older age also implies that their children are somewhat older, so that practically there is less role conflict. The higher education of the wives implies that economically it is more worthwhile for them to work than for the wives of male breadwinners.

It thus appears that when it is economically feasible and worthwhile, Israeli couples will be dual earners, but when there are more children to take care of, the children are younger, or the wives are trained for less lucrative jobs, couples will tend to be male breadwinner couples.

Occupational Dissimilarity Between Israeli Spouses

When we compared the occupations of American Jewish husbands and wives, we found a relatively high proportion of "cross-class" marriages; that is, marriages in which the occupations of husband and wife fall into different occupational "classes" (professional, academic, or managerial; skilled white collar such as sales and clerical; and blue collar or service occupations). Not only was there a high degree of occupational heterogeneity compared to other capitalist countries, but the direction of heterogeneity was striking, in which more of the heterogeneous marriages had wives in a higher occupational class than their husbands.

TABLE 7.14

Occupations of Husbands in Dual Earner and Male Breadwinner Couples, European-American Israeli (1988) and U.S. Jews (1990)

	Professional, Technical, Academic	Managerial, Administrative	Clerical, Sales	Service, Blue Collar	Total %	(Unweighted n)	Coefficient of Dissimilarity[a]
Israeli Jews:							
Male breadwinners	21.2	30.1	17.9	25.5	100.0	(431)	13.7
Dual earners	34.8	29.2	10.4	30.8	100.0	(314)	
U.S. Jews:							
Male breadwinners	39.1	20.1	21.5	19.3	100.0	(363)	6.4
Dual earners	44.5	17.9	17.3	20.3	100.0	(738)	

[a]For dissimilarity calculations, see note to Table 4.2.

Source: NJPS, 1990; 1988 special fertility survey (see text).

Among Israeli EA couples, the proportion of cross-class marriages (according to this same three-class grouping) is almost identical to that of American Jews: 43.4 percent. Furthermore, the proportion of heterogeneous marriages in which the wife has a higher occupation than her husband (25.3 percent) is also much greater than the heterogeneous marriages in which the husband has a higher occupation than his wife (18.1 percent). To some degree this is a result of the classification of the typically "female" occupations for women with at least some post-secondary education (teachers, social workers, nurses). But it is also a result of the lack of resistance to wives having higher occupations than their husbands. Both husband and wife seem to be cooperating in a common enterprise to support the family, and if the wife can be in a higher occupation, she will be. The considerations seem to be more practical (how much help will the family require to minimize the role conflicts, can they afford it, is it worthwhile economically) than ideological, and there seem to be few normative restrictions as to appropriate occupational status for wives in relation to their husbands—among Israeli as among American Jews.

JEWISHNESS AND GENDER EQUALITY
AMONG ISRAELI JEWS

In the previous chapter we found that Jewishness among American Jews was related to the secular achievement of both men and women: for both men and women, Jewishness was positively related to educational achievement, particularly in its more collective or public aspects of Jewish involvement. Jewishness was differentially related to the labor force activity of men and women: for men, it was related positively in its more collective and formal aspects of Jewish involvement; for women, a negative relationship was shown to be a result of the greater family roles of the more Jewishly involved, and there was little direct relationship between Jewish involvement and labor force activity. Contrary to our expectations, the more Jewishly involved did not exhibit more gender inequality in spousal relationships; in fact, there seemed to be a tendency toward greater equality in educational and occupational achievement among the more Jewishly involved and Orthodox couples. We concluded from this that gender inequality did not spill over from the religious arena to the secular and that the encouragement of secular achievement held for both men and women.

Given the unique ways in which Americans have adapted their Jewish involvement to the American setting, it is important to compare our findings to the effects of Jewishness on secular behavior in Israel to see whether the patterns we found are a result of the adaptation of Jewishness to the United States or related to Jewishness in general.

The comparison is not an easy one. As mentioned in the introduction to this chapter, many aspects of Jewishness that were measured in the American study were not appropriate for the Israeli setting. Living in a Jewish neighborhood and having predominantly Jewish friends tells us little about the person's religiosity when 85 percent of the population is Jewish, lives in communities segregated from non-Jews, and goes to school with Jews exclusively. Belonging to a formal Jewish organization or subscribing to a Jewish periodical mean little when almost all formal organizations in the country are "Jewish" and Hebrew newspapers are the national news carriers. Belonging to a denomination has no meaning when the only legitimized (recognized by the Israeli rabbinate) form of the religion is Orthodoxy. The focus of the comparison must be on ritual observance.

The data for this part of the analysis are also taken from the special fertility survey conducted in 1987–88. The indicators of religiosity and ritual observance that were asked included general evaluations of religiosity of the respondent, her spouse, and each of their parents; saying kiddush on Shabbat; not traveling on Shabbat; not eating *hametz*[27] on Passover; using separate meat and milk dishes; fasting on Yom Kippur; frequency of going to the *mikveh*;[28] frequency of husband's attendance at synagogue.[29]

In previous studies of Israeli religiosity (summarized in Kedem, 1991; see also Hartman, 1984), ritual observance in Israel has been considered one-dimensional. Factor analyses have resulted in a single factor rather than the two factors we found for American Jews and discussed in Chapter 6. Factor analysis[30] of the indicators of religiosity in the current Israeli study indicate a separation into two factors, in the directions found in the American study. However, the meaning of the second factor was not clear, and as nearly half (46.6 percent) of the variance was explained by the first factor, only it was used for further analysis. The indicators that had a high loading on this factor were the general questions about the religiosity of the respondent, her spouse, and each of their parents; travel on Shabbat; synagogue attendance; visiting the mikveh; keeping separate meat and milk dishes; and reciting kiddush on Shabbat (see Appendix II). This includes ritual observances of a traditional religious nature.

Religiosity and Educational Attainment Among Israeli Jews

Among American Jews, educational attainment had positive correlations with all of the Jewishness factors, but once age and gender were controlled, the ritual and Jewish background factors were not significantly related. We concluded that the positive Jewish orientation to religious education had been generalized to all education (including secular) among those whose Jewish involvement was broadened beyond the traditional religiosity. Here we consider whether a similar generalization has taken place in Israel or whether the indicator of religiosity, which is a very traditional ritualistic one, is not related, as the RITUAL factor in the American setting was not related to secular educational attainment.

Among the EA Israelis, the relationship between religiosity and educational attainment is significant only for the husbands. That is, among the more religious, the husbands are more educated ($r = -.298$, $\alpha < .01$);[31] however, there is no difference between the education of the religious or less religious wives. The significant relationship for husbands may be only because of learning in religious institutions of higher learning (*yeshivot*), which are included as years of formal schooling in the Israeli context and is more common among religious men in Israel than in the United States. Or it may be a generalization of the positive orientation to learning in the religion to the secular education, as in the United States.

Religiosity and Labor Force Activity Among Israeli Jews

Jewish involvement among American Jews was only weakly related to labor force activity. For men, it was mainly related to social contact with the Jewish community, and it was not clear whether Jewish involvement promoted labor force activity or labor force activity (at least in certain occupations) reinforced Jewish contact. For women, there was a negative relationship between Jewishness, especially the factors related to traditional rituals, and labor force activity, but further analysis showed that the relationship could be explained almost entirely by the positive relationship between Jewishness and family roles, on the one hand, and the negative relationship between family roles and labor force activity, on the other. Only the RITUAL factor retained a small but significant negative relationship with labor force activity when age, education, and family roles were controlled.

Among the EA Israeli women as well, when age, education, and family roles are controlled, the relationship between religiosity and labor force activity becomes insignificant (Table 7.15). The multiple regression model in Table 7.15 predicts wives' labor force activity[32] with the independent variables being education (both years of education and highest academic degree achieved); age; age at marriage, number of children, and age at first child; and the religiosity factor.

Age has the strongest relationship with labor force activity: between the ages of 22 and 39 (the ages of this sample), the older is the woman, the less active she is in the labor force. This is only partially related to how many children she has, as age continues to have a significant effect once

TABLE 7.15
Multiple Regression Analysis of Wife's Labor Force Activity,[a]
European-American Israeli Women, 1988

Independent Variable	Standardized Coefficient	Unstandardized Coefficient
Age	-.247***	-.356***
Years of education	.073	.033
Highest academic degree	.182**	.167**
Age at marriage	.005	.002
Age at birth of first child	-.186*	-.075*
Number of children	-.247***	-.356***
Religiosity	.058	.076
R	.349	
R²	.122	
(n)	(797)	

*p < .05.
**p < .01.
***p < .001.

[a]The dependent variable, labor force activity, was coded as follows: −1 = never participated in the paid labor force; 0 = participated in the past but not at the time of the survey; 1 = employed part-time; 2 = employed full-time.

Source: Special fertility survey (see text).

the number of children is controlled. How many children she has also is a strong deterrent to labor force activity. When she began to have children has an additional negative effect on labor force activity; women who begin to have children earlier seem to invest first in family roles and only later or intermittently in labor force roles, and this is expressed in a weaker attachment to the labor force. When she married has no relationship to labor force activity, as among American Jews.

Education is also related significantly and positively to labor force activity, but during these ages, family roles and life cycle stage are the more important factors. As among American Jews, the degree achieved is more important than the number of years invested in schooling.

The relationship between religiosity and labor force activity can be explained by the family roles invested in by more religious women, as among American Jews. Not even the small relationship between RITUAL and labor force activity remained after education, age and family roles were controlled among American Jews. This shows us again that the Jewish religion does not directly inhibit Jewish women from participating in the labor force; on the contrary, it takes a positive stand toward wives contributing to the household economy. However, traditional Jewish encouragement of having children indirectly restricts labor force activity at some ages. As can be seen in Table 7.16, more religious couples have more children among Israeli Jews, just as we saw that the more Jewishly involved American couples had more children (in terms of all Jewishness aspects).

Religiosity and Spousal Inequality Among Israeli Jews

Although we had expected to find religiosity related to greater spousal inequality, among American Jews we found no such relationship. Among the EA Israelis, however, the more religious are somewhat more conventional in spousal differences, and more unequal in the traditional directions (Table 7.16).

Despite no greater age difference between the more religious spouses than between less religious spouses, there is significantly greater difference in educational level and a significantly lower percentage of dual earners among the more religious. Some of this is related to the larger number of children among the more religious couples. However, it may also be related to the stronger definition of religious lifestyle among Israelis, so that some of the traditional influences of Judaism remain among the more religious in Israel with less transformation to a more secular lifestyle common among American Jews.

CONCLUSIONS

The purpose of this chapter was to test the extent to which the conclusions we reached about American Jews in previous chapters demonstrated

TABLE 7.16
Selected Couple Characteristics,
by Religiosity, European-American Israelis, 1988

Couple Characteristic	More Religious	Less Religious	(Significance of t)
Mean age difference	2.8	3.0	(.28)
% conventional education			
differences	76.5	64.3	(.00)
Mean education differences	1.2	–.1	(.00)
% dual earners	42.8	54.7	(.00)
Mean # children	2.8	2.2	(.00)

Source: Special fertility survey (see text).

orientations characteristic of American Jews in particular or all Jews as part of the same civilizational culture. We chose to compare these findings to the Israeli setting, where Jews are least exposed to some outside cultural influence on their secular or religious behavior. During the comparison, we came to the realization that being a dominant majority rather than a minority group has its own cultural and institutional ramifications that make comparisons and conclusions more difficult than expected. The difference in cultural origins and immigrant status between American and Israeli Jews directed us to narrow our comparison to subgroups similar to each other in ethnic background and immigrant status (i.e., second generation EA Israeli Jews compared to American Jews), from which the following conclusions are drawn.

With regard to gender differences in educational achievement, we find more equality among Israeli Jews than among American Jews—similar to what we found when comparing American Jews to the wider American population. The question is raised therefore as to how much of the gender difference is a function of the educational level rather than any cultural orientation. The positive relationship we saw between Jewish involvement in the American context and educational attainment was seen only for men in the Israeli context, and we could not be sure how much of this was due to religious rather than secular schooling.

The labor force activity of American and EA Israelis is very similar, and Israelis demonstrate an even greater tendency to gender equality in labor force activity than among American Jews, continuing the direction of difference we found between American Jews and the wider population of American whites. Education especially seemed to narrow gender differences among EA Israelis, whereas gender differences in the labor force participation of American Jews are apparent at all educational levels. Some of this could be explained by the more professionally channeled higher education in Israel, so that when higher education is achieved, even though it is among a smaller proportion of the population, it is put to better use in the labor market.

Similarly, Israeli women seem to utilize better their education for occupational achievement (i.e., they get higher occupational returns for their education than do American Jewish women), and therefore among EA Israelis with higher education there is greater occupational equality than among American Jews. This, however, is in the same direction that we saw when comparing American Jews to the wider American population—there are few cultural obstacles to occupational roles and within a high proportion of Jewish couples women have higher occupations than their husbands.

In both the Israeli and American contexts, Jewishness was related to more familistic roles; that is, having more children. As a whole, Israeli

Jews have more children and at younger ages than American Jews, which supports the continued association between familism and Judaism that has been part of the Jewish tradition. This tendency toward familism, however, did not have the same effect on women's labor force activity in the two contexts. In Israel, family and labor force roles are combined with greater frequency than among American Jews. However, since American Jews have fewer children and at later ages, their effect on labor force activity is reduced. Among Israeli Jews, part-time employment and a strong infrastructure of childcare facilitate the combination of mothering and labor force activity, without reducing or postponing children. This enables Israeli Jewish women to contribute to the economic well-being of the family alongside their spouses. However, in line with the more traditional Jewish heritage, their contribution seems to be motivated economically rather than by career commitment. Thus, a wife's labor force participation is related to husband's occupation more than among American Jews (but in the same direction: wives of professionals and scientific workers, who can afford substitute help better, are more likely to be in the labor force than other wives) and is more responsive to education and hence the economic value of her labor force participation.

Unlike American Jews, Israeli religious couples demonstrate greater spousal inequality in secular roles than less religious couples. Because the measure of religiosity in the Israeli study is limited, questions are raised about this difference that would require more extensive study, focusing on religiosity and its implications for secular behavior in the Israeli setting. Because the religiosity index reflects traditional ritual involvement in the Israeli context and is associated with a more defined lifestyle than among American Jews, it is possible that the more religious are more traditional in their marital patterns and that this perpetuates greater gender differences than in the less religious part of the population. It is also possible that the greater variation in number of children, and the higher burden of familial roles in the Israeli context, especially among the religious, is expressed in less investment in secular roles. A more comprehensive study based on a wider age range and larger sample would help to answer these questions.

CHAPTER 8

Conclusions

In this book we have analyzed the new data available from the 1990 National Jewish Population Survey about the comparative secular achievement of Jewish men and women, a high-achieving minority group in the United States. We consider whether Jewish men and women reach the same types and levels of economic achievement; how this achievement is related to their investment in economic roles, through educational background and labor force activity; and how it is related to their cultural or religious involvement as Jews. In particular we have considered whether their high educational level has resulted in greater gender equality in their economic roles and rewards; and whether Jewishness itself as a culture brings about greater or lesser gender equality in educational and economic activities and rewards.

The main thrust of our analysis can be expressed by the model in Figure 8.1, which summarizes both input into the labor force and the output of occupational rewards from labor force activity and the interrelation-

FIGURE 8.1
Model of Jewish Economic Achievement

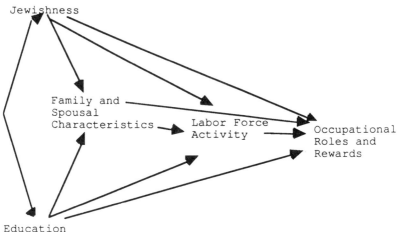

ships of the various factors involved. Education and Jewishness are two interrelated characteristics of input characterizing American Jews, which have both direct and indirect relationships to roles and rewards in the economic arena. The evaluation stresses how men and women react differently to these input factors, how the effect of these factors is mediated differently for men and women by the interaction of spousal characteristics within couple units, and how these differential relationships are related to observed gender differences in labor force roles and rewards. Some of our major findings are summarized here.

The interrelationship of Jewishness and education tends to be positive for both men and women. However, whether Jewishness brings about higher education or is reinforced by higher education was a question the present data could not answer. The relationship of Jewishness to labor force activity is a complex one, as certain aspects of Jewishness are related positively to labor force activity (especially the more social and contemporary expressions of American Jewishness) but others have a much weaker relationship, especially when education is controlled. Further, Jewishness is related negatively to labor force activity for women, unlike men; but this negative relationship turns out to be spurious, a result of the augmented family roles of more Jewishly involved women.

For both men and women, education is related positively to both labor force activity and occupational rewards in the form of occupational prestige; however, we show that for American Jews there are greater prestige returns to the education of men than women, which is one reason for the gap between the two. Investment in labor force roles in turn brings about differential rewards from labor force activity (i.e., occupational prestige), rewards that are also related directly to educational level (a positive relationship) and family roles (a positive relationship for men; a negative or nonsignificant relationship for women).

GENDER DIFFERENCES IN JEWISH SECULAR ACHIEVEMENT

Generally, Jewish men have higher educational and occupational achievement than Jewish women. Both Jewish men and women have higher achievements than their counterparts in the wider population. The relatively high occupational achievement of men is explained by a combination of higher education, certain aspects of Jewishness, and a strong positive support provided by marriage. Whether the latter is more or less than in the wider population was not an issue we could answer from available data but is certainly one worth exploring.

The relatively high occupational achievement of Jewish women compared to other women is also related to their high educational achievements and to some degree their smaller family size and efficient family
planning, which appears to ease the conflict with roles in the paid labor
force. The fertility and spacing of Jewish families was not the focus of the
current study. However, we did explore the strong importance of children
for Jews as a factor influencing the economic achievements of women,
finding that Jewish women were more apt to stay out of the labor force
longer with their preschool children than their counterparts in the wider
population and that the impact of family roles on economic activity
increased with Jewish involvement because of the augmented family and
parenting roles characterizing the more Jewishly involved.

The effect of marital roles per se on women's labor force activity surprisingly could be explained by other intervening variables. Marital
responsibilities per se do not seem to interfere with women's labor force
activity (nor does the family enhance her possibilities for economic
achievement, as it does for men). The weak effect of family size on labor
force activity and occupational achievement reflected the relatively small
family size of Jewish families (two children or fewer has relatively little
impact on labor force activity) as well as a low variation in family size; of
much more significance was the timing of first child. The ability of many
Jewish families to efficiently time their children appears to be one of
the secrets of Jewish women's success in the labor market and is a strategy for combining a high subcultural emphasis on traditional family
roles with the achievement orientation of the wider modern society.
Once Jewish families led in the transition from high to low fertility
through wider and more efficient use of contraceptives; today it appears
that they lead in the transition from single male breadwinner families to
dual earning families because of their ability to plan and control family
size and spacing.

Interestingly, the educational and occupational achievements of Jewish women far surpass other women's; and in fact, their achievements
surpass the majority of American men as well. In comparison to the wider
population of American men, in terms of educational attainment, labor
force activity, and occupational achievement, American Jewish women are
"emancipated." In comparison to Jewish men, however, Jewish women's
achievements show the traditional gender gap. Apparently Jewish women
compare themselves to Jewish men rather than to other women or to
men as a whole, which would explain Jewish women's intensive involvement in the women's movement, despite their impressive achievements
when compared to the wider population of women or men in the United
States.[1] The traditional gender gap between American Jewish men and
women is apparent especially at the higher levels of education, men hav-

ing significantly higher proportions attaining doctorates and professional degrees. So that as a whole Jews seem to have elevated the traditional gender gap to a higher level rather than having women catch up with men's achievements.

Such traditional differences are reinforced by the patterns of inequality found within Jewish couples, with men tending to be older, more educated, and more active in the labor force. Marriage in itself has no negative impact on women's achievements, but their education, labor force activity, and occupational prestige are affected negatively particularly by early entrance into parenting roles. Unlike women, men's educational achievements, labor force activity, and occupational prestige are enhanced by their marital roles, married men having higher achievement than unmarried men. Although marriage per se does not interfere with women's achievements, neither does it enhance their achievements which contributes to the resulting gender gap.

JEWISHNESS AND SECULAR ACHIEVEMENT
OF MEN AND WOMEN

Our exploration of Jewishness led us to develop a complex concept of Jewish involvement. We found that being Jewish was expressed in six different aspects of involvement, two expressing more closely the traditional religious aspects of Jewish observance, one expressing more contemporary ritual observances with communal aspects attached to them, two expressing involvement in formal and informal Jewish social circles and communal life, and one expressing Jewish background and learning. To some degree each of these aspects was related to the secular behavior (in education and labor force) of the Jewish men and women in our sample, which speaks to the persisting importance of religion in contemporary life, despite the secularization process that is assumed to be accompanying modernization. Along with this, we show that the aspects of Jewishness related to the secular behaviors central to our inquiry have been transformed from the more traditional ritual aspects in older cohorts to social and communal involvement in younger cohorts.

Generally we have shown that Jews who are "more Jewish" in this contemporary sense of involvement in various aspects of Jewish tradition or Jewish communal life are more educated and more active in the labor force than Jews who are not, whereas those with more traditional religious expressions tended to have lower education and labor force involvement particularly in older cohorts. In other words, Jews expressing more strongly the effect of their Jewish heritage are found to be more highly educated and in some ways more active in the labor force. In particular, the mainstream ways of expressing American Jewishness, socially and collectively being involved in being Jewish, do go together with higher education. We explained this difference generally as a transition from valuing Jewish education per se to valuing all education. Expressions of Judaism that are more typical of the non-Orthodox Jews in the United States are strongly related to educational achievement because of this generalization of the positive attitude toward education. More traditional or Orthodox Jews apparently have not made that transition or generalization, and in this sense we could not attribute the relationship directly to tendencies in the Jewish religion: those aspects closest to the "old" tradition were not related or related only weakly to educational achievement. However, there is a strong relationship between the more Orthodox expressions of Jewishness and achievement of Jewish education.

The relationship between Jewishness and labor force participation is mainly indirect, through accepted patterns of gender differentiation in the family. Married men tend to work harder in the labor force because of their acquired provider role; married women, on the other hand, spend more time with their children and curtail their labor force participation. Because Jewishness is related to a positive orientation to the family, Jewishness reinforces a conservative division of family labor between the genders. By affecting roles in the family, Jewish involvement indirectly affects men's and women's labor force behavior in opposing directions— men's labor force activity was related positively to Jewishness, but women's labor force activity was related negatively. Men's family roles are not expected to take time away from their labor force activity, but on the contrary increase their financial responsibilities, which are met through labor force activities; therefore Jewishness does not have a negative relationship with their labor force activity. Further, mainly the social aspects of Jewishness affect men's labor force participation, and their involvement in Jewish communal life is more through financial contributions (rather than volunteer time) or attending synagogue, neither of which takes time away from labor force activity. Men will be found more active in the labor force and at the same time more Jewish in this sense because successful men will be sought out for contributions and attracted to participate in Jewish organizations and synagogue by being offered higher positions in Jewish communal life.

The negative relationship between women's labor force participation and Jewishness disappeared when we controlled for family roles; that is, the negative effect of Jewishness on women's labor force activity is through their augmented family roles rather than a direct influence. The generally negative effect of Jewishness on labor force participation for women is not found in the case of education, because education rarely interferes with the fulfillment of familial roles. This lack of direct effect goes against the generally accepted opinion that Judaism inhibits women's equality with men. Even though Judaism reinforces the division of gender roles implicit in family and in particular parenting roles, it has no direct effect of differentiating men's and women's behavior in the economy. We found no evidence that Jewishness encouraged gender inequality between spouses, either, and found a relatively high degree of equality in labor force activity and occupational prestige between Jewish spouses.

Despite the different orientations of the main American Jewish denominations to gender equality in terms of religious roles and stratification, we found no spillover in terms of secular achievement in the anticipated directions. On the contrary, some of the strongest evidence of gender equality within couples was evidenced by American Orthodox, which would not be expected by their stand regarding gender and religious roles. This also is evidence that Judaism separates religious and secular arenas in its gender differentiation and has no overall patriarchal nature when it comes to women's access to roles and rewards.

AMERICAN AND ISRAELI JEWS

In our comparison of American and Israeli Jews we have seen that the tendencies to gender equality among Israelis of similar ethnic and immigrant background are somewhat greater in terms of education, labor force activity, and occupational distribution. Just as American Jewish women seem to be able to combine family and labor force roles more efficiently than the wider American population, Israeli women seem to combine family and labor force roles even more efficiently than American Jewish women. Overall, Israelis average less educational attainment than American Jews, but the returns to educational investment seem to be somewhat more equitable among Israeli Jewish men and women in terms of occupational achievement. Our findings reinforce our interpretation of the American Jewish data, which shows that there is a tendency toward gender equality in secular roles related to Jewishness; in the case of the Israelis, it is related to the institutions characterizing the Jewish state.

Israeli women have often been criticized for not investing more to change the gender inequality in their country. However, we have suggested several reasons for their relative complacency and for a doubtful prognosis with regard to increased activity in the future. In addition to the structural differences that facilitate combining family with labor force roles, the different male role in the Israeli situation, given the high frequency of reserve army duty and the generally lower standard of living, which makes life in general harder, may attenuate desires for equality with men; further, the institutionalization of the high value of familism makes family roles worthy of more social prestige than in the United States. Hence, although women may have no more access to monetary rewards relative to men than women in the United States, they may have greater access to social prestige accruing to their familial roles. In addition, in comparison to Israeli Jewish men, Israeli Jewish women with comparable qualifications are in many ways more equal than American Jewish women are to American Jewish men. All these factors help to explain the relative complacency of Israelis with regard to women's status and the lack of a widespread support for the women's movement in Israel.

One of our main purposes for bringing in the comparison to Israeli Jews was to test the extent to which the American Jewish patterns of behavior are influenced by their being a minority in a predominantly non-Jewish country (the "minority thesis"), as opposed to Israel where the predominant culture and population is Jewish. However, we found that the majority status of Israeli Jews increased the complexity of the comparison in several ways. As the predominant majority, Israeli Jews are responsible for the total societal functioning, which puts demands on the Israeli Jewish society that are not simply due to the absence of an outside political, economic, or cultural force within the country. These structural differences include, for instance, the responsibility for filling all economic roles, the distribution of higher educational opportunities according to the needs and resources of the country, and the responsibility for security of the citizens, which introduces the institution of the army and its manifold ramifications. These are needs of any country, whether Jewish or not, and the fact that Jews are responsible for these institutions in many respects does not make them "Jewish." Hence, the comparison is not necessarily the best (and certainly not the easiest) for testing the "minority thesis."

A better test of the "minority thesis" would probably be a comparison to other minority groups in the United States, particularly others who like the Jews have maintained their minority status self-consciously and voluntarily, preserving subcultural attributes that make them distinctive from the wider population.

CHANGES OVER COHORTS

As mentioned repeatedly throughout our analysis, year of birth has a double implication. It indicates age, or life cycle stage, and at the same time, birth cohort. Many of the gender comparisons changed over the life cycle, given the different implications of marriage and childbearing for men and women and the different patterns of retirement of men and women.

The implications for changes over birth cohort that we were able to extrapolate suggest increasing gender equality in younger cohorts in terms of educational attainment, labor force activity, and occupational roles and achievements. The dual earning pattern of couples is more common among younger cohorts, and there are fewer differences in education and occupational prestige among younger couples. These suggest that the tendencies indicated of gender equality in secular achievement among the Jews will continue into the future (assuming that patterns of inter-marriage do not alter the "Jewish" patterns significantly).

POLICY IMPLICATIONS FOR
THE AMERICAN JEWISH COMMUNITY

It can be expected that Jewish women will reach equality with Jewish men in terms of labor force roles and occupational achievement even sooner than their counterparts in the wider American population, given their strong educational qualifications, which are approaching men's in recent cohorts, the ability to manage family and parenting roles in such a way as to interfere minimally with labor force investment, and the absence of cultural impediments to engage in certain types of occupa-tional activities. Recognizing this, the Jewish community should take advantage of the highly skilled pool of Jewish women and incorporate their potential contributions into Jewish communal activities. Previous impediments to Jewish women's full participation in secular activities appear to stem not from the Jewish religion per se but from the social aspects of Jewishness that developed in congruence with the wider Amer-ican surroundings. To bring current Jewish social life into congruence with changes in the Jewish population and taking a cue from the strong leadership roles played by Jewish women in the movement toward secu-lar gender equality, Jewish formal organizations should find ways to attract women not only as auxiliary members alongside overwhelmingly male leadership but as leaders and managers of strong communal orga-nizations. Leaving aside the controversial question of ritual roles, which is being resolved within the different denominations in various manners, there are manifold ways to take advantage of the high caliber of human resources within the Jewish community, male and female alike. The Jew-ish community can find new ways to recruit high-skilled contributions of time and energy by offering greater rewards for what may continue to be dissimilar roles for men and women.

To facilitate the transition to dual earning families that Jewish fami-lies are showing, it is incumbent on the Jewish community to become leaders in childcare, part-time work, and other supportive infrastructures that allow the combination of strong family involvement alongside intensive labor force involvement.

Given the complexity of the differences between American and Israeli Jews that we uncovered in our attempt to make a straightforward comparison on a relatively well-defined topic, it would behoove the worldwide Jewish community to invest in greater communication between Jewish communities in an effort to increase the awareness of similarities and to gain an appreciation of differences and their sources. Israeli women have been criticized by American feminists—led in great part by American Jewish feminists—for settling for a less-than-desirable situation. It is obvious that the Israeli and American situations are far from comparable. The cultural and structural differences must be taken into consideration to understand different responses to what seem to be similar situations.

This is not a lesson for the Jewish community alone. An awareness of cultural differences between communities of women is growing, both within the United States and worldwide. Our comparison of gender equality among American and Israeli Jews has, we hope, highlighted some of the factors that must be taken into account when comparing one situation to another.

JEWISHNESS AND GENDER EQUALITY

Feminists have attacked Judaism for its gender inequality and patriarchal nature. In our exploration of the sources of gender inequality in Judaism, we found, on the contrary, the seeds for gender equality in terms of secular achievement and a legacy of active involvement of Jewish women throughout history in a variety of occupational roles. The 1990 NJPS data show that Jewish women share with Jewish men the distinctive high educational and occupational attainment in comparison to the wider American population. Although Jewish women's achievements do not equal Jewish men's achievements, they come closer to gender equality in terms of labor force activity and occupational achievement than men and women in the wider American population.

Another support of the Jewish tendency for equality in secular achievement comes from our comparison of American and Israeli Jews. Taking Israel to exemplify an environment characterized by the institutionalization of Jewish culture, "Jewish" patterns are even more evidenced among Israeli Jews. In this direction, our comparison shows an even greater degree of gender equality in educational and occupational attainment among Israeli Jews comparable in ethnic background and immigrant status to American Jews (second generation European-Americans) than among American Jews.

These patterns are tempered by the familism of the Jewish culture, which we see related both to the various ways in which American Jews are Jewishly involved and to the institutionalization of the Jewish culture in Israel. In the case of American Jews, entrance into the mothering role tempers both educational attainment and labor force activity, but the limited family size and the tendency to later childbearing minimize their impact and they have little effect on occupational achievement. In Israel, stronger familistic tendencies are combined with similar levels of labor force activity and occupational achievement, but the mechanisms facilitating the combination of roles are different. In Israel the strong familistic tendencies do not prevent activity in the labor force because of the widespread patterns of part-time employment and use of early childcare facilities.

That the tendency to gender equality in secular attainment is a Jewish pattern is supported by our comparison of American Jews with different types and extents of Jewish involvement. Both Jewish men and women more intensively involved in Jewish life have higher educational and occupational achievement. Our analysis of Jewish couples show that gender equality within families is not diminished by Jewish involvement.

Thus the patriarchal nature of the traditional Jewish religion does not appear to spill over into the secular arenas of activity; on the contrary, tendencies toward gender equality seem to be rooted in Jewish patterns of behavior.

Appendixes

APPENDIX I

Methodology of the
National Jewish Population Survey

Joseph Waksberg, Westat, Inc.

Large-scale sample surveys are frequently carried out in a number of dis-
crete steps and the National Jewish Population Survey (NJPS) followed
such a pattern. The steps consisted of determination of the subjects to be
included in the survey; development of specific question wording; testing
questions and procedures; decisions on survey procedures; preparation for
data collection, including recruitment and training of staff; sample selection; data collection; weighting and other aspects of data processing;
internal analysis of potential sources of errors; tabulations; analyses and
preparation of reports. This methodological report concentrates on the
technical aspects relating to sampling, survey procedures and data collection, weighting, and issues relating to accuracy of the data. There is a
brief description of the questionnaire development. Data analysis and
preparation of publications, both of the monographs and of less detailed
reports, are not part of the survey methodology and are not discussed
here.

GENERAL SURVEY PROCEDURES

The Council of Jewish Federations (CJF) established and supports a
National Technical Advisory Committee on Jewish population studies
(NTAC). At the time the NJPS was planned, the NTAC consisted of
researchers who worked for the CJF or local Jewish federations and outside demographers and statisticians interested in Jewish issues. The NTAC
endorsed an initial recommendation of the October 1987 World Conference on Jewish Demography in Jerusalem to conduct a U.S. National
Jewish Population Survey in the spring and summer of 1990. The CJF

concurred in this recommendation and agreed to support such a survey. The choice of 1990 was deliberate because it placed the survey at about the same time as the 1990 U.S. census, thereby ensuring maximum comparability between the Jewish survey data and census statistics. Further, the time period chosen for the conduct of the detailed interviews, late spring and early summer, both corresponded to the timing of the census and is a time when most college students could be reached in their families' residences or other dwelling places that are more permanent than dormitories or other college housing. The interviewing period is also the time that most sunbelt residents are in their more permanent homes.

The NTAC had independently come up with 1990 as the logical period for the survey as part of more general considerations of appropriate survey methodology. In a series of meetings in the decade leading up to 1990, the NTAC had discussed the many aspects of planning and implementing a Jewish population study and had submitted the following recommendations to the CJF:

- *That a large scale survey of the Jewish population be conducted in 1990.*

- *Data collection should be by telephone.* Over the past twenty to thirty years, survey researchers had demonstrated that the quality of responses to inquiries over the telephone were, for almost all subjects, about the same as for face-to-face interviews. Response rates to telephone surveys are generally lower than in face-to-face interviews, but the cost of telephone surveys is so much lower that the NTAC felt that the substantial cost advantage of a telephone survey more than compensated for the adverse effect on quality of a lower response rate.

- *A sample of 2,000 to 2,500 Jewish households should be selected by random digit dialing (RDD), without any use of federation or other lists of Jewish households.* RDD gives all households with telephones in the United States (both Jewish and non-Jewish) a known chance of selection into the sample so that lists are not necessary. Furthermore, it was the NTAC's judgment that the effort involved in trying to construct a national list and the likely small percentage of U.S. Jews that would be on the list would make the construction of the list counterproductive. It should be noted that households without telephones were not intended to be covered in the survey. In 1990, about 7 percent of U.S. households had no telephone. However, the percentage is undoubtedly much lower for Jewish households, and the NTAC did not believe their omission would have any detectable effect on the quality of the survey results. The survey also was to omit the nonhousehold population, principally persons in nursing homes, long-term hospital units, religious institutions, military barracks, and prisons. College students in dormitories (as well as those in private residences) were to be covered in the survey, usually as members of their parents' households.

- *Data should be collected only for the civilian population living in households.* This would omit the institutional and other nonhousehold population. The survey thus would exclude those in prisons, hospitals, nursing homes, hotels, religious institutions, and in military barracks. Estimates of the relatively small number of Jews in such places were added to the survey results for the estimate of the total number of Jews in the United States. However, their characteristics would not be reflected in the breakdowns of the totals by age, sex, and so forth.

- *A screening questionnaire that defines and identifies Jewish households should be administered to the sample of telephone households.* Because random digit dialing produces a sample of all U.S. telephone households, non-Jewish households would then be dropped and Jewish households retained for the survey.

- *That the survey include a wide variety of topics.* The NTAC developed a broad set of questions designed to shed light on the demographic, social, and economic characteristics of the Jewish population and to provide information on items of specific Jewish concern, such as inter-marriage, Jewish education, philanthropy, observances of Jewish rituals and practices, synagogue membership, utilization of social services, volunteerism, attitudes to certain issues of Jewish concern, and so on. The questions were divided into two groups: (1) ones for which reasonably accurate information for all household members could be provided by any adult in the household (e.g., age, education, observance, etc.) and (2) questions for which the accuracy of proxy responses would be in doubt (e.g., attitudes). For the first set of questions, data would be obtained for all members of the sample households. For the second group, the NTAC recommended that one adult be selected at random in each sample household and that the sample for these items should be considered as consisting of only the selected persons.

A second, and independent, partition of the questions was also made. In order to reduce the considerable interview length, the questionnaire was divided into a "core" component, to be asked in all sample households, and "modules" to be asked in subsamples of households. More specifically, respondents were randomly allocated to three equal subsamples, and each subsample was assigned one of the three following areas of inquiries:

1. Jewish identity
2. Social services
3. Philanthropy

• *After the survey information was collected, weights should be inserted into the data file.* The weights should be constructed so that when they are used in tabulations of the survey data, they provide approximately unbiased estimates of the U.S. Jewish population in each category shown in the tabulations.

• *The individual responses to the survey questionnaire as well as the appropriate weights should be entered onto a computer tape.* Copies of the tape would be available for researchers interested in making detailed studies of particular aspects of Jewish life.

• *A high priority was put on speed of data processing, tabulations of the data, and publication of the major results.* First a summary report would highlight the major findings in the survey, then a series of analytic studies would focus on particular topics.

• *The survey should be conducted outside CJF or its member organizations.* More specifically, a contract would be let by competitive bidding to a company experienced in the conduct of such statistical studies.

The CJF approved the NTAC recommendations, provided a budget for the survey, and asked the NTAC to make the necessary arrangements. A request for proposals (RFP) that described the work to be done, the procedures just outlined, and the scope of work was prepared and distributed to interested statistical and market research companies. A subcommittee of the NTAC reviewed the proposals submitted by organizations interested in carrying out the survey and selected the ones that were judged best. These organizations were invited to make personal presentations of their plans and their experience in such activities before the subcommittee. A contract was then awarded to a team consisting of ICR Survey Research Group and Marketing Systems Group (also known as Genesys Sampling Systems). The Marketing Systems Group was responsible for the sample selection and all weighting and estimation phases of the project. ICR was responsible for all other aspects of the survey, from questionnaire pretesting through data collection, coding, and data tape preparation.

The choice of ICR and Marketing Systems Group was based on a number of factors: understanding of the requirements of the study, the reputation of the team in doing high-quality work, experience with large-scale telephone sample surveys, an existing staff of experienced telephone interviewers and a system for training and supervising them, a capable statistician to oversee the sampling and related activities, and cost. A main, and overriding advantage of the team, was that they carried out, for other sponsors, a weekly RDD national household sample survey of 2,000 households. They agreed to add the screening questions that identified Jewish households to the questionnaire then in use. It was esti-mated that the approximately 100,000 households screened over the course of a year would supply the 2,500 responding Jewish households desired in the final sample. (The screening actually covered more than a year and consisted of over 125,000 households, which yielded over 5,000 households that indicated the presence of a Jewish member.) By attaching the screener questions to an existing national sample survey, the NJPS was able to avoid the expense of selecting and interviewing the very large sample needed to locate 2,500 Jewish households. Instead, the survey incurred only a fairly modest marginal cost of the added time to admin-ister the screening questions. If the NJPS had to pay the entire cost of selecting and screening more than 100,000 households, the additional cost probably would have been well over $1 million.

An additional advantage of using the ICR's ongoing weekly survey was that it provided flexibility in achieving the desired sample size. The amount of screening necessary to achieve a sample of 2,500 Jewish house-holds could be estimated only approximately in advance. With the weekly samples screened by ICR, a cumulative tally of Jewish households could be kept, and the weekly samples terminated before the end of the year if fewer than 100,000 households provided the required sample size or it could be continued for longer than a year if that was necessary.

SAMPLE SELECTION

The telephone numbers selected for the NJPS were based on random digit dialing and are a probability sample of all possible telephone numbers in the United States. The sampling procedure utilized a single-stage sample of telephone numbers within known residential working banks (the first two digits of the four-digit suffix, e.g., 212-555-XXxx). Telephone exchanges were strictly ordered by census geographic variables (i.e., Division, Metro/Nonmetro, Central City/Suburban, etc.), creating a sample frame with fine implicit geographic stratification. This procedure provides samples that are unbiased and in which all telephones have the same chance of selection. Because the random digit aspect allows for the inclusion of unlisted and unpublished numbers, it protects the samples from "listing bias"—the unrepresentativeness of telephone samples that can occur if the distinctive households whose telephone numbers are unlisted and unpub-lished are excluded from the sample. The RDD sample is referred to as the *screening sample*. It consisted of 125,813 households that were asked whether any household member was Jewish. (See the section on organiza-tion of collection activities for specific questions.) All qualified Jewish households were followed up with requests for the detailed interviews.

The household sample selection was accompanied by an automated scheme for scheduling callbacks for telephone numbers at which there was no response to the initial call. A three-callback rule was followed—the timing of the callbacks was scheduled by the computer to cover various times of the day, but within a narrow time frame. This narrow time frame was required by the short field period for each weekly survey. There were actually two weekly sample surveys, with 1,000 households in each survey. One weekly survey ran from Wednesday evening through Sunday evening; the second from Friday evening through Tuesday evening. The initial call and callback schedule ensured a minimum of two weekend attempts (if necessary) on each sample number.

The tight time schedule for the screening interviews undoubtedly reduced the response rate, as compared to a survey with more time for callbacks. (For example, persons on vacation during the survey week were never given an opportunity to respond.) However, the NTAC believed that the advantages of using an ongoing survey for screening outweighed the disadvantages.

PRESURVEY OPERATIONS

Two major sets of activities preceded the data collection. They consisted of the development and testing of the survey questions, and the interviewer training and briefing.

Development and Testing of Survey Instruments

Three stages of data collection were planned: screening, recontact, and in-depth interviewing. The questionnaires for all three phases were initially developed by the NTAC. These documents were then edited, reformatted, and programmed for CATI (computer assisted telephone interviewing) interviewing by ICR staff. The development phase included several questionnaire drafts and a series of "live" pretests.

CATI is a system in which the questionnaire has been entered into a computer, each interviewer is provided with a computer screen and keyboard, and the questions to be asked appear on the screen instead of having to be read from a paper questionnaire. The responses are entered directly into the computer. In addition to speeding up the data processing, CATI has the capability of carrying out editing for consistency and completeness of data and flexibility of operations. Almost all large-scale telephone surveys are now done via CATI.

All interviewing in both the screening, recontact/validation and the main study phases were conducted by professional interviewers via computer-assisted telephone interviewing. From an interviewing standpoint, the CATI system removes the potential for interviewer error relative to skip patterns and possible response options. Moreover, the CATI system provides inherent response editing capabilities relative to both range edits and conditional requirements based on prior responses. Computerized questionnaire control allows interviewers to better establish rapport with respondents and concentrate on responses rather than attempting to contend with the extreme complexity of the recontact and main study questionnaires.

Finally, CATI capabilities allowed for access to up-to-the-minute interviewing production measures, including production rates, refusal and refusal conversion rates, and results of dialing attempts.

In each pretest, personnel from NTAC and ICR monitored interviews as they were being conducted. Any unforeseen deficiencies in question content, sequencing, and nomenclature were corrected during this stage. In most cases, indicated changes were incorporated immediately, providing pretest capabilities during the same pretest session.

The final CATI questionnaires were reviewed and tested extensively by both NTAC and ICR personnel prior to "live" interviewing. In addition, the pretest data served as a "live" test of output, data format, edit checks, and such.

Interviewer Training and Briefing

All interviewers selected to work on the 1990 NJPS were personally briefed, trained and supervised during all hours of interviewing. In addition to participating in the standard ICR ten-hour interviewer training session, all interviewers who worked on the survey participated in a detailed briefing session developed specifically for this study.

This special briefing included an item-by-item discussion of each question and module contained in the interview; a discussion of special respondent "handling" for specific interview situations, including providing the CJF's telephone number to respondents who questioned the authenticity of the survey and suggesting that the CJF be called and a review of areas and issues relating to Jewish heritage including customs, holidays, and proper pronunciation of Hebrew words and phrases that interviewers would be likely to encounter during the course of the study. In addition to the briefing, written interviewer aids were provided and made available during all hours of interviewing.

ORGANIZATION OF DATA COLLECTION ACTIVITIES

For approximately one year preceding the survey, beginning in April 1989, ICR conducted Stage I of the National Jewish Population Survey.

This entailed incorporating a series of four screening questions into its twice weekly general market telephone surveys. The screening questions determined Jewish qualification and thus were the basis for the recruitment of households. The four screening questions in Stage I were asked in the following order:

1. What is your religion?
   If not Jewish, then . . .
2. Do you or anyone else in the household consider themselves Jewish?
   If no, then . . .
3. Were you or anyone else in the household raised Jewish?
   If no, then . . .
4. Do you or anyone else in the household have a Jewish parent?

This screening stage of the survey obtained information on the religious preference of 125,813 randomly selected adult Americans and the Jewish qualification of their respective households. It was determined initially that 5,146 households contained at least one person who qualified as "Jewish" or Jewishly affiliated as determined by the screening questions. Stage II, the inventory stage, consisted of attempts to recontact Jewish households to requalify potential respondents and solicit participation in the 1990 NJPS. The households classified as Jewish in the last three months of screening were omitted from Stage II because the Stage III interviewing was to follow so closely. Stage II included 4,208 households. During Stage II, a number of households that were initially classified as Jewish dropped out of the survey sample due to changes in household composition or to disqualification based upon further review.

Stage III, the final interviewing stage of the survey, yielded a total of 2,441 completed interviews with qualified respondents. The statistics reported here are drawn from these households. Through a process of scientific weighting procedures utilizing all 125,813 Stage I interviews, the sample of Jewish households represents about 3.2 million American households nationally.

The survey interviews collected information about every member of the household. Thus, the study was able to ascertain important personal information about 6,514 persons in the surveyed households. Appropriate weighting procedures indicate that the number of persons in the surveyed households represents about 8.1 million individual Americans, a number of whom are not themselves Jewish, reflecting the mixed composition of the households in the Jewish sample.

DATA COLLECTION: FIRST TWO PHASES,
SCREENING AND RECONTACT AND VALIDATION

Phase I. Screening

The entire screening phase was conducted as part of the ICR Survey Research Group's twice weekly telephone omnibus survey. The use of a telephone omnibus vehicle as opposed to a custom survey has obvious cost advantages; on the other side, there may be trade-offs relative to response rates; length of field period; placement of the screening questions on Jewish identity within the ever changing instrument; and so on. However, these were felt to be small.

As mentioned earlier, 125,813 screeners were completed for this project. Although no formal disposition of call results is available, it is known that the proportion refusing to participate in any given weekly survey averages about 45 percent. To assess the potential bias resulting from this response rate, two separate analyses were conducted. They are described in the final section.

Phase II. Recontact and Validation

The second phase of the study was conducted with respondents from Jewish households identified during the initial screening phase. This phase was designed to validate the initial screening process, initiate contacts with qualified households to explain the purpose of the study and gain cooperation, and provide a means of keeping in touch with the qualified respondents given the extended tune period between the initial screening and final interview.

The primary informational objectives of the recontact-validation phase were as follows:

1. Validate that the respondent or household was, in fact, Jewish,
2. Explain the purpose of the call and encourage respondents to participate in the in-depth study during the summer of 1990,
3. Collect detailed household data relating to age, sex, and relationship of each household member and type of residence and location,
4. Request and secure a third party reference to assist in the future recontact for the in-depth study.

Recontact phase interviewing was conducted over a fifty-two week period, from April 7, 1989 through April 2, 1990. The process was continuous, with most recontacts occurring within two weeks of the initial qualification in the screening phase.

On successful recontact, the household member who participated in the Screening Phase was asked to reverify the Jewish character of himself or herself and other household members relative to being Jewish, considering himself or herself Jewish, being raised Jewish, and having a Jewish parent.

Respondents were asked to participate in an in-depth main study phase interview to be conducted at a later date. This recruitment included an explanation of the study, the size of the study, an explanation of how and why they were selected to participate, and the naming of CJF as the study sponsor.

Substantial efforts were made to "convert" respondents who refused to participate. Respondents who refused to participate at the introduction or during the interview itself, were recontacted by specially trained interviewers. These interviewers used specially developed and proven techniques to convert refusals into participants. In some cases, alternative respondents within a given household were recruited to participate. In addition to specially trained interviewers, letters of explanation were mailed to refusals in an effort to establish credibility for the study and, in turn, to increase likely participation.

A household inventory of requalified Jewish households was created; this roster of household members included age and sex, along with each member's relationship to the primary contact person. Specifically, four questions were asked about each household member:

1. Name,
2. Age and sex,
3. Relationship to the respondent,
4. Religious qualification.

Additional information relating to household characteristics was also requested; specifically, the type of household unit (e.g., multiple family, single unit, apartment) and whether this particular unit was the primary residence or a seasonal or similar recreational dwelling.

Finally, information about third-party references (i.e., a relative or close friend) was requested for use in the event that respondents could not be reached at their original location. This third-party information was utilized to "track" the original respondents during the final phase of interviewing.

Not every Jewish household identified in the screening phase was included in the recontact phase. Specifically, households identified during the final three months of screening were excluded because of the rather short time until onset of the full national survey; it was thought that the risk associated with alienating respondents by attempting multiple contacts over a very short period of time outweighed the few households likely to be lost due to relocation.

In total, 4,208 Jewish households identified in the screening phase were included in the recontact phase. The results of attempted recontact are shown in Table AI.1. It should be noted that there was no strict call-back rule but rather "nonrespondent households" were continually recycled, with many receiving twenty attempts or more.

Over 81 percent of the screened and qualified households were successfully contacted and reinterviewed; of these, 15.5 percent did not requalify, and 6.3 percent disavowed knowledge of the previous interview. Just over 9 percent refused the recontact interview.

None of the original respondent households were excluded from the 1990 survey based on results of the recontact phase; the purpose here was to facilitate tracking of respondents and increase ultimate cooperation, not to requalify, validate, and reject sample households. Although the recontact data were retained, all sample households (including those that failed to qualify in Phase II) regardless of the outcome were again attempted during the final phase of interviewing.

PHASE III. MAIN STUDY, DATA COLLECTION

In the spring and summer of 1990, the third and final phase of data collection was undertaken. The survey instrument itself was initially developed by the NTAC, jointly pretested with ICR, and prepared for CATI interviewing by the ICR.

TABLE AI.1
Results of the Recontact Validation Phase

	Number	*Percent*
Total	(4,208)	(100.0)
Requalified and willing to particpate	2,124	52.1
Requalified and not willing	316	7.5
Not requalified	652	15.5
No such respondent	266	6.3
Refused at start	315	7.5
Refused during interview	75	1.8
Language barrier	27	0.6
Nonworking	135	3.2
Nonhouseholds	20	0.5
No Contact	278	6.6

In the main study phase, households that were identified as being Jewish in the screening phase were recontacted between May 8, 1990, and August 12, 1990, in an effort to complete the in-depth, detailed information requested on the Jewish character of the household, its members and related issues. Due to the considerable interview length (approximately thirty minutes), the questionnaire was divided into two parts: the "core" questionnaire and three shorter questionnaire "modules."

The core questionnaire was asked of all respondents. In addition to the core, respondents were randomly assigned to one of three groups and asked a series of more detailed questions relating to one of the following areas of inquiry (referred to as modules):

1. Jewish identity,
2. Social services,
3. Philanthropy.

The screening phase had identified a total of 5,146 Jewish households over more than fifteen months of interviewing and surveying a total of over 125,000 households. As Table AI.2 shows, 49 percent of these resulted in completed Phase III interviews; just over 15 percent refused to participate; and in only 13 percent of the cases was it impossible to contact any household members.

The most difficult and puzzling result, however, were the roughly 18 percent of respondents or households that failed to requalify; all of these respondents were recontacted a second time during Phase III, and all

TABLE AI.2
Results of the Main Study Phase

	Number	*Percent*
Total	(5,146)	(100.0)
Nonworking	366	7.1
Non-household	63	1.2
No answer or busy	191	3.7
Respondent no longer there	23	0.4
Answering machines	101	2.0
Refused at start	670	13.0
Refused during interview	126	2.4
Language barrier	21	0.4
Ineligible	146	2.8
Not requalified	908	17.6
Deleted or not used in interviews	25	0.5
Completed interview	2,506	48.7

failed to validate their replies in the screening phase. Later sections contain a discussion of this group of respondents and describe how they were used in estimating the size of the Jewish population.

It was also a standard practice to attempt conversion of all refusals, so that all of this group represents "double refusals." All telephone numbers reported as nonworking were verified and attempts to secure new numbers were made, although this was not very successful. No limit was placed on number of followup attempts, which explains the relatively low proportion of no answer and busy sample dispositions (<4%).

WEIGHTING PROCEDURES

Overview of Weighting Procedures

After the survey information was collected and processed, each respondent was assigned a weight. When the weights are used in tabulations of the survey data, the results automatically provide estimates of the U.S. Jewish population in each category shown in the tabulations.

The weighting method first ensured that key demographic characteristics of the adult population of the total weighted sample of the 125,813 screened responding households matched the most current estimates of these demographic characteristics produced by the Census Bureau. The weighting procedure automatically adjusted for noncooperating households as well as for those who were not at home when the interviewer telephoned and for households that lacked telephones or had multiple lines.

A second step in the weighting was carried out on the questionnaires completed in the recontact and validation phase and the main study phase of the study. This step made the weighted totals of completed questionnaires in each phase of the survey conform to the geographic and demographic profile of Jewish households at the earlier phases.

In addition, a separate weighting routine was established for each of the modules that was based on a subsample of the full set of Jewish households, so that the weighted total of each module corresponded to the full sample.

Detailed Description of Weighting

There were four stages in the preparation of the screening sample weights. First, households with more than one residential telephone number were assigned weights designed to compensate for their higher probabilities of selection—one-half for households with two telephone numbers, and one-third for households with three or more numbers. Second, cooperating households were poststratified, using eighteen geographic strata—nine census divisions, and two categories for in or out of metropolitan areas. In the third stage, a weight was derived by poststratifying the weighted counts of the population in the sample households, using geographic-demographic strata, to the best current estimates of those strata. The strata comprised census region (four), age by sex (twelve), education of respondent (three), and race, that is, white or other (two). The fourth stage was geographic poststratification at a state, metropolitan statistical area (MSA) or county level, depending on the size of the area. Individual counties with 75,000 or more households became individual strata. The remaining counties were grouped by individual MSAs or when necessary linked to a larger county (over 75,000 households) within the same MSA. Counties outside MSAs were grouped at the state level.

Following these weighting processes, completed screener interviews were classified by their initial level of Jewish qualification and the results of the subsequent data collection efforts. During the various interviewing phases, a significant number of Jewish households that were initially considered qualified subsequently became classified as non-Jewish. The largest proportion of these households were originally qualified because the respondents or others in the households "considered" themselves to be Jewish. Table AI.3 details weighted respondents by the basis for qualification and response category in the Phase II follow-up interview.

The critical issue was how to treat the "not qualified" in estimating the total number of Jewish households. The extreme alternatives were to

TABLE AI.3
Jewish Households Qualified by Screener,
by Reporting Status in Validation Interview

Reporting Status of Later Interviews	Basis of Qualification by Screener				
	Total	Religion	Consider	Raised	Parents
Total	3,753,000	1,737,000	1,347,000	195,000	474,000
	100.0%	46.3	35.9	5.2	12.6
Known Jewish households	1,896,000	1,167,000	460,000	80,000	189,000
	100.0%	61.6	24.2	4.2	9.9
Refused Phase III	506,000	242,000	176,000	29,000	59,000
	100.0%	47.9	34.8	5.8	11.6
Other nonresponse	563,000	200,000	246,000	29,000	88,000
	100.0%	35.4	43.8	5.1	15.7
Not qualified	789,000	128,000	466,000	57,000	138,000
	100.0%	16.2	59.0	7.2	17.5

ignore the requalification information altogether, essentially treating the "not qualified" as refusals or taking the additional information at "face value" and reducing the estimates of Jewish households by 789,000, to just under 3 million.

Of course, there were a wide range of options in between. To aid in the evaluation of this situation, a DJN (distinctive Jewish name) analysis was conducted on the respondents qualified through the screening process. The first step in this process was obtaining a reverse match for these telephone numbers; for each telephone number corresponding to a household that was listed in the white pages of any U.S. telephone directory, the name and address of the subscriber was obtained. The surnames were then matched against a data file of distinctive Jewish surnames provided by the NTAC. The results are shown in Table AI.4.

As is evident from the table, the not qualified segment exhibits strikingly different proportions of DJNs from the other groups. Based on this and related information, the determination was made that all respondents originally qualified on the basis of religion were most likely refusals and should remain as qualified Jewish households; conversely, among the other groups, the unweighted ratios of DJNs indicated a likely true qualification rate of 17.5 percent.

Based on these assessments, the estimated Jewish households were adjusted to those shown in Table AI.5. The impact of these adjustments were to reduce the estimates of Jewish households from 3.753 million to 3.208 million, a reduction of about 14.5 percent.

These adjustments to the weighted estimates of Jewish households required a two-phase adjustment to the weighted dataset:

1. The indicated proportions of not qualified respondents needed to be weighted downward to the indicated totals, whereas non-Jewish households required a compensatory weight to maintain total households in the entire screening sample.

TABLE AI.4
Percentage of Sample with Distinctive Jewish Surnames
(Base = Qualifiers with a Located Surname)

Reporting Status of Later Interviews	Basis of Qualification by Screener				
	Total	*Religion*	*Consider*	*Raised*	*Parents*
Known Jewish household	16.7	23.3	5.6	10.5	4.8
Refused Phase III	13.8	20.0	8.0	9.5	7.8
Other nonresponse	10.9	21.2	4.9	6.7	3.8
Not qualified	2.6	8.6	1.5	0.0	1.6

TABLE AI.5
Final Estimates of Jewish Households
Reflecting Adjustments to "Not Qualified" Call Results

Reporting Status of Later Interviews	Basis of Qualification by Screener				
	Total	Religion	Consider	Raised	Parents
Total	3,208,000 100.0%	1,737,000 54.1	963,000 30.0	148,000 4.6	360,000 11.2
Known Jewish households	1,896,000 100.0%	1,167,000 61.6	460,000 24.2	80,000 4.2	189,000 9.9
Refused Phase III	506,000 100.0%	242,000 47.9	176,000 34.8	29,000 5.8	59,000 11.6
Other nonresponse	563,000 100.0%	200,000 35.4	246,000 43.8	29,000 5.1	88,000 15.7
Not qualified	244,000 100.0%	128,000 52.4	82,000 33.6	10,000 4.1	24,000 9.9

2. The completed Phase III interviews were then weighted to the estimates of total Jewish households, for analyses based on Jewish households only.

The first step was accomplished by stratifying based on census division, and within the division, by (1) non-Jewish qualifiers, (2) households qualified by the screener as Jewish based on other than religion, who became "not qualified" in Phase III, and (3) all other Jewish households. The second group represent those respondents whose estimate of Jewish affiliation was to be adjusted in this process. The revised weights were substituted in the individual data records, completing reconciliation of the full screener data set.

The procedure just described was carried out for the full sample and is therefore applicable to the core questionnaire that was administered to all sample households. However, each sample data record also includes a module weight in addition to the household and population weights for the core questions. The weighting procedure for the modules duplicated that of the previous section; a poststratification scheme incorporating census region and level of Jewish qualification. A simple expansion factor to weight each module's sample total in each cell was computed, multiplied by the household weight, and incorporated into the sample record.

Separate population weights were also developed for the statistics obtained from the randomly selected adult in each household. Essentially, these weights incorporated the household weights multiplied by the number of adults in the sample households.

APPLICATION OF WEIGHTS

Given the character and complexity of the survey instrument itself, a determination as to which of the weights described previously to utilize for a particular statistic is not always apparent. The following explanation and examples should help in eliminating uncertainties.

Household weights should be used for developing estimates in the following types of situations:

1. Where the analysis, table, or distribution being produced is clearly based on household demographics. Examples include

   • The number of households by level of Jewish qualification,

   • Distributions of households by number of children, number of adults, number of Jewish adults, age of oldest member, or household income distributions,

   • Household distributions based on qualification of one or more members, such as "are you or any member of your household currently a member of a synagogue or temple?"

2. Where the analysis or distribution utilizes variables constructed from the roster of household members. Examples include

   • Age or educational attainment of all household members or subsets of all members,

   • Country of origin or employment status of all household members or adult household members.

The population weights are applicable only in those situations where the respondent answers to a specific question about himself or herself are to be utilized to represent all adult members in Jewish households. For example, opinions about various public issues, distributions of Jewish religious denomination or Jewish ethnicity, and personal attendance at Jewish religious services.

In certain rare situations users may need to devise their own weighting schemes to establish a fully weighted sample base. This is most likely to occur when the adult members of a sample household exceed the number for which data was requested. For example, detailed information as to marital status was requested for only four members 18 years of age and older. If a particular sample household had five members, there are a number of options depending upon one's objectives and the characteristics of the household:

   • A balance line of "not reported" could be incorporated into the tables being produced.

- The simplest weighting method would be to weight each of the four responses by 1.25 in addition to application of the household weight. Depending, however, on the characteristics of the member for which no data is available, alternative approaches might prove more desirable.
- If the missing number's data represented one of three adult children, a better approach might be to weight the data for the two children for which data is present by 1.5, while keeping the parent's weight at 1.0.
- Alternatively, one could compensate for the missing member information on an overall basis. For example, one could categorize all qualified members by age, sex, region, and so forth, using the household weights; categorize those for which data was reported in a similar matrix using the household weight; and finally compute a weight for each cell that would increase the base of those responding to the weighted total in the first matrix.

In most cases, the bias created by simply ignoring the small discrepancies will be minimal. However, the user needs to make these decisions on a case-by-case basis, possibly trying alternative methods and comparing the results.

Finally, the module weights should obviously be used for tabulations of items in any of the modules, regardless of whether simple totals of module items arc tabulated or there are cross-classifications with other nonmodule items.

ACCURACY OF DATA

Nonsampling Errors

All population surveys are subject to the possibility of errors arising from sampling, nonresponse, and respondents providing the wrong information, and the NJPS is no exception. The response rate to identify potential Jewish households, was approximately 50 percent. This is lower than most surveys that make efforts to ensure high quality strive to achieve. (The low response rate was partially caused by the contractor's need for each set of sample cases assigned for interview to be completed in a few days. This made intensive follow-up by the screener impractical.) The concern over the effect of nonresponse on the statistics is not so much on the size of the nonresponse, since this is adjusted for in the weighting, but on the likelihood that nonrespondents are somewhat different from respondents. Although variations in response rates by geography, age, sex, race, and educational attainment were adjusted for in the weighting, there was still the possibility that Jews and non-Jews responded at different rates.

To test whether this occurred at an important level, the telephone numbers of approximately 10,000 completed interviews and for about 10,000 nonrespondents were matched against telephone listings to obtain the household names, and the percentage of each group having distinctive Jewish names was calculated. The percentage for the completed cases was 1.38 percent and for the nonrespondents was 1.29. The difference between the two is well within the bounds of sampling error. Although distinctive Jewish names account for a minority of all Jews, this test does provide support for the view that nonresponse did not have an important impact on the reliability of the count of the Jewish population.

In regard to errors in reporting whether a person is Jewish, previous studies indicate that the errors are in the direction of understating the count of the Jewish population, although the size of the understatement does not seem to be very large. A particular concern in the NJPS was the fairly large number of cases where respondents in households reporting the presence of one or more Jews in the screening operation, reversed themselves in the detailed interview. Of all households reported as having Jews by the screener, 18 percent were reported as nonqualified in the detailed interview. There was a possibility that this was a hidden form of refusal, rather than errors in the original classification of the households or changes in household membership.

A test similar to the one on refusals was carried out for the nonqualified households. The telephone numbers for the 5,146 households who were reported as Jewish in the screening interview were matched against telephone listings, and those with distinctive Jewish names were identified. The detailed results of the match were reported already. They can be summarized as follows: in households that reported themselves as Jewish in the detailed interviews, 16.8 percent had DJNs. The rates were slightly smaller for refusals (13.9 percent) and for those who could not be contacted (10.9 percent). However, the percentage was only 2.9 percent for households who were reported as not Jewish in the detailed interview. It is, of course, possible that DJN households are less reticent than others in acknowledging to a telephone interviewer the fact that all or some of the household members are Jewish, but the evidence is that underreporting did occur, but not to a very serious extent. An adjustment in the weights of about 8 percent was made to account for the unreported Jews in the estimates of the total number of Jews. Because questionnaire information was not obtained for them, the statistics on characteristics of Jews may be subject to small biases if the Jewish nonqualifiers are very different from those who responded.

As mentioned earlier, other studies have reported that there is some understatement of reporting of Jewish heritage in interviews surveys. No adjustments were made for such possible understatement since firm data on its size does not exist. As a result, the estimate of the size of the Jewish population is probably somewhat on the low side.

It is not possible to quantify the effects of the relatively high nonresponse rates, the possibility that some respondents might have deliberately misreported their religious affiliations, errors arising from misunderstanding of the questions, or other problems in the data. As indicated, the test done with the presence of distinctive Jewish names did not detect any important problems. Furthermore, comparisons of the estimates of total Jewish population with the results of local area surveys carried out in or near 1990, did not show any important discrepancies. The screener questionnaire that inquired about Jewish affiliations also identified other major U.S. religious groupings, and estimates of their membership corresponded reasonably well with independent estimates of the membership.

Consequently, all of the tests we were able to carry out failed to turn up any major problems in the data. However, it seems reasonable to assume that persons who did not respond are somewhat different from respondents and the other potential sources of error must also have had some impact. When comparisons are made, either over time, or among subgroups of Jewish persons (e.g., between those with a relatively high level of Jewish education and others, persons with synagogue affiliation and unaffiliated, etc.), it would be prudent to avoid analyses or explanations of small differences, even if they are statistically significant. However, the evidence is that large and important differences do reflect real phenomena, and can be relied on.

Sampling Variability

Sample surveys are subject to sampling error arising from the fact that the results may differ from what would have been obtained if the whole population had been interviewed. The size of the sampling error of an estimate depends on the number of interviews and the sample design. For estimates of the number of Jewish households, the sample size is 125,813 screened households. The screened sample was virtually a simple random sample. As a result, it is very likely (the chances are about 95 percent) that the number of Jewish households is within a range plus or minus 3 percent around the estimate shown in this report. For estimates of the Jewish population, the range is slightly higher since sampling variability will affect both the estimate of the number of Jewish households and of the average number of Jews in those households. The 95 percent range is plus or minus 3.5 percent. These ranges are the limits within which the results of repeated sampling in the same time period could be expected to vary 95 percent of the time, assuming the same sampling procedure, the same interviewers, and the same questionnaire.

Unfortunately, due to the complex nature of the sample design and weighting method used in estimating the characteristics of the Jewish population, it is not possible to give a simple formula that will provide estimates of the standard errors for all types of estimates. To begin with, three basic samples are embedded in the survey:

1. The household sample can be considered as the equivalent of a simple random sample of 2,441 households.

2. For population statistics based on data reported for all household members, the sample size is 6,514. However, for most estimates of this type, the standard errors will be greater than what would be achieved with a simple random sample of 6,514 because of the presence of intraclass correlation; that is, the tendency of household members to be more alike than would be the case of persons chosen at random. The intraclass correlation introduces a design effect that should be superimposed on the simple formula for the standard error.

3. Population statistics based on data reported for only one household member, selected at random, are also based on a sample size of 2,441. However, because the chance of selection of any person depends on the number of adults in the household the sample is not equivalent to a simple random sample of 2,441. The varying probabilities of selection also create a design effect.

The standard error of an estimate of a percentage can be approximated by

$$\sqrt{D.p.(1-p)/Rn}$$

where p is the estimated percentage, D is the design effect, R is the proportion of Jews in the segment for which percentages are computed, and n is the sample size; that is, 2,441 or 6,514. When percentages are computed of all Jewish households or persons, R is equal to 1; when the base of the percentage is a subgroup of all households or persons (e.g., households observing certain rituals, all females, persons in a particular age group) the value of R is the fraction of all households or persons in that subgroup.

The value of D is 1 for household statistics. For population statistics, the value will depend on the item being estimated. Although it is possible to calculate an estimate of the value of D for each item (or, alternatively, a relatively unbiased estimate of the standard error), we assume most analysts will not want to make the fairly extensive effort needed for such calculations. Guidelines for approximating D follow:

- As stated earlier, D can be considered equal to 1 for household statistics.
- For items based on data reported for all household members, D will be in the range 1 to 2.7. It will be close to 1 for percentages based on a subset of the Jewish population (e.g., adult males, currently widowed persons, persons born abroad, disabled). At the other extreme, the value will be close to 2.7 on items on which household members are likely to have similar characteristics (e.g., the percentage of Jews who belong to conservative congregations). The 2.7 is the average size of Jewish households, and when D has this value, the effect on the standard error is to treat the statistic as a household item with a sample size of 2,441 rather than a population item. For other types of percentages, the value of D will be somewhere in the 1 to 2.7 range; the more alike members of a household are likely to be, the greater should be the value of D used in the calculations.
- The value of D is about 1.2 for items based on data reported for only one adult in the household. This design effect reflects the effect on sampling errors of having varying probabilities of selection, depending on the household size. For example, adults living in one-adult households will have twice the chance of selection as those in two-adult households, three times the chance as those in households containing three adults, and so forth.

It should also be noted that the value of n is lower for items in the modules asked for a subsample of respondents than for other items. Because the modules are based on a one-third subsample, the sample size of 2,441 and 6,514 are reduced to 814 and 2,171. When the sample sizes used in the base of percentages are obtained by simply counting the number of records used in the calculations, the count automatically provides the value of Rn, and it is unnecessary to calculate R, or to be concerned over whether or not the item is one of the modules.

APPENDIX II

Jewishness Factors

TABLE AII.1
Correlation Coefficients Between Jewishness Factors and Original Indicators,[a] U.S. Jews, 1990

Indicator	Jewishness Factors					
	CEREMONY	RITUAL	ASSOC	DENOM	FRATERNAL	JED
Lights Hannuka candles	.74890	.05697	.00291	.12144	.14195	.05863
Attends seder	.74273	-.00922	.03039	.11485	.18658	.11809
Fasts on Yom Kippur	.60598	.13353	.07229	.30665	.12865	.03169
Attends synagogue	.59842	.30997	.32707	.11886	.08920	.11951
Synagogue member	.58964	.14438	.38015	.14083	-.00111	.05301
Attends Purim carnival	.48673	.34056	.25727	-.14956	.04660	.11020
Does not use money on Shabbat	.04943	.74956	.03473	.03480	.12826	.11132
Fasts on Ta'anit Esther	-.00103	.72610	-.00633	-.01042	.14788	.30206
Uses separate meat and dairy dishes	.18567	.70484	.09194	.36332	.06493	-.08523
Buys Kosher meat	.22550	.65159	.08891	.36119	.09561	-.10359
Lights Friday night candles	.43117	.56513	.22018	.18918	.10498	-.02227
# of Jewish group memberships	.07410	.01196	.68016	.11988	.17286	.00254
Volunteer work for Jewish group	.26696	.16542	.61220	.03004	.06884	.04404
Contributes to UJA	-.10929	-.06098	.59049	.06283	-.12125	.04284
Subscribes to Jewish periodical	-.24364	-.07341	-.51332	-.03369	-.26196	-.07419
Celebrates Yom ha'Atzmaut	.32828	.28858	.47054	-.02544	-.00297	.03310

(continued on next page)

TABLE AII.1 (*continued*)

			Jewishness Factors			
Indicator	CEREMONY	RITUAL	ASSOC	DENOM	FRATERNAL	JED
Denomination raised	.06377	.05657	.10448	.73390	.11640	.14663
Personal denomination	.26820	.20551	.05569	.73217	.18577	.06959
Household denomination	.34410	.26836	.12234	.61597	.16775	.04098
Lives in Jewish neighborhood	.13496	.12561	.03425	.14058	.66513	.00204
Jewish neighborhood important	.25767	.25481	.04865	.10349	.63701	-.05459
Has Jewish friends	.25358	.06188	.25999	.16051	.61822	-.04446
Years formal Jewish education	.18418	.17691	.11493	-.06205	.03283	.66046
Had Bar or Bat Mitzvah or Confirmation	.15085	-.10847	.01007	.09689	-.25402	.59188
Type of Jewish education	-.08999	.16856	.05136	.27297	.13855	.58382
Eigenvalue	7.203	1.899	1.574	1.374	1.250	1.107
% of Shared Variance Explained	25.7	6.8	5.6	4.9	4.5	4.0

[a]Varimax rotation Kaiser normalization factor analysis.

TABLE AII.2
Correlation Coefficients Between Jewishness Factor
and Original Indicators,[a] Israeli Married Women, 1988

Indicator	
Husband's religiosity	.891
Respondent's religiosity	.875
Does not travel on Shabbat	.828
Visits mikveh	.791
Attends synagogue	.788
Husband's parents' religiosity	.684
Respondents' parents' religiosity	.662
Uses separate meat and dairy dishes	.646
Says kiddush on Shabbat	.512
Fasts on Yom Kippur	.155
Does not eat *hametz* on Passover	.139
Eigenvalue	6.074
% of Shared Variance Explained	46.6

[a]Varimax rotation Kaiser normalization factor analysis.
Source: Special fertility survey (see text).

APPENDIX III

Methods of Analysis

MULTIDIMENSIONAL SCALING

A multidimensional scale is derived for a set of n variables $x_1, x_2, \ldots, x_n$, for which correlation coefficients r_{ij} have been calculated for every possible pair (x_i, x_j), $i.j = 1, \ldots, n$ and $i = j$. The resulting set of correlation coefficients are arranged in a correlation matrix. The purpose of a multidimensional scaling analysis is to provide a graphical (geometric) representation of the order existing in the correlation matrix in the smallest possible Euclidian space. The distance between the points representing the variables in the graphical presentation is inversely related (orderwise) to the correlation coefficients between the variables represented by the points.

The purpose is not only to find a graphical representation of the correlation matrix, but to find the representation in the smallest possible space (i.e., the space with the fewest dimensions). The procedure is to find the best fitting presentation of the points for spaces of one, two, three, etc. dimensions. For each given m dimensional space ($m = 1, 2, \ldots$), a measure of how well the presentation fulfills the monotonicity condition is calculated. The measure used is called the *coefficient of alienation* (defined in Lingoes, 1966; a simple explanation of this measure is in Laumann, 1966, p. 93n). The smaller is this coefficient, the better the presentation. If the latter is small enough for $m = 1$ (usually a coefficient of .15 is the maximum that is acceptable), we can accept it as the final presentation; if it is not, we try the two-dimensional presentation, and so on, until the coefficient of alienation is acceptable. The presentation that is finally accepted expresses the structure of the interrelationships among the original variables. The configuration presented in Figure 2.1 has a coefficient of alienation indicating a close fit in one-dimension.

The interpretation of this structure is left open. Similar to the factor analysis methods, previous substantive knowledge is used to give meaning to the resulting structure. The final explanation given to the structure usually requires fewer dimensions than the original number of input variables.

See Schiffman, Reynolds, and Young (1981) and Kruskal (1964) for more discussion of the methodology involved.

APPENDIX IV

Profile of Israeli Society

The following tables give some background about Israeli society in 1990 on aspects relevant to our analysis. We present data about the population size and composition, current fertility rates, educational distribution, and labor force composition and rates. CBS is the Central Bureau of Statistics.

POPULATION

Size of Population

Population Group	%	(N in thousands)
Total	100.0	(4,821.7)
Jews	71.9	(3,946.7)
Non-Jews	18.1	(875.0)

Source: CBS (1991), Table 2.1.

Ethnic Composition of Population

Ethnic Background	%	(N in thousands)
Total Jews	100.0	(3,946.7)
Born in Israel	61.9	(2,442.9)
Father born in Israel	22.3	(880.9)
Father born in Asia-Africa	24.3	(958.7)
Father born in Europe-America	15.3	(603.3)
Born in Asia-Africa	15.0	(592.2)
Born in Europe-America	23.1	(603.3)

Source: CBS (1991), Table 2.22.

Immigration Status

Country of Origin	Period of Immigration	%	(N in thousands)
Asia-Africa	Total	100.0	(592.2)
	1980–1990	4.2	(40.4)
	1972–1979	2.8	(26.5)
	Up to 1971	88.7	(525.3)
Europe-America	Total	100.0	(911.5)
	1980–1990	31.3	(285.0)
	1972–1979	16.3	(148.7)
	Up to 1971	52.4	(477.8)

Source: CBS (1991), Table 2.22.

FERTILITY

The average number of children per Israeli-born Jewish woman is 2.69. It is slightly higher for the Asian-African born (3.09) and slightly lower for the European-American born (2.31) (CBS, 1991, Table 3.14).

EDUCATION

Educational Level of the Jewish Population

Ethnic Background	Median Years of Education	Median Years of Education (standardizing for age differences)
Total Jews	11.9	
Born in Israel	12.2	12.0
Father born in Israel	12.2	12.3
Father born in Asia-Africa	11.8	11.4
Father born in Europe-America	13.0	12.8
Born in Asia-Africa	9.4	11.0
Born in Europe-America	11.9	12.4
Men (total)	12.0	
Women (total)	11.8	

Source: CBS (1991), Table 22.2.

LABOR FORCE

Size of the Civilian Labor Force (N in thousands)

Population Group	Total	Males	Females
Total labor force	1649.9	979.9	669.5
Jews in labor force	1448.0	809.1	638.7
Non-Jews in labor force	201.3	170.8	30.5

Source: CBS (1992a), Table 4.

Ethnic Distribution of Labor Force

Ethnic Background	Total in Labor Force	Males in Labor Force	Females in Labor Force
Total Jews (%)	100.0	100.0	100.0
(N in thousands)	(1448.0)	(809.1)	(638.7)
Born in Israel (Total)	54.7	52.1	58.0
Father born in Israel	8.4	7.6	9.4
Father born in Asia-Africa	25.5	24.8	26.4
Father born in Europe-America	20.3	19.3	21.6
Born in Asia-Africa	21.5	24.2	18.3
Born in Europe-America	23.6	23.6	23.7

Source: CBS (1992a), Table 7.

Educational Composition of the Civilian Labor Force

Years of Education	Total Jews in Labor Force	Male Jews in Labor Force	Female Jews in Labor Force
Total %	100.0	100.0	100.0
(N in thousands)	(1448.0)	(809.1)	(638.7)
0–10	24.5	28.2	19.9
11–12	38.5	38.0	39.1
13–15	19.8	16.5	23.9
16+	16.9	16.9	16.9

Source: CBS (1992a), Table 12.

LABOR FORCE PARTICIPATION RATES

Ethnic Background and Educational Level
(% participating in the labor force out of total in each cell)

Ethnic Background	Total Jews	Male Jews	Female Jews
Total	53.6	61.2	46.4
Born in Israel	57.2	60.3	54.1
Father born in Israel	45.4	45.6	45.2
Father born in Asia-Africa	55.5	59.5	51.4
Father born in Europe-America	66.6	70.2	62.9
Born in Asia-Africa	53.6	68.6	39.2
Born in Europe-America	46.9	56.8	38.4
Years of Education:			
0–10	39.3	54.5	26.2
11–12	54.6	60.2	49.1
13–15	66.2	68.4	64.4
16+	74.7	72.8	77.2

Source: CBS (1992a), Tables 8 and 12.

Age, Sex, and Marital Status
(% participating in the labor force out of total in each cell)

Age	Total Jews	Males	Married Males	Females	Married Females
Total	53.6	61.2	74.9	46.4	53.7
18–24	37.9	31.5	56.8	44.6	55.6
25–34	74.3	81.1	84.2	67.5	64.5
35–44	78.8	87.8	89.1	70.1	68.5
45–54	75.3	89.5	89.5	61.7	61.0
55–64	52.8	75.7	77.8	33.1	33.1
65+	13.5	21.3	22.7	6.9	7.7

Source: CBS (1992a), Tables 8 and 27.

Occupational Distribution by Sex and Ethnic Background

		Born in Israel					
Occupation and Sex	Total	Total	Father Born in Israel	Father Born in Asia-Africa	Father Born in Europe-America	Born in Asia-Africa	Born in Europe-America
Total %	100.0	100.0	100.0	100.0	100.0	100.0	100.0
(N in thousands)	(1311.9)	(704.9)	(109.9)	(310.7)	(276.8)	(286.6)	(319.1)
Scientific, academic	9.3	8.7	8.3	2.9	15.5	3.8	15.5
Other professional, technical, and related	17.6	19.8	20.7	14.4	25.6	11.0	18.6
Administrative and managerial	5.8	5.7	5.5	3.5	8.3	5.5	6.4
Clerical	18.6	20.5	21.6	22.5	18.2	16.1	16.5
Sales	8.9	8.7	9.2	9.0	8.3	9.3	8.9
Service	13.2	11.6	12.9	14.8	7.0	20.7	10.0
Agricultural	3.4	3.8	6.1	2.8	3.7	3.1	2.6
Blue collar	23.3	21.2	15.7	30.1	13.4	30.5	21.5

(continued on next page)

Occupational Distribution by Sex and Ethnic Background (continued)

Occupation and Sex	Total	Born in Israel				Born in Asia-Africa	Born in Europe-America
		Total	Father Born in Israel	Father Born in Asia-Africa	Father Born in Europe-America		
Males:							
Total %	100.0	100.0	100.0	100.0	100.0	100.0	100.0
(N in thousands)	(746.3)	(382.9)	(56.8)	(173.2)	(149.5)	(182.8)	(179.8)
Scientific, academic	9.7	9.1	9.1	2.8	16.5	4.3	16.5
Other professional, technical, and related	11.6	13.1	12.3	9.7	17.3	7.4	12.6
Administrative and managerial	8.6	6.5	7.9	5.1	12.6	7.6	9.9
Clerical	10.6	9.9	11.5	9.7	9.6	12.1	10.5
Sales	10.3	10.7	12.4	10.3	10.7	10.6	9.4
Service	8.8	8.2	8.8	10.4	5.3	12.0	6.5
Agricultural	4.9	6.0	10.2	4.2	5.9	4.1	3.5
Blue collar	35.5	34.6	27.8	47.8	22.2	41.9	30.1

(continued on next page)

Occupational Distribution by Sex and Ethnic Background *(continued)*

Occupation and Sex	Total	Born in Israel			Born in Asia-Africa	Born in Europe-America
		Total	Father Born in Israel	Father Born in Asia-Africa	Father Born in Europe-America		

Occupation and Sex	Total	Total	Father Born in Israel	Father Born in Asia-Africa	Father Born in Europe-America	Born in Asia-Africa	Born in Europe-America
Females:							
Total %	100.0	100.0	100.0	100.0	100.0	100.0	100.0
(N in thousands)	(565.5)	(322.0)	(53.1)	(137.5)	(127.3)	(103.8)	(139.3)
Scientific, academic	8.7	8.3	7.5	3.1	14.3	3.1	14.1
Other professional, technical, and related	25.5	27.8	29.6	20.1	35.3	17.3	26.3
Administrative and managerial	2.2	2.4	3.0	1.5	3.3	1.9	1.9
Clerical	29.1	33.1	32.2	38.4	28.3	23.0	24.3
Sales	7.0	6.4	6.0	7.5	5.5	6.9	8.3
Service	19.1	15.6	17.1	20.3	9.0	35.9	14.4
Agricultural	1.3	1.2	(1.8)	(1.0)	1.2	1.3	1.5
Blue collar	7.1	5.2	2.8	8.1	3.2	10.7	9.1

Source: CBS (1992a), Table 56.

NOTES

INTRODUCTION

1. West and Zimmerman (1991).

2. There may be rewards other than those mentioned here that stem from performing a certain role, such as being interested in the job, satisfaction from doing a certain job, self-actualization. To the extent that these arise from intrinsic motivational factors rather than being allocated socially, they are not being considered here. This may be misleading, because "intrinsic" satisfactions are also socially developed. However, they are not related to the current book; and we have no data on them anyway.

3. Epstein (1988) summarizes most of the research to that date; Chafetz (1990) and Blumberg (1990) are among the more important works coming later.

4. The basic premises of Judaism are codified in the body of Jewish law, the *halacha*—"detailed rules and regulations, presupposed as divine commands in the holy books of the Bible, in turn expanded exegetically as legal commentaries on the Bible (that are technically its oral traditions) by the contributors to the Talmud and later rabbinical works" (Webber, 1983, pp. 144–145).

5. Heschel (1983, Introduction) suggests that the underpinning of a discriminatory, patriarchal outlook is the perception of women as "Other," because men's experience is taken as normative. The very specification of circumstances that grant women some sort of privileges or exemptions suggests (contrary to Heschel's interpretation) that the Jewish heritage does not take the male experience as normative, but rather recognizes a differentiation that has implications for the requirements made of women.

6. Although the first female Reform rabbi was not ordained until 1972.

7. Proverbs 31.

8. For example, Betty Friedan started us off with *The Feminine Mystique* in 1963; Gloria Steinem and Letty Cottin Pogrebrin were among the pioneering editors of *Ms.*

9. At the same time, a movement of feminism *within* Judaism developed. More detail about these developments can be found in Fishman (1993); Greenberg (1981, 1990); Heschel (1983); Koltun (1976); Schneider (1984); Umansky (1985).

10. For most analyses using weights, comparisons were made to the unweighted calculations, and means and distributions were very similar, attesting to the representativeness of the raw data.

11. The published data include Jews as part of the wider population, but because they are such a small proportion, their inclusion does not bias the conclusions significantly.

12.   Other rewards certainly can accrue from labor force roles, but we are limited in the information available for analysis. In the National Jewish Population Survey, for instance, respondents were asked about household income, but not how much each household member receives for his or her role in the labor force. Other rewards, such as health benefits or paid vacation were entirely neglected.

13.   It might be interesting to study whether the Jewish community allocates prestige differently than the wider society and whether this affects the occupational and educational aspirations of Jewish men and women. We are not aware of such a study to date.

CHAPTER 2. EDUCATION: GATEKEEPER TO GENDER EQUALITY IN THE ECONOMY

1.   Thus Brumberg (1986) notes, "By the early nineteenth century in Eastern Europe virtually all 'secular' studies had been eliminated from the schools maintained by Jews. . . . Entrenched orthodoxy opposed secular studies on religious grounds . . ." (p. 25). However, this was soon to change, with the Enlightenment.

2.   Even though compulsory elementary public education in the United States began as early as 1647 in the Massachusetts Bay Colony and spread slowly throughout most of the United States, the real impetus for public education came from two sources: industrialization during the nineteenth century and the consequent need for more educated labor; and large waves of immigration around the turn of the twentieth century, which resulted in a need to weld the new Americans into one people. Mississippi was the last state to pass legislation for compulsory elementary school attendance in 1918. As compulsory education and public elementary schools became more common around the turn of the century, the demand for higher public education also increased (Pulliam, 1990; Spring, 1991), so that by about 1910 the American secondary school was also being transformed from an elite to a mass public institution (Trow, 1977). The current universal compulsory system for grades K–12 was crystallized in the New Deal years (in the 1930s).

3.   For this reason, immigrant Japanese mothers to the United States, who push their children to achieve, are considered by some to be the "new Jews" of the United States.

4.   Immigration not only increases economic pressures but also increases familial roles, particularly those of women. The emotional stress of immigrating and trying to get adjusted to a new culture make the buffer role of the family more important than ever, and this is usually filled by women. Further, the brunt of resolving adjustment problems to daily conditions (such as shopping, schools, getting doctors and other services), usually falls on the shoulders of immigrant wives. Deprived of such supports as extended kin and familiar babysitters, familial roles become even harder. Through these increased familial roles, immigration may thus have an additional effect on the education of women, especially first generation immigrants. Girls may be called upon to share in these familial roles more than boys and therefore even the effect of immigration on children's education may be gender related.

5. "Girls appear to be more dependent on their mother's education and their perceptions of parental hopes for them, and less influenced by their own performance [or their own ability operating through their performance] than are boys" (Blake,1989: 204, referring to findings of Sewell et al., 1980).

6. In this context, the growth in Jewish women's studies offerings should be noted (Elwell, 1987).

7. Professional degrees include those in dentistry, medicine, law, chiropractice, optometry, osteopathy, pharmacy, podiatry, theology, and veterinary medicine.

8. Wherever possible in these comparisons, we have controlled for race to make the wider population more comparable to the Jewish subpopulation (which is almost entirely white).

9. Doctorate and first professional degrees were collapsed into a single category, as it was difficult to establish an order between them as to which was a "higher" degree.

10. Coefficients that show the weight of each individual independent variable in predicting or explaining the dependent variable. For example, how much do years of education predict the academic degree achieved, independent of the effect of age (which is controlled in the model). Nonstandardized coefficients may be compared between two populations if the models used are the same (identical dependent and independent variables) .

11. This may be a methodological artifact because number of years was linked to type of school (college, graduate school, etc.) and not a "clean" measure of number of years independent of academic degree.

12. Some bias may also be introduced by the fact that our sample excludes the institutionalized population (who are primarily elderly) .

13. According to NCES (1991b, p. 34), the proportion of male high school graduates completing college reached a maximum of 32.9 percent in 1976, dropped down to 27.7 percent in 1981, and has fluctuated around 28 percent since then.

14. Seventeen percent of the 65 and over cohort were born abroad, compared to only 4 percent of those under 25 (Goldstein, 1992).

15. See further discussion in Bianchi and Spain (1986), pp. 123–129.

16. This is true not only for women but for men as well, probably because of the additional financial pressure to leave school and work (see Marsiglio, 1986).

17. Because the range of education among the Jewish population is smaller, this may not be as much of a factor for Jewish separation. This is speculation on our part and might be interesting to follow up with an empirical study.

18. It would be interesting to find out whether the relationship between number of children and education in the wider population is also spurious and due to the age at which motherhood is entered as it is among Jews.

CHAPTER 3. LABOR FORCE PARTICIPATION OF AMERICAN JEWISH MEN AND WOMEN

1. Of course, the recent phenomenon of women returning to school at a later stage in the life cycle and the less common phenomenon of men adding to

their education later on in the life cycle happens among the Jewish population as it does in the wider population. However, it occurs in a small number of cases in the current sample and therefore we do not deal with it here.

2.   Sered (1992) discusses the "domestication" of religion among elderly Jewish women in Jerusalem. However, the notion of "domesticating" religion is one that would seem applicable to all Jewish women, particularly since their main religious roles apply to family life.

3.   How much a role the availability of childcare—specifically, Jewish childcare—plays in this preference is not yet clear.

4.   U.S. data based on Statistical Abstract (U.S. Bureau of the Census, 1991, Table 632) and U.S. Bureau of Labor Statistics, *Employment and Earnings* 37, no. 1 (January 1990): Table 3.

5.   Estimated by adding 6 (the age at which school is usually started) to the total years of education. Admittedly, this is a rough estimate, since some of the years may have been attained later on in life. However, most of the education is attained in these early years, and individuals rarely add to it. The growing phenomena of older women returning to school, for instance, is not unknown to our sample: 9 percent of the women currently attending college are 45 or over, presumably returnees to education. But they are too small in numbers to follow through in this sample.

6.   We assume that the increase in labor force participation rate at these ages reflects entrance into the labor force, as few people leave the labor force at these ages. When the participation rates peak and stabilize, we can assume that the period of entrance has more or less reached its end. Among women, the situation during these ages is somewhat more obscure, because some women leave the labor force when they marry and especially when they have children, even for a short period. The pattern is thus more complicated, especially for married women, and reflects a number of factors—both entrances and exits to the labor force during these ages.

7.   Calculated from 1987 data presented in Taeuber (1991), Table D4-1.

8.   Related to differentiated family roles, which will be discussed further later.

9.   Part-time work is generally considered less than 35 hours a week. However, in some occupations, a 35-hour work week is full time. Many of these are the traditional "female" occupations such as teaching. It may be that, at this age, women tend to enter traditionally "female" occupations which are easier to combine with family demands because of their frontal hours and vacation benefits.

10.   Calculated from Taeuber (1991), Table B1-20, 1988 data.

11.   We use here the age at first marriage as an indicator of family orientation, rather than an indicator of length of current marriage (which age at current marriage would give). For the 15 percent with multiple marriages, we do not calculate the number of years out of any marriage, although a more complete study might consider this as a further indicator of (lack of) investment in family roles.

12.   Due to the small number of cases, we lumped together all of the unmarried men (recognizing that their reasons for being unmarried vary).

13. T-test significant at *a* = .025.

14. Overall, married men are no less educated than unmarried men; on the contrary, in the previous chapter we showed that they have slightly more education than unmarried men. However, they may compress their educational attainment into fewer years or combine it with part-time employment once they are married.

15. T-test significant at *a* = .007.

16. Some unmarried women have children (87 divorced women, 10 separated women, and 133 widowed—the proportion of single mothers among the Jewish population is relatively small, *n* = 5), but the proportion of unmarried women with children is relatively small and are not separated in this analysis. Among the widowed women with children, 86 percent of the widowed are 60 or over and no longer participating in the labor force because of age, not childcare responsibilities.

17. T-test significance at *a* < .005. Married men have on the average 16.1 years of education, and unmarried men have 15.6 years of education. Because unmarried men are also significantly younger than married men, their lower education may be because they have not yet completed their education.

18. Married women have an average of 14.7 years of education compared to 15.0 for unmarried women (t-test significant at *a* < .077).

19. 0 = not working; 1 = part-time work; 2 = full-time work.

20. The high correlation between academic degree and years of education made it impossible to enter both in the same model, so the better predictor of labor force participation was used.

21. We tested for the existence of interactions with a multivariate analysis of variance and found only one interaction effect that was significantly related to labor force participation, that is, the effect of being married on labor force participation varies at different life cycle stages or for different cohorts, and therefore the interaction between marital status and age was significant.

22. Of course, this difference in itself has interesting implications, suggesting that among women not all the years of education they attain are relevant or useful for the labor force; what counts more is the actual degree achieved. For men, on the other hand, their participation is related more to the quantity (years) of education they achieve than to the actual degree they end up with.

23. This could also reflect a cohort difference, which can be tested when the younger cohort can be followed through to their behavior at a later stage of the life cycle.

24. We also did a multiple regression using the dichotomous participation variable as the dependent variable (even though this is not a legitimate use of regression). The resulting model had a poorer overall fit, but the actual standardized regression coefficients were practically identical to the ones presented.

25. No interactions were included in the model, because they were not significant.

26. See note 17.

27. Here we have presented the labor force participation rates for women 25–64 to minimize the low participation rates of women still in school or retired.

28. Table 3.8 is based only on women currently in the labor force and hence on different numbers than Table 3.9.

29.   It should be noted that the U.S. data include women of all marital statuses (single, married, divorced, separated, widowed), which may increase the proportion employed full-time.

30.   See explanation of age and retirement age indicators on p. 89.

31.   That is, the beta, or standardized regression, coefficient. The regression coefficients measure the independent effects of each variable (such as age) on the dependent variable (in this case labor force participation) when the other variables are controlled. The beta coefficient has been standardized, so that all independent variables can be compared as if they had the same range; the B coefficient is the raw or unstandardized coefficient and may be used to compare the effects of a variable across populations.

32.   Because of multicollinearity, age, age at marriage, and age at birth of first child could not be included in the same regression model. Because part of the effect of age is controlled by the retirement age variable, it was decided to omit age and include the other two in this regression showing the relationship of labor force participation to the timing of family roles.

33.   As the sample at older ages is relatively small, technical adjustments were made to arrive at these estimates (see note to Figure 3.10). It should be noted that the sample included only the noninstitutionalized population, which introduces some degree of bias at the older ages.

CHAPTER 4. OCCUPATIONAL ACHIEVEMENT OF AMERICAN JEWISH MEN AND WOMEN

1.   Research has shown sex differences in specific cognitive abilities—girls excelling in verbal ability and boys in visual-spatial and mathematical ability (Maccoby and Jacklin, 1974). At later ages, boys outperform girls on such tests as the SAT and the National Merit Scholarship Qualifying Tests, even when their grades are similar (M. Clark and Grandy, 1984; Rosser, 1989; Stockard and Wood, 1984; Wilder and Powell, 1989). International data is, however, less conclusive, suggesting that, although there may be gender differences in specific abilities, they are not necessarily linked to overall ability nor performance (Blake, 1989, p. 124).

2.   Unfortunately, the NJPS did not ask for individual income; therefore the occupational earnings, a common indicator of occupational reward, cannot be utilized here.

3.   The numbers reported here refer only to those considered Jewish by the definition in our first chapter, ages 25+, and therefore differ somewhat from the total Jewish sample reported on in Goldstein (1992). Although the specific numbers may differ, the conclusions we reach are generally the same.

4.   Three-digit grouping of occupations that employ at least one person in our sample.

5.   The coefficient of dissimilarity for the general U.S. population reported here is considerably smaller than that reported for 1980 in, for instance, Reskin and Hartmann, 1986; one reason for this is that our data is for whites only. A second reason is that we use 1990 data, and dissimilarity may indeed have decreased

considerably since 1980. Further, we use an eight group classification, which collapses several occupational categories into a smaller number of groups; and the fewer categories there are, the smaller is the dissimilarity coefficient.

6. Renzetti and Curran (1992) have shown that dissimilarity persists among the more highly educated for the wider American population as well.

7. The coefficients of dissimilarity in Table 4.6 differ from those in Table 4.5 because of different groupings of occupations and years of education. However, the general direction of findings is similar; that is, there is more gender dissimilarity among the less educated than among the more highly educated.

8. Limiting the analysis to those ages 25–64 to control for part-time workers due to student status or retirement.

9. See Papanek (1973), who introduced the concept of the "two-person career," and Fowlkes (1987).

10. It should be noted that the current occupations do not necessarily reflect the occupation at time of marriage; rather, we must consider the current occupation as an indication of the type of career that was developed, which may have started in a different level and field, related to how long ago the marriage took place.

11. ANOVA, $a = .001$.

12. It might be argued that the occupations of those 65 or over are misrepresentative of this age group since some of this age group has already retired, but it should be recalled that the most recent occupation is taken for those who are not currently working, and therefore the occupations of this older age group reflect their past occupations if they have already retired.

13. This does not necessarily reflect only those who remain in the labor force after age 65, as last occupation was reported for those who have ever worked, even if they were not working at the time of the survey.

14. Other occupational rewards, such as income, social power, and fringe benefits, were not measured in our survey on an individual basis. The only measure of income is for the household, rather than for the individual earner.

15. Research has shown that to some extent prestige evaluations of incumbents in an occupation vary to some extent by whether the incumbent is employed in what is considered a typical occupation for his or her sex (Jacobs and Powell, 1985). However, most research assigns the prestige score to all occupational incumbents (Wegener, 1992).

16. For those not currently working in the paid labor force, the prestige score was assigned according to the most recent occupation. The difference in prestige scores is significant at $a < .000$.

17. Significant ANOVA at $a < .000$.

18. $\alpha < .05$.

19. Other interactions were excluded in preliminary analysis either because of nonsignificance or because they caused multicolinearity in the model.

20. $\alpha < .001$.

21. In a stepwise regression, the independent variables are entered into the model in steps, allowing one to analyze the incremental effect as variables are added and not just the net effect when all other independent variables in the model are held constant.

22.   It should be noted that this is in contrast to findings about the attainment of income: although education seems to be the major determinant for income as it is for occupational prestige, Treiman and Terrell (1975) found that the income returns for education were equivalent for men and women. Here we find that women's prestige returns to education are smaller than for men.

CHAPTER 5. GENDER EQUALITY WITHIN JEWISH COUPLES

1.   But see Spencer (1992) and Chiswick's response to him (1992b).

2.   This does not imply that men and women were considered equivalent in terms of all facets of life nor in all stages of life. But in marriage, the mishnaic laws establish a certain equivalence that underlies the respective conjugal obligations and household responsibilities. For more detailed discussion of the mishnaic treatment of women in various stages and arenas of social life, see Wegner (1988).

3.   Only 49 of the couples were intermarried (i.e., one partner is Jewish by these criteria but not the spouse).

4.   More precise data on the separate income of husbands (not available here) would enable more precise conclusions. We base our conclusions here on indications from the occupation statistics.

5.   We would have liked to compare the occupations of wives who are currently working and wives who have worked in the past, but because of the variation among women who are not currently working in terms of when they last worked, the results of the comparison could be misleading, relating more to lack of labor force activity than to level of occupation.

6.   Measured by chi square = 110.34, $\alpha < .000$.

7.   Phi = .386, $\alpha < .000$.

8.   It should be noted that the managerial group is rather heterogeneous, including both managers of small businesses and executives in large corporations. As such, it is questionable whether all managers should be included in this upper/upper-middle-class group. More refined analysis is needed to separate out specific types of managers; however, the small numbers precluded our doing so here.

CHAPTER 6. ARE WE ONE?
HOW JEWISH INVOLVEMENT IS RELATED TO
GENDERED PATTERNS OF SECULAR ACHIEVEMENT

1.   Not all could be adequately identified because we were limited by the questions included in the survey. Some dimensions were not represented at all; for instance, there were no direct questions on "experiencing" Judaism, knowledge of Judaism, or specific doctrinal beliefs asked of the general sample. While there was one question asked about how literally the respondent believed in the Torah (Bible), it was only asked of a third of the respondents and less than 12 percent gave an answer. The quality of the indicators of other dimensions were questionable. For example, respondents were asked their Jewish "ethnicity," but the

number of Sephardis was apparently underrepresented in the sample. Other questions that were asked did not seem to fit into the general universe of content of Jewishness; for instance, how much contact the respondent had with Israelis or Israel seemed to be a relatively new component of Jewish identity, and its relationship to our topic of interest quite stretched, so we did not include the set of questions dealing with this area.

2. Factor analysis provides for each person in the sample a score on each one of the factors. This score is a weighted average of the person's answer to the questions about Jewish involvement, having a different set of weights for each factor. This score therefore represents the strength of Jewishness on each of the represented dimensions, as will be described.

3. A more comprehensive study could go into more detail on differences in the way individuals express their Jewishness and how it is related to the Jewish nature of the household.

4. All of these questions, except that about the frequency of attending synagogue services, were worded to determine whether anyone in the household did these acts or rituals.

5. Despite some dissension about the validity of the question about separate dishes, we included it because it correlated appropriately with other questions indicating this dimension of Jewishness. It apparently indicates a stricter observance of dietary laws than buying kosher meat, which a great many nonobservant and even non-Jewish consumers do in the United States, if we are to believe the advertisements of Hebrew National and Empire.

6. Although the same rituals traditionally focused on God and God's law, "modern" redefinitions give precedence to traditional themes of kinship and peoplehood, which are also incorporated in these celebrations. Even fasting on Yom Kippur is apparently seen more as an expression of solidarity with the Jewish people than a connection with God, if we are to follow its interpretation in Israel (see Sharot, 1991, on this point).

7. The first step in the factor analysis was orthogonal, which extracts independent factors. However, the second step, where we created the scores for each factor, allowed correlations between the factors. Because the indicators could have relatively high loadings on two factors, the same indicators could be included in more than one factor, and this explains some of the high correlations resulting from the second stage.

8. The Reconstructionists score between the Conservative and the Reform on each factor, but because of their small number are not included here.

9. Because of the nonlinear relationship of age to some of the Jewishness factors, we subdivided the age factor into dummy variables of age categories 25–34, 35–44, 45–54, 55–64, and 65+ (or for women 60+, i.e., retirement age). Because not all dummy variables could be entered into the model at one time, the middle category (45–54) was omitted.

10. Highest academic degree achieved was used as the education indicator because it had higher correlations with the other variables and its meaning was more clear-cut than number of years of education, which did not always signify completion of another stage of education as completion of an academic degree did.

11. For this table, the scores on each of the factors were trichotomized

into most involved, moderately involved, and least involved. The table presents the results for the most and the least involved.

12.   Denomination is handled separately later in the multivariate analysis.

13.   An exception is noted among the older men (55+) and women (45+), among whom those more involved in informal Jewish circles (FRATERNAL) are less educated. This may reflect a generational change in the relationship between informal Jewish involvement and education, informal involvement among younger cohorts perhaps reinforced by higher secular education (e.g., through Hillel and other Jewish groups on college campuses).

14.   The stronger relationship between education and Jewishness among the younger cohorts may be affected by the temporal proximity of the dependent and independent variables (as discussed previously). For the older cohorts, Jewishness on all factors except Jewish educational background is a measure of current Jewishness, which may have changed since the academic degree was achieved. For the younger cohorts, current Jewishness is temporally closer to the attainment of the academic degree, which may strengthen the relationship. In any case, the interaction must be controlled to properly understand the main relationship between Jewishness and education.

15.   There were not enough Reconstructionists to present the separate regression for them.

16.   The paucity of facilities for the Orthodox on most American university and college campuses—even where there are active Hillel chapters—also suggests that the Orthodox are not able to reinforce their way of expressing Jewishness in the secular setting.

17.   See, for example, Goodman-Thau (1991) and Heschel (1983).

18.   Gender was not considered as just another factor to be controlled by entering the sex variable into the model, because (1) preliminary analysis showed a strong effect on labor force participation of the interaction between Jewishness and gender; (2) age has a different relationship with labor force participation for men and women because of the different implications of family and parenting roles for each gender at different points of the life cycle; and (3) because of the relationship of Jewishness and family roles, the effect of Jewishness on labor force participation is also different for each gender.

19.   We have to remember that our population in this analysis is limited to those 25 and older. Otherwise, as we saw earlier, the negative effect of age on labor force participation would have been weakened.

20.   There is no appreciable difference in the mean number of children of women who have stronger or weaker Jewish backgrounds. Because, as we have explained previously, having Jewish training does not indicate how much one retains or accepts what one has been taught, nor do we control for quality or denomination of the Jewish education, this lack of effect does not mitigate the general conclusion that the more Jewishly involved also have more children. Also, as we see in Table 6-15, there is a relationship between having a Jewish background and how many children the woman has, which the summary of having or not having children does not show.

21.   Path analysis is a causal model for understanding relationships between variables. These causal relationships are represented in a path model which indi-

cates the direction of influence between variables. See Land (1968) for more detailed explanation of the method.

22. As is well-known, the path effects are the *net* effects of each independent variable on the dependent variable (compared with the correlation coefficient, which measures the total relationship between the variables, including indirect and spurious effects of other variables). See Land (1968) for a fuller explanation of the method of path analysis.

23. See Fishman (1993) for a discussion of women's roles in organized Jewish life.

24. Significant at $a < .01$.

CHAPTER 7. ARE WE ONE?
GENDER ROLES AND SECULAR ACHIEVEMENT
AMONG ISRAELI AND AMERICAN JEWS

1. A strong argument and rationale for using the civilizational paradigm to understand the Jewish case is made by Eisenstadt (1992).

2. Its self-sufficiency is compromised by its dependence on foreign aid, not unlike other new developing states, and worldwide Jewish contributions; and its employment of Arab labor.

3. Non-Jews make up approximately 12 percent of the labor force (Central Bureau of Statistics, 1990, Table E), concentrated primarily in blue-collar and service occupations. Because of the concentration of non-Jewish employment in non-Jewish towns, this percentage has an even lower effect on the country's labor market than the 12 percent would indicate.

4. The "Jewishness" of its institutions depends to a great extent on the political balance between the "more Jewish" and the "less Jewish," at least in terms of religious observance.

5. The first results of this study came out while our book was in its final stages, and the data have not yet been released for public use. However, future analyses might well shed light on a number of issues we raise here.

6. Women are exempted from army service if they are married, religious, or illiterate; only about 50 percent actually serve in the army.

7. Central Bureau of Statistics (1992), Table 2.25.

8. Central Bureau of Statistics (1991), Table 3.17.

9. For more detail about the ethnic differences in social status see Ginor (1979), Kraus and Hodge (1990), and Smooha (1978).

10. The authors acknowledge the help of the Hebrew University Data Bank and the principal investigator, Eric Peritz, for making available the data set. The survey was sponsored by the United Nations Fund for Population Activities (Isr.85/PO/274). See Peritz and Baras (1992) for more detail about the study.

11. The Israeli public school system offers two kinds of schools for Jewish children in grades kindergarten through high school, a secular one and a religious one (the Arab sector is separate). They differ in the approach to the study of the Bible and the extent to which religious subjects are learned. However, both

include instruction in Jewish subjects. For more discussion on the Israeli school system, see Peled (1981) and Krausz (1989).

12.   The current situation of higher education in Israel may change in the near future, as a result of a government initiative to upgrade the current private colleges (*michlallot*) to the status of the public universities (i.e., granting B.A.s). However, for the period of concern to us here, it has not changed yet.

13.   Central Bureau of Statistics (1992b), Table 3.6 (1990 data).

14.   Ibid., Table 2.25 (1990 data).

15.   Ibid., Table 3.16.

16.   Ibid., Table 3.14.

17.   Immigrant generation was not controlled here, because of the small numbers in the sample.

18.   In the total Jewish population of Israeli men, the labor force participation rate of men with low education is even higher than among second generation EA Israelis, perhaps because a higher proportion have finished their education while the second generation EA with low education may still be in school.

19.   American Jewish women with less than ten years of education participate more than men with the same level of education, but since there are very few of them, no serious conclusion should be drawn from this.

20.   Separate data for second generation Israelis of European-American background were not published by marital status.

21.   Among second generation European-American Israeli Jewish women aged 25–39, labor force participation is lower for women who have children than women who do not (using data from the 1988 fertility survey); and in the total population, when age is controlled (without controlling for ethnic background), women with no children participate more than women with children at every stage of the life cycle (Central Bureau of Statistics, 1992a, Table 86).

22.   The number differs from that presented in Table 4.2 (30.2) because of a slightly different occupational classification used for comparative purposes.

23.   Not controlling for ethnicity, as published data were not available.

24.   This is not to suggest that no problems are involved in doing so: the case of the Israeli "superwoman" (e.g., Swirski and Safir, 1991) is much lamented.

25.   Due to small numbers, both first and second generation wives of European-American background are included.

26.   Differences significant at $\alpha < .001$.

27.   Bread and bread products.

28.   Ritual bath, which according to Jewish *halacha* is to be visited by women after each menstrual period.

29.   According to Jewish *halacha*, men are commanded to attend synagogue prayers on a daily and weekly basis; as a time-bound commandment, women are exempt from this except on certain holidays. In the United States, especially in the non-Orthodox denominations, the distinction between men's and women's obligations with regard to synagogue attendance is not observed; therefore, in the American survey a general question about synagogue attendance did not differentiate between men and women. In the Israeli context, where Orthodox traditions prevail, it was more appropriate to ask about husband's synagogue attendance.

30. Principle components varimax rotated Kaiser normalization factor analysis.

31. The negative relationship is a result of the wording of the religiosity items: the more religious, the lower is the factor score.

32. The dependent variable, labor force activity, was coded as follows: −1 = never participated in the paid labor force; 0 = participated in the past but not at the time of the survey; 1 = employed part-time; 2 = employed full-time.

CHAPTER 8. CONCLUSIONS

1. Alternatively, Jewish women might be motivated by the inequalities in the religion for intense involvement in the women's movement. However, this seems less plausible, since the early women's movement in which Jewish women were forerunners, addressed secular inequalities before consciousness about religious and spiritual concerns had even been raised.

BIBLIOGRAPHY

Acker, Joan. 1980. "Women and Stratification: A Review of the Literature." *Contemporary Sociology* 9: 25–39.

Alexander, Bobby C. 1987. "Ceremony." *The Encyclopedia of Religion*, vol. 3, pp. 179–183. New York: Macmillan.

Allen, Carole, and Herman Brotman. 1981. *Chartbook on Aging in America*. Washington, DC: Administration on Aging.

Almquist, E. 1987. "Labor Market Gender Inequality in Minority Groups." *Gender and Society* 1, no. 4: 400–414.

American Association of University Women (AAUW), Educational Foundation. 1992. *How Schools Shortchange Girls*. Wellesley, MA: Wellesley College Center for Research on Women.

Atchley, R. C., and S. Miller. 1983. "Types of Elderly Couples." In T. H. Brubaker (ed.). *Family Relations in Later Life*. Newbury Park, CA: Sage.

Atkinson, M. and B. Glass. 1985. "Marital Age Heterogamy and Homogamy, 1900 to 1980." *Journal of Marriage and the Family* 47, no. 3: 685–691.

Bar-Yosef, Rivka, and Ilana Shelach. 1970. "The Position of Women in Israel." In Schmuel N. Eisenstadt, Rivka Bar-Yosef, and Chaim Adler (eds.), *Integration and Development in Israel*, pp. 639–672. Jerusalem: Israel Universities Press.

Baskin, Judith (ed.). 1991. *Jewish Women in Historical Perspective*. Detroit: Wayne State University Press.

Baum, C., P. Hyman, and S. Michel. 1976. *The Jewish Woman in America*. NY: Dial Press.

Becker, G. 1981. *A Treatise on the Family*. Cambridge, MA: Harvard University Press.

Berger, P. 1967. *The Sacred Canopy*. Garden City, NY: Doubleday.

Bergmann, Barbara R. 1986. *The Economic Emergence of Women*. New York: Basic Books.

Berk, Sarah F. 1985. *The Gender Factory*. New York: Plenum.

Berman, Saul. 1976. "The Status of Women in Halakhic Judaism." In E. Kolton (ed.), *The Jewish Woman: New Perspectives*, pp. 114–128. New York: Schocken.

Bernstein, Deborah. 1990. *Struggle for Equality*. NY: Praeger Publishers.

Bianchi, Suzanne M., and Daphne Spain. 1986. *American Women in Transition*. New York: Russell Sage Foundation.

Bielby, W., and D. Bielby. 1992. "I Will Follow Him: Family Ties, Gender-Role Beliefs, and Reluctance to Relocate for a Better Job." *American Journal of Sociology* 9: 1241–1267.

Blake, Judith. 1989. *Family Size and Achievement*. Berkeley: University of California Press.

Blumberg, R. 1984. "A General Theory of Gender Stratification." In R. Collins (ed.), *Sociological Theory, 1984*, pp. 23–101. San Francisco: Jossey-Bass.

——. (ed.). 1990. *Gender, Family and Economy: The Triple Overlap*. Newbury Park, CA: Sage.

Bose, Christine. 1973. *Jobs and Gender: Sex and Occupational Prestige*. Baltimore: Johns Hopkins University Center for Metropolitan Planning and Research.

——. 1985. *Jobs and Gender: A Study of Occupational Prestige*. New York: Praeger.

Brubaker, T. H. 1985. *Later Life Families*. Newbury Park, CA: Sage.

Brumberg, Stephan. 1986. *Going to America, Going to School*. Westport, CT: Greenwood.

Bryson, R., et al. 1978. "Family Size, Satisfaction and Productivity in Dual-Career Couples." In J. Bryson and R. Bryson (eds.), *Dual-Career Couples*. New York: Human Sciences.

Carter, M. J., and S. B. Carter. 1981. "Women's Recent Progress in the Professions, or Women Get a Ticket to Ride after the Gravy Train Has Left the Station." *Feminist Studies* 7 (Fall): 476–504.

Central Bureau of Statistics, 1988. *Labor Force Surveys, 1988*. Jerusalem: Keter Press.

——. 1990. *Education and Socio-Economic Characteristics of the Population*. 1983 Census of Population and Housing Publications, No. 24. Jerusalem: Keter Press.

——. 1991. *Statistical Abstract of Israel, 1991*. Jerusalem: Keter Press.

——. 1992a. *Labor Force Surveys, 1990*. Jerusalem: Keter Press.

——. 1992b. *Statistical Abstract of Israel, 1992*. Jerusalem: Keter Press.

Chadwick, B., and T. Heaton (eds.) 1992. *Statistical Handbook on the American Family*. Phoenix: Oryx Press.

Chafetz, Janet Saltzman. 1990. *Gender Equity: An Integrated Theory of Stability and Change*. Sage Library of Social Research, vol. 176. Newbury Park, CA: Sage.

Chiswick, Barry. 1983. "The Earnings and Human Capital of American Jews." *Journal of Human Resources* 18: 313–336.

——. 1986. "Labor Supply and Investment in Child Quality: A Study of Jewish and Non-Jewish Women." *The Review of Economics and Statistics* 47 (November): 4.

——. 1991. "The Economic Status of American Jews: Analysis of the 1990 National Jewish Population Survey." Paper presented at the Conference on Policy Implications of the 1990 National Jewish Population Survey, Los Angeles.

——. 1992a. "The Postwar Economy of American Jews." In Peter Medding (ed.), *A New Jewry? America Since the Second World War*, pp. 85–101. Studies in Contemporary Jewry: An Annual, Vol. 8, Institute of Contemporary Jewry, Hebrew University of Jerusalem. New York: Oxford University Press.

——. 1992b. "Labor Supply and Investment in Child Quality: A Study of Jewish and Non-Jewish Women: A Reply." *Review of Economics and Statistics* 74: 726–727.

————. 1993. "The Skills and Economic Status of American Jewry: Trends over the Last-Half Century." *Journal of Labor Economics* 11: 229.

Clark, M., and J. Grandy, 1984. *Sex Differences in the Academic Performance of Scholastic Aptitude Test Takers*. New York: College Entrance Examination Board.

Clark, R. L. 1988. "The Future of Work and Retirement." *Research on Aging* 10, no. 2: 169–193.

Cohen, S. 1983. *American Modernity and Jewish Identity*. New York: Tavistock Publications.

————. 1988. *American Assimilation or Jewish Revival?* Bloomington: Indiana University Press.

———— and Paul Ritterband. 1988. "The Utilization of Jewish Communal Services in Queens and Long Island." Manuscript, New York: United Jewish Appeal/Federation of Jewish Philanthropies.

Cole, Stephen. 1986. "Sex Discrimination and Admission to Medical School, 1929–1984." *American Journal of Sociology* 92, no. 3: 549–567.

Condran, Gretchen, and Ellen Kramarow. 1991. "Child Mortality Among Jewish Immigrants to the United States." *Journal of Interdisciplinary History* 22: 223.

Coser, R. L., and G. Rokoff. 1971. "Women in the Occupational World: Social Disruption and Conflict." *Social Problems* 19: 535–554.

Cox, Harold G. 1993. *Later Life*, 3d ed. Englewood Cliffs, NJ: Prentice-Hall.

Cramer, James C. 1980. "Fertility and Female Employment: Problems of Causal Direction." *American Sociological Review* 49: 234–247.

Curran, Barbara. 1985. *The Statistical Lawyers Report: A Statistical Profile of the U.S. Legal Profession in the 1980s*. Chicago: American Bar Foundation.

————. 1986. *Supplement to the Statistical Lawyers Report: A Statistical Profile of the U.S. Legal Profession in the 1980s*. Chicago: American Bar Foundation.

Cusick, T. 1987. "Sexism and Early Parenting: Cause and Effect?" *Peabody Journal of Education: Issues on Sex Equity and Sexuality in Education* 64: 113–131.

Deckard, Barbara S. 1979. *The Women's Movement: Political, Socioeconomic, and Psychological Issues*. New York: Harper and Row.

DellaPergola, Sergio. 1980. "Patterns of American Jewish Identity." *Demography* 17: 261–273.

Desai, Sonalde, and Linda Waite. 1991. "Women's Employment During Pregnancy and After the First Birth: Occupational Characteristics and Work Commitment." *American Sociological Review* 56: 551–556.

Dexter, Carolyn. 1985. "Women and the Exercise of Power in Organizations: From Ascribed to Achieved Status." In A. H. Stromberg and B. A. Gutek (eds.), *Women and Work: An Annual Review*, Vol. 1, pp. 239–258. Beverly Hills, CA: Sage.

Diament, Carol (ed.). 1989. *Jewish Marital Status*. New York: Hadassah, The Women's Zionist Organization of America.

Dick, Thomas P., and Sharon Rallis. 1991. "Factors and Influences on High School Students' Career Choices." *Journal for Research in Mathematics Education* 22: 281.

Dugger, Karen. 1991. "Social Location and Gender-Role Attitudes: A Comparison of Black and White Women." In J. Lorber and S. Farrell (eds.), *The Social Construction of Gender*, pp. 38–59. Newbury Park, CA: Sage.

Eisenstadt, S. N. 1992. *Jewish Civilization*. Albany: SUNY Press.

Elazar, Daniel J. 1976. *Community and Polity: The Organizational Dynamics of American Jewry*. Philadelphia: Jewish Publication Society.

Elwell, Sue (ed.). 1987. *The Jewish Women's Study Guide*, 2nd ed. New York: Biblio Press.

England, Paula. 1979. "Women and Occupational Prestige: A Case of Vacuous Sex Equality." *Signs* 5, no. 2: 252–265.

——— and George Farkas. 1986. *Households, Employment and Gender*. New York: Aldine.

Epstein, Cynthia Fuchs. 1988. *Deceptive Distinctions: Sex, Gender and the Social Order*. New Haven, CT: Yale University Press.

Faludi, S. 1991. *Backlash: The Undeclared War Against Women*. New York: Crown.

Fenstermaker, Sarah, Candace West, and Don Zimmerman. 1991. "Doing Gender." In Rae Lesser Blumberg (ed.), *Gender, Family and Economy: The Triple Overlap*, chapter 12. Newbury Park, CA: Sage.

Finke, Roger, and Rodney Stark. 1992. *The Churching of America, 1776–1990: Winners and Losers in our Religious Economy*. New Brunswick, NJ: Rutgers University Press.

Fishman, Sylvia Barack. 1993. *A Breath of Life: Feminism in the American Jewish Community*. New York: The Free Press.

Fowlkes, M. 1987. "The Myth of Merit and Male Professional Careers: The Roles of Wives." In N. Gerstel and H. Gross (eds.), *Families and Work*, Ch. 17. Philadelphia: Temple University Press.

Fox, John, and Carole Suschnigg. 1989. "A Note on Gender and the Prestige of Occupations." *Canadian Journal of Sociology* 14: 353–360.

Friedan, Betty. 1963. *The Feminine Mystique*. New York: Dell.

Gabriel, Susan L., and Isaiah Smithson (ed.). 1990. *Gender in the Classroom: Power and Pedagogy*. Urbana: University of Illinois Press.

Geerken, M., and W. Gove. 1983. *At Home and at Work: The Family's Allocation of Labor*. Beverly Hills, CA: Sage.

Gerson, Kathleen. 1985. *Hard Choices: How Women Decide About Work, Career and Motherhood*. Berkeley: University of California Press.

Ginor, Fanny. 1979. *Socio-Economic Disparities in Israel*. Tel-Aviv: Transaction Books.

Glass, Jennifer, and Valerie Camarigg. 1992. "Gender, Parenthood, and Job-Family Compatibility." *American Journal of Sociology* 98: 131–151.

Glenn, S. 1990. *Daughters of the Shtetl: Life and Labor in the Immigrant Generation*. Ithaca, NY, and London: Cornell University Press.

Glock, C., and R. Stark. 1965. *Religion and Society in Tension*. Chicago: Rand McNally.

Goldscheider, Calvin. 1986. *Jewish Continuity and Change: Emerging Patterns in America*. Bloomington: Indiana University Press.

——— and A. Zuckerman. 1984. *Transformation of the Jews*. Chicago: University of Chicago Press.

Goldsmith, Elizabeth B. (ed.) 1989. *Work and Family: Theory, Research, and Applications*. Newbury Park, CA: Sage.

Goldstein, Sidney. 1992. "Profile of American Jewry: Insights from the 1990 National Jewish Population Survey." In D. Singer and R. Seldin (eds.), *American Jewish Yearbook 1992*, pp. 77–173. New York and Philadelphia: The American Jewish Committee; The Jewish Publication Society.

———— and Barry Kosmin. 1991. "Religious and Ethnic Self-Identification in the United States 1989–90: A Case Study of the Jewish Population." Paper presented at the Population Association of America Annual Meeting, Washington, DC.

Goodman-Thau, Eveline. 1991. "Challenging the Roots of Religious Patriarchy and Shaping Identity and Community." In B. Swirski and M. Safir (eds.), *Calling the Bluff on Equality: Women in Israel*. New York: Pergamon Press.

Greenberg, Blu. 1981. *On Women and Judaism*. Philadelphia: The Jewish Publication Society of America.

————. 1992. "Women Today—An Orthodox View." in Steven T. Katz (ed.), *Frontiers of Jewish Thought*. Washington, DC: B'nai B'rith Books.

Greenhaus, J. H., and N. J. Beutell. 1985. "Sources of Conflict Between Work and Family Roles." *Academy of Management Review* 10: 76–88.

Haaga, John. 1989. "The Revival of Breastfeeding in the United States, 1963–81." The RAND Corporation, Santa Monica, CA, unpublished manuscript.

Hartman, Harriet. 1983. "Women's Roles in Israeli Society." Ph.D. dissertation, Hebrew University of Jerusalem, Department of Sociology [Hebrew].

———— and Moshe Hartman. 1990. "Immigration and Married Female Immigrants' Labor Force Behavior." *Israel Social Science Review* 7: 1.

————. 1993. "How Equal is Equal?" *Contemporary Jewry* (Fall).

Hartman, Moshe. 1971. "Patterns of Labor Force Participation: A Multivariate Analysis." Ph.D. Dissertation, University Microfilms, The University of Michigan.

————. 1984. "Pronatalistic Tendencies and Religiosity." *Sociology and Social Research* 68, no. 2.

———— and Harriet Hartman. 1985. "International Migration Mobility and Wives Labor Force Participation." Paper presented at the International Sociological Association Research Committee on Social Stratification, Boston.

———— and Harriet Hartman. 1993. "More Jewish, Less Jewish: Implications for Education and Labor Force Characteristics." Paper presented at American Sociological Association annual meeting joint session with Association for the Social Scientific Study of Jewry.

————, Vered Kraus, and Harriet Hartman. 1989. "Prestige Evaluations of Masculine-Phrased and Feminine-Phrased Occupational Titles." Paper presented at the International Sociological Association Research Committee Meeting on Stratification and Mobility, Stanford, CA.

Hatch, Laurie. 1992. "Gender and Work at Midlife and Beyond." In Jon Hendricks and Lou Glasse (eds.), *Gender and Aging*, Ch. 11. Amityville, NY: Baywood Publishing.

Hayward, Mark, William R. Grady, and Steven McLaughlin. 1988. "The Retirement Process Among Older Women in the U.S.: Changes in the 1970s." *Research on Aging* 10, no. 3: 358–383.

Hazleton, Leslie. 1977. *Israeli Women: The Reality Behind the Myths.* New York: Simon and Schuster.

Heckman, James J., and Robert J. Willis. 1977. "A Beta Logistic Model for the Analysis of Sequential Labor Force Participation of Married Women." *Journal of Political Economy* 85: 27–58.

Henry, Emily, and Sondra Taitz. 1983. *Written out of History.* Fresh Meadows, NY: Biblio Press.

Herberg, Will. 1956. *Protestant, Catholic, Jew.* Garden City, NY: Doubleday.

Herman, Simon. 1977. *Jewish Identity: A Social Psychological Perspective.* New Brunswick, NJ: Transaction Books.

Hertz, R. 1986. *More Equal than Others: Women and Men in Dual-Career Marriages.* Berkeley: University of California Press.

———. 1991. "Dual-Career Couples and the American Dream: Self-Sufficiency and Achievement." *Journal of Comparative Family Studies,* no. 22, 2: 247–263.

Hertzberg, Arthur. 1989. *The Jews in America.* New York: Simon and Schuster.

Herz, Dianne. 1988. "Employment Characteristics of Older Women." *Monthly Labor Review* (September).

Heschel, Susannah (ed.). 1983. *On Being a Jewish Feminist.* New York: Schocken.

Heuvel, A. V. 1989. "Are There Really Only Two Types of Women: Labor Force Participants and Nonparticipants?" Paper presented at the American Sociological Association Meetings, San Francisco.

Hewlett, S. 1987. *A Lesser Life: The Myth of Women's Liberation in America.* New York: Warner Books.

Himmelfarb, H. 1982. "Research on American Jewish Identity and Identification." In M. Sklare (ed.), *Understanding American Jewry.* New Brunswick, NJ: Transaction Books.

Hochschild, Arlie. 1989. *The Second Shift.* New York: Avon Books.

Hodge, R. W. 1981. "The Measurement of Occupational Status." *Social Science Research* 10: 396–415.

Hout, M. 1978. "The Determinants of Marital Fertility in the United States, 1960–1970: Inferences from a Dynamic Model." *Demography* 15: 139–159.

———. 1982. "The Association Between Husbands' and Wives' Occupations in Two-Earner Families." *American Journal of Sociology* 83, no. 2.

Hudis, Paula. 1976. "Commitment to Work and to Family: Marital-Status Differences in Women's Earnings." *Journal of Marriage and the Family* 38: 267–278.

Hunter College, Women's Studies Collective. 1983. *Women's Realities, Women's Choices.* New York: Oxford University Press.

Hyman, Paula. 1983. "The Jewish Family: Looking for a Usable Past." In Susannah Heschel (ed.). *On Being a Jewish Feminist,* pp. 19–26. New York: Schocken.

———. 1991. "Gender and the Immigrant Jewish Experience in the United States." In Judith Baskin (ed.), *Jewish Women in Historical Perspective,* ch. 10. Detroit: Wayne State University Press.

Izraeli, D. 1992. "Culture, Policy, and Women in Dual-Earner Families in Israel." In S. Lewis, D. Izraeli, and H. Hootsmans (eds.), *Dual Earner Families: International Perspectives,* pp. 199–246. London: Sage Publications.

Jacobs, Jerry. 1989. *Revolving Doors: Sex Segregation and Women's Careers.* Stanford, CA: Stanford University Press.
—— and Brian Powell. 1985. "Occupational Prestige: A Sex-Neutral Concept?" *Sex Roles* 12: 1061–1071.
Jencks, Christopher, Marshall Smith, Henry Acland, Mary Jo Bane, David Cohen, Herbert Gintis, Barbara Heyns, and Stephan Michelson. 1972. *Inequality: A Reassessment of the Effects of Family and Schooling in America.* New York: Basic Books.
Jones, Elise F. 1981. "The Impact of Women's Employment on Marital Fertility in the U.S., 1970–75." *Population Studies* 35: 161–173.
Kalmijn, Mathhijs. 1991a. "Shifting Boundaries: Trends in Religious and Educational Homogamy." *American Sociological Review* 91, no. 56 (December): 786–800.
——. 1991b. "Status Homogamy in the United States." *American Journal of Sociology* 97: 496–523.
Karp, Abraham J. 1976. *Golden Door to America: The Jewish Immigrant Experience.* New York: Penguin Books.
Katz, Jacob. 1973. *Out of the Ghetto: The Social Background of Jewish Emancipation, 1770–1870.* New York: Schocken.
Katz, Ruth, and Yohanan Peres. 1986. "The Sociology of the Family in Israel: An Outline of Its Development from the 1950s to the 1980s." *European Sociological Review* 2: 148–159.
Kedem, P. 1991. "Dimensions of Jewish Religiosity in Israel." In Z. Sobel (ed.), *Tradition, Conflict and Innovation: Jewishness and Judaism in Contemporary Israel*, pp. 251–273. Albany: SUNY Press.
Koltun, Elizabeth (ed.). 1976. *The Jewish Woman: New Perspectives.* New York: Schocken.
Kominski, Robert, and Andrea Adams. 1992. "School Enrollment—Social and Economic Characteristics of Students: October 1990." *Current Population Reports*, Series P-20, no. 460. Washington, DC: Bureau of the Census.
Korman, A. K. 1988. *The Outsiders: Jews and Corporate America.* Lexington, MA: Lexington Books.
Kosmin, Barry, Sidney Goldstein, Joseph Waksberg, Nava Lerer, Ariella Keysar, and Jeffrey Scheckner. 1991. *Highlights of the CJF 1990 National Jewish Population Survey.* New York: Council of Jewish Federations.
Kraus, Vered, and Robert W. Hodge. 1990. *Promises in the Promised Land: Mobility and Inequality in Israel.* New York: Greenwood Press.
Krausz, E. (ed.) 1989. *Education in a Comparative Context.* Studies of Israeli Society, vol. 4. New Brunswick, NJ: Rutgers University Press.
Kruskal, J. B. 1964. "Multidimensional Scaling by Optimizing Goodness of Fit to a Nonmetric Hypothesis." *Psychometrika* 29: 1–27.
Kuznets, Simon. 1972. *Economic Structure of U.S. Jewry: Recent Trends.* Jerusalem: Institute of Contemporary Jewry, Hebrew University.
Land, Kenneth. 1968. "Principles in Path Analysis and Causal Inference." In E. Borgatta (ed.), *Sociological Methodology 1969*, Ch. 2. San Francisco: Jossey-Bass.
Laumann, Edward O. 1966. *Prestige and Association in an Urban Community.* New York: Bobbs-Merrill.

Leibowitz, Arleen. 1974. "Education and Home Production." *American Economic Review* 64: 243–250.

Leiulfsrud, H., and A. Woodward. 1988. "Cross-Class Families: Review Essay." *Acta Sociologica* 31, no. 2: 175–180.

Lengermann, Patricia Madoo, and Ruth A. Wallace, 1985. *Gender in America: Social Control and Social Change.* Englewood Cliffs, NJ: Prentice-Hall.

Levy, Shlomit, Hanna Levinsohn, and Elihu Katz. 1993. *Beliefs, Observances and Social Interaction Among Israeli Jews.* Jerusalem: Louis Guttman Israel Institute of Applied Social Research.

Lewin, Alisa G. 1992. "Married Women's Labor Force Participation and Part-Time Employment in Israel." Paper presented at the American Sociological Association annual conference, Pittsburgh.

Lewis, S. 1992. "Introduction: Dual-Earner Families in Context." In S. Lewis, D. Izraeli, and H. Hootsmans (eds.), *Dual Earner Families: International Perspectives*, pp. 1–18. London: Sage Publications.

Lewis, S., D. Izraeli, and H. Hootsmans (eds.). 1992. *Dual Earner Families: International Perspectives.* London: Sage Publications.

Liebman, Charles, and Steven Cohen. 1990. *Two Worlds of Judaism: The Israeli and American Experiences.* New Haven: Yale University Press.

Lingoes, James C. 1966. "New Computer Developments in Pattern Analysis and Non-Metric Techniques." In *Proceedings of the IBM Symposium, Computers in Psychological Research, Blaricum, the Netherlands.* Paris: Gauthier-Villars.

Lipset, Seymour Martin. 1995. *Exceptionalism: The Persistence of an American Ideology.* New York: Norton.

Lopata, H. Z. 1993. "The Interweave of Public and Private: Women's Challenge to American Society." *Journal of Marriage and the Family* 55: 176–190.

Lorber, Judith, and Susan Farrell (eds.). 1991. *The Social Construction of Gender.* Newbury Park, CA: Sage.

Lyon, David. 1985. *The Steeple's Shadow: On the Myths and Realities of Secularization.* London: SPCK.

Maccoby, E., and C. Jacklin. 1987. "Gender Segregation in Childhood." In H. Reese (ed.), *Advances in Child Development and Behavior*, pp. 239–288. New York: Academic Press.

MacLeod, Jay. 1987. *Ain't No Makin' It.* Boulder, CO: Westview Press.

Mael, Fred. 1991. "Career Constraints of Observant Jews." *The Career Development Quarterly* 39: 341–349.

Mare, Robert. 1991. "Five Decades of Educational Assortative Mating." *American Sociological Review* 56: 15–32.

Marini, Margaret M., and Mary C. Brinton. 1984. "Sex Typing in Occupational Socialization." In B. Reskin (ed.), *Sex Segregation in the Workplace: Trends, Explanations, Remedies*, pp. 192–232. Washington, DC: National Academy of Sciences.

Marsiglio, W. 1986. "Teenage Fatherhood: High School Accreditation and Educational Attainment." In A. Elster and M. Lamb (eds.), *Adolescent Fatherhood.* Hillsdale, NJ: Lawrence Erlbaum Associates.

Mason, K., and Lu, Y. 1988. "Attitudes Towards Women's Familial Roles: Changes in the United States, 1977–1985." *Gender and Society* 2: 39–57.

Matras, Judah, and Gila Noam. 1987. "Schooling and Military Service: Their Effects on Israeli Women's Attainments and Social Participation in Early Adulthood." *Israel Social Science Research* 5: 29–43.

McGuire, Meredith. 1992. *Religion: The Social Context*, 3d ed. Belmont, CA: Wadsworth.

McLaughlin, Steven. 1978. "Sex Differences in the Determinants of Occupational Status." *Sociology of Work and Occupations* 5, no. 1: 5–30.

———, Barbara Melber, John Billy, Denise Zimmerle, Linda Winges, and Terry Johnson. 1988. *The Changing Lives of American Women*. Chapel Hill: University of North Carolina Press.

Meiselman, Moshe. 1978. *Jewish Woman in Jewish Law*. New York: Yeshiva University Press.

Mocanachie, M. 1989. "Dual-Earner Couples: Factors Influencing Whether and When White Married Women Join the Labor Force in South Africa." *The South African Journal of Sociology* 20, no. 3.

Moen, Phyllis. 1985. "Continuities and Discontinuities in Women's Labor Force Activity." In G. Elder, Jr. (ed.), *Life Course Dynamics: Trajectories and Transitions, 1968–1980*, pp. 113–155. Ithaca, NY: Cornell University Press.

———. 1992. *Women's Two Roles: A Contemporary Dilemma*. Westport, CT: Greenwood.

Monson, Rela Geffen. 1992. "Women Today—A Non-Orthodox View." In Steven T. Katz (ed.), *Frontiers of Jewish Thought*. Washington, DC: B'nai B'rith Books.

Morantz-Sanchez, Regina Markell. 1985. *Sympathy and Science: Women Physicians in America*. New York: Oxford University Press.

Nakao, Keiko, and Judith Treas. 1990. "Computing 1989 Occupational Prestige Scores." *GSS Methodological Report*, no. 70.

National Center for Education Statistics (NCES). 1991a. *The Condition of Education, 1991*. Vol. 1, *Elementary and Secondary Education*. Washington, DC: U.S. Department of Education.

———. 1991b. *The Condition of Education, 1991*. Vol. 2, *Postsecondary Education*. Washington, DC: U.S. Department of Education.

———. 1991c. *Digest of Education Statistics, 1991*. Washington, DC: U.S. Department of Education.

———. 1993. *Digest of Education Statistics, 1993*. Washington, DC: U.S. Department of Education.

Neusner, Jacob. 1987. *Death and Birth of Judaism*. New York: Basic Books.

Nilson, L. 1976. "The Occupational and Sex-Related Components of Social Standing." *Sociology and Social Research* 67: 392–404.

Oakes, Jeanne. 1985. *Keeping Track*. New Haven, CT: Yale University Press.

O'Barr, Jean (ed.). 1989. *Women and a New Academy: Gender and Cultural Context*. Madison: University of Wisconsin Press.

O'Connell, Martin, and Amara Bachu. 1992. *Who's Minding the Kids?: Child Care Arrangements, Fall 1988*. Washington, DC: U.S. Bureau of the Census.

O'Dea, T. F. 1966. *The Sociology of Religion*. Englewood Cliffs, NJ: Prentice-Hall.

Papanek, H. 1973. "Men, Women and Work: Reflections on the Two-Person Career." *American Journal of Sociology* 78: 852–872.

Pavalko, Ronald M. 1988. *Sociology of Occupations and Professions*, 2d ed. Itasca, IL: Peacock.

Peled, Elad. 1981. "Israeli Education." In E. Ignas and R. J. Corsini (eds.), *Comparative Educational Systems*. Itasca, IL: Peacock.

Peritz, Eric, and Mario Baras (eds.). 1992. *Studies in the Fertility of Israel.* Jewish Population Studies, No. 24. Jerusalem: Institute of Contemporary Jewry, Hebrew University of Jerusalem, and Demographic Center, Ministry of Labour and Social Affairs.

Philips, B. 1991. "Sociological Analysis of Jewish Identity." In D. Gordis and Y. Ben-Horin (eds.), *Jewish Identity in America*, pp. 3–26. Los Angeles: University of Judaism.

Philliber, William W., and Dana Hiller. 1983. "Changes in Marriage and Wife's Career as a Result of the Relative Occupational Attainments of Spouses." *Journal of Marriage and the Family* 45: 161–170.

Philliber, William W., and Dana Vannoy-Hiller, 1990. "The Effect of Husband's Occupational Attainment on Wife's Achievement." *Journal of Marriage and the Family* 52 (May): 323–328.

Phillips, Ruth M. 1981. "Women in Medicine." In Betty Justice and Renata Pore (eds.), *Toward the Second Decade*, pp. 49–56. Westport, CT: Greenwood.

Pogrebrin, Letty C. 1991. *Deborah, Golda and Me.* New York: Crown.

Pulliam, John. 1990. *History of Education in America*, 5th ed. New York: Macmillan.

Renzetti, Claire M., and Daniel J. Curran. 1992. *Women, Men and Society*, 2d ed. Boston: Allyn and Bacon.

Reskin, Barbara F. 1993. "Sex Segregation in the Workplace." *Annual Review of Sociology* 19: 241–270.

——— and Heidi Hartmann. 1986. *Women's Work, Men's Work: Sex Segregation on the Job*. Washington, DC: National Academy of Sciences.

——— and Patricia A. Roos. 1990. *Job Queues, Gender Queues: Explaining Women's Inroads into Male Occupations*. Philadelphia: Temple University Press.

Reszke, I. 1984. *Social Prestige and Gender.* Warsaw: Polish Academy of Sciences.

Rindfuss, Ronald R., Larry L. Bumpass, and Craig St. John. 1980. "Education and Fertility: Implications for the Roles Women Occupy." *American Sociological Review* 45: 431–447.

Ritterband, Paul. 1990. "Jewish Women in the Labor Force." Report prepared for the American Jewish Committee, mimeo.

Roberts, Keith. 1990. *Religion in Sociological Perspective*, 2d ed. Belmont, CA: Wadsworth.

Roos, Patricia. 1985. *Gender and Work: A Comparative Analysis of Industrial Societies.* Albany: State University of New York Press.

Rosenfeld, Rachel A., and Kenneth L. Spenner. 1992. "Occupational Sex Segregation and Women's Early Job Career Shifts." *Work and Occupations* 19: 424–449.

Rosenthal, Robert, and Lenore Jacobson. 1968. *Pygmalion in the Classroom.* New York: Holt, Rinehart and Winston.

Rosser, P. 1989. *The SAT Gender Gap.* Washington, DC: Center for Women's Policy Studies.

Rytina, Nancy F., and Suzanne M. Bianchi. 1984. "Occupational Reclassification and Changes in Distribution by Gender." *Monthly Labor Review* 107: 11–17.

Sadker, Myra, and David Sadker. 1989. *Teacher, School and Society*, 2d ed. New York: Random House.

Scanzoni, John. 1970. *Opportunity and the Family*. New York: The Free Press.

Schiffman, S. S., M. L. Reynolds, and F. W. Young. 1981. *Introduction to Multidimensional Scaling: Theory, Methods and Applications*. New York: Academic Press.

Schneider, Susan Weidman. 1984. *Jewish and Female: Choices and Changes in Our Lifes Today*. New York: Simon and Schuster.

Sered, Susan Starr. 1992. *Women as Ritual Experts: The Religious Lives of Elderly Jewish Women in Jerusalem*. New York: Oxford Univerity Press.

Sewell, W. H., R. M. Hauser, and W. C. Wolf. 1980. "Sex, Schooling and Occupational Status." *American Journal of Sociology* 86: 551–583.

Shalvi, Alice. 1988. "Equality for Women in Today's Israel?" *Middle East Review* 20, no. 4: 21–25.

Sharot, Stephen. 1991. "Judaism and the Secularization Debate." *Sociological Analysis* 52, no. 3: 255–275.

Siegel, Paul. 1971. "Prestige in the American Occupational Structure." Ph.D. dissertation, University of Chicago.

Silverman, P. 1987. "Family Life." In P. Silverman (ed.), *The Elderly as Pioneers*, pp. 205–223. Bloomington: Indiana University Press.

Skinner, D. 1984. "Dual Career Family Stress and Coping." In P. Voyndanoff (ed.), *Work and Family*, pp. 261–271. Belmont, CA: Mayfield.

Sklare, Marshall. 1972. *Conservative Judaism: An American Religious Movement*. New York: Schocken.

Slavin, S. L., and M. S. Pratt. 1982. *The Einstein Syndrome: Corporate Anti-Semitism in America Today*. Lanham, MD: University Press of America.

Smooha, Samuel. 1978. *Israel: Pluralism and Conflict*. London: Routledge and Kegan Paul.

Soldo, Beth J., and Emily M. Agree. 1988. "America's Elderly." *Population Bulletin* 43, no. 3. Washington, DC: Population Reference Bureau.

Sørenson, A., and S. McLanahan. 1987. "Married Women's Economic Dependency. 1940–1980." *American Journal of Sociology* 93, no. 3: 659–687.

Spencer, B. G. 1992. "Labor Supply and Investment in Child Quality: A Study of Jewish and Non-Jewish Women: A Comment." *Review of Economics and Statistics* 74: 721–725.

Spring, Joel. 1991. *American Education: An Introduction to Social and Political Aspects*, 5th ed. New York: Longman.

Stark, R., and W. Bainbridge. 1985. *The Future of Religion: Secularization, Renewal and Cult Formation*. Berkeley: University of California Press.

Steinberg, Stephen. 1974. *The Academic Melting Pot*. New York: McGraw-Hill.

——— . 1981. *The Ethnic Myth: Race, Ethnicity and Class in America*. Boston: Beacon Press.

Stewart, M., K. Prandy, and R. M. Blackburn. 1980. *Social Stratification and Occupations*. London: Macmillan.

Stockard, J. 1980. "Gender Equity and Education." *Annual Review of Research in Education.*

——— and J. Wood. 1984. "The Myth of Female Underachievement: A Reexamination of Sex Differences in Academic Underachievement." *American Education Research Journal* 21: 825–838.

Sweet, James A., and Larry L. Bumpass. 1987. *American Families and Households.* New York: Russell Sage Foundation.

Swirski, Barbara, and Marilyn Safir (eds.). 1991. *Calling the Bluff on Equality: Women in Israel.* New York: Pergamon Press.

Taeuber, Cynthia. 1991. *Statistical Handbook on Women in America.* Phoenix: Oryx Press.

Taeuber, Cynthia, and Victor Valdisera. 1986. *Women in the American Economy.* U.S. Bureau of thje Census, Current Population Reports, Series P-23, No. 146. Washington, DC: U.S. Government Printing Office.

Theodorson, George A., and Achilles G. Theodorson. 1969. *Modern Dictionary of Sociology.* New York: Apollo Editions.

Thomas, D. L., and M. Cornwall. 1990. "Religion and Family in the 1980s: Discovery and Development." *Journal of Marriage and the Family* 52: 983–992.

Treiman, D. J., and K. Terrell. 1975. "Sex and Status Attainment: A Comparison of Working Women and Men." *American Sociological Review* 40: 174–200.

Trow, Martin. 1977. "The Second Transformation of American Secondary Education." In Jerome Karabel and A. H. Halsey (eds.), *Power and Ideology in Education.* New York: Oxford University Press.

Ultee, W., and R. Luijkx. 1990. "Educational Heterogamy and Father-to-Son Occupational Mobility in 23 Industrial Nations." *European Sociological Review* 6, 125–149.

Umansky, Ellen M. 1985. "Feminism and the Reevaluation of Women's Roles Within American Jewish Life." In Yvonne Yazbeck Haddad and Elison Banks Findly (ed.), *Women, Religion and Social Change*, pp. 477–494. Albany: SUNY Press.

U.S. Bureau of the Census. 1990. *Statistical Abstract of the United States*, 109th ed. Washington, DC: U.S. Government Printing Office.

——— . 1992. *Statistical Abstract of the United States*, 111th ed. Washington, DC: U.S. Government Printing Office.

U.S. Bureau of Labor Statistics. 1990. *Employment and Earnings* 37, no. 1.

——— . 1991. *Employment and Earnings* 38: 11.

——— . 1994. "Work and Family: Promotions among Women." Report no. 868. Washington, DC: U.S. Government Printing Office.

Vera, H., D. Berardo, and F. Berardo. 1985. "Age Heterogamy in Marriage." *Journal of Marriage and the Family* 47, no. 3: 553–566.

Vetter, L. 1989. "The Vocational Option for Women." In S. Harlan and R. Steinberg (eds.), *Job Training for Women: The Promise and Limits of Public Policies*, pp. 91–113. Philadelphia: Temple University Press.

Voydanoff, P., and R. F. Kelly. 1984. "Determinants of Work-Related Family Problems Among Employed Parents." *Journal of Marriage and Family* 46: 881–892.

——— . 1985. "Work/Family Role Strain Among Employed Parents." *Family Relations* 34: 367–374.

Waite, Linda, G. W. Haggstrom, and D. E. Kanouse. 1985. "Changes in the Employment Activities of New Parents." *American Sociological Review* 50: 263–272.

Waite, Linda, and Kristin A. Moore. 1978. "The Impact of an Early First Birth on Young Women's Educational Attainment." *Social Forces* 56: 845–865.

Waite, Linda, and Ross Stolzenberg. 1976. "Intended Childbearing and Labor Force Participation of Young Women: Insights from Non-recursive Models." *American Sociological Review* 41: 235–252.

Walsh, Mary Roth. 1977. *"Doctors Wanted: No Women Need Apply": Sexual Barriers in the Medical Profession, 1835–1975.* New Haven, CT: Yale University Press.

Webber, Jonathan. 1983. "Between Law and Custom: Women's Experience of Judaism." In P. Holden (ed.), *Women's Religious Experience: Cross-Cultural Perspectives*, pp. 143–162. London: Croom-Helm.

Weber, Max. 1963. *The Sociology of Religion*, trans. Ephraim Fischoff. Boston: Beacon Press [originally published in 1922].

Wegener, Bernard. 1992. "Concepts and Measurement of Prestige." *Annual Review of Sociology* 18: 253–280.

Wegner, Judith Romney. 1990. *Chattel or Person: The Status of Women in the Mishnah.* New York: Oxford University Press.

Weinberg, S. S. 1988. *The World of Our Mothers.* New York: Schocken Books.

Weller, Robert. 1969. "The Employment of Wives, Role Incompatibility and Fertility." *Milbank Memorial Fund Quarterly* 46: 507–526.

West, Candace, and Don Zimmerman. 1991. "Doing Gender." In Judith Lorber and Susan Farrell (eds.), *The Social Construction of Gender*, Chapter 1. Newburg Park, CA: Sage.

Wilder, G., and K. Powell. 1989. *Sex Differences in Test Performance: A Survey of the Literature.* College Board Report 8903, ETS RR 89-4. New York: College Board Publications.

Wilson, Bryan. 1976. *Contemporary Transformations of Religion.* New York: Oxford University Press.

Winter, Bill. 1983. "Survey: Women Lawyers Work Harder, Are Paid Less, but They're Happy." *American Bar Association Journal* 69 (October): 1384–1388.

Wright, Erik Olin, Karen Shire, Shu-Ling Hwang, Maureen Dolan, and Janeen Baxter. 1992. "The Non-Effects of Class on the Gender Division of Labor in the Home: A Comparative Study of Sweden and the United States." *Gender and Society* 6, no. 2 (June): 252–282.

Zborowski, M., and E. Herzog. 1962. *Life Is with People: The Culture of the Shtetl.* New York: Schocken.

NAME INDEX

Acker, Joan, 153
Adams, Andrea, 35, 175
Agree, Emily M., 110
Alexander, Bobby C., 51, 202
Allen, Carole, 110
Almquist, Elizabeth, 2, 3, 62
American Association of University
  Women (AAUW), 23, 24, 29
Atchley, Robert C. , 113
Atkinson, Maxine, 166, 173

Bachu, Amara, 108
Bainbridge, William, 213
Baras, Miriam, 347
Bar-Yosef, Rivka, 9
Baskin, Judith, 169
Baum, Charlotte, 8, 62, 169, 228
Berger, Peter, 3, 213, 234
Bergmann, Barbara R., 96, 115, 116,
  121
Berk, Sarah F., 45
Berman, Saul, 9, 11
Bernstein, Deborah, 255
Beutell, Nicholas J., 61
Bianchi, Suzanne M., 4, 40, 44, 50,
  51, 54, 55, 83, 122, 142, 339
Bielby, Denise, 168
Bielby, William, 168
Blackburn, Robert M., 143
Blake, Judith, 23, 339, 342
Blumberg, Rae, 3, 337
Bose, Christine, 153
Brinton, Mary C., 115
Brotman, Herman, 110
Brubaker, Timothy H., 113
Brumberg, Stephan, 24, 25, 26, 338
Bryson, Rebecca, 167, 188
Bumpass, Larry L., 15, 54

Camarigg, Valerie, 116, 132
Central Bureau of Statistics (CBS),
  270, 330, 347, 348
Chadwick, Bruce, 166, 179
Chafetz, Janet Saltzman, 1, 2, 337
Chiswick, Barry, 4, 63, 100, 110,
  146, 169, 213, 220, 344
Clark, Mary J., 342
Clark, Robert L., 110
Cohen, Steven, 30, 199, 202, 203,
  208, 213, 240, 249, 250, 251, 252
Cole, Stephen, 46
Condran, Gretchen, 73
Coser, Rose L., 121
Cramer, James C., 62
Curran, Barbara, 115, 120, 207, 343
Cusick, Thomas, 45

DellaPergola, Sergio, 15
Desai, Sonalde, 72, 83, 96
Dexter, Carolyn, 115
Diament, Carol, 209
Dugger, Karen, 62

Eisenstadt, Shmuel N., 13, 198, 250,
  347
Elazar, Daniel J., 234
Elwell, Sue, 339
England, Paula, 70, 116, 153
Epstein, Cynthia Fuchs, 337

Faludi, Susan, 167
Farkas, George, 70, 116
Farrell, Susan, 3
Fenstermaker, Sarah, 2
Finke, Roger, 213

Fishman, Sylvia Barack, 25, 28, 62, 63, 96, 97, 116, 169, 208, 228, 234, 337, 347
Fowlkes, Martha, 182, 188, 343
Fox, John, 153
Friedan, Betty, 337

Gabriel, Susan L., 29
Geerken, Michael, 168, 184
Gerson, Kathleen, 61, 73, 74
Ginor, Fanny, 347
Glass, Becky, 173
Glass, Jennifer, 116, 173, 132
Glenn, Susan A., 116, 169
Glock, Charles, 197, 199, 202, 203, 204
Goldscheider, Calvin, 4, 15, 18, 26, 55, 116, 199, 203, 208, 213, 214, 233
Goldsmith, Elizabeth B., 62
Goldstein, Sidney, 4, 15, 68, 110, 115, 118, 173, 339, 342
Goodman-Thau, Eveline, 346
Gove, Walter R., 167, 184
Grady, William R., 110
Grandy, Jerilee, 342
Greenberg, Blu, 337
Greenhaus, Jeffrey H., 61

Haaga, John, 83
Haberfeld, Yitzhak, 153
Haggstrom, Gus W., 74
Hartman, Harriet, 117, 155, 168, 188, 220, 256
Hartman, Moshe, 117, 155, 168, 188, 203, 220, 238, 265, 284
Hartmann, Heidi, 116, 121
Hatch, Laurie, 110, 111
Hauser, Robert M., 23
Hayward, Mark, 110
Hazleton, Leslie, 255
Heaton, Tim B., 166, 179
Heckman, James L., 188
Herberg, Will, 198
Herman, Simon, 198
Hertz, Rosanna, 167, 184

Hertzberg, Arthur, 8
Herz, Dianne, 110
Herzog, Elizabeth, 24, 214
Heschel, Susannah, 337, 346
Heuvel, Audrey V., 154
Hewlett, Sylvia, 64, 96
Hiller, Dana, 184
Himmelfarb, Harold, 199, 203
Hochschild, Arlie, 73, 75, 133, 160
Hodge, Robert W., 117, 347
Hootsmans, Helen, 178
Hout, Michael, 62, 168
Hudis, Paula, 132
Hunter College, 28
Hyman, Paula, 8, 12, 62, 234

Izraeli, Daphna, 168, 178

Jacklin, Carol N. 342
Jacobs, Jerry, 37, 42, 115, 122, 343
Jacobson, Lenore, 23
Jencks, Christopher, 23
Jones, Elise F., 102, 108

Kalmijn, Mathhijs, 166, 167, 175
Kanouse, David E., 74
Karp, Abraham J., 8, 27
Katz, Jacob, 13
Katz, Elihu, 253
Kedem, Peri, 203, 283
Kelly, Robert F., 61
Kleemeier, Robert W., 110
Koltun, Elizabeth, 337
Kominski, Robert, 35, 51, 175
Korman, Abraham K., 119, 245
Kramarow, Ellen, 73
Kraus, Vered, 117, 347
Krausz, Ernest, 348
Kruskal, Joseph B., 327
Kuznets, Simon, 110, 118

Land, Kenneth, 347
Laumann, Edward O., 327

Leibowitz, Arleen, 83
Leiulfsrud, Hakon, 189
Lengermann, Patricia Madoo, 142
Levy, Schlomit, 253
Lewin, Alisa G., 270
Lewinsohn, 253
Lewis, Suzanne, 2, 64, 178
Liebman, Charles, 30, 202, 203, 208, 213, 249, 250, 251, 252
Lingoes, James C., 327
Lipset, Seymour Martin, 4, 228
Lopata, Helen Z., 182
Lorber, Judith, 3
Lu, Yu-Hsai, 4, 155, 168
Luijkx, R., 166
Lyon, David, 208

Maccoby, Eleanor E., 342
MacLeod, Jay, 24
Mael, Fred, 245
Marini, Margaret M., 115
Marsiglio, William, 339
Mason, Karen, 4, 155, 168
Matras, Judah, 254
McGuire, Meredith, 3, 207
McLanahan, 166
McLaughlin, Steven, 8, 28, 29, 40, 110, 153
Meiselman, Moshe, 9
Michel, Sonya, 8, 62
Miller, Sheila J., 113
Mocanachie, M., 168, 178, 184
Moen, Phyllis, 61, 62, 63, 64, 73, 74, 155
Monson, Rela Geffen, 10, 208
Moore, Kristen A., 54
Morantz-Sanchez, Regina Markell, 43

Nakao, Keiko, 117, 145, 146
National Center for Education Statistics (NCES), 37, 339
Neusner, Jacob, 203
Nilson, Linda, 153
Noam, Gila, 254

O'Barr, Jean, 29
O'Connell, Martin, 108
O'Dea, Thomas, 213
Oakes, Jeanne, 23

Papanek, Hanna, 174, 182, 343
Pavalko, Ronald M., 85
Peled, Elad, 348
Peritz, Eric, 347
Philliber, William W., 167, 184, 188
Phillips, Bruce, 43, 199, 203
Pogrebrin, Letty Cottin, 16, 255, 337
Powell, Krusten, 342, 343
Pradt, Mary S., 119, 245
Prandy, Kenneth, 143
Pulliam, John, 338

Rapoport, 188
Rapoport, 188
Reilly, Mary, 51
Renzetti, Claire, 115, 120, 207, 343
Reskin, Barbara F., 115, 116, 121
Reszke, Irena, 117, 146
Reynolds, M. Lance, 327
Rindfuss, Ronald R., 54
Ritterband, Paul, 73, 208
Roberts, Keith, 197, 213
Rokoff, G., 121
Roos, Patricia A., 81, 116, 132, 134, 135, 159
Rosenfeld, Rachel A., 116, 132, 136
Rosenthal, Robert, 23
Rosser, Phyllis, 342
Rytina, Nancy F., 122, 142

Sadker, Myra, 29
Sadker, David, 29
Safir, Marilyn, 255, 348
Scanzoni, John, 165
Schiffman, Susan S., 327
Schneider, Susan W., 208, 209, 337
Sered, Susan, 207, 208, 340
Sewell, William H., 23, 339

Shalvi, Alice, 255, 270
Sharot, Stephen, 199, 203, 208, 345
Shelach, Ilana, 9
Shenhav, Yehuda, 153
Siegel, Paul, 153
Silverman, Philip, 113
Skinner, Denise, 168
Sklare, Marshall, 202
Slavin, Stephen L., 119, 245
Smithson, Isaiah, 29
Smooha, Samuel, 347
Soldo, Beth J., 110
Sørenson, Aage, 166
Sørenson, Annamette, 166
Spain, Daphne, 4, 40, 44, 50, 51, 54, 55, 83, 339
Spencer, Byron G., 344
Spenner, Kenneth L., 116, 132, 136
Spring, Joel, 338
St. John, Craig, 54
Stark, Rodney, 199, 202, 203, 204, 213
Steinberg, Stephen, 15, 26, 30, 213
Steinem, Gloria, 337
Stewart, Andrew, 143
Stockard, Jean, 27, 342
Stolzenberg, Ross, 61, 74, 102
Sweet, James A., 15
Swirski, Barbara, 255, 348
Suschnigg, Carole, 153

Taeuber, Cynthia, 102, 153, 340
Terrell, Katherine D., 344
Theodorson, George A., 117
Theodorson, Achilles G., 117
Treas, Judith, 117, 145, 146
Treiman, Donald J., 344
Trow, Martin, 338

U.S. Bureau of Labor Statistics, 154, 178, 340
U.S. Bureau of the Census, 270, 340
Ultee, Wout C., 166
Umansky, Ellen M., 10, 16, 20, 337

Valdisera, Victor, 153
Vannoy-Hiller, Dana, 167, 188
Vetter, Louise, 29
Voydanoff, Patricia, 61

Waite, Linda, 54, 61, 72, 74, 83, 95, 102
Wallace, Ruth A., 142
Walsh, Mary Roth, 43
Webber, Jonathan, 9, 13, 337
Weber, Max, 207
Wegener, Bernard, 145, 148, 343
Wegner, Judith Romney, 10, 62, 169, 170
Weinberg, Sidney S., 169, 208, 228, 344
Weller, Robert, 2, 62
West, Candance, 2, 337
Wilder, Gita, 342
Wilson, Bryan, 3
Wolf, W. C., 23
Wood, J. Walter, 342
Woodward, Arthur, 189
Wright, Erik Olin , 165, 189

Young, Forrest W., 327

Zborowski, Mark, 24, 214
Zimmerman, Don, 2, 337
Zuckerman, Alan, 4, 26, 55, 214

SUBJECT INDEX

Academic degree, 30, 89, 339, 345
  gender differences in, 35–36
  labor force participation and,
    85–87, 86
  occupational prestige and, 147–48,
    153
  U.S. whites, 33, 34
  U.S. Jews, 33, 33
Achievement orientation, 228, 242
Age (*see also* cohort)
  as cohort, 38, 64, 98
  education and, 37–44, 220
  Jewishness and, 208–9, 210, 346
  labor force participation and, 89,
    97–98, 137–145, 238, 342
  occupational prestige and, 155
Age at first birth
  education and, 45, 51
  labor force participation and, 95
  occupation and, 136
  occupational prestige and, 162
Age at marriage, 340
  age homogamy and, 173–74
  education and, 45, 49
  labor force participation and, 70–73
  occupation and, 135–36
Age homogamy, 172–74, 277–78
  U.S. Jews compared to U.S. total
    population, 173
  U.S. Jews compared to Israeli Jews,
    277–78
Age of first child
  labor force participation and, 107
Age of youngest child
  labor force participation and, 95,
    99–102
American Jews (*see* U.S. Jews)
Army service (*see* Israeli Army)

Breadwinner
  male, 178, 180–82, 279–80
  female, 179, 180, 279–80

Childcare, 44, 83, 95–96, 340
  in Israel, 270, 296, 298
Children (*see also* number of
    children, age at first birth, age
    of first child, age of youngest
    child)
  women's labor force participation
    and, 4, 95
Cohort (*see also* age)
  education and, 37–44
  Jewishness and, 210
  life cycle and, 17, 38, 295
Comparable worth, 3
Conservative Judaism, 10, 201,
    204–5, 222, 227

Denomination (*see also* Conservative
    Judaism, Orthodox Judaism,
    Reconstructionist Judaism,
    Reform Judaism), 201, 204–5,
    207, 214, 221–22, 227
  gender roles and, 244
Diaspora, 10, 199, 202
Divorce
  labor force participation and, 75
Dual earners, 1, 170, 178, 227, 296
  children and, 179
  compared to other couples,
    178–182, 279–80
  Jewishness and, 170, 241–42
  life cycle and, 179
  occupations of, 188–93

Dual earners *(continued)*
  U.S. Jews compared to Israeli
    Jews, 279–80
  U.S. Jews compared to U.S. total
    population, 178–80

Education, 5, 23–60
  age and, 37–44, 220
  age at first birth and, 45, 51–54
  age at marriage and, 45, 49–51
  changes for white U.S.s, 40
  gender differences in, 28–32,
    34–60, 291–92
  gender roles and, 23, 28–30
  family roles and, 25, 30, 36,
    44–56, 261–64
  Israeli, 257–64, 347–48
  Jewish *(see* Jewish education)
  Jewishness and, 212–17
  Judaism and, 13–14, 24–26
  labor force participation and, 6,
    82–88, 169–70, 265–66
  marital status and, 46–49
  measurement of, 30
  number of children and, 44,
    54–56, 263–64
  occupation and, 122–29, 143
  occupational prestige and, 147–48,
    150, 159
  religious, 24
  women's, 13, 14, 217–19
  U. S., general, 15, 338
  U.S. Jews, 31–60
    changes in, 37–44, 55
    compared to U.S. white
      population, 32–36, 40–41,
      47–49, 58
    compared to Israeli Jews, 257–64
  U.S. white population, 32–34
Educational homogamy, 167, 169,
  174–78, 279
  Jews compared to U.S. total
    population, 175
  U.S. Jews compared to Israeli
    Jews, 278, 279
Enlightenment, 25

Family roles, 1, 7, 14
  attitudes toward, in Judaism,
    9–13, 229, 298
  attitudes toward, in Israel, 255
  education and, 25, 30, 44–56,
    261–64
  gender roles and, 16–17
  Israeli, 245
  Jewishness and, 241, 290
  labor force participation and, 15,
    61, 62, 63, 73–81, 95, 167,
    235, 267, 284–86, 288, 293,
    348
  occupation and, 132–37, 167
  occupational prestige and, 152,
    161–62, 242
Family size *(see* number of children,
  children, fertility)
Feminism
  Israelis and, 294, 297
  Judaism and, 297
  U.S. Jews and, 15–16, 169,
    291–92
Fertility *(see* number of children,
  family roles)
  of U.S. Jews, 4

Gender differences
  in education, 28–31, 290–92
  Israeli compared to U. S. Jews,
    259–61
  in labor force participation,
    61–114, 266–67
  in occupational prestige, 147,
    153–62
    education and, 153
  in occupations, 271–77
  Jewishness and, 282–88
Gender discrimination in labor
  market, 116
Gender roles, 1–7
  changes over time, 296
  children and, 63
  education and, 23, 28
  ethnic variation, 2, 3, 62
  in economy, 1

in family, 16–17, 165–94
in U. S., 14–16
Jewishness and, 9–11, 217–48
Judaism and, 9
labor force participation and,
67–68, 73–81
life cycle and, 67–68
occupations and, 7
religious variation, 3
societal rewards and, 2
GI bill, 15, 57
Golda Meir syndrome, 255
GSS (General Social Survey, NORC),
168

Halacha
gender roles and, 9
Higher education (*see* education)
Holocaust, 198
Homogamy
age, 172–74, 277–78
educational, 167, 169, 174–78,
278–79
Hours of work, 84, 85, 93, 93–95,
270–71, 340
age and, 93–94
age of youngest child and, 101–2,
106–7
education and, 87, 93–94
Israeli Jews and, 270–71
marital status and, 93
number of children and, 98
age of mother and, 99
occupation and, 130–31
occupational prestige and, 148,
151, 160
Human capital, 115–16, 134, 135,
137, 147–48, 153, 158

Immigration
education and, 8, 15, 26–27
gender roles and, 27
labor force participation of women
and, 8
of U.S. Jews, 26

Income, 344
Israel
education, 347
non-Jews in, 347
Israeli army, 253–54, 258, 294
women's participation in, 347
Israeli Jews, 18, 20, 249–88,
329–36
compared to U. S. Jews, 249–88
education of, 257–64
immigration and, 256–57
labor force participation of,
284–86
Jewishness and, 202–3
profile of, 329–36
Israeli students, 254

Jewish culture
women's occupational roles and,
116
Jewish education, 25, 28, 204
secular education and
Jewish identity (*see* Jewishness)
Jewishness, 18, 197–248
age and, 208–9, 210
education and, 212–27, 292–93
family roles and, 208, 229, 241,
290, 293–94
gender and, 207–8, 210
gender differences in occupational
prestige and, 243
labor force participation and,
228–42, 284–86, 292–94
marital status and, 210–12
measurement of, 199–207,
324–26, 345
in Israel, 282–86, 326
occupational prestige and,
242–47
of Israeli Jews, 202–3, 326
self-employment and, 246
Jewish organizations, involvement in
occupational prestige and, 243

Kashrut, 200–1, 202

Labor force, entrance into, 66–71
Labor force participation, 5, 61–114
  age and, 5, 66, 78–81, 88, 89, 91,
    97–98, 106, 109, 137–45, 187,
    238, 284–85, 342, 343
  age at first birth, 95–96, 107–10
    changes over cohorts, 108–9
  age at marriage and, 70–73, 285
  age of youngest child and, 63–64,
    99–102, 104, 185
  age of mother and, 104, 106
  education of mother and, 100,
    104
  children and, 95–109
  differences between spouses (see
    dual earners, breadwinners
    male, breadwinners female)
  education and, 6, 66–67, 69–70,
    82–88, 92, 265–66
    children and, 102–9
    family roles and, 83
  family roles and, 6, 15, 61, 62, 63,
    73–81, 95, 235, 267, 284–86,
    288, 293, 348
  gender gap and, 66–67, 73–81,
    84–86, 110–13, 266–67
  hours of, 68, 93
  Israeli Jews, 264–71, 284–86
  Jewishness and, 228–42, 292–94
  Judaism and, 62
  life ccle and, 61–62, 69–70, 73–74
  marital status and, 73–81, 293
    age and, 68, 75–77, 92
  number of children and, 70–71,
    95–99, 185, 187, 269–71,
    285–86, 291
  spousal influence on, 168, 182–88
  U.S. attitudes towards wives', 168
  U.S. Jews, 65
    U.S. Jews compared to U.S.
      whites, 65, 65–66, 67, 68,
      77–78, 81–82, 87–88,
      100–1, 110–11
    U.S. Jews compared to Israeli
      Jews, 264–71
  U.S. whites, 65–66
  wives', 169, 178–88

Law degrees, 42
Life cycle, 10, 61–63, 148, 155–56,
  210–12

Marital status, 340
  education and, 46, 341
  Jewishness and, 210–11
  labor force participation and,
    73–82, 89, 91, 267–68, 291
  occupation and, 132–35
  occupational prestige and, 155,
    160–61
Mate selection, 16, 165, 167, 169
Medical degrees, 42–43
Mikveh, 9, 283
Mishnah, 169
Minority thesis, 18
Modernization, 197, 213–14
Multi-dimensional scaling, 327

NJPS (National Jewish Population
  Survey), 1990, 19
  methodology of, 301–22
NJPS (National Jewish Population
  Survey), 1970–71, 113
Number of children
  education and, 263–64
  Jewishness and, 241, 346
  labor force participation of women
    and, 95–99, 269–71,
    285–86, 291
  age of mother and, 96–98
  occupation and, 136–37, 291
  occupational prestige and, 162

Occupation, 115–45
  age and, 137–45, 343
  age at marriage and, 135–36
  age at first birth and, 135–36
  changes in, 137–45
  education and, 122–29, 143
    changes in, 143–45
  family roles and, 116, 132–37,
    133, 247, 276–77, 340

gender differences in, 115, 116–44, 271–77
hours of work and, 130–31, 340
Jewishness and, 245–47
male breadwinners' compared to dual earners', 182
marital statu and, 132–35
number of children and, 136–37
sex segregation in, 115, 120–22, 273–77
spousal influence on, 168
U.S. Jews compared to U.S. whites, 118–19, 122
U.S. Jews compared to Israeli Jews, 271–77
women's entrance into, 142–43
Occupational dissimilarity, 121–22, 125, 342–43
changes in, 137–45
education and, 123, 125–29, 273–76
hours of work and, 130–31
Jewishness and, 243
marital status and, 134–35
Occupational prestige, 7, 117, 145–64, 343
age and, 148–49, 152, 155, 159–60
age at first birth and, 162
age at marriage and, 162
changes in, 152
education and, 150, 159
family roles and, 150, 152, 161–62
gender differences in, 153–62, 290–92
age and, 159
education and, 156
hours of work and, 148, 151, 155, 156, 160
marital status and, 157, 160–61
Jewishness and, 242–45
marital status and, 152, 155, 157, 160
measurement of, 117
number of children and, 162
occupation and, 146
spousal influence on, 191–93

U.S. Jews', 145–62
compared to all U. S. population, 146–47, 291
work hours and, 151, 155, 156, 160
Occupational structure of U. S., 14
of Israel
Orthodox Judaism, 10, 201, 203, 204–5, 216, 219, 221–22, 225, 227, 233, 244, 293, 294, 346

Part-time work (*see also* hours of work), 340
in Israel, 270–71, 276
occupation and, 130–31, 133
occupational prestige and, 154–55
Path analysis, 238–41, 346–47
Protestant ethic, 62, 228
Provider role, 70, 74

Reconstructionist Judaism, 10, 227, 245, 346
Reform Judaism, 10, 201, 204–5, 222, 224, 227, 245
Religious leadership, 10
Religiosity (*see also* Jewishness), 198–99
gender and, 207–8
in Israel, 253, 283–86
occupation and, 245
labor force participation and, 284
Retirement, 6, 64, 111
education and, 111–12
labor force participation and age at, 89–91, 92, 109–13
marital status and, 112–13
Ritual observance, 200–1, 202–3

Sample, 19, 171
Secularization, 197, 213, 215, 217
Self-employment, 110, 246
Socioeconomic status
education and, 27–28

Spousal equality, 165–94
  age, 172–74
  educational, 174–78, 225–27,
    279–80
  family roles and, 171
  labor force participation, 178–82,
    279–80
  occupational, 188–91, 280–82
  occupational prestige, 191–93,
    244–45
  Jewishness and, 241–42, 244–45,
    279–82, 286, 288
Synagogues, 198
  attendance/membership, 201

Title IX, 15, 29, 37, 43

U.S. Jews, 7
  as minority group, 8, 18, 249–50
  characteristics of, 250–51
  compared to Israeli Jews, 249–88,
    294–95
  discrimination against, 15
  education of, 4
  fertility and, 4
  family roles and, 4

Weighting, 19, 304, 308, 313–18, 337
Women rabbis, 10–11, 243

Yiddish, 199

Zionism, 198–99